Are You Ready?

Are You Ready?

By Harold Camping

Vantage Press, New York

First Edition
Are You Ready?

Published by Vantage Press, Inc.
516 West 34th Street, New York, New York 10001

Manufactured in the United States of America
ISBN 0-533-10932-9

Library of Congress Catalog Card No.: 93-94226

Contents

Preface

On a Monday evening in February, 1993, I returned home from hosting another of the daily Open Forum programs. I was grateful in my soul that two days earlier at a Saturday banquet, I had had the privilege of addressing a large and enthusiastic group of Family Radio supporters, solemnly warning them that September, 1994, could very well be the end of the world. With that in mind, it is incumbent upon each one of us to be sure that we are ready to meet God. Never before in the history of the world are more than five billion people individually and collectively at risk. To wait and see if Christ's return is indeed to be in the fall of 1994 is not enough. This is so because if Christ did come, and all the Biblical evidence points to this likelihood, those who "waited to see" would be caught without salvation. It would be guaranteed that they would have to face the Judgment Throne of God, be found guilty of their sins, and plunged into Hell forevermore.

And this Monday evening on the Open Forum program, I was able to continue to warn.

But then suddenly something happened that shook me into the reality of the extreme urgency of time. My wife greeted me with the information that she had just had a lengthy call from a long-time friend of ours, Pastor Bartel Huizenga. He called from a hospital in San Francisco to let us know that the next morning he would undergo an operation to have a fast-growing tumor removed from his brain. Bart Huizenga was retired but when he preached for our church a few months earlier, he had no physical disabilities. Bart Huizenga, although a year younger than I, was suddenly threatened by a physical situation that could very well take his life, and indeed did take his life a few months later.

And then on this fateful Monday evening an hour after I heard the shocking news about Bart, the phone rang. Family Radio's Vice President Scott L. Smith was on the line. He had just received the news that Family Radio's Secretary-Treasurer Mr. Richard Van Dyk had suffered a heart attack and was now in a hospital in Dallas, Texas. What was going on? "Rich," as Scott and I called him, had been at the same banquet that I had attended the previous Saturday. He and my wife and I had had a restful Sunday praising God for what God was doing through Family Radio. I had taken him to the airport that Monday morning, and he appeared to be in the so-called "pink of health." Rich was very careful about diet, exercise, vitamins, etc.

And now he, too, was in a hospital, a breath away from eternity. What was happening?

And then I understood. I was being reminded that many people in the world today will not be alive in September of 1994. Each and every day almost 200,000 people die. They die for thousands of different reasons. But they die.

In fact, not one of us can know that we will be alive tomorrow. Not one of us is guaranteed another day. Therefore, the urgency to be ready to meet God is now! We must be ready **now** for eternity.

And so even as I write this sequel to *1994?* I solemnly declare: Even though it strongly appears that September, 1994, is the end for the whole human race, you and I must be ready now. **You or I could easily be one of the almost 200,000 people who will die in the next twenty-four hours or in any twenty-four hour day between now and the end of the world.**

By God's mercy He has given mankind the Gospel which tells us how important it is that we become ready to meet God.

The Bible is the Gospel, which sets forth God's divine plan for the human race. Because man was created in the image of God, he was created accountable for his actions. God decreed that if man rebelled against God, man would have to bear the penalty for his sin, which is death. This death is primarily two-fold: First, he would come under the curse of God and be alienated from God. After man sinned, the effects of this curse were that man became completely infected with sin and could not live forever on this earth. Man became totally rebellious against God; he became a citizen of Satan's dominion. Satan was an angel who, together with many other angels, rebelled against God at the time our first parents sinned.

The second aspect of this death is intimately associated with the curse that God put on mankind because of sin. Man became subject to the wrath of God. God's perfect, divine law decreed that the payment for sin was death and the ultimate consequence of this death was Hell. Mankind, each and every human being, on the last day of this earth's existence, must stand for trial. If any sin is found in him, the law of God calls for eternal damnation for that individual. Since each and every human being who has ever existed has sinned, that is the terrible condition of mankind. Every human being is on the path to Hell. He will stand for judgment before an angry judge, the Lord Jesus Christ, against whom mankind has rebelled. Because Christ is perfectly just and righteous, He must carry out the demands of God's perfect law by sentencing each and every sinner to eternity in Hell.

The good news is that God, in His perfect love, has provided a way of escape from Hell. The way of escape is found in God Himself in the person of the Lord Jesus Christ, who took on a human nature by being born of the virgin Mary. Because God became a human being, He became qualified to be a substitute or a stand-in for sinful humans.

For Christ to be our substitute, it was necessary to put on Him the sins of each and every person that He came to save. When He took upon Himself these sins, He became subject to the perfect law of God that demanded eternal damnation as the penalty for sin.

Christ, the sin-bearer of those He came to save from the wrath of God, came under the sentence of Hell. This is what the atonement, the cross, and salvation are all about. In A.D. 33, Christ was found guilty of the sins of all who would ever become saved. In the space of three days and three nights, God poured out His wrath on Him. This wrath was the equivalent of the eternal damnation of each and every person whom Christ came to save.

Because Christ was God as well as man, God could so intensify the suffering of Christ as He paid the penalty of the wrath of God, that by Sunday morning, He could and did arise from the tomb, proving that He as the God-man had completely satisfied the demands of the law, which decreed eternal damnation for sinners.

This in a nutshell is what the Bible is all about. It comes to mankind with the warning that each and every one of us is a sinner and, therefore, rightly subject to the awful wrath of God. It tells us that at the end of the world, God will judge each and every human being. They will be found guilty because not one person has lived without sin. Each person will be found guilty, and he will be removed into Hell, where he will experience the wrath of God forevermore. We, of course, do not understand the severity of this penalty because we do not understand how wrong, how rebellious, and how awful sin is. But whether we understand or not, the penalty for sin is eternal damnation.

On the other hand, there is the tremendous good news that those who trust in Jesus Christ as their Savior will not experience the wrath of God. Because Jesus has already paid for their sins when He went to the cross, they stand perfectly righteous before God. They do not have to be judged on the last day; instead, they will be with Christ forevermore in the new heavens and the new earth, which God will create at the end of time, after He has destroyed the present universe.

This book, like the book *1994?*, has as its primary mission the task of serving as a warning that this is the awful predicament of every human being.

But it also is a declaration that there is still hope. It is still the day of salvation. But that day is drawing to a close with great speed. Never in the history of the world has there been such urgency to cry to God for His mercy. May it be that many who read this book will yet experience the grace and mercy of eternal God.

Introduction

In September of 1992 the book *1994?* became available wherever books are sold. Based entirely upon the Bible, it is designed to strongly emphasize that the end of the world could well take place in September of 1994. In it a great amount of Biblical data is set forth to show the great likelihood that this will happen. Path after path is set forth that focuses on the year 1994 as the last year for planet earth and for the entire present universe. The big message of the book is to sound the warning that Judgment Day is almost here.

The book *1994?* was carefully written for two major purposes. The first purpose was to sound the alarm. Judgment Day is almost here. Each and every individual in the world is in serious trouble with God because of his sins. And time to find a solution to his sin by trusting in the Lord Jesus as his Savior has almost come to an end.

The second purpose was to present to the thousands of dedicated Bible students the Biblical data that has lead to the conclusion that September, 1994, in all likelihood will be the end of the world. Any student of the Bible can be in error. The Biblical principle that God has established is that any doctrine declared by one prophet is to be judged by the other prophets (I Corinthians 14:29). Every believer is a prophet, and he exercises his prophetic role at the time he witnesses to others what he believes the Bible teaches. But because he is not infallible and may have misunderstood the teaching of the Bible, other believers are to check his teaching by also carefully examining the Biblical evidence that gives rise to the doctrine being offered.

This is, therefore, a major purpose of publishing the book *1994?* Many other believers can critique what was written in order that corrections can be made if any or all of the material is in error.

The book *1994?* has been available to readers for more than a year. During this year, many have studied it very carefully. Additionally, during this year, I have continued to search for anything and everything the Bible might offer that speaks to the question of the timing of the return of Christ. In fact, this continued study has resulted in the publication of this book, *Are You Ready?*, which is a follow-up to the book *1994?*

During the past year as many students of the Bible have been carefully examining the ideas and conclusions set forth in the book *1994?*, one would think that if these conclusions are in error there would be an increasing sense of uneasiness in the hearts of many. There would be a feeling and a growing awareness that this whole study is somehow incorrect in that there are too many inconsistencies, too many "far-fetched" ideas, too much speculation.

The fact is, however, just the opposite has been the case. Individual after individual has written to me or talked with me offering further corroboration, further Biblical evidence that validates the conclusion of the extreme likelihood of the end of the world sometime in September of 1994.

This, too, has been my personal experience. As I carefully prepared the material set forth in this book, *Are You Ready?*, I have found increasing corroboration that the material set forth in the book *1994?* is accurate.

The reaction to the book *1994?* of those who are in the church has been very interesting. A small percentage has received it gladly. Whether they agree or not to all of the material set forth, they are delighted to contemplate the wonderful fact that Christ's return could possibly be that near.

On the other hand, a great many people have refused to come near the book. One of their main arguments is that we cannot know anything at all about the timing of Christ's return. They insist that Christ's coming is to be like a thief in the night and therefore we are not to look in the Bible for any information that might relate to the timing of Christ's return. They use such a verse as Mark 13:33: "Take ye heed, watch and pray: for ye know not when the time is."

They use Acts 1:7 to convince themselves that we should not think about these things: "And he said unto them, It is not for you to know the times or the seasons, which the Father hath put in his own power."

In fact, the Bible is very clear that we cannot know the day or the hour. When Jesus stated in Mark 13:33 that we cannot know when the time is, He added in verse 35, as further explanation:

Watch ye therefore: for ye know not when the master of the house cometh, at even, or at midnight, or at the cockcrowing, or in the morning.

These statements of midnight, cockcrowing, etc., have to do with the hours of the day. And indeed, we cannot know the day or the hour.

When Acts 1:7 is correctly translated from the Greek, it does not say, "It is not **for** you to know the times . . . ." Rather, more correctly it should have been translated, "It is not **of** you to know the times . . . . " That is, any knowledge we might receive does not come from our own thinking. It must come from God. If it is to come from God, it must come from the Bible.

God does divide the peoples of the world into two groups insofar as the knowledge of His return is concerned. On the one hand are all of the unsaved for whom Christ's coming is as a thief in the night. I Thessalonians 5:2-3 says it so succinctly:

> For yourselves know perfectly that the day of the Lord so cometh as a thief in the night. For when they shall say, Peace and safety; then sudden destruction cometh upon them, as travail upon a woman with child; and they shall not escape.

On the other hand, there are those who have trusted in Christ. Their knowledge of Christ's return is altogether a different situation. I Thessalonians 5:4-5 declares:

> But ye, brethren, are not in darkness, that that day should overtake you as a thief. Ye are all the children of light, and the children of the day: we are not of the night, nor of darkness.

By this statement we know that the believers are to have an entirely different knowledge concerning the details of Christ's return from that of the unbelievers. But if they are the children of light, from where are they to receive light relating to Christ's coming? Our only source is the Bible. Effectively God is commanding us to search the Bible for information concerning the day of the Lord. As we search the Bible we will receive much light. In fact, Ecclesiastes 8:5 declares: "Whoso keepeth the commandment shall feel no evil thing: and a wise man's heart discerneth both time and judgment."

More than that, in II Peter 3:12, God admonishes us by the words:

Looking for and hasting unto the coming of the day of God, wherein the heavens being on fire shall be dissolved, and the elements shall melt with fervent heat?

The next two verses further underscore the posture of the believers "looking":

Nevertheless we, according to his promise, look for new heavens and a new earth, wherein dwelleth righteousness. Wherefore, beloved, seeing that ye look for such things, be diligent that ye may be found of him in peace, without spot, and blameless.

Where is the believer to be looking? Not in the sky, not in the philosophies of men, not in his own feelings. He is to look in the Bible. Like the Bereans of Acts 17:10-11, we are to search the Scriptures. And as our knowledge of the day of the Lord increases, as we receive more and more light on the subject, we should not be afraid of what we learn. Rather, we should rejoice and desire more than ever to sound the warning to the world.

I am afraid that many church people would like to think that we are not to know anything at all about the timing of Christ's return. They want to be like the heathen - His coming will be like a thief in the night. They are afraid to expose the light of the Bible on the question.

Believers should be looking for the end of the world and Christ's return. If "believers" do not want to know, there are at least three possibilities as to why they do not want to know.

(a) They are misled by their church or by their pastor.
(b) They are afraid to face the reality of Hell.
(c) They love this world more than Christ.

If (b) or (c) is true it may be that they are not saved. If (a) is true, they might be saved but are not necessarily saved.

It is imperative that each individual immediately tests himself concerning these three options.

Test No. 1. The Bible has much to say about Judgment Day and the eternal damnation that follows. Am I ready to hear about, think about, and talk freely and easily about this subject? After all, if I have been saved, Hell is no threat to me any longer since Jesus has fully paid for my sins, and I will, therefore, never stand before the Judgment Throne of God.

But if that subject is something that frightens me so that to even think about it is unacceptable to me, there is a strong likelihood that I am still unsaved.

If your honest answer is "No!," you should seriously question if you are saved.

Test No. 2. Do I find it difficult to hear about, think about, or freely talk about the soon return of Christ and the end of the world because:

1. I want to see my children grow up?
2. I want to finish my education?
3. I first want my business to succeed?
4. I first want a long-planned vacation?
5. I want that new home I have desired for so many years?
6. There is any plan that is more important to me than the fact that if Jesus does come, I will have the most important and wonderful goal of my life realized?

If the answer to any of these questions is "Yes," you should seriously question if you are saved.

Test No. 3. When I look honestly at myself, do I truly find an ongoing and earnest desire to do the will of God? That is, when I discover in my life a practice that is contrary to the Bible, am I miserable in my soul until I repent of that practice? Likewise, if I find I hold a Bible doctrine that cannot easily be defended by the Bible (even though it was taught to me by a beloved pastor or Bible teacher), am I willing to set that doctrine aside and seek for more wisdom from the Bible concerning the subject matter of that doctrine?

If the answer is "No!," you should seriously question if you are saved.

Many are quite offended when it is suggested that they are to carefully examine themselves to make certain that they are saved. But isn't it wonderful that it is still the day of salvation? We can still cry to

God for mercy. We can still repent. We can still fill our souls with the bread and water of the Bible. How merciful God is that all of this is still possible.

It is imperative that our self-examination be done without delay. It is almost the end of time as we know it. Hebrews 2:3: "How shall we escape, if we neglect so great salvation; which at the first began to be spoken by the Lord, and was confirmed unto us by them that heard him."

Indeed, wonderfully, the book *1994?* also emphasizes that even though time has almost run out, it is still the day of salvation. If there were ever a time to make certain of one's salvation, it is now. Really, the big message of the book *1994?* is not the likelihood that the end of the world could come in September of 1994. **The big message is: Are you ready to meet God? This is the pressing question that every human being should insistently face.**

After *1994?* was published, a number of questions arose that justify further discussion. One question is: Shouldn't more information be developed that shows how God uses numbers in the Bible? Historically, theologians have little to offer as to the purpose of God's usage of a great many numbers in the Bible.

A related question is: What Biblical justification do we have to see spiritual truth in God's use of numbers?

Another question that should be addressed is that of the chronology of the kings of Judah and Israel. Based on the Biblical data, shouldn't we be able to know very precisely how each of their reigns fit into the Biblical calendar?

A further question that could stand more analysis is the meshing of our calendar (the Julian or Gregorian) with the calendar of the Bible. If this is not done with great accuracy, the calendar paths from the date of creation, the flood, Abraham, etc., will be in jeopardy.

In the process of supplying answers to these questions, we have been enabled to find many more calendar paths that focus on 1994 as the year in which God in all likelihood will end the world.

Because the signs spoken of in the Bible that show we are near the end of the world continue to dramatically unfold as each day goes by, a chapter has been included to remind us of the more prominent signs. Moreover, because the single greatest focus on 1994 as the year for Christ's return is the Jubilee information in the Bible, a further discussion of that event is also included.

In seeking a title for this book, the real question that must be asked of every person in the world - *ARE YOU READY?* - continues to pound in my ears. Therefore, this book has been entitled ARE YOU READY? Hopefully it will be an assist to anyone who still has doubts about the reality of the world coming to an end.

Are You Ready?

Chapter 1.
The Signs that Show Us that
We Are There

When we study the Bible, we find certain absolute truths that are tremendously important. Among them are:

1. This world will come to an end (Matthew 24:29; II Peter 3:10).
2. The end will come at the close of the New Testament era (I Peter 4:7; I Corinthians 10:11).
3. At the end Christ will return to gather all those who have believed on Him (Mark 13:26-27; I Corinthians 15:51-52).
4. At the end every unsaved human being will be judged and condemned to spend eternity in Hell for his sins (John 5:28-29; Revelation 20:12-13).
5. At the end God will destroy this world by fire, the whole universe will melt with fervent heat, and God will then create new heavens and a new earth (II Peter 3:12-13; Revelation 21:1).
6. All those who have trusted in Christ as their personal Lord and Savior will be with Him forever in the new heavens and new earth (John 14:2-3; I Thessalonians 4:16-17).
7. There must be an end-time generation who will be living at the time that the end occurs.

The Bible is crystal clear on these issues. The only thing that we do not know is exactly when the end of the world will come.

Biblical information in the book *1994?* as well as in this volume, which is a sequel to *1994?*, indicates that we can know much about the timetable of the end of the world. This is particularly true once we have come to understand the calendar given in the Bible.

But completely apart from the calendars of the Bible that show us the likely month and year of Christ's return, the Bible speaks of many signs that indicate when that end is very near.

In Matthew 24:3 the disciples asked Jesus the question that is the ultimate question in man's mind. They asked: "Tell us, when shall these things be? and what shall be the sign of thy coming, and of the end of the world?" They effectively were asking: Can we tell by events that are happening in the world that the end of the world is almost here?

Throughout history mankind has asked this question. Because he is created in the image of God, he senses that there will be a time when he must answer to God for the manner in which he has lived his life. Usually, when the trauma he or his nation is enduring is especially terrible, both in its size as well as in its duration of time, he begins to wonder if "doomsday," as he frequently expresses it, has almost come.

The Bible gives a number of signs that show mankind that the end has almost come.

In fact, the Bible gives a number of signs that show mankind that the end has almost come. These signs will not help us in knowing the likely month and year when Christ will return, but they do offer corroboration to the conclusions we can arrive at by projecting the calendar of the Bible to its Biblical suggested end. In *1994?* as well as in this sequel to that book, we have found an immense amount of data that focuses on September, 1994, as the likely month and year for the end.

Returning to the signs that may be in evidence showing that we are almost at the end of time, we are directed by the Bible to at least seven signs that we should examine. Some of these have been mentioned or even detailed in the book *1994?* but they will still be listed and briefly examined in this chapter so that we may be altogether aware of them. We will discover that by these signs alone, completely apart from any understanding of the numbers found in the Bible, we can be very certain that we are very near the end of this world.

Israel has become a Nation

The first sign that we will consider is that Israel has again become a nation.

In Matthew 24:32-33, we read:

Now learn a parable of the fig tree; When his branch is yet tender, and putteth forth leaves, ye know that summer is nigh: So likewise ye, when ye shall see all these things, know that it is near, even at the doors.

In the Bible, God frequently typifies individuals or nations by certain kinds of trees. Believers are typified by the palm tree or the olive tree. Other trees, such as the cedar tree or the sycamore tree, can be a metaphorical reference to nations of the world.

When we study the matter of the fig tree, we learn that it refers to a nation or a person under the curse of God. Jesus is called a fig tree in John 1:48 because He had become a curse for us. In that context Nathanael, who was a picture of believers, was under the fig tree in the sense that Jesus, who had taken upon Himself Nathanael's sins, ruled over Nathanael as Christ rules over all believers.

> *The only other entity to which the fig tree can refer*
> *is the nation of Israel.*

The only other entity to which the fig tree can refer is the nation of Israel. They are typified in the Bible by a fig tree because even though for 2100 years they had been God's special people, they, too, came under the curse of God so that it as a nation could never turn to Christ as Messiah. This curse was dramatized by Jesus when He cursed the physical fig tree in the account found in Mark 11:12-21.

But Matthew 24:32 indicates that when the fig tree would put forth leaves it would be a sign that the return of Christ was very near.

Amazingly, after almost 2000 years, the fig tree appears alive and well. In 1948, Israel again became a nation among the nations of the world. The fig tree is in leaf. However, the Bible predicted there would be no fruit and as a direct fulfillment of that prophecy we see no evidence of any desire on their part as a nation to acknowledge Jesus as their Messiah. To be in fruit must relate to a nation that has come to trust in the God of the Bible and His salvation program.

But the fig tree is in leaf and, therefore, we know the time has come very close for the return of Christ. He is near, even at the doors.

False Prophets Have Arisen

Sign number two is that false prophets featuring signs and wonders have arisen.

In Matthew 24, Jesus repeatedly makes reference to false Christs arising as a sign that the end of the world is near. In Matthew 24:24, He declares:

> For there shall arise false Christs, and false prophets, and shall shew great signs and wonders; insomuch that, if it were possible, they shall deceive the very elect.

We discussed this sign at length in the book *1994?*, but let it suffice us to say that never before has there been such a worldwide interest in signs and wonders, that is, in miracles, as there is in the present day. The dramatic rise in interest and involvement with the matter of miracles is clearly given as a sign that the end of the world is almost here.

The dramatic rise in interest and involvement with the matter of miracles is clearly given as a sign that the end of the world is almost here.

The Falling Away

Sign number three is the falling away of the church.

In II Thessalonians 2:3, we read of two events that must take place before Christ returns. The first is that there will be a falling away of the church. This event, too, has been discussed at length in the book *1994?* Perhaps we can summarize the apostasy or falling away that is so pervasive in the churches of our day by noting the general indictment that most churches are no longer under the authority of the Bible. True, a great many churches still speak of the "inerrant" or "infallible Word of God," and many still declare that the Bible is their authority.

But when we examine these churches in action, we find that the Bible is no longer their authority. Their authority for the salvation plan they teach or the practice they hold is not the Bible. Instead, their authority is what the pastors have learned in seminary or the church fathers have declared to be true. A great many churches have their "Confessions" or their "Systematic Theology" as the statement of final authority.

This does not mean that a church should not have a "Confession" or follow the Systematic Theology that has been taught in seminary. Indeed, every church has a statement of doctrinal principles which it believes to be Biblical. Therefore, it tries to follow these principles. But when it refuses to change or modify these principles when they can be shown to be in error, then it is obvious that the "Confession" or the Systematic Theology is the ultimate authority rather than the Bible.

A most distressing phenomenon is that virtually never do we hear of congregations and denominations looking in the mirror and asking: "Where have we gone wrong?" On the contrary, as we repeatedly see the shift toward women deacons and pastors, more interest in miracles, less and less preaching on hell and damnation, etc., etc., we can know that more frequently any reevaluation that is going on in churches is moving them away from the Bible rather than toward its authority.

This falling away is particularly awful because it comes at a time when so many people are literate and have access to a Bible. It comes at a time when so many study helps, such as concordances, are easily available. It comes at a time when so many excellent means of communication are available. All of these should mean a tremendous increase in Bible understanding all over the world.

Amazingly, just the opposite is happening. Instead of an increase in Bible knowledge, in most churches there is a falling away from truth. The Bible increasingly is no longer the final authority. It has become supplanted by the church and the ideas of men as the ultimate authority. Thus, it is no wonder that few today have a healthy fear of God. The Gospel that is preached to a high degree has degenerated into a religion that is pleasing to the ears of men.

> *This stubborn continuation on a path going away from truth and moving toward further apostasy that is so common in churches and denominations in our day is predicted in the Bible and is further evidence that we must be well into the final tribulation period.*

Significantly, this stubborn continuation on a path going away from truth and moving toward further apostasy that is so common in churches and denominations in our day is predicted in the Bible and is further evidence that we must be well into the final tribulation period. In II Thessalonians 2:11, God declares that He will send them (the church) strong delusion that they should believe a lie. We read:

> And for this cause God shall send them strong delusion, that they should believe a lie.

In Jeremiah 6:2 God describes Zion the church as a delicate woman who has fallen. In this Book, the church is typified by ancient Israel which came under the judgment of God because of their continued sins. This judgment was physical as God brought Babylon against Judah to destroy it. But it is a picture of the church of our day as God brings Satan against it to destroy it spiritually.

The Book of Lamentations is a lament or a funeral dirge in which the church weeps over its destruction by God as its destroyer. In Lamentations 1:13 we read:

> From above hath he sent fire into my bones, and it prevaileth against them: he hath spread a net for my feet, he hath turned me back: he hath made me desolate and faint all the day.

The "he" is definitely God. The "me" is the church. This verse is teaching that God has put a net or snare on the church so that it turns away from truth even as II Thessalonians 2:11 teaches that God will send a strong delusion. Thus, it is not at all surprising that churches are not turning to truth. They are snared by God to remain in their apostasy and even to turn back to greater apostasy.

A church that does not operate with the Bible as the ultimate and final authority will increasingly develop doctrines and practices contrary to the Bible. This result is guaranteed to follow because no matter how intelligent men may be, their ideas are both sin-tainted and completely limited compared with the infinite perfect truth presented by God in the Bible. Moreover, the practice of denying the ultimate authority of the Bible guarantees the removal of the blessing of God on that church. The result can only be rapid increasing apostasy even as we are seeing it happen in so many churches in our day.

> *The practice of denying the ultimate authority of the Bible guarantees the removal of the blessing of God on that church.*

The Antichrist

Sign number four is that the man of sin is revealed.

A fourth sign in evidence that we are very near the end of time is that the man of sin, the Antichrist, has been revealed.

Throughout the New Testament era, it was fairly generally taught that the man of sin spoken of in II Thessalonians 2 would be some great political or religious (or a combination of both) world leader. Thus, in his day, Kaiser Wilhelm was spoken of as the Antichrist. Earlier than that one of the popes of the Roman Catholic Church was regarded as the Antichrist. During the Second World War, Hitler and Mussolini shared the spotlight as being the Antichrist.

> *Through His Word, God the Holy Spirit has revealed that Satan is the Antichrist.*

But in every instant these conclusions proved false because the world continued on its way. However, in our day, we have come to know without question who the Antichrist is. Through His Word, God the Holy Spirit has revealed that Satan is the Antichrist. As I John 4:3 teaches, the Antichrist was already in the world before the Bible was completed and he is to come.

There we read:

And every spirit that confesseth not that Jesus Christ is come in the flesh is not of God: and this is that spirit of antichrist, whereof ye have heard that it should come, and even now already is it in the world.

Only Satan can meet the qualifications of this verse. He was already in existence almost 2000 years ago when this statement was written. And he is to come near the end of the world. Therefore, the Antichrist must be Satan himself.

This makes abundant sense. The Bible constantly speaks of two kingdoms: that of Christ and that of Satan. Christ is the head of the true kingdom of God. His followers are called Christians and prophets. Satan as the pseudo-Christ or Antichrist heads up the other kingdom. In the Bible his followers are called antichrists or false prophets. Because Satan is the master deceiver, he masquerades as Christ so that the spiritually unwary are snared into following him when they are convinced in their own minds that they are following Christ.

In II Thessalonians 2:3-4, we read how Satan rules in congregations and churches.

> Let no man deceive you by any means: for that day shall not come, except there come a falling away first, and that man of sin be revealed, the son of perdition; Who opposeth and exalteth himself above all that is called God, or that is worshipped; so that he as God sitteth in the temple of God, shewing himself that he is God.

The temple is the body of believers. They are found in churches and congregations all over the world. But these churches have become false churches because they are no longer faithful to the Bible. So Satan has taken control as the man of sin.

> *Satan is called a man because in Isaiah 14, he is typified by the king of Babylon.*

Satan is called a man because in Isaiah 14, he is typified by the king of Babylon. Verse 4 declares:

> That thou shalt take up this proverb against the king of Babylon, and say, How hath the oppressor ceased! the golden city ceased!

And then as the passage continues to talk about the king of Babylon, verses 12-14 state:

How art thou fallen from heaven, O Lucifer, son of the morning! how art thou cut down to the ground, which didst weaken the nations! For thou hast said in thine heart, I will ascend into heaven, I will exalt my throne above the stars of God: I will sit also upon the mount of the congregation, in the sides of the north: I will ascend above the heights of the clouds; I will be like the most High.

Theologians correctly have concluded that these verses refer to Satan, who headed up the angels who rebelled against God at the beginning.

But then in verses 15-16, the Bible speaks of Satan as a man:

Isaiah 14:15-16: Yet thou shalt be brought down to hell, to the sides of the pit. They that see thee shall narrowly look upon thee, and consider thee, saying, Is this the man that made the earth to tremble, that did shake kingdoms.

Satan is spoken of as a man because he is typified by a man, the king of Babylon. God uses the king of Babylon as a picture of Satan because the kingdom of Satan is called Babylon. This is seen clearly in Revelation 17 and Revelation 18. Revelation 18:2 is an example:

And he cried mightily with a strong voice, saying, Babylon the great is fallen, is fallen, and is become the habitation of devils, and the hold of every foul spirit, and a cage of every unclean and hateful bird.

Since Satan is typified by the king of Babylon because he rules over the spiritual Babylon, and since he is called "a man" in Isaiah 14, therefore, God picks up this idea by calling him the "man of sin" in II Thessalonians 2.

The fact that we know that Satan is indeed the man of sin, the Antichrist, therefore, assures us that the end of the world has drawn very near.

The fact that we now know that Satan is indeed the man of sin, the Antichrist, therefore, assures us that the end of the world has drawn very near.

Curiously, we can know that the Antichrist is Satan. Yet most theologians and pastors are still looking for a great world leader of some kind who will be in-filled by Satan. However, Satan as usual comes as the master deceiver. The Bible tells us that he is the father of lies. He does not come, so to speak, with a red suit and forked tail. He comes as an angel of light. In II Corinthians 11:13-15, God describes how we are to recognize him:

> For such are false apostles, deceitful workers, transforming themselves into the apostles of Christ. And no marvel; for Satan himself is transformed into an angel of light. Therefore it is no great thing if his ministers also be transformed as the ministers of righteousness; whose end shall be according to their works.

Because Satan is a spirit he must come through those who follow him. Yes, even they who are false teachers and preachers are also completely deceived. They are convinced that they are ministers of Christ while in fact they are ministers of Satan, who works through them as the Antichrist.

They can be known because they are bringing false gospels. And in their blindness they fully believe they will recognize the Antichrist when he will come.

Through the false doctrines and false gospels that are everywhere in our day, Satan is bringing spiritual havoc to the churches, even as the Bible predicts.

Only when we read the Bible very carefully can we know that he has come as the Antichrist. And through the false doctrines and false gospels that are everywhere in our day, he is bringing spiritual havoc to the churches even as the Bible predicts. Because very frequently he is not recognized as the Antichrist, many teachers and preachers are lulled into spiritual unconsciousness thinking that we cannot be near the end of time because the Antichrist must still be revealed.

Running To and Fro

Sign number five is that many shall run to and fro.

Another sign that we are very near the end of the world is indicated by the language of Daniel 12:4:

> But thou, O Daniel, shut up the words, and seal the book, even to the time of the end: many shall run to and fro, and knowledge shall be increased.

This verse clearly speaks of the end of the world and emphasizes that "many shall run to and fro." What does this mean? Does this mean that the abundant air travel of our day, which makes possible speedy trips to almost any part of the world, is a sign that we are near the end of time?

A search of the Bible assures us that that is not what God has in mind by the phrase "run to and fro." Instead, we find in Amos 8:11-12 the declaration:

> Behold, the days come, saith the Lord GOD, that I will send a famine in the land, not a famine of bread, nor a thirst for water, but of hearing the words of the LORD: And they shall wander from sea to sea, and from the north even to the east, they shall run to and fro to seek the word of the LORD, and shall not find it.

These verses teach that running "to and fro" has to do with the scarcity of the true Gospel that will exist in the world at the end of time. Because increasingly the churches that should be presenting the true Gospel have fallen away, it has become extremely difficult for believers to find churches that bring the whole counsel of God and still practice the principle that the Bible is the ultimate authority.

It has become extremely difficult for believers to find churches that bring the whole counsel of God and still practice the principle that the Bible is the ultimate authority.

Moreover, Satan is loosed and he is blinding the spiritual eyes of so many. In addition, God Himself is sending unto them "strong delusion, that they should believe a lie" (II Thessalonians 2:11). Thus, those who are running to and fro looking for truth, in reality do not want truth. Even as they run to and fro seeking truth, they more often than not reject it even when they hear it.

Additionally, in their quest for truth, frequently they are seeking for it in places far removed from the Gospel. Such activities as the New Age movement and similar occult practices attest to this.

This sign is dramatically in evidence in our day.

Knowledge Shall Increase

A sixth sign is that knowledge shall increase.
In Daniel 12:4, we read:

But thou, O Daniel, shut up the words, and seal the book, even to the time of the end: many shall run to and fro, and knowledge shall be increased.

Knowledge shall increase as a sign that we are near the end of time. What knowledge is this? Is this the secular knowledge that has increased so spectacularly in our day? By means of faster and faster computers, scientists have been enabled to expose secrets of this universe that previously have not been known to man. An understanding of DNA, gene technology, superconductors, fiber optics, etc., etc., are a tiny sample of the extensive knowledge that scientists are amassing as they probe this world that God has created. And every day there are new discoveries. Indeed, it appears that God has taken all of the limitations away insofar as where man can go as he pursues this kind of knowledge. One cannot help but wonder: If the Lord would tarry even a few years, what else will man discover?

The tragedy of all this discovery, which God is allowing in our day, is that it is not causing man to glorify God. As each new discovery comes to light, mankind ought to exclaim in breathless wonder "What a wonderful Creator God is, as evidenced by such a complex and beautiful creation!" Instead, with each new discovery, mankind reacts like they are the creator of what they have discovered.

> *Truly man's rebellion against God is magnifying with each new discovery.*

Instead of praising God, they increasingly conclude that they are learning to be the masters of their fate. They convince themselves that they are increasingly in control of their destiny. Truly man's rebellion against God is magnifying with each new discovery!

But this is not the kind of knowledge spoken of in Daniel 12:4. In the Bible's definition of knowledge, God has in mind a knowledge of God and His Word. Therefore, while it is true that this is a time when physical knowledge is on the increase, it is also a time when a knowledge of the Word of God is on the increase.

This does not mean that more and more people are coming to know God. The Bible definitely teaches that the opposite is true. As we approach the end, fewer and fewer people are becoming saved.

But amongst those who are saved there is a great increase in the understanding of the Bible. For example, a great many of the teachings declared in the book *1994?* and in this sequel to it have been known to believers only the last few years. It seems very apparent that in our generation God has taken the "lid off" of a greater knowledge of the physical universe, and so, too, God has taken the "lid off" of a greater understanding of the Word of God.

Theology's High-Water Mark

Theology (the study of God) reached its high-water mark during the Reformation or shortly thereafter. It was during that period of history that such notable men as Calvin and Luther lived. It was the period from which we received the confessions that have helped to stabilize the church. The Augsburg Confession, the Heidelberg Catechism, the Canons of Dort, the Belgic Confession, and the Westminster Confession were all written several hundred years ago, shortly after the Reformation.

Study of the writings of these men and of the confessions indicate that the church had come to a fairly accurate understanding of the basic doctrines of the Bible: The authority of the Bible; its infallible, inerrant nature; God revealed as three distinct persons even though there is only one God; the doctrines of grace which have to do with the nature of the atonement and man's salvation; doctrines concerning creation and the end of the world, at which time the unbelievers would be judged and removed into Hell while the believers would be with Christ forevermore in the new heavens and the new earth, were quite accurately understood.

> *It appears that some doctrines that were held were not quite as Biblical as they could have been.*

This is so even though it appears that some doctrines that were held were not quite as Biblical as they could have been. For example, it was not commonly held that believers receive their new resurrected souls at the moment of salvation; that there are no special rewards given in eternity to believers who work especially hard for Christ after they are saved; that believers will never stand before the Judgment Throne of God; or that there cannot be any saving efficacy in the signs of water baptism and communion.

Even so, God in His mercy had given the church an excellent understanding of such important doctrines as the sovereignty of God, election and predestination, eternal damnation, and the incarnation of Christ.

But as we view history it appears that God had set some kind of limit on how much Bible knowledge would be understood during most of the history of the church. As the decades and centuries that followed the Reformation unfolded, a further and greater understanding of the Bible did not continue. Any activity relating the possibility of further Biblical understanding was normally in a direction away from the truth of the Bible. For example, the so-called premillennial idea of Christ's return gained countless adherents even though it can be readily shown to be totally contrary to the Bible.

In fact, any preacher or church that in our day holds tenaciously to the doctrines promulgated during that earlier period of the Reformation, when many of the confessions were formed, is looked upon as being especially careful in their understanding of the Bible.

> *Therefore, the Bible is a Book that could be insistently studied for many lifetimes without ever plumbing the depths of the spiritual riches that can be found in it.*

This is a very curious situation. The Bible is God's Word to mankind and has come to us from an infinite God. Therefore, it is a book that could be insistently studied for many lifetimes without ever plumbing the depths of the spiritual riches that can be found in it. It is indeed strange, therefore, that truth that has been faithfully derived from the Bible froze at the Reformation level. Throughout these past hundreds of years, with far more literacy, far more Bibles, far better communication methods, and far more study helps, one would think that a great harvest of spiritual fruit would have flowed from the Bible. God, of course, is in control of this, and obviously it was not His plan that new truth should continuously flow from the Bible.

> *It is God's plan that knowledge of His Word would be on the increase near the end.*

But now we are very close to the end of time. It is God's plan that knowledge of His Word would be on the increase near the end. Therefore, we should not be surprised at what we are learning about the numbers God has placed in the Bible. We should not be surprised at the new insights many believers are receiving, insights that relate to the timing and the details of the end of the world.

> *Who would dare to say that he has uncovered Bible truth of which such men as John Calvin and Martin Luther were unaware?*

It is true, however, that pastors and teachers of the Bible who have received their training in schools that have departed from the truth that the Bible is the final authority are greatly offended by the charge that the church, to an increasing degree, is no longer faithful to the Bible. Pastors who are very conservative in that they were trained in the doctrines developed and set forth during the Reformation and who rigorously hold to the long-standing confessions are also offended. After all, who would dare to say that he has uncovered Bible truth of which such men as John Calvin or Martin Luther were unaware?

That, however, is the nature of the Bible. In our day, if one diligently and faithfully continues to search it out, always ready to be obedient to what he discovers, always making certain that what he discovers harmonizes with that which already has been shown to be trustworthy truth, he is bound to come up with additional truth.

The question then remains: Should the one who has come forth with additional truth that is harmonious with the whole Bible be looked upon as arrogant, heretical, etc.? Or should his findings be carefully examined by searching the Bible as others check out what he has found?

In any case, it cannot be denied that we are living in a day when Biblical knowledge is on the increase. If there were ever a time when a Bible student should seriously study the Bible, it is in our day.

Homosexuality

A seventh sign that shows in dramatic fashion that we are at the end of the world is the fact that the homosexuals have come out of the closet, that is, they openly boast of their sin.

> *It is very striking that the sin that was especially featured at the time Sodom and Gomorrah were destroyed was that of homosexuality.*

It is very striking that the sin that was especially featured at the time Sodom and Gomorrah were destroyed was that of homosexuality. When God, who had taken on the appearance of two men, came to warn the city and Lot's family of the impending judgment on these cities, the Bible records the reaction of the men of the city to these two visitors. We read of this sad event in Genesis 19:4-11:

> But before they lay down, the men of the city, even the men of Sodom, compassed the house round, both old and young, all the people from every quarter: And they called unto Lot, and said unto him, Where are the men which came in to thee this night? bring them out unto us, that we may know them. And Lot went out at the door unto them, and shut the door after him, And said, I pray you, brethren, do not so wickedly. Behold now, I have two daughters which have not known man; let me, I pray you, bring them out unto you, and do ye to them as is good in your eyes: only unto these men do nothing; for therefore came they under the shadow of my roof. And they said, Stand back. And they said again, This one fellow came in to sojourn, and he will needs be a judge: now will we deal worse with thee, than with them. And they pressed sore upon the man, even Lot, and came near to break the door. But the men put forth their hand, and pulled Lot into the house to them, and shut to the door. And they smote the men that were at the door of the house with blindness, both small and great: so that they wearied themselves to find the door.

The phrase "that we may know them" indicates the desire of the men of the city to have sexual relations with the two visitors. This is underscored when Lot in desperation offers his two virgin daughters in order to hospitably protect the visitors.

God points to the destruction of Sodom and Gomorrah as a picture or representation of the final judgment. Luke 17:28-30:

Likewise also as it was in the days of Lot; they did eat, they drank, they bought, they sold, they planted, they builded; But the same day that Lot went out of Sodom it rained fire and brimstone from heaven, and destroyed them all. Even thus shall it be in the day when the Son of man is revealed.

> *Today, homosexuality is increasingly being taught and practiced as an alternative lifestyle that should be acceptable to all people.*

Mysteriously in our day the identical sin that was boldly practiced in Sodom just before its destruction is boldly being practiced all over the world. Today, homosexuality is increasingly being taught and practiced as an alternative lifestyle that should be acceptable to all people.

One would think that when the plague of AIDS began to sweep through the world, being evidenced to a high degree in the homosexual community, that this would so shame those who practiced this sin that they would again hide themselves from the eyes of the public.

Amazingly, the very opposite is the case. The homosexuals have used the AIDS plague to obtain the pity and compassion of the world and at the same time advertise this kind of lifestyle as being quite normal and acceptable.

As we indicated in *1994?* (pages 207-214), the AIDS plague which was predicted in Romans 1:24-27, serves two very important purposes. They are:

1. The AIDS plague together with the fact that homosexuality is increasingly being accepted as a viable lifestyle is a dramatic sign that the world is ripe for judgment.

2. It is a judgment predicted in the Bible which can readily be seen by all men, thus indicating the Bible's predictions concerning future judgments do come true. In like manner, the repeated predictions of the Bible concerning the judgment of the last day will also certainly come to pass.

By these seven signs which are dramatically in evidence in our day, God is assuring us that we are at the time of the end of the world.

Let me ask you: **Are you ready to meet God?** To test this question, let me present this situation: Suppose you went to the doctor tomorrow for a health test, and a few days later, he told you that you had a terrible, incurable illness that would certainly take your life in the next thirty days. After the initial shock of such a disclosure, would you begin to be increasingly at peace and in happiness that soon you would be leaving this life, with all its tears and sorrows, and entering into the glorious presence of your Savior?

Or would you find an increasing bitterness and resentment in your soul that your life is being so quickly cut off? Such a careful examination can help you to know if you are ready to meet God.

My dear friend, if you have any doubts at all about your salvation, cry to God for His mercy. The fact that you can still read this indicates that it is still the day of salvation. But time is running out - fast!!

Chapter 2.
The Jubilee Year

In the book *1994?*, references were made to the Jubilee. Because of the nature and character of this important year and its identification with the end of the world, we should look at it more carefully and in greater detail than we had done in the book *1994?*

Even before we examine the Biblical information about the Jubilee year, we should ask the question: The laws concerning the Jubilee and its observance are part of the Old Testament ceremonial system; what does that have to do with the New Testament era and the end of time?

The Feast Days Directly Relate to the Unfolding of the Salvation Plan

That is a fair question in that we know from the Bible that once Christ went to the cross, we are no longer to offer sacrifices or observe special days such as the seventh day Sabbath or new moons or other feast days. Therefore, we definitely know that throughout the New Testament era we are not to observe the Jubilee year.

> *We discover that while we are not to observe these special days, God does recognize them as He unfolds His salvation plan.*

But having said this, we look again at the Bible and we discover that while we are not to observe these special days, God does recognize them as He unfolds His salvation plan. We learned in the book *1994?* that the day that Jesus was announced as the Lamb who takes away the sin of the world was the first day of the seventh month of the Jewish calendar, the day that was a new moon called the feast of the trumpets.

Moreover, the day that Jesus was crucified as the Lamb of God was the very day the priests were slaughtering the lambs in the temple in their observance of the Passover Day called for in the Old Testament ceremonial laws.

Of course, these were events that took place on the Old Testament side of the cross. Now we are in the New Testament era. But God assures us that the spiritual application of the Old Testament feast days goes on into the New Testament era. This is proven by the fact that fifty days after the Passover was the feast of weeks at which time the initial harvest was recognized as a special day called Pentecost.

> *While the Jews were observing Pentecost as an Old Testament ceremonial feast day, God was observing it in its spiritual fullness, and the initial harvest of 3000 souls was brought into the temple, which is the body of Christ.*

It was on Pentecost day fifty days after the cross and, therefore, well into the New Testament era that the Holy Spirit was poured out, which we read about in Acts 2. While the Jews were observing Pentecost as an Old Testament ceremonial feast day, God was observing it in its spiritual fullness, and the initial harvest of 3000 souls was brought into the temple, which is the body of Christ.

Indeed, God is clearly demonstrating that the Old Testament feast days have literal application in the New Testament era. But the application is not to be done by the church or by man's efforts. It is to be done by God.

When Was the Jubilee Year?

Therefore, when we read Leviticus 25 and Leviticus 27, which have so much to say about a Jubilee year, we wonder what God's application of this event might be in the New Testament era.

To discover the New Testament application of this year requires that first we know when it was to be observed in the Old Testament era. This is very important because the application by God of the feast of trumpets on the first day of the seventh month of the Jewish calendar, Tishri 1, when Jesus was announced, the Passover on the fourteenth day of the first month of the Jewish calendar, Nisan 14, when Jesus was crucified, and the feast of weeks fifty days later, when the Holy Spirit was poured out, all occurred on the exact day called for by Old Testament law.

Likewise, the Old Testament law demanded that the Jubilee year be observed at a very precise time which was set forth by God Himself. We turn to Leviticus 25 to determine this time. In Leviticus 25:2, we read:

> Speak unto the children of Israel, and say unto them, When ye come into the land which I give you, then shall the land keep a sabbath unto the LORD.

Verses 8 to 11a continue with the information:

> And thou shalt number seven sabbaths of years unto thee, seven times seven years; and the space of the seven sabbaths of years shall be unto thee forty and nine years. Then shalt thou cause the trumpet of the jubile to sound on the tenth day of the seventh month, in the day of atonement shall ye make the trumpet sound throughout all your land. And ye shall hallow the fiftieth year, and proclaim liberty throughout all the land unto all the inhabitants thereof: it shall be a jubile unto you; and ye shall return every man unto his possession, and ye shall return every man unto his family. A jubile shall that fiftieth year be unto you.

To determine the year during which the Jubilee was to be observed requires that we know the year Israel came into the land of Canaan.

To determine the year during which the Jubilee was to be observed requires that we know the year Israel came into the land of Canaan. That year was to be a Sabbath year and was to be followed by a series of seven seven-year periods with the next year after that being the Jubilee year.

From our very careful study of the Biblical calendars, we found from the Biblical data that Israel entered the land of Canaan in the year 1407 B.C. (see page 298, *1994?*). As called for in the above verses, the year 1407 B.C. was, therefore, a Sabbath year.

This year was to be followed by a series of seven seven-year periods, the last year of each seven-year period was also to be a Sabbath year. Thus, the sequence of years was as follows:

Entrance into the land of Canaan, <u>1407 B.C.</u>, a Sabbath year.

1. 1406, 1405, 1404, 1403, 1402, 1401, <u>1400</u>, a Sabbath year.

2. 1399, 1398, 1397, 1396, 1395, 1394, <u>1393</u>, a Sabbath year.

3. 1392, 1391, 1390, 1389, 1388, 1387, <u>1386</u>, a Sabbath year.

4. 1385, 1384, 1483, 1382, 1381, 1380, <u>1379</u>, a Sabbath year.

5. 1378, 1377, 1376, 1375, 1374, 1373, <u>1372</u>, a Sabbath year.

6. 1371, 1370, 1369, 1368, 1367, 1366, <u>1365</u>, a Sabbath year.

7. 1364, 1363, 1362, 1361, 1360, 1359, <u>1358</u>, a Sabbath year.

The next year was the fiftieth year, and it was to be the Jubilee year. Thus, 1357 B.C., which immediately followed the year 1358 B.C., was the first Jubilee year. The sequence of seven seven-year periods was then repeated so that 1307 B.C. became the next Jubilee year. From then on, therefore, every year ending in 57 or 07 was a Jubilee year. Thus, 7 B.C., when Christ was born, was also a Jubilee year.

When we project the Jubilee year into the New Testament era, we know the next Jubilee year after 7 B.C. was 44 A.D. (7 + 44 - 1 = 50). Remember, because there is no year 0, when we are determining the duration of time between an Old Testament event and a New Testament event, we are to add the Old Testament years to the New Testament years and subtract 1.

> *We can be certain, therefore, that if we project the Jubilee years into the New Testament era, the year 1994 is a Jubilee year.*

Since 44 A.D. was a Jubilee year, the year 94 A.D., which came fifty years later, was also a Jubilee year. Thus, every New Testament year ending in 44 or 94 would be a Jubilee year. We can be certain, therefore, that when we project the Jubilee years into the New Testament era, we find the year 1994 is a Jubilee year.

The Significance of the Jubilee Year

Having established when the Jubilee year occurred, we next wonder about the significance of the Jubilee year. Leviticus 25:10 declares:

And ye shall hallow the fiftieth year, and proclaim liberty throughout all the land unto all the inhabitants thereof: it shall be a jubile unto you; and ye shall return every man unto his possession, and ye shall return every man unto his family.

In Leviticus 27:24, the Bible says:

In the year of the jubile the field shall return unto him of whom it was bought, even to him to whom the possession of the land did belong.

Historically, during the Old Testament era, every fifty years at the time of the Jubilee year, all debts were forgiven, all Jews who had sold themselves as slaves in payment for debt were set free, and all land went back to the original owners. Every financial arrangement had to have these principles in mind.

> *Spiritually, the Jubilee year was without question*
> *pointing to the end of the world.*

Spiritually, the Jubilee year was without question pointing to the end of the world. True, in a sense we experience the Jubilee year spiritually at the time we become saved. At that moment, all of the debt that we owe God because of our sins is forgiven. We definitely come into the liberty of salvation.

But the Bible indicates that the believers will inherit the earth. We read in Matthew 5:5: "Blessed are the meek: for they shall inherit the earth." Of course, it will not be this earth in its present sin-cursed state. Instead, it will be a redeemed earth, in which no curse or corruption will be found. In the Garden of Eden, mankind was given this present earth, but when he rebelled against God, he lost this possession and became a slave of Satan. The proof that he has lost his ownership of this earth is dramatically seen every day all around us. A man works hard all his life and finally owns many acres of land. But then he dies. Abruptly his ownership has come to an end. On the last day, he will be resurrected, judged, and removed into a place called Hell. He will never have further ownership of this earth.

But for believers, a far more glorious future is coming. It is true that now we may own little or nothing of the earth. As a matter of fact, God declares of believers in Hebrews 11:13:

> These all died in faith, not having received the promises, but having seen them afar off, and were persuaded of them, and embraced them, and confessed that they were strangers and pilgrims on the earth.

> *However, when the end of the world comes,*
> *the believers will again become the*
> *owners of earth.*

However, when the end of the world comes, the believers will again become the owners of earth. It will not be the earth in its present sin-cursed form; it will be a glorious new heaven and new earth. Then full liberty will be established as called for in Romans 8:21-23:

Because the creature [creation] itself also shall be delivered from the bondage of corruption into the glorious liberty of the children of God. For we know that the whole creation groaneth and travaileth in pain together until now. And not only they, but ourselves also, which have the firstfruits of the Spirit, even we ourselves groan within ourselves, waiting for the adoption, to wit, the redemption of our body.

This liberty, which is partially given to us at the time we become saved, will be total at the end of the world. At that time our salvation is completed in that we receive our resurrected body and the new heaven and new earth becomes our habitation. Then the creation itself is set at liberty from the bondage of corruption it was placed under because of Adam's sin. Simultaneously, the believer's liberty is completed.

> *Thus, we can know that the Jubilee year has everything to do with the end of the world when the earth itself will be delivered from the bondage of corruption and the believers will all experience the removal of the last bondage they are under - that of sin and a corrupted body.*

Thus, we can know that the Jubilee year has everything to do with the end of the world when the earth itself will be delivered from the bondage of corruption and the believers will all experience the removal of the last bondage they are under - that of sin and a corrupted body. Moreover, they will at that time no longer be pilgrims and strangers on this earth but will receive their inheritance of this earth as the new heavens and the new earth.

The Jubilee and the Ram's Horn

Returning to Leviticus 25, we find some very significant words, which when compared to the same words in Joshua 6 and Exodus 19, direct us down another path to the end of the world.

In Leviticus 25, the word "Jubilee" is found fifteen times. In fourteen of these times, it is the Hebrew word "*yobel*." The word "*yobel,*" however, is translated "ram's horn" in Joshua 6:4, 5, 6, 8, 13. What does a ram's horn have in common with Jubilee? Very much, as we shall discover when we look carefully at the context in which "ram's horn" is found in Joshua 6.

In Joshua 6, God records for us the destruction of Jericho. It was indeed a very unusual way that God prescribed to bring about its destruction. Jericho was a walled city. Its inhabitants were safe within its walls. From the top of the walls, they could repulse almost any enemy attack. Therefore, as long as they had sufficient food and water and they carefully guarded the gate to city, they were safe.

But it was not God's plan that Israel surround the city for a long time so that eventually the city would have to surrender because their food and water were gone. God prescribed an altogether different attack plan. It is described in Joshua 6:3-5:

> And ye shall compass the city, all ye men of war, and go round about the city once. Thus shalt thou do six days. And seven priests shall bear before the ark seven trumpets of rams' horns: and the seventh day ye shall compass the city seven times, and the priests shall blow with the trumpets. And it shall come to pass, that when they make a long blast with the ram's horn, and when ye hear the sound of the trumpet, all the people shall shout with a great shout; and the wall of the city shall fall down flat, and the people shall ascend up every man straight before him.

Israel was to go around the city once each day for six days, with seven priests blowing trumpets made of the horn of a ram, the ark following them (verses 8, 11). No other sound was to be made (verse 10). On the seventh day, they were to encompass the city seven times. When the city had been encompassed the seventh time on the seventh day, the priests were to blow a loud blast with the ram's horn trumpets and the people who were marching around the city were to give a simultaneous loud shout. At that moment the walls would fall flat and Israel's army could easily destroy the city.

But the ram's horn trumpets are called "yobel" which is the identical word translated "jubilee" in Leviticus 25. Does this destruction of Jericho, therefore, relate in any way to the Jubilee of 1994?

> *Does this destruction of Jericho, therefore, relate in*
> *any way to the Jubilee of 1994?*

Indeed it does. Please note how many times Israel encircled the city before the walls fell. Yes, a total of thirteen times. Once each of six days plus seven times on the seventh day equals a total of thirteen times.

Thirteen Encirclements of Jericho - 13,000 Years

When does the last Jubilee of the world take place? At the end of 13,000 years. We surely can see the parallelism. What happened to the inhabitants of Jericho, except for Rahab and her family, is declared in verse 21: "And they utterly destroyed all that was in the city, both man and woman, young and old, and ox, and sheep, and ass, with the edge of the sword."

Who is destroyed by being cast into hell at the end of 13,000 years? Each and every one who is unsaved. Who was kept alive when Jericho was destroyed? Rahab and her family. Who does not come into judgment at the time of the end of the world? All the believers, of whom Rahab and her family are a picture, will be safe from destruction.

What did the ark represent? It should have been in the holy of holies in the tabernacle where no eye could see it. But God had commanded that it, too, go around the city. Thus, those who were to be destroyed could see it as they peered over the wall. And all Israel could see it. Why was the ark out there in the open for every eye to see? Remember, the ark represents Christ Himself. And on the last day, when God brings His judgment on the world, every eye will see Christ as the Judge of all the earth. The presence of the ark at the fateful end of Jericho clearly points to Christ coming to judge the world on the last day.

> *The sound of the Jubilee after thirteen*
> *encirclements brought the moment of judgment*
> *upon the city.*

What happened at the moment the walls fell? Joshua 6:5 declares that when the priests made a long blast with the ram's horn, the people shouted with a great shout, and the walls fell flat. The sound of the Jubilee after thirteen encirclements brought the moment of judgment upon the city. Can we see why the words ram's horn and Jubilee are the same word? Jubilee identifies with judgment even as the judgment at the end of the world is in a Jubilee year.

Jubilee and the Shout at the End of the World

There is another parallel. In Leviticus 25, the Hebrew word translated "Jubilee" is always the word "*yobel,*" which as we have seen is translated "ram's horn" in Joshua 6. That is the case in every instance except in Leviticus 25:9: "Then shalt thou cause the trumpet of the jubile to sound on the tenth day of the seventh month, in the day of atonement shall ye make the trumpet sound throughout all your land." This verse contains the word Jubilee, but in this instance, the Hebrew word translated "Jubilee" is not "*yobel.*" It is the word "*teruah.*" The word "*teruah*" is normally translated "shout" in the Bible. See, for example, Numbers 23:21, I Samuel 4:5-6, and Ezra 3:11-13.

In two very auspicious verses in Joshua 6, the Hebrew word "*teruah*" is translated "shout." In Joshua 6:5, we read: "all the people shall shout with a great shout [*teruah*]; and the wall of the city shall fall down flat."

The second usage of the word shout as a translation of "*teruah*" is in verse 20, where we read: "and the people shouted with a great shout [*teruah*], that the wall fell down flat."

> *Just as the Jubilee, which is also translated from the world "teruah" brings the world to an end, so the shout (teruah) of the people brought Jericho to its end.*

The great shout (*teruah*) of the people signified the end of Jericho. Just as the Jubilee which is also translated from the word "*teruah*" brings the world to an end, so the shout (*teruah*) of the people brought Jericho to its end.

Can we see why Leviticus 25:9 uses the word *"teruah"* for "Jubilee"? We could paraphrase it this way: "Then thou shalt cause the trumpet of the shout (*teruah*-Jubilee) to sound on the tenth day of the seventh month, in the day of atonement . . . ."

We are reminded of that very pertinent verse recorded in I Thessalonians 4:16 in which God is describing events that will occur at the end of the world. We read: "For the Lord himself shall descend from heaven with a **shout**, with the voice of the archangel, and with the **trump** of God: and the dead in Christ shall rise first." Notice the "shout" and the "trumpet." These words tie the clear message of I Thessalonians 4:16 to the end of Jericho in a very graphic way.

The walls of Jericho fell flat after thirteen encirclements, and at the moment of the sound of the trumpet and the great shout. So, too, at the end of the 13,000 years, the trumpet will sound and a shout will be heard as Christ comes to judge this earth.

Indeed, the destruction of Jericho at the end of thirteen encirclements identifies with the Jubilee at the end of 13,000 years. Indeed, the destruction of Jericho identifies with the end of the world.

The Day of Atonement and the Jubilee

Significantly, the word "teruah" which we have learned is translated both "shout" and "jubilee" is found in Leviticus 25:9, which also tells us which day the "shout" or "jubilee" was to sound. That day was to be the tenth day of the seventh month, which was the day of atonement. The day of atonement points directly at the cross. It is on that day that Christ atoned for our sins.

But the cross identifies with the Passover, Nisan 14. In fact, to this present day there is no part of God's salvation plan that literally falls on the day of atonement as does the Passover and the feast of Pentecost.

> *Therefore, the day of atonement identifies altogether in its most complete sense with the end of the world.*

But we must also be aware that the atonement is more than the fact that Christ has endured the wrath of God for our sins. It is not complete in every sense of the word until every believer's salvation is complete and he has inherited the new heaven and new earth. Therefore, the day of atonement identifies altogether in its most complete sense with the end of the world.

We, therefore, are not surprised to discover that the trumpet of the Jubilee was to sound on the day of atonement which was Tishri 10 of the Jewish calendar. As we learned in the book *1994?*, all of the Biblical evidence points to the end of the world coming in the seventh month. In all probability it could be on September 15, which is the date for the day of atonement in 1994. In the book *1994?* we learned that it also could be sometime during the timing of the feast of tabernacles which follows from September 20 to September 27. As we learned in our study found in *1994?*, we dare not decide which exact day it will be, but the evidence shows that in all likelihood it must be from the earliest on September 15, the day of atonement, to no later than September 27, the last day of the feast of tabernacles.

God Appears to Ancient Israel

Interestingly, the word "yobel," which helps to relate the destruction of Jericho to the judgment at the end of the world, is found in one other place in the Bible. In this instance, it is translated "trumpet." In Exodus 19:13, we read: "There shall not an hand touch it, but he shall surely be stoned, or shot through; whether it be beast or man, it shall not live: when the trumpet [*teruah*] soundeth long, they shall come up to the mount."

The setting of this verse is very significant and also relates to the end of the world. Three months earlier, the nation of Israel had left Egypt. They were at the base of Mount Sinai. God instructed Moses that God was going to come down upon Mount Sinai in the presence of the people. Verse 11 declares: "And be ready against the third day: for the third day the LORD will come down in the sight of all the people upon mount Sinai."

The people were to be ceremonially cleansed in preparation for this event, and they were instructed not to touch the mount lest they die. Then, when the trumpet (teruah in verse 13) sounded louder and louder, the whole mountain was covered with smoke. We read the dramatic language of verses 16-18:

And it came to pass on the third day in the morning, that there were thunders and lightnings, and a thick cloud upon the mount, and the voice of the trumpet exceeding loud; so that all the people that was in the camp trembled. And Moses brought forth the people out of the camp to meet with God; and they stood at the nether part of the mount. And mount Sinai was altogether on a smoke, because the LORD descended upon it in fire: and the smoke thereof ascended as the smoke of a furnace, and the whole mount quaked greatly.

> *Lightnings, fire, smoke, earthquakes - this is the language of Judgment Day.*

Lightnings, fire, smoke, earthquakes - this is the language of Judgment Day. Then, too, God will come down in the presence of all the peoples. Then, too, there will be the sound of the trumpet. Then, too, those who touch the mount will die; that is, those who are subject to hellfire because they have not been saved will experience the second death, eternal damnation.

Indeed, this account identifies with Jubilee. This is so because Jubilee is identified with Judgment Day. At the time the believers are set at liberty, the unsaved come into judgment.

How awful all of this is. Are you ready to meet God? God coming down on Mount Sinai at the sound of the Jubilee (the trumpet), and God causing the walls to fall flat so that Jericho could be destroyed, are but tiny examples of what will happen at the end of the world. Then it will not be a single mountain that will quake greatly, it will be the whole earth. It will not be two million people hearing the sound of the trumpet and the voice of God and seeing God as a consuming fire, it will be more than five billion people.

In Hebrews 12:25-29, we read of the parallelism between the event recorded in Exodus 19 and the end of the world:

See that ye refuse not him that speaketh. For if they escaped not who refused him that spake on earth, much more shall not we escape, if we turn away from him that speaketh from heaven: Whose voice then shook the earth: but now he hath promised, saying, Yet once more I shake not the earth only, but also heaven. And

this word, Yet once more, signifieth the removing of
those things that are shaken, as of things that are made,
that those things which cannot be shaken may remain.
Wherefore we receiving a kingdom which cannot be
moved, let us have grace, whereby we may serve God
acceptably with reverence and godly fear: For our God
is a consuming fire.

The "once more" when Christ will shake the earth and the
heaven is the end of the world. Of, friend, what will happen to you?

Like Rahab and her family, who escaped the destruction of
Jericho, will you be spared judgment because Christ had become your
Savior? I use the verb "had become" because when God comes down
in the Jubilee, it will be too late for anyone to become saved. Those who
are not ready will without question be subject to judgment and eternal
damnation.

Dear friend, don't delay. Today it is still the day of salvation.
Now is the time to beg God for His mercy. Now is the time to turn from
your sinful ways and cry mightily to God. The days are slipping away
fast. **The end is upon us.**

We have begun to see the startling information that the Bible
presents to us. Both in the book *1994?* and already in this volume, we
should be amazed at what we can learn.

But before we continue our search for more nuggets of truth
hidden within its holy pages, we will serve ourselves well by taking a
little time to stand back and analyze how we can understand the Bible
to the highest possible degree. When we read the Bible, we see many
puzzling statements. At times, we are instructed by the Bible to look
for a spiritual meaning in the Biblical statement. We know the whole
Bible has to do with the message of salvation. Yet so many sentences
and even whole paragraphs appear to teach us little or nothing about
the salvation message. As we continue our study, we should spend
some time to find fundamental principles from the Bible that will guide
us in our study.

Chapter 3.
Understanding the Bible

The constant concern of the child of God who dearly loves the Lord is to know and to do the will of God. He recognizes that the Bible is the sourcebook of truth. It is the only authority that discloses the will of God for his life, but the Bible is often difficult to understand.

One might ask, "How can I, as a student of the Word, reach into the treasures of truth that comprise the Bible? Many verses seem irrelevant; many seem impossible to understand. Learned theologians frequently have great differences of opinion concerning what the Bible teaches: How can I determine which teacher, preacher, or theologian is leading me correctly? Must I be limited to blindly following a teacher, knowing that he is a fallible human being and therefore subject to error?"

"What about the problems that arise from the different translations of the Bible? How can I know which ones are trustworthy? Do I dare trust paraphrases, which seem to make the Bible easier to understand?"

We should spend a little time answering some of these questions by presenting a few basic principles that should be kept in mind as we study the Bible.

In so doing, may it be that we have a fresh appreciation of the wonderful Word that God has given to us. This Word is the Bible. May we also have a better basis upon which to understand the Biblical information that relates to the time and character of the end of the world.

Hermeneutics

Hermeneutics is the science of biblical interpretation. Many learned and scholarly books have been written regarding the principles of hermeneutics. Every believer should be concerned with the subject, because it relates to the process by which we derive spiritual truth from the Scriptures.

ur desire that we might clearly understand a few basic
proper Biblical interpretation. By so doing, we will also
see the wealth of information God gives that helps us to
hrist's return as well as to help us understand many more
details concerning His return. These principles are taken from the
Bible; the Bible requires that we keep these in mind. They will be
carefully examined as we proceed in our study and are as follows.

1. We must remember that the Bible, in its entirety, is the Holy
Word of God. Every word, every phrase, is God-breathed. "Holy men
of God spake as they were moved by the Holy Ghost" (II Peter 1:21).
It is imperative that we remember that the Old Testament is just as holy
and important and uniquely the Word of God as the New Testament.

> *Each book, each paragraph, each sentence, each*
> *word, and each letter of each word, is exactly as*
> *God intended it to be.*

The Bible is not just any book. It has no peer. God moved holy
men of old to write as He guided them. The Bible in its original
autographs (that is, in the original documents that were written), is
exactly the message that God intended for man. Each book, each
paragraph, each sentence, each word, and each letter of each word, is
exactly as God intended it to be. We must, therefore, approach the
Bible with holy awe. This is God's message to man.

Because the Bible is God's book, only God can open our eyes
to see the truths set forth on its pages. Sometimes the truths are very
clearly seen, sometimes they are revealed only by diligent search in the
Bible, and sometimes they remain hidden, regardless of our desire to
know everything God has revealed in the Bible. Because God reveals
truth, we must go humbly to the Scriptures; we must beseech the Lord
that truth be revealed to us, for it is God, the Holy Spirit, who leads us
into truth, through the Bible.

> *We must approach the Bible with an earnest desire
> to be obedient to the precepts and rules in the
> Scriptures.*

Furthermore, we must approach the Bible with an earnest desire to be obedient to the precepts and rules in the Scriptures. In matters of doctrine and practice we should be ready to be obedient to anything and everything we read in the Bible.

2. The Bible is its own interpreter. We compare spiritual things with spiritual (I Corinthians 2). To understand a word or a phrase or a concept in the Bible, we must determine how that same word, phrase, or concept is used everywhere else in the Bible. Thus, the Bible becomes its own dictionary; it becomes its own commentary. While such diligent comparison requires much work on the part of the student of the Bible, it is the only way to come to a true understanding of the biblical message. (*Young's Analytical Concordance* and *Strong's Exhaustive Concordance* help immeasurably in this respect because they give every word used in the original languages and where the words are found in the English King James Bible.)

Because the Bible is its own interpreter, we must leave no stone unturned in becoming acquainted with the Bible. There is no short cut. We must spend much time reading the Bible. To try to learn truths in greater and greater detail and not be exposed to all that God has written in the Bible is foolish. The Bible must be read and re-read.

Any conclusion that we come to from reading a particular verse or passage must be tested for its validity by checking that conclusion against everything else the Bible offers concerning the subject. Only when the conclusion is found to be in harmony with all that the Bible teaches can we know that we are on the path of truth.

3. When we allow God's Word to guide us in formulating principles of Bible interpretation, we find that the Bible has different levels of meaning. As we study a verse in the Bible, we must remember that while it may have only one level of meaning, it may have as many as three.

The first level is historical. When Jesus taught using parables, He was not describing historical events. With few exceptions, such as these parables, the Bible gives us an exquisitely accurate account of events and conversations which actually occurred in history.

The second level of meaning in the Bible concerns moral and spiritual teachings. When a particular historical event is viewed in the light of the commandments of God as they are found throughout the Scriptures, we may look upon the event as an example of an application of God's laws.

> *The whole Bible is, in fact, the Gospel of the Lord Jesus Christ.*

The third level of meaning relates to the Gospel of salvation. This is the dominant and most important message of the Bible. The whole Bible is, in fact, the Gospel of the Lord Jesus Christ. The Bible reveals God's wonderful message of salvation.

Thus, there are at least three basic principles that must be kept in mind to study the Bible. They are summarized as follows.

1. The Bible alone and in its entirety is the Word of God.

2. The Bible is its own interpreter.

3. The Bible normally displays more than one level of meaning or significance.

We will look at these three principles in greater detail. A thorough understanding of these principles will prepare us to receive the rich and wonderful truths that are hidden within the Bible.

> *We will see that the Bible alone and in its entirety is the Word of God.*

The Bible Alone and in its Entirety Is the Word of God

The first principle to examine in greater detail is that the Bible alone and in its entirety is the Word of God. In the examination of this principle, let us ask, "What is the true Gospel?" As we answer this question, we will see that the Bible alone and in its entirety is the Word of God. It alone and in its entirety is the Gospel of the Lord Jesus Christ.

What is the true Gospel? No evangelical believer needs to struggle for an answer to this question. The true Gospel has everything to do with the Lord Jesus Christ. If we recognize Him as Lord and Savior, we have the true Gospel. The Bible declares in I John 4:2-3:

> Hereby know ye the Spirit of God: Every spirit that confesseth that Jesus Christ is come in the flesh is of God: And every spirit that confesseth not that Jesus Christ is come in the flesh is not of God: and this is that spirit of antichrist, whereof ye have heard that it should come; and even now already is it in the world.

God says through the Apostle Paul in I Corinthians 15:1-4:

> Moreover, brethren, I declare unto you the gospel . . . how that Christ died for our sins according to the scriptures; And that he was buried, and that he rose again the third day according to the scriptures.

Does it follow then that anyone who holds these truths must be a follower of the Gospel and is to be accepted as a brother in Christ? Must we recognize as followers of the true Gospel any church or denomination that is ready to make these principles part of its statement of faith?

Does Satan have the True Gospel?

Unfortunately, the question is not quite that simple. Satan and the demons admit that all these things are true of Christ. For instance, the demon in Mark 1:24 said of Jesus in the flesh: "I know thee who thou art, the Holy One of God." In Luke 4:41 God informs us:

And devils also came out of many, crying out, and saying, Thou art Christ the Son of God. And he rebuking them suffered them not to speak: for they knew that he was Christ.

These devils are not saved nor are they to become saved; and yet, in their declaration, they apparently satisfy the criteria of I John 4:2-3 for those who are of the Spirit of God. Jesus speaks of false prophets in Matthew 7:15-23. In verses 22 and 23 He says of them:

Many will say to me in that day, Lord, Lord, have we not prophesied in thy name? and in thy name have cast out devils? and in thy name done many wonderful works? And then will I profess unto them, I never knew you: depart from me, ye that work iniquity.

We can see, therefore, that someone may use the name of Christ, do work in the name of Christ, and thus appear to identify with the Christ of the Bible, but he is not necessarily a follower of the true Gospel of Jesus Christ.

The false prophets appear to satisfy the criteria set forth in I John 4:2-3. We can see, therefore, that someone may use the name of Christ, do work in the name of Christ, and thus appear to identify with the Christ of the Bible, but he is not necessarily a follower of the true Gospel of Jesus Christ.

This line of thinking may leave us in shambles. How are we to recognize the true Gospel if we cannot trust those who say they preach Christ and who do their work in the name of Christ? Can we trust no one?

As you can see, the question, "What is the true Gospel?" is not as easy to answer as you may have thought.

We must find the answer to this question! How dreadful it would be if we followed a false prophet who brought a false gospel and we trusted that it was the true Gospel. We could end up in hell - confident that we were saved while believing in something other than the true Gospel. We must find the answer to the question concerning the nature of the true Gospel.

Where Can We Learn of Christ?

In seeking for the answer to this important question, we might also ask, "How do we know about Christ? Where do we learn of Him?"

Immediately and correctly the answer one gives is, "Of course, we learn about Christ from the Bible. It, as the Word of God, is our source of information concerning Jesus and the salvation He offers."

> *The Bible is the only authority by which we can know what to believe about Christ.*

How true this answer is! The Bible is the only authority by which we can know what to believe about Christ. This principle is clearly presented in the Bible. We read about the nature of the Gospel in I Corinthians 15:1-4. Verses 3 and 4 say:

> For I delivered unto you first of all that which I also received, how that Christ died for our sins according to the scriptures; And that he was buried, and that he rose again the third day according to the scriptures.

In the phrase "according to the scriptures," God declares that the Bible is the authority of the Gospel.

In Luke 24:13-48 Jesus discusses His resurrection with the two disciples on the road to Emmaus. Significantly, He indicates to them that the authority for His actions is the Scriptures. In verses 44-46 we read:

> And he said unto them, These are the words which I spake unto you, while I was yet with you, that all things must be fulfilled, which were written in the law of Moses, and in the prophets, and in the psalms, concerning me. Then opened he their understanding, that they might understand the scriptures, And

said unto them, Thus it is written, and thus it behoved Christ to suffer, and to rise from the dead the third day.

The principle of the ultimate authority of the Scriptures is seen in the temptation of Christ by Satan. Again and again, when Satan tempts Jesus, our Savior replies, "it is written" (Luke 4:4, 8, 10).

> *The knowledge we have concerning Christ or God's plan of salvation must be firmly based on the Bible.*

Thus, the Bible is the authority that tells us about the Gospel. It is the source book of truth. The knowledge we have concerning Christ or God's plan of salvation must be firmly based on the Bible.

All of the Bible Is the Word of God

Having established the principle that the Bible is the authority of the Gospel of salvation, the next obvious question is: "How much of the Bible must we trust to know that we are following the true Gospel?" More specifically, we might ask: "Based on I Corinthians 15:1-4 and I John 4:2-3, if we believe Christ has come in the flesh and we trust in His death and resurrection, can we be sure we are following the true Gospel? Can we have the true Gospel regardless of what we believe concerning creation, the end of the world, hell, predestination, etc?"

The answer to these questions is found in II Timothy 3:16:

All scripture is given by inspiration of God, and is profitable for doctrine, for reproof, for correction, for instruction in righteousness.

God indicates by this statement that the whole Bible is the Word of God. Therefore, it gives us, in its entirety, information concerning the Gospel. The whole Bible is the Word of God. The Bible, in its entirety, is the revelation of God's will for man. Every doctrine taught in it is an essential part of the revelation of the Gospel.

The Old and New Testaments Are of Equal Importance

The Old Testament is equal in importance to the New Testament. When Jesus declared in Luke 24:46 and Luke 4:4, "it is written," He used as His authority that part of the Bible that today we call the Old Testament. God states in II Timothy 3:16 that, "All scripture is given by inspiration, . . . and is profitable for doctrine, . . . " He is speaking especially of the Old Testament because it was the only Bible available to the church at that time.

The importance of the relationship between the Old Testament and the New Testament church is underscored by the language of I Peter 1:10-12:

> Of which salvation the prophets have inquired and searched diligently, who prophesied of the grace that should come unto you: Searching what, or what manner of time the Spirit of Christ which was in them did signify, when it testified beforehand the sufferings of Christ, and the glory that should follow. Unto whom it was revealed, that not unto themselves, but unto us they did minister the things, which are now reported unto you by them that have preached the gospel unto you with the Holy Ghost sent down from heaven; which things the angels desire to look into.

In this statement, God emphasizes the principle that the Old Testament was written to be as important to us today as it was to Old Testament Israel. Note in verse 12 the words, "not unto themselves" (meaning the Old Testament believers), "but unto us they did minister" (that is, to believers in this present day). The Old Testament must be read and studied as carefully as the New Testament.

The Old Testament must be read and studied as carefully as the New Testament.

We learned from II Timothy 3:16 and I Peter 1:10-12 that the whole Bible is the Word of God. We must not countenance the idea that we are to follow only the New Testament. Every word in the entire Bible is the Word of God.

The Bible Is to be Obeyed

Because the Bible is God's revelation, it is to be obeyed. God emphasizes this principle in I John 2:3-4, where we read:

> And hereby we do know that we know him, if we keep his commandments. He that saith, I know him, and keepeth not his commandments, is a liar, and the truth is not in him.

The Bible is the law book or rule book that presents the commandments, which are to be obeyed. This is the reason that the devils can believe and acknowledge that Jesus is the Christ who has come in the flesh and yet they are subject to eternal damnation. They are correct concerning the doctrines of Christ but by no means are they ready to be obedient to anything and everything that is in the Bible.

> *Only a child of God, a person born of the Holy Spirit, actually confesses the truths of I John 4:2-3, for only he is ready and willing to be altogether obedient to the Gospel.*

In I John 4:2 we read: "Every spirit that confesseth that Jesus Christ is come in the flesh, is of God." The key word is "confess." We commonly use this word to mean a simple and open admission of truth, but the Bible's use implies not only admission of the truth, it also implies identification with that truth. Therefore, only a child of God, a person born of the Holy Spirit, actually confesses the truths of I John 4:2-3, for only he is ready and willing to be altogether obedient to the Gospel.

When we read about the false prophets in Matthew 7:15-23, we discovered that although they claimed to identify with the Christ of the Bible, they were unsaved. In that context (verse 21), Jesus declares:

Not every one that saith unto me, Lord, Lord, shall enter into the kingdom of heaven; but he that doeth the will of my Father which is in heaven.

The false prophets did not do the will of God, and therefore we know that their gospel could not be trusted. God is teaching that the true Gospel is intimately associated with obedience to the Bible, because the Bible is the record of God's will.

Therefore, two principles can be firmly and safely stated.

1. The whole Bible is the Word of God. It is the ultimate authority and the Word of God.

2. A follower of the true Gospel is ready to be obedient to anything and everything in the Bible. It is the authority to which we are to submit.

God summarizes these principles in Revelation 22:19 where He warns:

And if any man shall take away from the words of the book of this prophecy, God shall take away his part out of the book of life, and out of the holy city, and from the things which are written in this book.

The Bible Alone Is the Word of God

We must face other questions: "Is the Bible alone the Word of God? Does the Holy Spirit lead men to truth by means other than the Bible? For example, is it possible for God the Holy Spirit to speak to me in a dream or in a vision?"

As we examine these critical questions, we must be guided by the Biblical account of the experiences of the early New Testament church. Their Bible was what is now called the Old Testament. Occasionally, people received additional revelations of the will of God by such means as dreams, visions, or angel visitations; for instance, Peter received a vision concerning the proclamation of the Gospel to the Roman centurion, Cornelius. Peter's obedience to this vision added the information given in the vision to the written Word. The vision provided knowledge of the will of God.

The Apostle Paul and the Apostle John also received information through visions. These visions provided help in knowing the will of God.

In the church at Corinth, there were those who received additional information regarding the will of God from a phenomenon called "tongues." Those who received the gift of tongues spoke in an unknown language, "mysteries" in the spirit (I Corinthians 14:2). What they received from God could have been in the form of praise, prayer, or additional revelation. When this happened in the assembly, they were commanded to seek from God interpretation of the message, so that the whole congregation could be edified. They were edified because this information was a declaration of the will of God and could be considered an addition to the written Word. The combination of the written Word and the Word received in the "tongue" gave them more complete knowledge of the will of God (to which they were to be obedient).

Therefore, the question that faces us is: "Can it be possible today that God is supplying additional revelations of His will by tongues, visions, or dreams?" The answer to this question must be found in the Bible.

While the Bible was being written, additions were made to it as holy men spoke, being moved by the Holy Spirit (II Peter 1:21). Then God completed the written Word, and when He came to the last chapter of the last book of the Bible, He declared (in Revelation 22:18):

> For I testify unto every man that heareth the words of the prophecy of this book, If any man shall add unto these things, God shall add unto him the plagues that are written in this book.

With this declaration, God effectively ended the possibility of any further revelation from Himself. With the completion of the New Testament we were given a more extensive revelation than that enjoyed by the church at Corinth. With the writing of the Book of Revelation, we have the entire New Testament and the Old Testament; and to the Old and the New Testaments, nothing is to be added. Never again would God give divine information by means of a dream, a vision, a tongue, or an angel visitation. God has given the complete account of His will.

> *The Bible alone is the authority under which the Gospel stands. The true Gospel is circumscribed by the Bible.*

Thus, we have another principle concerning the nature of the true Gospel: The Bible alone is the authority under which the Gospel stands. The true Gospel is circumscribed by the Bible. There is no other source of divinely articulated or verbalized truth.

> *The Bible alone and in its entirety is the Word of God.*

We may combine the foregoing principles into one statement: **The Bible alone and in its entirety is the Word of God**. The true Gospel is completely identified with and has as its authority the Bible alone and in its entirety.

Some might argue, "But Revelation 22:18 speaks of "this book." This book must refer to the Book of Revelation. Therefore, this verse does not end further additions to the Bible; rather, it limits further expansion only of the Book of Revelation."

A bit of reflection will show the failure of this reasoning. If we assume that the phrase "this book" refers only to the Book of Revelation, then in fact it must relate to the whole Bible. The Bible is one cohesive whole. A verse or chapter added to or taken from the Book of Revelation is added to or taken from the Bible - the Book of Revelation is an integral part of the whole Bible. In Revelation 22:7-9 we read:

> Behold, I come quickly; blessed is he that keepeth the sayings of the prophecy of this book. And I John saw these things, and heard them. And when I had heard and seen, I fell down to worship before the feet of the angel which shewed me these

things. Then saith he unto me, See thou do it not: for I am thy
fellowservant, and of thy brethren the prophets, and of them
which keep the sayings of this book: worship God.

In these verses God speaks of those who "keep the sayings of this
book." We cannot keep the sayings of any part of the Bible unless we
understand the meaning of those sayings. We cannot understand the
meaning of any part of the Bible unless we view the verses in question
in the light of the whole Bible. Thus, to "keep the sayings of this book"
must mean to become involved with the teachings of the whole Bible.
Therefore, "this book" must be the whole Bible.

What about Direct Bible Quotations Coming to Us?

Others will insist, "But the information I received in a vision or
tongue was a direct quotation from the Bible. Therefore, it was not an
addition to the Bible."

This argument is also invalid, as can be shown, for example, in
Acts 2:17-21, where the Apostle Paul under the guidance of the Holy
Spirit quotes from Joel 2:28-32. Can Acts 2:17-21 be removed from
the Bible because it is not an addition to the Word of God - it is a
duplication of something already in the Bible? Immediately we know
that we cannot do this. Acts 2:17-21 is as important a part of the Word
of God as Joel 2:28-32. Many verses, phrases, and even chapters are
duplicated in the Bible, but each one is an important part of the Word
of God.

---

*If someone believes he has received a direct
revelation from God in which the Bible is quoted,
he would be attempting to add to the Word of God.*

If someone believes he has received a direct revelation from
God in which the Bible is quoted, he would be attempting to add to the
Word of God. He would be guilty of violating the command given in
Revelation 22:18.

Praying in a Tongue

One observation of those who are interested in tongues is that when they pray in a tongue, they cannot be adding to the Scriptures. They fail to realize that there are many prayers in the Bible, including prayers by David, Solomon, and Ezra. As these men prayed, they were guided by the Holy Spirit to say the words that have been written in the Bible, the Word of God. While they prayed to God, God used them to write the Word of God. Likewise today, if someone claimed to pray in a tongue inspired by the Holy Spirit and that God guided him as to what he prayed, then his prayer would just as certainly be the Word of God as are the prayers recorded in the Bible.

Therefore, anyone who claims to pray in a tongue is adding to the Word of God, and anyone who thinks he receives a revelation from God in a tongue, in a dream, or in a vision, is adding to the Word of God. The principle of Revelation 22:18 will be violated by anyone who attempts to pray in a tongue.

> *If one has a gospel that starts with the Bible and then adds what is believed to be divine truth from other sources, such as dreams or visions, he is following a gospel other than the true Gospel.*

In Revelation 22:18-19 we have a clear statement by which we can know whether or not we follow the true Gospel. The true Gospel is circumscribed by the Bible. If one has a gospel that starts with the Bible and then adds what is believed to be divine truth from other sources, such as dreams or visions, he is following a gospel other than the true Gospel.

The Authority Regarded as Divine Establishes the Gospel

What is the divine authority that structures and determines the nature of the true Gospel? The Bible. We read a verse in the Bible and interpret it by focusing the whole Bible upon it. We are to interpret

Scripture by Scripture, or as I Corinthians 2:13 puts it, by "comparing spiritual things with spiritual."

If one believes that the Bible is the Word of God, and believes that some other book is also divine revelation, then his authority is a wider authority than the Bible alone. If someone believes the Bible is the Word of God, but also believes that a dream, vision, or tongue is a revelation from God, then his "gospel" is wider than the Bible. He will interpret any Bible verse not according to the rest of the Bible only, but also in light of the information received in the dream or vision.

We can begin to understand why false gospels differ in many points of doctrine from the Gospel based only on the Bible. The doctrines we hold are the products of the authority under which we place ourselves.

A judge who tries a case under the law of the United States will come to a different conclusion than the judge who tries the same case under the law of Canada plus the law of the United States. The second judge has a wider and therefore a different authority than the first.

If I receive a vision that I believe has come from God, and that vision is related to a particular doctrine, it is apparent that I will regard the information of the vision as the latest, clearest, and most important information in regard to that doctrine. I will believe this regardless of what the Bible offers concerning that doctrine. Even if it disagrees to some extent with the Bible, I will consider the vision a truth that modifies what the Bible teaches. I will be following the same principle of interpretation as that which applies to the New Testament modifying truths in the Old Testament. My conclusion concerning the doctrine will be influenced by my vision.

It should now be apparent how important it is to know what our authority is. If it is less than the whole Bible or more than the whole Bible, we will no longer have the true Gospel, which is the Gospel of salvation.

Every Religion has an Authority

Every religion or gospel is under an authority - an authority its followers believe is the Word of God. The Muslim religion, for example, looks upon the writings of Mohammed as being of divine origin. These writings, therefore, are the final authority in matters of doctrine and practice in that religion. Those who have the Mormon gospel believe that the Bible is the Word of God, but they are convinced that the writings of Joseph Smith, in "The Book of Mormon," are also divine. Consequently, the authority that structures and determines this gospel is the combination of the Bible and "The Book of Mormon."

We live in a day when many people believe that God continues to bring revelations by dreams, visions, voices, or tongues. Those who are interested in these activities have an authority that structures and determines their gospel; their authority is a combination of the Bible and the messages which they believe are from God. This gospel, too, is structured and determined by what is considered to be a divine source of truth.

From these examples, we can see that those who believe that the Bible alone and in its entirety is the Word of God have one Gospel, and those who believe the Bible is the Word of God but who also believe that God brings additional revelations today have a different gospel. The most recent revelation in such a gospel has the greatest impact upon its doctrines. For example, in the true Gospel, we do not dare say that we understand the Old Testament unless we have carefully studied the New Testament. The New Testament interprets the Old Testament. The New Testament shows that the ceremonial laws have been completed in Christ; therefore, we are not to observe the Old Testament Sabbaths or the Old Testament Passover. It shows us that God's decree that adultery is sin has been strengthened to include thoughts of lust. The later revelation sheds more light on the earlier one, and it is the final word.

Those who believe that God brings revelations today place great importance on the content of the revelations. For them, the later revelations are the last word, and they influence their view of the Bible, which they believe is part of the revelation of God. As a result, their understanding of many biblical passages is different from the understanding of those who believe that the Bible alone and in its entirety is the Word of God.

> *The true Gospel has as its authority the Bible alone
> and in its entirety. There is no other divine source
> of God's Word.*

The true Gospel has as its authority the Bible alone and in its entirety. There is no other divine source of God's Word. There can be no later additions to the Word of God. The true Gospel, which has as its authority the Bible alone and in its entirety, is different from a gospel which includes in its authority revelations which may have come after the Bible was completed. These other gospels may use ideas, phrases, and words from the true Gospel, but they are false because they have an authority other than the true Gospel. Many different gospels employ such terms as "the blood of Jesus," "the cross," "the resurrection," "heaven," "hell," and "Holy Spirit," etc., but the use of these Biblical words does not guarantee that the true Gospel is being taught. Only by following the Gospel that has its authority circumscribed by the Bible can we know that we have the true Gospel.

Does the Bible Contain the Word of God?

Some theologians declare that the Bible **contains** the Word of God; this implies that parts of the Bible are not the Word of God. Effectively, they make themselves or their churches the ultimate authority: they decide what parts of the Bible are the Word of God. Rather than being subject to the Word of God, they are ruling over the Word of God. They have a narrower authority than the whole Word of God. It is important that we recognize that the whole Bible is the Word of God!

Early in this study, we raised the question, "What is the true Gospel?" We learned that the true Gospel is circumscribed by the Bible. It is based on the principle that the Bible alone and in its entirety is the Word of God. The Bible is the complete written presentation of the Gospel.

> *God is saying that those who add to the words of*
> *this book are subject to eternal damnation; they are*
> *therefore unsaved.*

This conclusion has ominous implications for many congrega-tions and denominations; it tells of enormous consequences for today's evangelical community. The importance is stressed in the warning of Revelation 22:18-19, where God declares that anyone who widens the authority by "adding to the words of this book," is subject to the plagues written in "this book." The plagues relate to God's wrath being visited on those who are subject to hell. God is saying that those who add to the words of this book are subject to eternal damnation; they are therefore unsaved. They do not understand the true Gospel of salvation.

By the same token, anyone who has a narrower authority upon which his gospel is based (he believes that only parts of the Bible are the Word of God), is warned by Revelation 22:19 that he, too, is subject to eternal damnation. Specifically, God declares, "God shall take away his part out of the book of life, and out of the holy city . . . ." How important it is that we recognize what constitutes the true Gospel.

God states the same warning in slightly different language in Galatians 1:8-9. God declares through the Apostle Paul:

> But though we, or an angel from heaven, preach any other gospel unto you than that which we have preached unto you, let him be accursed. As we said before, so say I now again, If any man preach any other gospel unto you than that ye have received, let him be accursed.

The double warning indicates the certainty of the curse! It emphasizes the seriousness of being sure that we are following the true Gospel, for to be under the curse of God is to be subject to hell.

One might theoretically accept divine truth as coming from the Bible only, yet in actuality, regard certain doctrines or practices of his church or denomination as inviolate. He insists on holding a doctrine regardless of what the Bible indicates; effectively, he has placed that doctrine on a level of authority equal with the Bible. He has inadvertently widened the authority of the Bible, and for this reason, he could never come to an agreement with those who more carefully practice by the principle that the Bible alone is the ultimate authority.

The Authority of the Bible Is Narrowed by Some Who Claim the Whole Bible Is God's Word

There are those who narrow the authority of the Bible by insisting that certain passages of the Bible apply only to the historical situation in which they are originally found. For example, they conclude that we need not obey I Corinthians 14:34, which teaches that women are not to speak in the congregational worship service. They argue that this verse speaks of a problem unique to the culture of that day and, therefore, is not applicable to believers today. They conclude that it is not applicable because we live in a culture which is different from the one that existed at the time of the church of Corinth.

Let us examine this conclusion. If the statement of I Corinthians 14:34 is applicable only to the culture of that day, then Jesus' statement in the conversation with Nicodemus in John 3 does not apply to us today, because Nicodemus was an Old Testament Jew. None of us is an Old Testament Jew. Also, the Old Testament would have no application for us today, because it was addressed to ancient Israel or nations such as Babylon. They were entirely different cultures from the cultures we have today. Moreover, the Book of Romans would have no application for us today, because it was written to the church at Rome almost 2,000 years ago. Philippians, Colossians, and the New Testament epistles would have no application for us. All of Jesus' teachings would also have to be set aside in view of the fact that He was addressing individuals who lived in a culture different from ours.

A conclusion that allows us to set aside certain passages because they seem to be associated with a cultural problem of long ago and therefore is said to have no application for our lives today, effectively, destroys the authority of the Bible. It is a direct violation of II Timothy 3:16:

All scripture is given by inspiration of God, and is profitable for doctrine, for reproof, for correction, for instruction in righteousness.

That conclusion would narrow the authority of the Bible in that no longer is the whole Bible the Word of God. God, in fact, placed these accounts in the Scriptures so that the principles would be laid down for the church throughout its history. I Corinthians 14:34 is as applicable to churches today as it was in the days of the church at Corinth.

The question at issue is: Are we ready to be obedient to the Bible? If we are not prepared to be obedient, we can destroy the authority of the Bible by such stratagems as the decision that a passage had meaning only for the culture of the day in which it was written. We must never lose sight of the fact that the whole Bible is the Word of God and is therefore to be obeyed.

> *We should know the Biblical basis for every doctrine we teach.*

This principle underscores the importance of constant Bible study for all who teach or preach God's Word. We should know the Biblical basis for every doctrine we teach. If we find that a doctrine does not have adequate Biblical authority, or that there are passages in the Bible that appear to contradict a doctrine we teach, it is imperative that we resolve these differences before we continue to teach that doctrine. We who believe that we have been called to teach or preach have a grave responsibility to be as accurate as possible in the Word of God. God declares in James 3:1: "My brethren, be not many masters [teachers], knowing that we shall receive the greater condemnation."

The seriousness of being a teacher of the Word of God cannot be over-emphasized. Teachers and preachers of the Word of God should search the Word of God unceasingly so that what is said to the class or congregation will be as true and trustworthy as possible. A teacher or a preacher must be ready to correct the doctrine he teaches at any time, if he finds it is contrary to the Word of God.

May our Lord give to all those who love Him and wish to be obedient to Him the wisdom and humility to submit to the authority of the Bible.

Thus far in our study we have discovered that the Bible alone and in its entirety is the verbalized, articulated Word of God. We will study another principle of Bible interpretation, that is, we are to interpret the Bible by the Bible.

Chapter 4.
The Bible Is its Own Interpreter

The second principle we shall examine is the truth that the Bible is its own interpreter. This truth is of great consequence, for it determines the method by which we examine each verse of the Holy Scriptures.

When Bible teachers disagree on a doctrine, frequently one of them will say, "Well, he has his opinion, his interpretation, and I have mine. Therefore, we don't see this verse in the same way."

If this teacher's statement is correct and conclusive, we can do almost anything we wish with the Bible. We become free to read the Bible and make our own personal judgments as to what God means in every verse. Unfortunately, this is the thinking behind the writing of paraphrased Bibles; this is the thinking that has influenced some of the newer translations of the Bible.

This makes man the ultimate judge and the final authority. It effectively declares that God has written words and phrases that we call the Bible but which depend upon us, as teachers, to decide what God means; thus, the reader has the final say as to what is truth.

This kind of "anything goes" thinking has spawned cults and false gospels which prevail all over the world. A teacher interprets verses according to a preconceived idea and then tries to show that his gospel is Bible-based.

This condition exists in many of our churches and congregations. One of the most puzzling phenomena currently facing the church is that theologians of various denominations are so far apart in their understanding of doctrines supposedly related to or derived from the Bible. A result of this is that Lutherans remain Lutheran from generation to generation, Baptists remain Baptist, Presbyterians remain Presbyterian, Methodists remain Methodist, etc. A basic reason for the existence of different denominations is that each denomination has reached a different conclusion concerning doctrines.

For example, some denominations hold the premillennial view from generation to generation. Other denominations hold the postmillennial view from generation to generation, and others hold the amillennial view through generations.

> *There can be only one true account of the return of Christ.*

There can be only one true account of the return of Christ, so at least two of the foregoing views must be wrong and unbiblical. The return of Christ and the end of the world simply cannot take place in three different ways.

Only One True Doctrine of Salvation

The same problem exists with other doctrines. For instance, there are differences between denominations in the teachings of the nature and character of salvation and the meaning of baptism. One would think that as diligent students of the Scriptures, who love the Lord and continue to search the Bible, they would come closer and closer to each other as they grow closer to the fulness of the truth. If this were the condition in each denomination, all denominations would gradually agree more and more. Yet year follows year, and there is no rapprochement of any kind.

This phenomenon is a result of the fact that the Bible is not fully relied upon as the source of absolute truth. The Bible is often regarded as just another of the various disciplines or philosophies of the secular world. One can understand the proliferation of different schools of thought in the secular world, because in the disciplines of music, art, and philosophy there is no absolute truth. Each discipline is allowed to exist independently of the others and is accepted just as it stands.

> *When we deal with the Bible, however, we are dealing with absolute truth. Anything that is taught, any doctrine that is held, that is not in agreement with truth is false.*

When we deal with the Bible, however, we are dealing with absolute truth. Anything that is taught, any doctrine that is held, that is not in agreement with truth is false. In short, any doctrine not in agreement with absolute truth is a lie. If a teacher or pastor declares to his congregation, "Thus saith the Lord," when the Lord has not said that, he is mouthing doctrines that are out of man's mind rather than God's. We immediately sense how reprehensible this is.

If well-meaning, learned theologians teach three different answers to the same question, we are forced to conclude that someone is teaching that which is false. This is an exceedingly serious matter - no child of God wants to preach lies. It is a matter that will not go away by itself.

There is evidence that these differences in understanding Biblical doctrine exist today. What is the problem? We can both understand the problem and find its solution.

> *Each denomination believes that its presuppositions reflect Bible truth, and the teachers and pastors cling tenaciously to them.*

Theological Presuppositions

The problem is that theologians and pastors are taught to come to the Bible from the perspective of the already established theological position of the church or denomination to which they belong. A Baptist is taught to come to the Bible with Baptist presuppositions; a Lutheran comes to the Bible with Lutheran presuppositions. One who is Reformed, comes with a Reformed perspective. Theological presuppositions govern the way the Bible student interprets and understands the Bible. Each denomination believes that its presuppositions reflect Bible truth, and the teachers and pastors cling tenaciously to them. They are convinced that perspectives from other denominations are most likely incorrect and are not to be considered or followed, although they readily acknowledge that each denomination has a right to exist. They believe their own denominations' presuppositions are the most accurate, and they remain with them. The consequence is that the Baptist remains a Baptist, the Lutheran remains a Lutheran, the Presbyterian a Presbyterian, etc.

  Unfortunately, most theologians come to the Bible in much the same way that students come to social science classes - art, music, and philosophy. For example, there are many schools of philosophy: the Eleatic school of philosophy, the Ionian school of philosophy, Byzantine philosophy, Arabic, and Western philosophy, to name a few. Each philosophy has its original thinkers, faithful followers, and **some** truth in it. Ordinarily, followers of one school of philosophy accept the rightful existence of and potential contribution of other schools. No one would conclude that the philosophy he follows has absolute truth. He follows a particular school of philosophy because he believes that it is more acceptable than any other.

> *They feel they are being honest if they*
> *remain faithful to their particular*
> *denominational presuppositions.*

  Most theologians approach the Bible the same way. They do not regard the Bible as the law book of absolute truth. It is a book to be viewed from their denomination's school of thinking. They contend that there are various schools of thought (denominational presuppositions) that relate to how the Bible is to be interpreted. The school of thought followed will influence conclusions derived from the Bible. They feel they are being honest if they remain faithful to their particular denominational presuppositions. It is believed that theologians of other denominations are faithful to the Word if they remain faithful to their denominational presuppositions. In this way, the study of the Bible is viewed as an activity similar to the study of social sciences.

  May the study of the Bible be regarded as a social science? Is it not the book of absolute truth? Only when a student realizes it is absolute truth does he understand what the Bible is. If he has not come to this realization, in essence he is teaching less than the truth - he is teaching falsehoods.

The Bible Alone Is Absolute Truth

Theologians should recognize that the Bible teaches absolute truth. Is it not true that the conclusion that all men are sinners is absolute truth? This is also the case in regard to conclusions such as: the certainty of death, burial and resurrection of Jesus; God created the world, Christ will come to judge the world, there will be a New Heaven and a New Earth; and salvation is possible only through the atoning work of Jesus Christ.

> *It is incumbent upon the pastor and the teacher to study the Bible until he has found the absolute truth of every aspect of the Gospel.*

These teachings are absolute truth. They are taken from the Bible, which is the Book of absolute truth. Therefore, it is incumbent upon the pastor and the teacher to study the Bible until he has found the absolute truth of every aspect of the Gospel. Only then can he be sure that he is not teaching a lie.

The Bible is unrelated to the social sciences and cannot be studied in the same manner. It must be approached analytically, as one would approach an engineering book or a law book, even though the engineering book or law book does not begin to have the level of truth that is contained in the Bible - the Bible has no peer. It is absolutely true in all its aspects. We must carefully, prayerfully, and diligently search out the truth. As we do, God Himself will lead us into the truth.

The Church has Placed Itself above the Bible

Now we can see what the church has done. Inadvertently, by approaching the Bible as social sciences are approached, the church has placed itself above the Bible. Theologians within these churches would vigorously deny this assertion. They would maintain that the Bible is altogether infallible and inerrant and is the only authority on which they can lean and structure doctrine.

This claim might be made confidently, but the sad fact is that in practice it is altogether negated because too frequently the theologian comes to the Bible with his denomination's presuppositions. With this approach, the Bible is no longer the ultimate authority; the denominational presuppositions are the ultimate authority.

The argument is made that each presupposition is derived from the Bible, and therefore the Bible is actually the ultimate authority. In practice, however, the presupposition is never questioned by most theologians. They treat their presupposition as being inviolate; it belongs to that denomination and must never be tampered with. The fact, however, is that if we are to find truth, the presuppositions have to be examined and critiqued as vigorously as any doctrine that we claim to have received from the Bible.

> *We must go to the Bible with no prejudices and no presuppositions whatsoever. We must let the Bible alone guide us into truth.*

The solution to this problem is: We must go to the Bible with no prejudices and no presuppositions whatsoever. We must recognize that we are human beings with feet of clay; we have sin-tainted minds. Our minds are finite and not like the infinite mind of God. We must hold the position, "let God be true, but every man a liar" (Romans 3:4).

It could be argued that the preliminary statements of solution and principles of Bible interpretation presented in this study are presuppositions. However, the question at issue is: These statements come from where? Are they Biblical teachings? Can it be demonstrated that they originate in the pages of Holy Writ, or are they just someone's theory? If they cannot be shown to be derived from the Bible, they should be corrected. No presupposition should be retained if it is not in complete harmony with the Bible.

There is agreement among various denominations that the Bible is true, that the Bible is the infallible Word of God, and that it is the only rule for doctrine and practice. There is also agreement that we cannot trust our minds, and that we must put every thought under the searchlight of the Word of God. This is what the Bible clearly teaches.

> *Stubbornly holding wrong doctrine in the light of the Scriptures is the most serious problem in the church today.*

If theologians would come to the Bible with no more than these common presuppositions, and humbly let the Bible lead them into truth, there would be increasingly more agreement between those who are children of God, regardless of denominational background. Truth is truth. An incorrect doctrine does not agree with the Scriptures. Stubbornly holding wrong doctrine in the light of the Scriptures is the most serious problem in the church today.

If we are truly children of God, at the moment of salvation we received our resurrected souls in which we never wish to sin again. Even though our unsaved bodies continue to lust after sin, there is within us a constant and earnest desire to do the will of God. As we read and study the Bible, we learn more and more about how we can live in accord with God's will. Because we have this intense desire to do God's will, we become greatly troubled when we discover that we have been holding wrong doctrine. If we read a Bible verse that appears to contradict a doctrine we hold, we will become concerned. Our new nature (our resurrected soul), has an intense desire to be true to God's Word. This concern will not disappear until we have re-examined this doctrine and we are comfortable with all that the Bible teaches concerning it.

The tragic other side of the coin is that if we persist in a sinful practice after reading statements in the Bible that show the practice is sinful, we should wonder whether or not we are really saved.

> *"How can I be a child of God and blatantly continue holding wrong doctrine?"*

Can a Saved Pastor Persistently Teach Lies?

If we continue to hold and teach wrong doctrine after we read Scripture that suggests it is wrong, we must ask the logical and fair question, "How can I be a child of God and blatantly continue holding wrong doctrine?" The seriousness of this question cannot be overestimated.

It may be that as we humbly approach the Bible, and let God lead us into truth, we find that a doctrine or a series of doctrines taught in our church as denominational presuppositions are indeed true to the Word of God. In this case, we are assured that the church fathers who presented these doctrines did their work well. The Holy Spirit enlightened their hearts and minds to truth.

If I may insert a personal note. I was brought up in a church that is Reformed in doctrine. While I had heard about the so-called five points of Calvinism, I had never been taught well enough so that I could go to the Bible to prove any of these five points that concern themselves with the doctrines of grace. The fact is, I can recall reading essays by learned authors on these doctrines in my younger days in some of our church papers and being very confused by what I read.

However, in my role as host of the "Open Forum" program, people ask me questions concerning the Bible, "live" on the air, and I have had to face with great zeal the whole question of the nature of salvation. When I was finally able to ferret out all the Biblical teachings concerning the nature of salvation, to my utter delight I found that the five points of Calvinism were in agreement with everything that I had found in my independent studies of the Scriptures. The Reformers of old had done their work well and accurately.

The Confessions Are Not Infallible

On the other hand, in my personal experience I have also found that other historical statements of the church are not as Biblical. For example, today we have confessions like the Heidelberg Catechism, the Canons of Dort, the Belgic Confession and the Westminster Confession. While I have a very high regard for these confessions of the church (because in many cases they have been hammered out in the crucible of a church facing apostasy or heresy, and because in the main they can be tested and found to be quite accurate insofar as the Scriptures are concerned), nevertheless, there are statements in some of them which I believe can be shown to be incorrect insofar as the Bible is concerned.

Do we dare to disagree with the confessions? We must dare to disagree if we can show from the Scriptures that the confession is incorrect.

Do we dare to disagree with the confessions? We must dare to disagree if we can show from the Scriptures that the confession is incorrect. Otherwise, the confession becomes an authority higher than the Bible.

As long as we are on the subject of confessions, I think it is appropriate to make this statement: The confessions have served the church exceedingly well in that they have provided stability at times when theologians might have become careless in their study of the Scriptures. They can give a church a lot of security. On the other hand, they can also do a great disservice to the church if the confession is looked upon as being inviolate. We must realize that the confession is the work of man, not the work of God. Only the Bible is the work of God. In 1618-1619, the reformed churches of Europe adopted a confession called the "Belgic Confession" to help the churches maintain faithfulness to the Bible. I am tremendously pleased with Article VII of the Belgic Confession, which reads:

THE SUFFICIENCY OF THE HOLY SCRIPTURES TO BE THE ONLY RULE OF FAITH

We believe that those Holy Scriptures fully contain the will of God, and that whatsoever man ought to believe unto salvation is sufficiently taught therein. For since the whole manner of worship which God requires of us is written in them at large, it is unlawful for any one, though an apostle, to teach otherwise than we are now taught in the Holy Scriptures: **nay, though it were an angel from heaven**, as the apostle Paul says. For since it is forbidden to **add unto or take away anything from the Word of God,** it does thereby evidently appear that the doctrine thereof is most perfect and complete in all respects.

Neither may we consider any writings of men, however holy these men may have been, of equal value with those divine Scriptures, nor ought we to consider custom, or the great multitude, or antiquity, or succession of times and persons, or councils, decrees or statutes, as of equal value with the truth of God, since the truth is above all; **for all men are of themselves liars, and more vain than vanity itself.** Therefore we reject with all our hearts whatsoever does not agree with this infallible rule, which the apostles have taught us, saying, **Prove the spirits, whether they are of God. Likewise: If any one cometh unto you, and bringeth not this teaching, receive him not into your house.**

This article of the Belgic Confession accurately presents the Biblical principle that nothing can stand above the Bible. It reminds us that accurately dealing with the Bible is of phenomenal importance. The importance of the Bible being the ultimate authority cannot be "swept under a rug." It cannot be said, "That is your opinion. I have my opinion." The issue is whether we are going to be true prophets of God or false prophets.

> *The issue is whether we are going to be true prophets of God or false prophets.*

The prophets of Baal on Mount Carmel were convinced that they had truth when they cut themselves and cried to their god to burn the sacrifice on the altar. Their zeal, sincerity, and conviction could not change the fact that they were false prophets. The prophets and Pharisees of Jesus' day, together with Saul of Tarsus, were convinced that they had truth, and they did everything possible to stop the spread of the Gospel, as taught by the Rabbi, Jesus. They could not be faulted for their zeal, sincerity, or conviction, but they were false prophets. The followers of Jesus were the true prophets. To be a true prophet in our day, it is imperative that we humble ourselves and approach the Bible with the recognition that only God is true, and every man is a liar. We all have within us the possibility of self-deception.

> *Every teacher must go humbly before the Lord and ask forgiveness for that which was taught that was untrue.*

Even after we are saved, we have sin-stained minds. No one on this side of the grave can know truth perfectly. The most careful teacher can at times be in error. Every time we teach in error, we are teaching a lie. Every teacher must go humbly before the Lord and ask forgiveness for that which was taught that was untrue. We all see through a glass darkly.

Teaching and the Christian Life

Teaching doctrine is analogous to living our Christian lives. We saw earlier that as we study the Bible, and we find sin in our lives, our earnest desire is to turn away from that sin. We ask the Lord's forgiveness, and we ask Him to strengthen us as we turn away from that sin. The life of the believer is one of constant learning as he discovers how to live an increasingly more holy life before God.

Each teacher and each pastor should continually be learning doctrine. He can never say there is nothing more to learn. If he has stopped learning, he might as well be dead. We repent of sinful practices as we discover them in our lives, and if we discover we have held and taught an unbiblical doctrine as we study the Bible, we should ask the Lord's forgiveness and turn away from that unbiblical teaching.

Obviously, this is easier said than done. When we repent of unbiblical practices, we usually have the approbation of our congregation, and this encourages us to take the new path. However, when we discover that a denominational presupposition is not Biblical or we discover that a doctrine we hold is unbiblical, and we turn away from it, we risk bearing the wrath of colleagues and the wrath of the congregation. We may appear to them to be heretics because we no longer adhere to that particular denominational presupposition or doctrine. A consequence may be that we are driven out of the denomination.

This consequence may seem strict and unwarranted, but that is how monolithic denominations are in regards to what they believe. It is only God's grace working in one's life that enables him to courageously face the consequences of coming closer to truth.

I cannot help but comment on the fact that churches, to a high degree, have figured out how to have a comfortable existence, where everything is agreeable and happy. This makes one wonder why Jesus said in Matthew 5:10-12:

> Blessed are they which are persecuted for righteousness' sake: for theirs is the kingdom of heaven. Blessed are ye, when men shall revile you, and persecute you, and shall say all manner of evil against you falsely, for my sake. Rejoice, and be exceeding glad: for great is your reward in heaven; for so persecuted they the prophets which were before you.

Did Jesus mean the kind of persecution that occurs only in Communist countries? Was he speaking of dreadful bloodlettings by political authorities?

> *The Bible anticipates that church leaders will be the first to denounce those who make a stand for the truth.*

The persecution recorded in the Bible, when the prophets were killed and New Testament Christians were taken to Jerusalem and cast into prison, is persecution by church leaders. The Bible anticipates that church leaders will be the first to denounce those who make a stand for the truth. People do not change. They do not want the truth any more today than they did at any other time in history. We should expect that if we hold to the truth, we will experience persecution. In our land, physical bloodletting is not fashionable, but it is permissible to scandalize, to vilify those who hold to the truth.

The other side of the coin is, if all appears beautiful, complacent, and secure, then we can wonder, "Do we really have the truth?" Remember that Jesus said, "Woe unto you, when all men shall speak well of you!" (Luke 6:26).

This is not to suggest that we seek persecution. It is to remind us of the fact that persecution is reasonably normative for the true believer. When a pastor discovers that a cherished doctrine of his church is not as Biblical as it should be, he can expect persecution as he begins to preach more faithfully to the Word of God.

The Modern Ecumenical Movement

There is a significant agreement developing today between denominations that historically were quite adamant in their "go-it-alone" understanding of cardinal doctrines of the Bible. The growing unity centers around doctrines that can be shown to be unbiblical. Unity is increasingly found in connection with doctrines such as divorce and remarriage after divorce, the right of women to rule and speak within the congregation, birth control, and the responsibility of the church to physically feed and clothe the hungry masses of the world. Doctrines that favor miraculous healing and additional revelation from God are finding greater approval across denominational lines.

> *One cannot help but wonder if this is the end product of a church age in which the churches have become careless with the Bible because of presuppositions.*

This is an amazing phenomenon in view of the fact that this latter-day unity is based on principles that are contrary to the Bible. One cannot help but wonder if this is the end product of a church age in which the churches have become careless with the Bible because of presuppositions. When bringing judgment, God first blinds theologians so that they begin to rewrite the rules of the Bible. As a final judgment on the church prior to Judgment Day, He will allow the churches to be overcome by false gospels - gospels in which it is taught that there is more to divine revelation than the Bible alone.

We have wandered beyond the scope of our study, and we should now return to the question: How are we to understand the Bible? How are we to interpret the difficult passages of the Bible? God gives us the answer to this question in I Corinthians 2:13:

> Which things also we speak, not in the words which man's wisdom teacheth, but which the Holy Ghost teacheth; comparing spiritual things with spiritual.

In this statement God rejects the idea that we can interpret the Scriptures to make them agree with what we have in our minds or our denominational doctrine. Our thinking, our opinion, our ideas, these are of no value. Only the Bible, the source book of spiritual truth, can guide us to a solution, to a true understanding of any verse. God Himself, in the person of the Holy Spirit, will lead us into truth if we humbly look to Him for guidance (John 16:13). The sword of the Spirit, as He leads us into truth, is the Word of God - called the Bible. An understanding of any part of the Bible must be reached by searching the rest of the Scriptures for help to gain the proper understanding.

> *An understanding of any part of the Bible must be reached by searching the rest of the Scriptures for help to gain the proper understanding.*

Some verses seem to be easily understood, but there are many that are difficult, and yes, even seemingly contrary to other verses. The verses that seem to be easily understood: How can we be sure that we understand them correctly?

Understanding Matthew 25:31

For example, in Matthew 25:31 God is surely speaking of a time when all nations will literally stand before Him. At that time, all those who have done good works, such as fed the hungry, clothed the naked, and visited the sick will go into heaven to be eternally with the Lord Jesus Christ. It seems that this passage teaches that our salvation is based on our good works. This passage is a convincing "proof" passage for those who believe that their good works make a contribution towards their salvation.

However, those who have read more widely and more carefully in the Bible immediately become uneasy with the conclusions of the last paragraph. They argue, "But doesn't the Bible say that we are saved by grace and not by works?" Indeed, they are correct. Salvation is by grace alone. Our works are the proof, or evidence, or result, of God's saving power in our lives.

How do we know that salvation is by grace and not by works? How do we know that whatever Matthew 25:31-46 is teaching, it is not teaching that our good works are the basis of, or grounds for, our salvation? We know this because many other verses in the Bible teach and emphasize that salvation is altogether of grace. Ephesians 2:8-10 is one passage that teaches that salvation is altogether of grace. There we read:

> For by grace are ye saved through faith; and that not of yourselves; it is the gift of God: Not of works, lest any man should boast. For we are his workmanship, created in Christ Jesus unto good works, which God hath before ordained that we should walk in them.

Many theologians today subscribe to the hermeneutical principle that if a verse makes sense as it is read, seek no other sense. In other words, if the verse appears to be straightforward and clear, and if a conclusion as to what it is teaching immediately can be found, then you can be sure that you are on safe ground in teaching this conclusion.

> *Every conclusion, regardless of how solid it appears to be, must be tested to determine if it is in harmony with the rest of the Bible.*

However, this hermeneutical principle is Biblically invalid. **Every conclusion, regardless of how solid it appears to be, must be tested to determine if it is in harmony with the rest of the Bible.**

How Are We to Understand Isaiah 2:4?

Isaiah 2:4 declares:

And he shall judge among the nations, and shall rebuke many people; and they shall beat their swords into plowshares, and their spears into pruninghooks: nation shall not lift up sword against nation, neither shall they learn war any more.

It certainly seems that this verse is teaching that there will be a time on this earth when universal peace will prevail - when warfare between nations will have come to an end. The believer who holds the premillennial view thinks this will occur during a future 1,000 year reign of Christ, when He is supposed to rule from Jerusalem. The postmillennial believer does not see Christ returning to this earth to reign, rather, he sees a future golden age when the Christian Gospel will pervade the world and nations will cease all warfare. In either case, the conclusion that at a future time war will stop seems to harmonize with some other conclusions concerning future events. Thus, it seems easy to conclude that this verse, which speaks of a cessation of warfare, is clear and understandable.

Is it so easy to understand? In Matthew 24:6-8 God speaks of wars and rumors of wars as the beginning of sorrows, and He describes the final tribulation period as the last event prior to Christ's return and Judgment Day. No possibility is offered in these verses for a time of political peace on this earth.

The heart of man is desperately wicked, as we are informed in Jeremiah 17:9, and we are told in James 4:1-2:

From whence come wars and fightings among you? come they not hence, even of your lusts that war in your members? Ye lust, and have not: ye kill, and desire to have, and cannot obtain: ye fight and war, yet ye have not, because ye ask not.

> *The Bible does not allow the conclusion that universal peace will come upon this earth at some future time.*

The Bible does not allow the conclusion that universal peace will come upon this earth at some future time. World peace is an impossible idea in the face of the corrupt nature of mankind.
What does Isaiah 2:4 teach? The answer is found in the passages of the Bible that speak of peace. For example, we read in Isaiah 40:1-2:

> Comfort ye, comfort ye my people, saith your God. Speak ye comfortably to Jerusalem, and cry unto her, that her warfare is accomplished, that her iniquity is pardoned: for she hath received of the LORD's hand double for all her sins.

In this revealing passage, God shows us that the cessation of war that He has in view is not between political nations; it is between the dominion of Satan, to which we belong before we are saved, and the kingdom of God, which we enter into when we become saved. Christ came as the Prince of Peace. Before we were saved we were slaves of Satan; we were at war with God. After we became saved, we were at peace with God. Isaiah 2:4 speaks of the coming of the Messiah to bring spiritual peace to this world. All who believe on Him have come into this peace. Before we were saved, we were a nation at war with the nation which is the kingdom of God. When we become saved, we become part of the kingdom of God, and therefore we are at peace with God. We have become servants of God, who care for the spiritual needs of this world. This is the import of the language which describes believers who use plowshares and pruninghooks.

> *When we become saved, we become part of the kingdom of God, and therefore we are at peace with God.*

This understanding of Isaiah 2:4 agrees with all that the Bible teaches. This understanding came only after we realized that the verses, which apparently were quite clear, had to be examined in the light of the entire Bible. Only then could we be satisfied with our understanding of these verses or any verses.

Thus, we can see that the hermeneutical principle that declares, "If the verse in question makes common sense as it is read, then seek no other sense," violates a fundamental scriptural principle. **Regardless of how clear a verse may appear to be, the doctrinal conclusion we derive from that verse should not be taught as Gospel truth unless it has been checked against anything and everything else in the Bible that might relate to that conclusion.**

> *They do not take the time to see if it harmonizes with everything else the Bible teaches on the subject.*

Theologians frequently fall into a snare because they violate the principle that conclusions concerning one part of the Bible must be checked with the rest of the Bible. They study a verse or a passage and come to a conclusion but they do not take the time to see if it harmonizes with everything else the Bible teaches on that subject.

The very structure of theological study often fosters unbiblical conclusions. One theologian is an expert in Greek, another is an expert in Hebrew, one in the Old Testament, another in the New Testament. One is considered to have his expertise in the doctrines of Christ, another in the doctrines of the Holy Spirit, and still another in the doctrine of the end times. Theological courses are set up on various subjects so that there is a course in soteriology (the doctrine of salvation), another in christology (the doctrine of Christ), and another in eschatology (the doctrine of the last things), etc.

Structuring theological truth does not necessarily result in wrong conclusions, but it frequently does. For example, it is possible for a theological professor to find many verses that deal with the nature and purpose of the church, and by studying these verses, a theologian may become an expert in ecclesiology (the doctrine of the church). He may come to and teach conclusions that appear Biblical as he views them in the light of the verses that speak about the church. He may have an earnest desire to be faithful to the Bible. No one would fault his integrity as he teaches all that he has learned from the Bible.

However, if he has not tested his conclusions to see if they are in harmony with all that the Bible teaches concerning the nature of salvation, the nation of Israel, the end time, the Holy Spirit, and everything else in the Bible, the likelihood is that some of his conclusions concerning the church will be invalid.

He may have done theologically what the designer of a building may do. He designs a building with beams to carry certain stresses and forces but he fails to see if the foundation design is capable of carrying the same stresses and forces. This practice would soon result in the failure of the building. Any designer knows that he must carefully design all parts of the structure to make sure that each beam, and each bolt, etc., will be able to sustain the stresses and forces that will be upon the building. Only then will the building be safe.

> *Any conclusion we reach based on our understanding of a particular verse or verses must be tested for scriptural integrity by everything in the Bible that relates to these verses.*

Similarly, any conclusion we reach based on our understanding of a particular verse or verses must be tested for scriptural integrity by everything in the Bible that relates to these verses.

We must look to the Bible to interpret Scripture. We cannot look at Matthew 25:31-46 and understand it unless we examine it in the light of everything else the Bible teaches regarding the subject matter in these verses. Only then can we know that these verses are a parable which teach spiritual truth related to salvation.

Comparing Scripture with Scripture

This is the method of interpretation the Bible tells us to use, as I Corinthians 2:13 declares:

Which things also we speak, not in the words which man's wisdom teacheth, but which the Holy Ghost teacheth; comparing spiritual things with spiritual.

God is spirit, and salvation is God's spiritual program whereby those who are spiritually dead are reconciled to God. They become spiritually alive. God's Word is the sword of the Spirit, and we must realize that to compare spiritual things with spiritual is to compare one part of the Bible with every other part of the Bible. Thus, we are correct in our conclusion that we are to interpret the Bible with the Bible. We are to compare everything in the Bible with everything else in the Bible that may relate to the verse or word being studied. After we have examined the word, phrase, or verse in question in the light of the rest of the Bible (so that we know we are in agreement with the whole Bible), we are ready to teach the meaning of this verse or word.

> *The student of the Bible must become increasingly expert in the whole Bible. It means that he must unceasingly study every aspect of Bible truth.*

This means that the student of the Bible must become increasingly expert in the whole Bible. It means that he must unceasingly study every aspect of Bible truth. This is a life-long endeavor, and it requires constant diligence and perseverance. There will be times when it will be necessary to set aside previously held conclusions that do not stand under the scrutiny of the whole Bible. This requires grace and humility, but it is essential if truth is to be served.

The Bible Is its Own Dictionary

If we continue to study every aspect of the Bible, we will discover that the Bible is its own dictionary. If we wish to know the meaning of a word in the Bible, we do not go to a dictionary of Greek or Hebrew (the original languages of the Bible). To do so would be useless. The meanings of words have changed during the last two thousand years to such a degree that it would be a wonder if any of the words used in the Bible had the same meaning today.

We must find all the verses in the Bible in which the word in question is found; then, we see how it is used in these verses. Based on this information, we can begin to discern its meaning and know how it is used in the verse being studied.

> *To discover the meaning of a verse, it is necessary to do a study of the words and concepts in the verse to see how they are used throughout the Bible.*

To discover the meaning of a verse, it is necessary to do a study of the words and concepts in the verse to see how they are used throughout the Bible. By this means, we can bring the whole Bible to bear on the verse in question.

Occasionally we find a word in the original Hebrew or Greek which is used only once in the entire Bible. In this case, it cannot be compared with its use in other parts of the Bible. However, we can be sure that the content of the word will convey a truth which is found in other places in the Bible. Therefore, it is from the Bible that we can know the parameters that prescribe how we are to understand the word.

The use of Biblical words in ancient secular writings may help in finding the meaning of some words, but the secular record must never be considered as trustworthy as the Bible. The Bible's use of the word must be the final authority in determining its meaning.

Only infrequently is it impossible to determine the meaning of a Hebrew or Greek word. It is best to leave it in its original language and trust that at a future date God will open the eyes of a Bible student to learn its meaning.

The Bible Is its Own Grammar Book

The Bible is its own grammar book. The careful student may begin to understand tenses, moods, and voices in Hebrew and Greek by studying these languages in the ancient secular accounts. It is conventional for the Bible student to go to Hebrew-English and Greek-English dictionaries for this purpose, but conclusions based on secular evidence cannot stand until they are subjected to the scrutiny of the Bible.

Ideally, the rules of grammar and the meanings of words should be derived entirely from the Bible, because the Bible alone must stand as the final authority in all matters of which it speaks. This includes concepts, ideas, and truths and the form in which these ideas, concepts, and truths are presented. The Bible would be less than the Word of God if this were not so because the grammar and the words are the means by which Bible truth is presented.

> *The serious Bible student should be relentless in his study of the Bible.*

The serious Bible student should be relentless in his study of the Bible. Only as it increasingly becomes part of his life will he be able to draw closer and closer to the rich storehouse of truths which is the Bible.

A peril of the Bible teacher is that he may be impressed with the fact that a great many theologians agree on a particular doctrine. It is easy to simply trust that the judgment of these theologians is accurate. Unfortunately, however, theologians frequently build on what other theologians have said rather than checking the Scriptures to make sure that previous theologians have been accurate. Wonderfully, God has given us His Word so that any belief, regardless of how widely held it may be, can be analyzed and checked against the Scriptures.

When Elijah stood on Mount Carmel, he stood alone against hundreds of other prophets who agreed theologically, but Elijah was right and they were wrong. Consensus is never a basis for truth.

The Bible is the revelation of God's will to man. God is the author. God used human authors - they spoke out of their own experience, training, environment, culture, and personality - but they were used of God to produce the Bible, and what they penned, right down to the word and the letters of each word, was the precise word God desired to use as the revelation of His will. Whether Paul or Jesus or Jeremiah or an unnamed scribe spoke or wrote, what was written was God's Word.

Before we can know the truth of any verse or phrase in the Bible, we must compare the conclusion we have reached concerning that word or phrase against the rest of the Bible. Only when we find that the conclusion is in harmony with everything else the Bible teaches can we be sure that we are on the path of truth.

Red Letter Editions of the Bible

We are currently besieged with Bibles called "Red Letter Editions," in which the words Jesus spoke are printed in red and the rest of the Bible is printed in black letters.

Whatever the purpose of the publishing houses in printing these Red Letter Editions, the impact on the reader is devastating. The reader cannot help but think that the words Jesus spoke are more important than the other words because they are emphasized by red type and consequently set off from the rest of the Bible. Thus, the reader unconsciously adopts the principle that the Bible has two levels of authority: the first and most important being the words that Jesus spoke. The second level of authority would be everything else.

A word spoken by Paul or Isaiah or any of the men of God used to pen the Holy Scriptures has equal authority with the words spoken by the Lord Jesus Christ.

This conclusion is contrary to the Bible and effectively undermines the authority of the Bible. The Bible declares that all Scripture is given by inspiration of God. Therefore, a word spoken by Paul or Isaiah or any of the men of God used to pen the Holy Scriptures has equal authority with the words spoken by the Lord Jesus Christ. It is wise, if possible, to use Bibles that are printed only in black.

> *There is a marvelous oneness and cohesiveness throughout the Bible that makes it a joy to study and contemplate.*

The Bible Is One Truth

Because God is the author, there is a marvelous oneness and cohesiveness throughout the Bible that makes it a joy to study and contemplate. Words and phrases used in one book are to be studied in the light of words and phrases used elsewhere in the Bible.

For example, the meaning of the Greek word *kamno* used by the Holy Spirit in James 5:15, is to be interpreted in light of its use in two other New Testament passages, Hebrews 12:3 and Revelation 2:3. In Hebrews 12:3, the word *kamno* is translated "wearied," and in Revelation 2:3, *kamno* is translated "faint," so the context clearly indicates that this word is related to spiritual weariness. No suggestion is offered that it relates to physical illness. Thus one can discover the meaning in the obscure passage, as James 5:15, by the use in the clearer passages.

When we carefully read James 5:15, we discover that three blessings were experienced by the one who had been subject to *kamno*, and they all relate to salvation: 1) he has become saved; 2) he has been raised up; 3) his sins have been forgiven. These three phrases relate to salvation. James 5:14 employs the Greek work *astheneo*, which is translated "sick" in our Bible, but we find by the use of the word *astheneo* in other places in the Bible that it can refer to any kind of spiritual or physical illness. Because God used the word *kamno* in verse 15 and not *astheneo*, we know that physical healing is not in view in this passage; the focus is on salvation.

Interpreting Scripture with Scripture Helps Us to Understand Matthew 12:36

The statement in Matthew 12:36 can be easily misunderstood if we do not practice the principle of comparing Scripture with Scripture. In Matthew 12:36 Jesus lays down the principle that "every idle word that men shall speak, they shall give account thereof in the day of judgment." Does this mean that believers will have to give an account before God? By looking at the word "judgment" in light of everything else the Bible offers, we know that believers do not come into judgment. Let us see why this is so.

> *The demands of the law of God recorded in II Corinthians 5:10 have been met by Christ on behalf of all who believe on Him.*

The Greek word used in Matthew 12:36 and translated "judgment" in the King James Bible is the word *krisis*. This word is used in John 5:24, where Christ declares, "He that heareth my word, and believeth on him that sent me, hath everlasting life, and shall not come into condemnation; but is passed from death unto life." The word translated "condemnation" is the word *krisis*, the same word used in Matthew 12. Thus, we are assured that those who place their trust in Christ do not give an account before the judgment throne. To expand the thought, we know that the reason we do not come into judgment is that Christ became sin for those who place their trust in Him, and He has already been judged for those sins. Believers cannot be judged for sins that have been taken care of by our Savior. Effectively, believers have already stood before the judgment throne of God to answer for their sins. They did so in the person of Jesus Christ, who as their substitute, was laden with their sins, was found guilty of those sins, and was punished for those sins. The demands of the law of God recorded in II Corinthians 5:10 have been met by Christ on behalf of all who believe on Him. This verse declares:

> For we must all appear before the judgment seat of Christ; that every one may receive the things done in his body, according to that he hath done, whether it be good or bad.

These are just a few of the great number of examples that could be offered that indicate that we must carefully examine words in the light of their use throughout the Bible to discover their true meaning. Since God is the author of the Bible, we know that every word in the original languages was chosen carefully, regardless of whether Luke, Jeremiah, or Moses was the human author, because we know that God is infallible in all that He does. We can place implicit trust in the Bible.

The Bible Is Infallible

One must understand that only the original autographs are to be considered infallible. As originally penned in Hebrew, Greek, and Aramaic, they are the articulation of the perfect will of God.

The scribes who copied the originals for later generations had a deep sensitivity to the holiness and uniqueness of the Word of God. Even after hundreds of years, copies were such faithful reproductions of the original manuscripts that one can consider the copies to be virtually infallible.

God has provided access to some ancient copies, some of which, in the case of the Old Testament, were made prior to the appearance of the New Testament writings. As a result, translators have a superbly accurate Bible from which to work.

> *The task of the translator is to translate as faithfully as possible.*

The task of the translator is to translate as faithfully as possible. It is an exacting and difficult job to be absolutely true to the original because languages are not parallel in structure or in meaning of individual words.

Most words in the Bible have equivalent words in the language into which they are being translated. Most phrases in the original texts lend themselves to rather accurate translation without dropping or adding words. In the King James and American Standard versions, any words added by the translators to help work out the translation were *italicized*. This warns the reader that the *italicized* word is not found in the original language.

Bibles are available in most of the major languages of the world. These Bibles are well translated and we may consider them to be almost as infallible as the original texts. Because Hebrew and Greek texts are available for study and comparison, students of the Word can examine the original language to check the translators' faithfulness. *Young's Analytical Concordance* and *Strong's Exhaustive Concordance* assist non-Greek and non-Hebrew students to study God's use of individual words as found in the original language. Our Lord has certainly blessed us!

To Paraphrase or Not to Paraphrase

It has been claimed that paraphrased editions of the Bible are valuable tools for effective evangelism. This claim is made by many who testify of its validity because someone became a Christian after reading a paraphrased edition.

Is this conclusion valid? Has God guided men in our day to develop more readable Bibles so that His work of saving people will be assisted in the closing days of the earth's existence? Or, instead of being a blessing, will the paraphrases prove to be sinful and God's wrath will be poured out on the church for its audacious use of such books? These questions must be examined carefully and candidly for we are currently being besieged by paraphrased editions of the Bible.

> *God did not intend to write the Bible to be always easily understood.*

God is infinitely wise. He could have written the Bible simply, so that no one could misunderstand it. God did not intend to write the Bible to be always easily understood. It is true that some verses give readily understood truth, but many verses which appear to be easily understandable are actually difficult to grasp in their full meaning. The Bible declares in Proverbs 25:2, "It is the glory of God to conceal a thing: but the honour of kings is to search out a matter."

In Proverbs 1:5-6 God informs us:

A wise man will hear, and will increase learning; and a man of understanding shall attain unto wise counsels; To understand a proverb, and the interpretation; the words of the wise, and their dark sayings.

These are warnings that the Bible may not be as clear as we would sometimes like to think. We are being advised in these verses that we have to search out the truth. The Bible tells of such difficulties, as Jesus declares in Mark 4:11-12:

And he said unto them, Unto you it is given to know the mystery of the kingdom of God: but unto them that are without, all these things are done in parables: That seeing they may see, and not perceive; and hearing they may hear, and not understand; lest at any time they should be converted, and their sins should be forgiven them.

He adds in Mark 4:34, "But without a parable spake he not unto them: and when they were alone, he expounded all things to his disciples."

The difficulty in understanding the Word is highlighted by the different teachings in the evangelical community concerning important subjects, such as God's sovereignty, election and predestination, the total depravity of man, particular atonement versus free will, the security of believers, baptism, the Lord's Supper, the final tribulation, the return of Christ, and rewards. One may begin to wonder: can anyone really find truth in the Bible?

> *The Word of God is to be accepted first by*
> *faith and not because one*
> *understands it.*

One must realize that the Word of God is to be accepted first by faith and not because one understands it. God's command to Abraham to sacrifice his son, Isaac, made no sense whatsoever. Killing his son would contravene every promise God had made to him, but Abraham obeyed in blind faith. The Bible is to be accepted by faith. Only then will it be the living Word that leads to salvation. Then it will be the Sword of the Spirit which He will use to lead into all truth. As

we humbly trust the Word of God, the Holy Spirit will slowly lead us
to truth by His Word.

In paraphrased editions, one senses the following attitude: A
scribe has been given a message by the King. He is mandated to give
the message to the populace. The scribe listens to the King's message
and realizes it is difficult to understand. He reasons that a better
conveyance of truth would be simpler language. He receives the
message, rewrites it in his own words, and gives it to the people. He
fails to realize that the King, in his perfect wisdom, gave the message
exactly as he did with precise purpose in every word.

The audacity, the temerity, the arrogance of this scribe! He did
not deliver the King's message; he made himself more authoritative and
wiser than the King.

> *It is God who applies His Word to the hearts of*
> *those who are to be saved.*

This is what paraphrase translators and those who use them
have done. They are insensitive to the nature and character of the Word
they are communicating. They have lost their awareness of the holiness
of God's Word. They have forgotten that saving people is God's work.
Evangelists do not sell the Gospel; they do not snare people into
salvation; they do not save people. The Christian is to faithfully witness
from God's Word as He has given it. It is God who applies His Word
to the hearts of those who are to be saved. As the witness brings the
Word, there is a clear line of demarcation between the Bible and the
preaching. The Bible is infallible; the preaching may be open to
question.

The fact that someone becomes convicted of sin by reading a
paraphrase is no rationale for its use. God spoke truth in the Bible
through cursed Balaam (Numbers 23 and 24) and wicked Caiaphas
(John 11:49-52). He used a donkey to convey His Word (Numbers
22:28-30), but the sins of these men were not excused or covered.
Today, too, God can use a statement that approximates His Word to
accomplish salvation, but that does not excuse the sins of those who
have lost their sensitivity to the holiness of God's Word and substituted
the work of man for God's Word. God's elective decree is that the one

who was saved while reading a paraphrase would have been saved while reading the Bible.

One might ask, are paraphrases helpful in any way? For example, do they render a useful service when used as a commentary?

Unfortunately, our minds are not dependable. We may realize that the paraphrase is not the Bible, but subconsciously we accept its statements as we accept the Bible - but it is not the Bible. The paraphraser rewrites a phrase (in his own words) according to what he believes is a logical and proper interpretation. If his understanding of the phrase is Biblical, he will isolate one particular truth that God intended to be in the original phrase. However, rewriting sets aside the full depth of meaning that God intended to make available in the phrase. In other words, the Bible is emptied of much of its content. If the paraphraser interprets incorrectly, he presents as Biblical truth that which is a lie. Because it is in a format which purports to be the Bible, the reader accepts a falsehood as truth. He clutters his mind with information which at best is merely part truth and at worst is altogether false. What Christian would dare to become a part of this kind of activity? The faithful and safe way to go is to reject paraphrases without delay.

Rewriting the Bible in simple English (or in simplified form in any other language), will be considered sin by few people. Few read the Bible extensively or intensively. Few are ready to be obedient to what the Word declares. We live in the days prophesied by our Lord in Hosea 4:6:

> My people are destroyed for lack of knowledge: because thou hast rejected knowledge, I will also reject thee, that thou shalt be no priest to me: seeing thou hast forgotten the law of thy God, I will also forget thy children.

God's wrath will surely be visited upon us for this sin.

Chapter 5.
The Bible has More than One
Level of Meaning

Thus far in our study, two important principles have been discovered that must be kept in mind as we study the Bible. They are:

1. The Bible alone and in its entirety is the Word of God.
2. We are to interpret Scripture with Scripture.

Keep these principles in mind and truth will be found from the Bible.

The use of words and phrases must be studied in individual sentences, the context in which the sentence is used, and how they are used elsewhere in the Bible. The more familiar the student is with the entire Bible, the more he will be helped in his study.

We must recognize that the Bible is God's Word. The Holy Spirit leads us into truth. If we study diligently and pray that God will open our spiritual eyes to truths hidden within the Word, we will grow in grace.

We will now look at a third principle, which is of great importance. It, too, must be understood to realize the spiritual riches of the Bible. That principle is that the Bible ordinarily has more than one level of meaning. These levels are:

1. The historical setting.
2. The moral or spiritual teaching.
3. The salvation account.

These levels of meaning will now be examined in greater detail.

The Bible Is Absolutely Accurate in its Record of Historical Events

Many people have the notion that because the Bible is God's Word concerning salvation, it is not trustworthy in areas of history, science, and other fields of learning. However, the Bible is a revelation from God as He spoke through holy men of old; we know that it must be true and dependable.

A favorite target of attack is the creation of the earth. The Bible declares that God created the universe in six days. When we search the Bible, we find this statement abundantly supported. There is no encouragement for the theory that more than six 24-hour days was required.

> *These scientific conclusions are not even a fraction*
> *as accurate as the majestic statements of the Bible*
> *that tell of God's creation of the*
> *heavens and the earth.*

Modern science has concluded that the world is billions of years old. Is this conclusion valid? The scientific conclusions about the origin of the universe are based on exceedingly scarce evidence. No present-day scientist lived then, and the written record goes back only about five thousand years. The modern-day scientist views the meager available evidence in the light of assumptions he is forced to make. Obviously, his conclusions are no more accurate than the assumptions, or "educated guesses," on which he based his view. It is impossible that these scientific conclusions can be a fraction as accurate as the majestic statements of the Bible that tell of God's creation of the heavens and the earth.

The Bible records a flood that destroyed everything that had the breath of life from off the face of the earth. This flood covered the highest mountain (Genesis 6 to 9). To suggest that this may have been a localized flood is to deny the authority of the Scriptures.

The Bible says that in Peleg's day the earth was divided (Genesis 10). This historic event is seen in scientific evidence that indicates that the earth once had one continent which broke up into the smaller continents now known.

> *Unless the Bible shows that an event or conversation is to be understood as non-historical, it is absolutely dependable that every conversation and every historical incident recorded in the Bible actually took place.*

Unless the Bible shows that an event or conversation is to be understood as non-historical, it is absolutely dependable that every conversation and every historical incident recorded in the Bible actually took place. Archeological evidence may not prove the existence of a particular nation named in the Bible, and an incident may be unusual, nevertheless, we have no right to suggest that what the Bible has recorded is not authoritative.

When the Bible speaks of the nation of Israel passing through the Red Sea, and the "waters were a wall unto them on their right hand and on their left" (Exodus 14:22), it would deny the truth of God to suggest that anything but a miracle occurred. God altered the physical laws to make the waters stand as a wall. The Bible says a prophet named Jonah was cast into the sea and swallowed by a fish. To suggest that this is not an historical event is to repudiate God. The Bible speaks of the bodily resurrection of the Lord Jesus Christ. Be assured that these events actually happened in history.

The Bible is impeccably accurate in what God gives us concerning historical events - the facts He brings to our attention - and it is certain that the Bible is equally accurate about future events. The return of the Lord Jesus Christ in glory, the rapture of believers on the last day to go to be with Him, the destruction by fire of the present universe, the creation of New Heavens and a New Earth as the eternal dwelling place of born-again believers, and the removal of the unsaved into a place called hell where they will suffer eternally in payment for their sins - all these things are to be understood as future events. They are just as certain to take place as it is certain that the historical events recorded in the Bible took place.

> *To deny the historical accuracy of the Bible in
> its record of creation and the flood will lead to
> questions regarding future events.*

It must be emphasized that to deny the historical accuracy of the Bible in its record of creation and the flood will lead to questions regarding future events, such as the destruction of the world by fire and the removal of the unsaved into eternal damnation. God gives a warning in II Peter 3:3-7, 10, 13:

> Knowing this first, that there shall come in the last days scoffers, walking after their own lusts. And saying, Where is the promise of his coming? for since the fathers fell asleep, all things continue as they were from the beginning of the creation. For this they willingly are ignorant of, that by the word of God the heavens were of old, and the earth standing out of the water and in the water: Whereby the world that then was, being overflowed with water, perished: But the heavens and the earth which are now, by the same word are kept in store, reserved unto fire against the day of judgment and perdition of ungodly men.... .

> But the day of the Lord will come as a thief in the night; in the which the heavens shall pass away with great noise, and the elements shall melt with fervent heat; the earth also, and the works that are therein, shall be burned up. . . .

> Nevertheless we, according to his promise, look for new heavens and a new earth, wherein dwelleth righteousness.

God's purpose for writing the Bible was not to give us a book on history or science. It was to reveal His salvation plan, and God did this in an historical context. His plan comes to fruition in history. When God selects historical incidents or conversations through which the salvation program will shine, it is absolutely certain that the incidents and conversations, as recorded, are accurate and trustworthy.

The Bible is much more than an account of historical events. It has a second level of meaning which is concerned with teaching moral and spiritual values.

The Bible Teaches Moral and Spiritual Values

II Timothy 3:16: "All scripture is given by inspiration of God, and is profitable for doctrine, for reproof, for correction, for instruction in righteousness: . . . ." God gives moral and spiritual principles and guidelines in the Bible by which we are to live and have a more abundant life. In His condescending love and mercy God gave to the human race, which is made in His image, a written revelation of how to live happily and effectively in the world.

> *When he sins, the believer is deeply troubled; within his own personality, he will feel violated.*

The believer in Christ, he who has received his eternal resurrected soul (also called "spirit"), from the moment of his salvation will have an ongoing desire to be obedient to God. He will heed the admonitions and exhortations of the Bible because he loves God, who is doing the admonishing. When he sins, the believer is deeply troubled; within his own personality, he will feel violated. In his body he continues to lust after sin, but in his soul, where he has been born from above, he wants to never sin again. God in the person of the Holy Spirit indwells him. He has become a child of God and the Holy Spirit will bring him under conviction if he does not confess and turn from sin.

This process is sometimes called "growing in grace" or growing in "sanctification." It is the experience of every child of God. It is the process by which the child of God will do good works; that is, he will do works pleasing to God. These works are neither a cause nor a basis for salvation. They are an expected result of salvation. Ephesians 2:8-10 beautifully expresses this principle:

For by grace are ye saved through faith; and that not of yourselves; it is the gift of God. Not of works, lest any man should boast. For we are his workmanship, created in Christ Jesus unto good works, which God hath before ordained that we should walk in them.

To receive maximum value from the guidelines for life presented in God's Word, keep three principles in mind.

1. The Bible is the final authority.

2. The Bible must be read with a view to being obedient to what is found therein.

3. The Bible interprets and explains the rules that God has laid down.

> *The Bible is the standard God established for the well-being of mankind.*

Many rules for man's conduct may be read in the Bible. For example, the Bible says that we should seek the kingdom of God and His righteousness. It declares that we are not to commit adultery. It emphasizes that we are to be holy just as our heavenly Father is holy. Rules of conduct are found throughout the Bible. The Bible is the standard God established for the well-being of mankind.

The Bible records hundreds of historical situations which can be examined in light of these rules to discover the blessings that come with obedience and the curse that comes with disobedience. This encourages and helps avoid the consequence of living in violation of these rules. It gives the accounts of Joseph and Daniel and the blessings that came to them as they obeyed God, and the accounts of Israel and Judah, who came under God's judgment because of disobedience. God declares in I Corinthians 10:11:

Now all these things happened unto them for ensamples; and they are written for our admonition, upon whom the ends of the world are come.

This information is valueless unless it is recognized that the Bible is the Word of God. There is no higher authority which abrogates, invalidates, or explains the Biblical statement. It is totally trustworthy and dependable.

> *We must look upon the examples and declarations of the Bible with a view to being obedient to them.*

We must look upon the examples and declarations of the Bible with a view to being obedient to them. We can know that the Bible is the authoritative Word of God, but only by surrendering to all that we find in Scripture will we begin to see the implications and ultimate value of its truth. The Bible is more than just a rule book; it is the living Word of God. Humbly and obediently approach the Bible as the Word of God, and it becomes the sword of the Spirit as God applies His Word to our lives. We will never be able to interpret the Bible properly nor see the riches of His Word, unless we come to it with an earnest desire to be obedient to what is found there.

God declares, "Thou shalt not kill," but we cannot know what He means unless we examine everything in the Bible that relates to killing. Then we can be sure that God does not mean do not kill animals. On the contrary, there are times when the Bible insists that even human life must be taken.

It is imperative that the whole Bible be read and investigated to gain understanding of the moral and spiritual laws God has given.

> *When we, as unsaved sinners, go to the Bible and are ready to be obedient to all that is found there, we discover that we do not measure up to God's standards.*

When we, as unsaved sinners, go to the Bible and are ready to be obedient to all that is found there, we discover that we do not measure up to God's standards. This should bring us to our knees and make us cry out for deliverance from our sins, through the Lord Jesus

Christ, who is presented as the Redeemer. To the extent that man lives in conformity to the laws of the Bible, he will enjoy the blessings of God, but he will never know the highest blessing and happiness - eternal life - if he does not become obedient to the command to believe on the Lord Jesus Christ.

It has been shown that the Bible is impeccably accurate in its record of historical events. Through these events and the direct commands in Scripture, God gives us moral and spiritual values.

The Bible Is the Gospel of Grace

The third level of meaning persistently shines through the Scriptures: The Bible is the presentation of the Gospel of grace. Unquestionably, this is the most important purpose of the Bible. It was written that mankind might know of its need of a Savior. God declares in John 20:31, in regard to signs that Jesus performed:

> But these are written, that ye might believe that Jesus is the Christ, the son of God; and that, believing, ye might have life through his name.

Without Christ we are condemned to eternal damnation because of our sins.

God tells mankind about our terrible predicament through His salvation program. He discloses to us that without Christ we are condemned to eternal damnation because of our sins. Wonderfully, God shows us the escape that He provided through the Lord Jesus Christ.

The presentation of the Gospel message is given to us in two basic ways: (1) by means of statements which speak directly to the question of salvation; and (2) by means of historical events and phrases which are types or figures of God's salvation program. These two methods of Gospel presentation will be examined.

God Speaks Directly to the Matter of Salvation

Almost from the beginning of the Bible, statements are made that speak directly to the question of salvation. In Genesis 3:15 God declares that there would be enmity between Satan and the woman, and between his seed and her seed, and that Satan's head would be bruised. This reflects the enmity that exists between the kingdom of Satan and the kingdom of Christ. Christ is the seed of the woman, who vanquished Satan by going to the cross.

God gives additional insight, in Genesis, of His salvation program when He declares that the scepter would not depart from Judah. This Biblical language tells us that a King would come from Judah, and that this King would be intimately related to salvation.

God gives more information about His salvation program in Psalm 103, where He speaks of Himself as the Savior who "forgiveth all thine iniquities" and "redeemeth thy life from destruction." In Isaiah 53, God is more specific; He describes the coming Savior as One who would become a Man of Sorrows, upon whom God would lay our sins.

> *In the New Testament the proclamation of the salvation program comes to its most complete revelation.*

In the New Testament the proclamation of the salvation program comes to its most complete revelation. The first four books of the New Testament present the Lord Jesus Christ as our Savior. John the Baptist's introduction of Him was, "Behold the Lamb of God who taketh away the sin of the world." John 3:16 contains a beautiful and specific promise: "For God so loved the world, that he gave his only begotten Son, that whosoever believeth in him should not perish, but have everlasting life."

The revelation of the Gospel program continues in the epistles. Under the inspiration of the Holy Spirit, the Apostle Paul and others wrote to various churches and in detail revealed the grand declaration of salvation.

The Bible as a whole is a book that presents the glorious Gospel of salvation through the Lord Jesus Christ. Anyone who reads it with a humble attitude and realizes that it is the Word of God can be convicted of his sin; and by His Word, God will draw him into the kingdom of Christ.

The Gospel of Grace Is Frequently Hidden

The Bible makes many statements that bear directly on the message of salvation, but the message is not always immediately apparent - sometimes it is hidden within the Biblical language. We must realize that the message of salvation is the most important message of the Bible. We would expect, therefore, that it would shine through every page of the Bible.

Earlier in our study we saw that the Bible can be trusted implicitly, including when it speaks from an historical standpoint. We discovered that the Bible frequently gives moral and spiritual values, which if observed, assure happiness on this earth. We learned that the major presentation of the Bible is the Gospel of God's grace as revealed through the Lord Jesus Christ, our Savior. It is this level of meaning - salvation - that is frequently seen in clear language.

> *The message of salvation can be found hidden within historical conversations and incidents in the Bible.*

The message of salvation can be found hidden within historical conversations and incidents in the Bible. The hidden aspects of this third level of meaning must be examined in addition to the first level of meaning (the historical aspects), and the second level of meaning (the moral and spiritual teachings).

Historical events, words, phrases, and concepts in themselves do not appear to speak of the message of salvation; nevertheless, we know that the Bible is the Word of God. We know that the intent of the Bible is to bring men face to face with their need of a Savior. We realize that God put nothing in the Bible incidentally or coincidentally or casually. It was not God's purpose to write the Bible to give us a history lesson. God did not write the Bible merely to give us moral and spiritual lessons so that mankind might live more comfortably on earth.

> *The great predicament of mankind is that he is going to hell because of his sins.*

The great predicament of mankind is that he is going to hell because of his sins. This is a major facet of the most important message of the Bible. The rest of the message is that by believing in Christ we can escape this terrible predicament.

Much of the Bible superficially appears to have no direct relationship to God's salvation plan; however, as noted, there is ample evidence in the Bible that its central purpose is to bring God's salvation plan to the attention of the human race.

Is it possible that only those statements that speak directly of the message of salvation are considered relevant to the salvation message? Is the balance of the Bible simply the historical framework in which the Gospel message is cast?

The Bible provides answers to these questions. This is what will be developed as the study continues. God teaches us how to handle the words, phrases, and concepts which at first appear to have no direct relationship to His salvation plan.

The Ceremonial Laws Pointed to Aspects of God's Salvation Program

One major way in which God hid the salvation message is in the ceremonial laws. For example, in the Old Testament God instituted the Passover Feast. This was first observed when Israel went out of Egypt, and the angel of death killed the firstborn in homes that did not have the lamb's blood on the doorpost. The blood of that lamb provided salvation from physical death for the firstborn of their homes. The Bible clearly teaches that that historical event is a picture of the salvation provided through the Lord Jesus Christ. He is our Passover. He is the Lamb which was slain so that we would not come into eternal damnation.

> *By means of the ceremonial laws God has hidden*
> *the salvation message within the Scriptures.*

In addition to the observance of feast days which anticipated the coming of the Lord Jesus Christ, the ceremonial laws included offerings, sacrifices, food laws, planting laws, and a host of regulations. These are types or figures or representations of spiritual truths which relate to some aspect of salvation. By means of the ceremonial laws God has hidden the salvation message within the Scriptures. An understanding of the spiritual meaning of each aspect of the ceremonial laws will improve the understanding of the salvation message.

God's Salvation Plan Is Taught by Means of Parables

Let us look at another Biblical means of understanding the salvation message. When Christ was on earth He declared from time to time that He was about to speak in a parable. He then proceeded to give the parable and concluded His presentation with the spiritual meaning. In these parables Christ presented an earthly story with a heavenly meaning. These parables paralleled the ceremonial observances of the Old Testament, which were earthly observances with a heavenly meaning. The ceremonial laws, therefore, were historical parables; they were earthly experiences of the Israelites that pointed to a spiritual aspect of salvation.

> *Certain historical incidents were recorded in the*
> *Bible so that we might, through them, understand*
> *spiritual truth that relates to salvation.*

In addition to ceremonial observances and parables, God uses historical events to teach spiritual lessons. God shows us in the Scriptures that certain historical incidents were recorded in the Bible so that we might, through them, understand spiritual truth that relates to salvation. These historical events effectively were, therefore, historical parables.

In Genesis we read of Hagar bearing Ishmael by Abraham and the subsequent expulsion of Hagar and Ishmael from the home of Abraham and Sarah. In Galatians 4, God calls attention to this historical event to teach the spiritual truth that we have either a salvation that leads to spiritual bondage (typified by Hagar and Ishmael), or a salvation that leads to spiritual freedom (typified by Sarah and Isaac). It is not the purpose of this study to develop this particular truth, but you can read about it in Genesis 21:9-14 and Galatians 4:21-31.

In Malachi 4 God speaks of the coming of Elijah, and in Matthew 11:11-14 our Lord shows us that the Elijah He referred to was John the Baptist. Therefore, God is indicating that Elijah typified John the Baptist.

These pertinent Biblical illustrations demonstrate that the message of salvation is greatly expanded throughout the Scriptures. It is far beyond the clear declarations of salvation as stated in John 3:16, Isaiah 53, and the epistles.

When God indicates that He is speaking in parables, that an historical event or a person is a type of an aspect of salvation, or that the ceremonial law points to the Lord Jesus Christ, then it is safe to develop spiritual truth from these Scriptural accounts. Do we dare go beyond this and surmise that other historical events, personalities, and concepts might have a spiritual dimension? Are they types and figures of some aspect of the salvation proclamation? The Bible will guide us to the answers.

> *The use of parables was a common teaching method of the Lord Jesus Christ.*

In Mark 4 God says, "without a parable spake He not unto them." The use of parables was a common teaching method of the Lord Jesus. In the four Gospels, Jesus sometimes made the point that He was speaking in a parable, for example, in the parable of the sower in Luke 8.

On other occasions, He did not emphasize that He spoke in a parable. He would say, "the kingdom of heaven is . . . " and proceed with a story. This is a parable even though Jesus did not specifically use that word.

Another example is the story He told of the rich man and Lazarus in Luke 16. The Bible does not say that it is a parable, but when carefully studied, it is discovered that it must be a parable. If it were an historical event, it would be full of contradictions. For example, we are told that the rich man dies and is buried; therefore, his body is in the grave. Yet, in the next few verses we find that in hell he is described as having eyes and a tongue. However, when his body was buried, he was buried with his eyes and tongue. How then did his eyes and tongue get into hell when his body is in the grave?

Other contradictions are seen in this story if it is assumed that it is an actual historical event. When viewed as a parable (an earthly story with a heavenly meaning), then the contradictions disappear, and we realize that Christ is not giving us a chronological outline of what happens when we die. He is pointing out important spiritual concepts concerning what happens when someone dies without Christ.

From these examples it has been shown that God does not necessarily specifically say that a Biblical passage is a parable or that it is meant to indicate spiritual truth which relates to salvation.

God has given pertinent examples of the Bible's teaching methods by specifically indicating that either a parable is in view or that an historical event symbolizes spiritual truth. These examples show us the path we ought to follow. They direct us to God's teaching method. We must apply the teaching method to our Bible study.

Do we have any additional Biblical validation to proceed in this fashion? Can we search for the salvation message in passages that appear to be historical?

We might approach these questions in this way: in John 20 Jesus speaks of the miracles He did, and He declares in verse 31:

> But these are written, that ye might believe that Jesus is the Christ, the Son of God; and that, believing, ye might have life through his name.

Jesus specifies that these miracles were done so that through the record of them we might come to salvation. When Jesus actually performed the miracles, they were in themselves historical events that appeared to be unrelated to the salvation program.

> *The healing of a sick man in itself has nothing to do with the salvation program.*

The healing of a sick man in itself has nothing to do with the salvation program; however, based on the principle in John 20:31, Christ insists that He performed this miracle so that we might know about salvation. The Bible declares that without a parable, Jesus did not speak to them (Mark 4:34); these miracles were historical parables. They are earthly stories - actual historical events - with a spiritual meaning, in the same way that the parable of the sower is an earthly story with a heavenly meaning. This conclusion agrees with the principle in Mark 4:34, that "without a parable spake he not unto them."

A question persists: Jesus performed miracles that can be regarded as historical parables, but what about the Old Testament? Scripture says that Jesus always taught with parables; it was His teaching method, but the Bible is filled with records of historical events, phrases, and concepts.

In I Peter 1:11 we read that the Spirit of Christ spoke through the Old Testament prophets:

> Searching what, or what manner of time the Spirit of Christ which was in them did signify, when it testified beforehand the sufferings of Christ, and the glory that should follow.

This verse says that the Old Testament is as much the Word of Christ as the New Testament. This is not surprising because John 1 declares that Christ is the Word. Jesus spoke directly when He was on earth; He spoke directly throughout the Bible because He is the Word of God. The declaration of Mark 4:34, "without a parable spake he not unto them" applies to the whole Bible.

God reinforces this, for example, in Psalm 78:1-3:

Give ear, O my people, to my law: incline your ears to the words of my mouth. I will open my mouth in a parable: I will utter dark sayings of old; Which we have heard and known, and our fathers have told us.

In Proverbs 1:5-6 God informs us:

A wise man will hear, and will increase learning; and a man of understanding shall attain unto wise counsels; To understand a proverb, and the interpretation; the words of the wise, and their dark sayings.

These sayings parallel what we have read concerning Jesus' teaching method (the use of parables), and this helps us to understand how God has presented truth in the Bible.

> *Historical events are, in effect,*
> *historical parables.*

God declares the Gospel of salvation on every page of the Bible. At times the presentation of the salvation message is clear. At other times, God has hidden the salvation message within the record of historical incidents and concepts. God teaches through the use of parables. Historical events are, in effect, historical parables.

God had literally millions of historical events and concepts from which to choose and to record. Of all that He could have written, particular events were recorded in order that we might know that Jesus is the Christ and through Him we have salvation.

To assist us in understanding God's teaching method, the Bible gives examples. For instance, at times Jesus said, "This is a parable." The Bible might declare that a particular historical event has deeper spiritual meaning, but it must be remembered that these are examples. God is intimating that in similar fashion we are to attempt to find the salvation message in all the Scriptures.

It is taught in many seminaries and elsewhere that one should not look for deeper spiritual meaning unless the Bible expressly indicates that we are to do so. However, these teachers inevitably find, to some degree, that God's teaching method employs the use of parables far beyond what He has declared to be parables.

Many of these teachers do not hesitate to acknowledge that a New Testament statement such as "the kingdom of heaven is . . . " is a parabolic statement even though the Bible does not say it is a parable. They do not hesitate to look at Boaz in the Book of Ruth as a figure of Christ, the Redeemer, but nowhere in the Bible is there a declaration that Boaz is to be considered a figure of Christ.

They may consider Joseph, who became prime minister of Egypt, a type of the Lord Jesus Christ. Nowhere in the Bible is Joseph said to be a type or figure of our Savior. They may see the leprosy of Naaman the Syrian as a figure or type of sin, etc. Without realizing it, these people are moving in the direction of correct Biblical interpretation.

If Boaz is a representation of Christ, it must be decided whom Ruth and Naomi represent, and who or what is represented by the other kinsmen, the cities, and the other historical elements in the written account. If Joseph is a figure of the Lord Jesus Christ, what do the other elements represent that are interwoven in the historical account of Joseph in the Old Testament? The answers must be pursued by each believer as he attempts to unravel the salvation story from these historical events.

> *When a statement in the Bible appears to have no direct bearing on salvation, we must look for a deeper spiritual meaning of that statement that relates to salvation.*

When a statement in the Bible appears to have no direct bearing on salvation, we must look for a deeper spiritual meaning of that statement that relates to salvation. We many not discover what the salvation teaching is, but that does not mean that it is not there, hidden within the historical account.

Jesus the Lamb of God

Please consider for a moment John the Baptist's announcement of Jesus as the Messiah. For hundreds of years, Israel had been waiting for the promised Messiah. Finally, the all-important day had come for Jesus to be announced to the world. We read in John 1:29 that when John the Baptist saw Jesus approaching, he declared: "Behold the Lamb of God, which taketh away the sin of the world."

What kind of statement is that? Jesus was not a lamb. He was God Himself who had taken on a human nature by being born of the virgin Mary. It is true that He had come to take away sins. That part of the announcement is plausible. But He was not a lamb. He was not an animal.

However, John the Baptist was speaking under the inspiration of the Holy Spirit. Therefore, what he is announcing has to be true. The idea of a lamb has to be understood in some spiritual sense. Obviously, this is so if the statement in John 1, "Behold the Lamb of God," is true because Jesus was not an animal.

Where are we to go to find help with this puzzle? Of course, we are to search the Bible. And in so doing, we do find the answer to our puzzle. Throughout the Old Testament, lambs were sacrificed on altars as a type or representative of the coming Messiah. Even as a perfect lamb was chosen from the flock and then offered as a burnt offering to God, so, too, the perfect Jesus was to be offered to God as a burnt offering. That is, He was to be laden with the sins of all who would believe on Him, and God would pour out His wrath on Him as He paid the penalty of eternal damnation on behalf of those whose sins He bore. Indeed, every one of the thousands of lambs that were sacrificed during the previous 11,000 years of earth's history was pointing to Christ as THE LAMB OF GOD who would take away the sins of the world.

> *In this most important announcement of our Savior, God shows us how the Bible was written.*

Thus, in this most important announcement of our Savior, God shows us how the Bible was written. "Behold the Lamb of God, which taketh away the sin of the world." The phrase "Lamb of God" is allegorical. It relates altogether to the Gospel of salvation. We can know this when we use the rest of the Bible to teach us what the spiritual meaning of the phrase might be.

The phrase "takes away the sin of the world" is not at all allegorical. This statement directly and plainly relates to the Gospel of salvation.

Thus, we find that the whole statement relates entirely to the message of salvation. We also learn how we are to understand the teaching of Mark 4:33-34, "with many such parables spake he the word unto them . . . . But without a parable spake he not unto them." In the short statement of John 1:29, in which God declares the message for which the Jews had been waiting for hundreds of years, God announces that the Messiah has finally come. How significant it is that God has couched the message in a way that we see in it how God spoke in parables. Moreover, to understand it requires us to search the Bible for direction.

Numerous conversations, events, and personalities are recorded in the Bible that point to the Lord Jesus Christ or to some other aspect of salvation. These historical personalities and events are like parables. Millions of conversations and events that could have been incorporated into the Bible were not. God specifically chose those that are written down because they relate to and teach some aspect of His salvation program.

God Keeps Us Humble

Many passages do not easily reveal the wealth of truth hidden within them. The diligent Bible student may spend hours with one verse or passage, but not discover the deeper spiritual meaning which he suspects is hidden there. This is God's way of keeping us humble as we study the Bible. Often we will have to admit that we do not know the full teaching of a particular passage. Another student at another time may receive the insights we sought in that passage. Like the Bereans, the child of God will continue to search the Scriptures to find the nuggets of truth that God in His grace might reveal to him.

> *The golden thread that runs through the Bible is the declaration that there is a way to escape damnation.*

The Bible is God's message of salvation to the human race. The golden thread that runs through the Bible is the declaration that there is a way to escape damnation. God selected each conversation and historical incident in the Bible to present an aspect of His marvelous redemption plan. The message of salvation may be hidden deep within the Biblical language, but it is the task and joy of the believer to search out this passage.

Generally, if a Bible statement relates directly to an aspect of the message of salvation, there is no deeper spiritual meaning. For example, when the Bible speaks directly of salvation, spiritual rule in the church, obedience of believers to Christ, the return of Christ, or Judgment Day, we are not to look for deeper meaning. These subjects are in themselves the basic message of the Bible.

When the Bible tells us about Abraham seeking a wife for Isaac, David fleeing from Saul, Jesus healing the sick, and the shipwreck of the Apostle Paul, it is certain that these messages are included to teach us about salvation. We discover this by regarding these accounts as historical parables.

The more diligently we study the Bible to understand the fundamental doctrines of God's salvation plan, the better equipped we will be to search out the deeper spiritual meanings hidden within the historical events.

We will find that a beautiful harmony exists between the spiritual meaning and the message of salvation of a passage. This will appear in the measure that our interpretation harmonizes with the truth of the Gospel message.

> *Many theologians and pastors have inadequate knowledge of the message of salvation.*

Unfortunately, many theologians and pastors have inadequate knowledge of the message of salvation. As a result, they have extreme difficulty in finding the heavenly meaning hidden within the earthly stories. They ridicule the principle that God has hidden the salvation message within historical statements. This criticism does not invalidate the principle that the salvation message is found in the deeper spiritual meaning of an event.

Is it dangerous to attempt to discover spiritual meaning within the Bible? Will this lead to fanciful interpretations? Would it be better to leave this idea and cease from any attempt to find the Gospel declaration on every page of Scripture?

These are serious questions. We never want to read anything into the Scriptures that God never put there. As we seek out this third level of meaning within the Biblical account, it is important to remember these three rules:

1. **The spiritual meaning must relate to the Gospel of salvation.** Salvation is the message of the Bible. It will not do to look at an historical account and try to identify it with certain political nations or a contemporary phenomenon. The spiritual meaning always relates to the Gospel program. This is seen in the parables of Jesus and in the Old Testament presentation of the ceremonial law.

Many theologians realize that the ten horns of the dragon of Revelation 13 and Revelation 17 represent something, but they have decided that they represent the ten nations of the European Common Market.

We can know that their conclusion is erroneous. Political nations of Europe and economic factors in our world have nothing to do with salvation. If nations are involved in God's salvation plan, only two nations can be in view: the nation that is called the kingdom of God and the nation that is called the kingdom of Satan, which includes all the political nations of the world.

The ten horns of the dragon in Revelation 13 and Revelation 17 cannot refer to the kingdom of Christ; they must refer to the dominion of Satan. The number ten spiritually signifies completeness. In this instance, it signifies the completeness of Satan's rule in the world prior to Judgment Day.

When this is understood, all the Biblical passages which concern the ten horns are harmonized.

2. **Within an historical situation, to identify words or concepts with spiritual truth, we must have Biblical validation.** For example, we frequently find the words "stone" and "rock" in the Bible. Due to the fact that in many verses a stone or a rock is identified with the Lord Jesus Christ, we can attempt to make this application in an historical situation. We have seen that a "sower" can be identified with one who brings the Gospel, and "seed" can be identified with the Word of God.

3. If we have reason to believe that the third level of meaning is within a particular historical statement - that it can apply spiritually to the Gospel - **the conclusions we derive from our analysis of that historical situation must be in agreement with everything else the Bible teaches concerning the nature of salvation**. If we reach a conclusion that is contrary to the teaching of the rest of the Bible concerning salvation, we immediately know that we have not correctly understood the spiritual meaning of the passage.

If these three rules are carefully observed, we will be on safe ground as we study the Bible to discover its deeper spiritual meaning.

Do we run grave risks in attempting to spiritualize statements of the Bible? Some have done this and they ended up with wrong teachings concerning the message of salvation. We must be exceedingly careful in how we deal with the Holy Scriptures. The Word of God is never to be considered a mere plaything of men.

Many have expressed the fear that "spiritualizing" the Bible will lead people away from the true Gospel. This can happen only when we violate the three rules outlined above. If these rules are strictly followed, the understanding of the Gospel of salvation can be nothing but what the Bible teaches.

> *Every theologian, Bible teacher, and preacher*
> *living today looks for the deeper spiritual meaning*
> *whenever he is able to do so.*

Every theologian, Bible teacher, and preacher living today looks for the deeper spiritual meaning whenever he is able to do so.

Anyone who analyzes the ceremonial laws in order to understand the character of the coming Messiah and His salvation program is looking for deeper spiritual meaning. Anyone who suggests that Joseph (who was sold into Egypt by his brothers, eventually became the prime minister of that country, and saved his family from starvation), was a great type of Christ, has begun to find the deeper spiritual meaning within the historical context. No one can Biblically fault the idea that we are to look for the deeper spiritual meaning within the historical context.

Those who say that they accept the Bible literally and would not dare spiritualize (that is, look for a deeper spiritual meaning relating to salvation), actually do spiritualize when it is convenient; for example, what theologian would dare teach that the beast that comes from the sea and has seven heads and ten horns is a literal physical beast? Even though the Bible does not say that the beast is to be considered a picture or figure of some aspect of God's salvation plan, theologians correctly see it as a representative of Satan or of his dominion.

> *We receive our reward when we find that a particular historical account unfolds into a dramatic and beautiful picture of salvation.*

We have no other choice than to examine every passage of the Bible to discover deeper spiritual truth. This requires hours of exceedingly diligent work, God wrote the Bible in such a way that we are encouraged to search the Scriptures. We receive our reward when we find that a particular historical account unfolds into a dramatic and beautiful picture of salvation.

The spiritual meaning may be obvious, as it is in Isaiah 53, the Gospel of John, and the epistles. It may be hidden in parables, as it is in Matthew 13. It may be hidden in the ceremonial laws of the Old Testament; it may be buried more deeply in the historical events and conversations of the Bible. These historical events were chosen by God for inclusion in the Bible because of the deeper spiritual truths of salvation which are hidden within them.

The dominant message of the Bible is salvation, but the Biblical writing of the earthly story may appear awkward. Through this awkwardness, God provides the message of salvation. This particular language is necessary in order to reveal the beautiful truth of the parables.

Moses: A Representative of the Law

The Bible's historical events were chosen by God to hide within them deeper spiritual truths concerning salvation. For example, in Deuteronomy 34 we read that God buried Moses and no one ever found his sepulchre. No one else in the Bible was treated in this peculiar fashion. We may be puzzled because Moses struck the rock when God had commanded him to speak to it, and he was not permitted to enter the land of Canaan. This seems like cruel punishment for a faithful leader like Moses. These two events can be understood when we grasp the fact that in these passages God presents Moses as a figure or representative of the law, and the land of Canaan is a picture of salvation.

> *God's action in punishing Christ ended the law's demands. Thus, the believer does not enter into salvation by keeping the law.*

Joshua, who led the children of Israel into the land of Canaan, is presented as a figure of the Lord Jesus Christ, who brings us into salvation. The law ends when salvation begins. Moses, who typified the law in this context, died without entering into the Promised Land; keeping the law cannot bring us into salvation. When God subjected Christ to hell for our sins, the demands of the law that the penalty be paid for sins was fulfilled. God's action in punishing Christ ended the law's demands. Thus, the believer does not enter into salvation by keeping the law. In that sense, the law (typified by Moses) is dead to the believer. Instead, he enters into heaven by the grace of God (typified by Joshua).

The account of Moses when he struck the rock (and water came forth to satisfy the thirst of the Israelites), can be understood if we see Moses as a figure of the law. The rock is a figure of Christ. The water is the Gospel that flows from Christ. Moses (the law) struck the rock (that is, the law brought judgment on Christ), therefore, water (the Gospel of salvation) could flow from the rock (from Christ) to satisfy the thirst (the spiritual thirst) of those who drank the water.

Another example of what may appear to be awkward language is found in the Book of Ruth. Ruth and Orpah, daughters-in-law of Naomi, said to Naomi in Ruth 1:10, "Surely we will return with thee unto thy people." In the historical context they would not have used the word "return" - it implies that they had been there previously. However, God chose this word because these two women are a picture of the human race. The human race began with God in the Garden of Eden and through the Lord Jesus Christ they return to God.

Awareness of the principle that within the historical record God has hidden deep spiritual truths which concern the nature of salvation should cause a Bible translator to be exceedingly careful about the words he uses. He should never substitute an original word with another word that appears to him to be more convenient or salutary. For example, in the original languages God frequently used the word "blood" in phrases such as "the shedding of blood." Some translators have actually substituted the word "death" for the phrase "shedding of blood." The shedding of blood does emphasize death; nevertheless, the word "blood" has implications beyond the word "death," and this kind of substitution should not be made.

When, for example, the Bible describes a distance in cubits, like 200 cubits, the translator should never estimate how many feet there are in 200 cubits and substitute the word "feet" for cubits. The number 200 is God-breathed, and it has within it spiritual implications.

> *Throughout the Bible, numerous historical conversations, events, and personalities are types or figures which point to the Lord Jesus Christ or an aspect of the salvation program.*

Throughout the Bible, numerous historical conversations, events, and personalities are types or figures which point to the Lord Jesus Christ or an aspect of the salvation program. These historical personalities and events are to be looked upon as parables.

Historical events are types or shadows of God's salvation program; thus, these historical events are in effect historical parables.

The study will continue with an examination of a few historical personalities and events that have hidden within them the third level of meaning, which relates to the Gospel of salvation.

Historical Personalities and Events and the Gospel of Salvation

Some events and personalities which point to Christ and the salvation message are obvious. Moses, who is sometimes presented as a figure of the law ("Moses and the prophets"), is also presented as a figure of our Savior. When he led the children of Israel out of Egypt, he was shown to be a type of Christ, who leads us out of the bondage of sin and into the security of salvation. In Deuteronomy 18:15 Moses, under the inspiration of the Holy Spirit, declared: "The LORD thy God will raise up unto thee a Prophet, from the midst of thee, of thy brethren, like unto me; unto him ye shall hearken." That Prophet was the Lord Jesus Christ, who was "like unto" or typified by Moses.

David is another type of Christ. As shepherd and as king, he was a figure of Christ, who is the Good Shepherd and the King who rules over the kingdom we enter when we are saved. When David penned the words of Psalm 69, he was speaking of his personal experiences, but by the inspiration of the Holy Spirit he was anticipating the sufferings of Christ, who spiritually, and to a much greater degree, would go through the same experiences.

> *Citizenship in heaven (salvation), is the land of spiritual rest for those who follow the Lord Jesus Christ.*

Joshua, who led the children of Israel out of the wilderness and into the land of Canaan, is another type of the Lord Jesus Christ. This is shown particularly in Hebrews 4. Canaan was the land of physical rest for those in the nation of Israel who followed Joshua. Citizenship in heaven (salvation), is to be in the land of spiritual rest for those who follow the Lord Jesus Christ. The name Joshua (Hebrew) is identical to the name Jesus (Greek) in the New Testament.

The nation of Israel is frequently presented to us in the Bible as a type of those who are to believe in the Lord Jesus Christ. This is seen in the language of Galatians 3 where God declares in verse 7, "Know ye therefore, that they which are of faith, the same are the children of Abraham," and in verse 29, "And if ye be Christ's then are ye Abraham's seed, and heirs according to the promise." Israel in the flesh, also called national Israel, is the physical seed of Abraham, but in Galatians 3 God says that eternal Israel consists of those who are in Christ, regardless of nationality.

The list of types and shadows which is displayed in the Old Testament is a long one. Egypt, for example, is presented as a figure of being in bondage to sin, the way we are before we are saved. The passage of Israel through the Red Sea under the leadership of Moses is a beautiful picture of the redemption provided for us through the Lord Jesus Christ.

The wilderness sojourn of Israel is a dramatic picture of the sojourn of believers in the wilderness of this world while they travel towards the completion of salvation - the return of Christ on the last day. The entrance of Israel into the land of Canaan is a picture of our entrance into the fulness of salvation when we receive our resurrected bodies on the last day.

In the New Testament, God continues to provide numerous types and figures that appeared throughout history and pointed to aspects of the salvation program. The Bible declares in John 20:30-31:

And many other signs truly did Jesus in the presence of his disciples, which are not written in this book: But these are written, that ye might believe that Jesus is the Christ, the Son of God; and that believing ye might have life through his name.

God is saying that certain miracles were recorded in the Bible so that we might believe that Jesus is the Christ, the Son of God. The records provide us with insights into the nature of salvation. Jesus' healing of the blind is a good example: Jesus brought physical sight to the physically blind, and He brought spiritual sight to the spiritually blind.

The Gospel in the Raising of Lazarus

One of the most significant miracles that Jesus did was raise Lazarus from the dead. In this miracle, recorded for us in John 11, the Bible tells us that Jesus stood outside the tomb of Lazarus and "cried with a loud voice, Lazarus, come forth" (verse 43). Lazarus, who had been dead for four days, whose body had no will or life of its own, mysteriously, marvelously, incomprehensibly responded to the command to come to physical life.

> *Before we are saved, we are as spiritually dead as Lazarus was physically dead.*

In like manner, Jesus commands us to be saved, to come into spiritual, eternal life. When we are unsaved, we are as spiritually dead as Lazarus was physically dead. Lazarus had no will or capacity of his own to respond to the command of Jesus, and we have no desire or will within our lost souls to respond to His command to be saved.

The Bible teaches in Romans 3:11, "there is none that seeketh after God." Ephesians 2:1 indicates that we "were dead in trespasses and sins." How can a spiritual corpse respond to the Gospel call?

Incomprehensibly, there are those who hear the Gospel, respond, and believe. As Lazarus was raised from physical death, we are "risen with Christ" (Colossians 3:1). In Christ we are raised from spiritual death into spiritual life.

The Gospel in the Book of Ruth

The Book of Ruth gives an accurate record of events of history; however, the book was written in the genre of a parable in which God gives us insights into the marvelous salvation provided through the Lord Jesus Christ.

The cursed Moabite woman, Ruth, represents all who by nature are under the curse of sin but who respond to the Gospel. Boaz, the kinsman-redeemer who bought and married Ruth, is a picture of the Lord Jesus Christ, who purchased us so that we might become His bride. Orpah, Ruth's sister-in-law, who decided to stay in Moab, typifies those who hear the Gospel and are attracted to it, but who decide to stay in their old lives rather than follow the Lord Jesus Christ.

Naomi represents national Israel. During a famine, she and her family left Bethlehem and went to live in the land of Moab. As a result, her husband and sons died, and she was left a widow. In similar fashion, national Israel repeatedly turned away from God and as a result was cut off from being the wife of God. A seed was raised up for the family of Naomi through the marriage of Boaz and Ruth; and Christ, our Redeemer, came from Israel. The son born to Boaz and Ruth was also called a kinsman-redeemer (Ruth 4:14). He, too, was a figure of Christ.

Nehemiah, the Cupbearer of the King

Another Old Testament historical parable that teaches the Gospel is the record of Nehemiah. Nehemiah, who was the cupbearer of King Artaxerxes, went to Jerusalem to rebuild the wall. He is a dramatic picture of the Lord Jesus Christ. The cupbearer would die if the king's drink was poisoned. Christ died as the result of drinking the cup of God's wrath, which He did to save the sinners who were to become children of the King. Nehemiah's work was to rebuild the wall of Jerusalem. Christ's work on the cross built the Holy City, the New Jerusalem, which includes all who believe in Him as Savior.

Abram, a Figure of Christ

In Genesis 12 is the account of Abram when he went to Egypt because there was a famine in his land. While he was in Egypt, Pharaoh thought that Sarai was Abram's sister, and he took her into his house. This historical event is a picture of the marriage between Christ (typified by Abram), and His people (typified by Sarai). Sarai was not only the half sister of Abram, she was also his wife. Similarly, we who believe in Christ are called His brothers and His bride. The world of sin, represented by Egypt, desires to have the bride of Christ (Sarai). Abram was afraid that Pharaoh would kill him to obtain Sarai; Satan wanted Christ killed because he thought that as a result he could have the bride of Christ.

God presents the Gospel in the Old Testament in numerous ways, including the use of the historical parable. God meant it when He declared in Hebrews 4:2 that the Gospel was preached to Old Testament Israel as well as to us.

We and the Thieves on the Cross

God also uses historical parables in the New Testament. For example, the two thieves who were crucified with Christ - at first, they both reviled Christ but one of them came to believe in Him. The other thief continued to revile Him until he died.

> *We are like the two thieves in that, by nature, we*
> *are in rebellion against God.*

This is a picture of the Gospel as it is preached to all mankind. We are like the two thieves in that, by nature, we are in rebellion against God. Left to ourselves, we revile Him and refuse to turn to Christ. Most of the human race lives and dies in this rebellion, just as did the thief who died in unbelief.

There are those who hear the Word and respond to it. They become born-again believers. They are represented by the thief who submitted to the authority of Christ, and pleaded, "remember me when thou comest into thy Kingdom." In gracious compassion, Christ declared, "Today shalt thou be with me in paradise" (Luke 23:42-43).

The thief who responded to Christ brought the Gospel to the other thief. He said, in Luke 23:40-41:

> But the other answering rebuked him, saying, Dost not thou fear God, seeing thou art in the same condemnation? And we indeed justly; for we receive the due reward of our deeds: but this man hath done nothing amiss.

This is a picture of believers who, immediately upon becoming born again, have an earnest desire to share the Gospel.

These Signs Will Follow the Believers

Two verses of Mark 16 are dramatic proof of the principles set forth in this study. In verses 17 and 18 God declares:

And these signs shall follow them that believe; In my name shall they cast out devils; they shall speak with new tongues; They shall take up serpents; and if they drink any deadly thing, it shall not hurt them; they shall lay hands on the sick, and they shall recover.

Some theologians see the fulfillment of these verses in the fact that the apostles were empowered by God to heal the sick and cast out devils. In II Corinthians 12:12 we read:

Truly the signs of an apostle were wrought among you in all patience, in signs, and wonders, and mighty deeds.

Additionally, when Paul was shipwrecked on the Island of Melita, while he gathered sticks for a fire, a viper fastened on his hands. He shook it into the fire and was not harmed. This is looked upon as a fulfillment of Mark 16:18, that they shall pick up serpents.

The problem with the conclusion of these theologians is that it does not agree with the prophecy of Mark 16:17, which declares that **these signs shall follow them that believe**. The Bible does not declare that these signs will follow the apostles. Rather, it says these signs will follow those who believe. That is, they will be in evidence wherever believers are found.

There is no possibility of making sense of these verses if they are to be understood physically as they stand.

However, unless we understand the principle set forth in this study that is derived from Mark 4, that Christ spoke in parables, and without a parable He did not speak with them, we have no way of understanding these verses. The fact is, many doubt that a good part of Mark 16 even belongs in the Holy Canon. It is easy to sympathize with them if we expect verses 17 and 18 to be understood as physical truth. There is no possibility of making sense of these verses if they are to be understood physically as they stand.

However, when we look upon these five signs that follow believers to discover the spiritual meaning hidden within them, we not only find harmony with the rest of the Bible, but we can also know that only God could have written these verses. Indeed, we can be certain that without question these verses are an integral part of the Holy Canon.

The first sign that will follow those who believe is that in Christ's "name shall they cast out devils." This is a figure that points to those who will become saved when the Gospel is sent forth by believers. Those who are not saved are in Satan's dominion. When they become saved, it is as if devils have been cast out of them. That is, they are no longer under the power of Satan. They have been translated into the kingdom of Christ. The miracle that people are saved from Satan's power takes place wherever the Gospel is proclaimed by believers. Indeed this sign always follows those who believe.

> *The language of the believer is that of the kingdom of God.*

The second sign that follows believers is that they shall speak with new tongues. The spiritual meaning of this figure is found in the fact that each nation has its own language. The language spoken by the unsaved (regardless of political language), is that of the dominion of Satan. The language of the believer is that of the kingdom of God. Even if the same English or German or French words are used in both kingdoms, the language used by the believer is different from that of the unbeliever. The words may be the same, but their meanings and applications to the speaker will be quite different. We are reminded of the Old Testament prophecy of Psalm 40:3: "He hath put a new song in my mouth," and Psalm 98:1: "O sing unto the LORD a new song." Indeed, wherever believers are found, we find them speaking with new tongues.

The third sign that will follow those who believe is that they will take up serpents. In the Bible the serpent typifies Satan (Rev. 12:9). Before we are saved, we are under Satan's power. He rules over us; but when we become saved, we rule over him. To use the figure of Mark 16:18, we are like the snake handler who takes up the snake. Wherever believers are found, there will be those who rule over Satan as they plunder his house of those who are being saved.

The fourth sign that follows those who believe is "if they drink any deadly thing, it shall not hurt them." When we become saved, we drank the pure water of the Gospel. To listen to a false gospel is to drink poison. For example, in Deuteronomy 32:32-33, God faults ancient Israel for their idol worship by declaring:

> For their vine is of the vine of Sodom, and of the fields of Gomorrah: their grapes are grapes of gall, their clusters are bitter: Their wine is the poison of dragons, and the cruel venom of asps.

However, because believers can never lose their salvation, if they should drink the poison by listening to a false gospel, they cannot lose their salvation. This principle is true wherever believers are found.

The fifth sign that follows those who believe is "they shall lay hands on the sick, and they shall recover." Spiritually, when believers share the Gospel with others, they are ministering to those who are spiritually ill. The Gospel applied by the Holy Spirit by means of the witnessing of believers brings spiritual healing, for God says in I Peter 2:24b, 25a, "by whose stripes ye were healed. For ye were as sheep going astray." This principle is also true and will be in evidence wherever there are believers.

Thus, we see that these five signs literally follow all who believe, but we must understand them in their spiritual dimension. Because we can come to such a beautiful understanding of these verses once we apply the Biblical principle that Christ spoke in parables, we have certain vindication that this principle must be seriously considered wherever the Bible gives historical information that in itself does not relate to the Gospel message.

1. The deeper, spiritual meaning must relate to some aspect of the Gospel of salvation.

2. The spiritual identification of elements within the parable of the historical account must be found in the Bible and must have Biblical validation.

3. The spiritual conclusion must be in total agreement with everything in the Bible that relates to the nature of salvation.

Put Coals of Fire on Your Enemies

The last illustration is in Romans 12:20, where we read:

Therefore if thine enemy hunger, feed him; if he thirst, give him drink; for in so doing thou shalt heap coals of fire on his head.

The Bible consistently teaches that there are two kingdoms in this world, and they are at enmity with each other.

The Bible consistently teaches that there are two kingdoms in this world, and they are at enmity with each other. One is the kingdom of Satan; the other is the kingdom of God, and the Lord Jesus Christ is the head. In the Biblical sense, every unsaved person is an enemy of every born-again believer, but God admonishes us to love our enemies.

In Romans 12:20 God says that we are to feed our enemies and give him drink. The food we are to give is the wonderful Word of God, the bread of life. The water is the Gospel of the Lord Jesus Christ. Those who hunger and thirst after righteousness shall be filled.

In the Old Testament, if anyone touched the altar where the coals were, he became ceremoniously cleansed. In Isaiah 6, Isaiah became cleansed when the coals of fire from the altar touched his lips. When we present the Gospel to someone who becomes saved, we effectively have touched that individual with coals of fire from the altar and made him or her spiritually clean. The phrase "on his head" signifies that this cleansing encompasses the whole being of the person.

Do Not Plow with an Ox and an Ass Together

An example of a Biblical passage with three levels of meaning will now be examined. The procedure for a long passage is the same as will be done here for a short passage, Deuteronomy 22:10: "Thou shalt not plow with an ox and ass together."

First, this was a command to ancient Israel and it required obedience. They literally were not to plow land with an ox and a donkey yoked together. If anyone did this, he was in rebellion against God. Whether or not they could see the rationale of the command was irrelevant; they were to be obedient. It was a command that had an historical level of meaning.

Second, it teaches moral and spiritual truth, perhaps in the sense that it would be cruel to harness a small donkey to a large ox. However, the command prohibits harnessing an ass with an ox; they were not to harness a large donkey and a small ox, even if they were of more equal size.

On a deeper level , we know that in the Old Testament an ox was a clean animal, and the ass or the donkey was an unclean animal. Clean animals typified the people who were to become clean through the blood of the Lord Jesus Christ. The unclean animals typified those who were of the world and would remain in rebellion against God. In II Corinthians 6:14 God commands, "Be ye not unequally yoked together with unbelievers." In Luke 16:13 Jesus laid down the same principle with the words:

> No servant can serve two masters; for either he will hate the one, and love the other; or else he will hold to the one, and despise the other. Ye cannot serve God and mammon.

This is an integral part of the Bible's message. It is a moral principle that applies to the entire human race and to which every believer will attempt to adhere as he grows in sanctification. It is the same principle that is presented in Deuteronomy 22:10, when the Israelites were not to plow with an ox and an ass together. Thus, this verse has the first level of meaning, historical, and the second level of meaning, moral or spiritual.

It also has the third level of meaning; that is, it relates to the Gospel of salvation; it relates to the essential nature of salvation.

In the Bible, oxen were frequently offered as burnt offerings or as blood sacrifices. Therefore, oxen, like sheep, often typified and pointed to the Lord Jesus Christ, who represented a burnt offering by shedding His blood for our sins. Could the ox in Deuteronomy 22:10 be a reference to our Lord?

If so, what about the ass? It was never offered as a burnt offering. Nothing in the Bible suggests that it represents our Lord. It is found, however, that the ass does typify someone. It typifies people who need salvation. In Exodus 34:20 we read:

> But the firstling of an ass thou shalt redeem with a lamb: and if thou redeem him not, then shalt thou break his neck. All the firstborn of thy sons thou shalt redeem. And none shall appear before me empty.

> *A lamb represents Christ as well as the believer who is redeemed by Christ.*

In this passage, the ass was to be redeemed by a lamb. A lamb represents Christ as well as the believer who is redeemed by Christ. Therefore, the ass can be seen to represent the unbeliever. The ass that was not redeemed was to have its neck broken; that is, it was to be killed. This is a picture of everyone who is unsaved. If we are not redeemed by the Lamb of God, Jesus, we must face death - eternal death in hell.

We have scriptural validation to believe that the ox represents Christ, and the ass represents the one who needs salvation. Why are they not to be yoked together? After all, in one sense we are yoked to Christ, as Matthew 11:29-30 teaches:

> Take my yoke upon you, and learn of me; for I am meek and lowly in heart: and ye shall find rest unto your souls. For my yoke is easy, and my burden is light.

We are yoked to Him in that we are "in Christ." We have become spiritually identified with Him, who is our substitute; He made payment for our sins.

> *Christ, and Christ alone, has done all the work. We can contribute nothing to our salvation.*

We are not yoked to Him as though we were working with Him to accomplish our salvation. Christ, and Christ alone, has done all the work. We can contribute nothing to our salvation. We cannot say that God has done all that He could do and the rest is up to us. We are saved by grace and grace alone. The spiritual meaning of the command that prohibits yoking an ox and an ass together is an historic parable that points to the truth that we are saved by Christ's work alone and not by our own.

This cryptic verse, Deuteronomy 22:10, opens us a wealth of information when examined for the three levels of meaning. The Bible is a rich mine when carefully studied verse by verse.

Summary

The Bible alone and in its entirety is the Word of God. It is the Gospel of Jesus Christ. Anyone who does not follow this principle follows another gospel. He will be under a different authority than that related to the true Gospel. His doctrinal conclusions will be in error, and he will not relate to the salvation that leads to eternal life.

The Bible is its own interpreter. In the measure that we are able to view a particular verse of Scripture or a particular doctrine in the light of the entire Bible, is the measure we will be on the path to accurate interpretation.

The Bible frequently has three levels of meaning. The first is historical; the second is moral or spiritual; and the third is that which relates to the essence of the Gospel of salvation. For these reasons, a Bible translator must be exceedingly careful that, in his desire to make plain the historical or moral teaching of a verse, he does not obscure or remove the spiritual or Gospel meaning.

In relation to the third level, any spiritual meaning found within a passage must be in agreement with these three principles:

1. The deeper, spiritual meaning must relate to the Gospel of salvation.

2. The spiritual identification of elements within the parable or historical account must have Biblical validation.

3. The spiritual conclusion must be in total agreement with everything in the Bible that clearly relates to the nature of salvation.

Finally, the Bible is the ultimate authority. It is to be obeyed. Read it with a view to being obedient to everything found within its pages.

When the nature of Biblical writings is understood, rich and wonderful truth is found hidden within the pages of the Bible. May it be the experience of each of us to learn from the Bible, which is the repository of truth.

Having set forth some basic principles which we are to keep in mind as we study the Bible, we shall now continue our quest for truth to help us understand the whole chronology of history. This will in turn help us to know if we are indeed on a Biblical path regarding the timing of the end of the world.

One part of the Biblical chronology is the Biblical record of the reigns of the kings of Judah and Israel. The language of the Bible concerning the duration of these reigns is very confusing. Can we harmonize all of the Biblical data so that the reign of each king will be properly placed in the calendar of history? We will do this as we continue our study.

By accurately determining where each king fit into the calendar of history, we will also discover many new paths that focus on the year 1994 as the likely year for the end of the world.

Chapter 6.
The Kings of Israel and Judah

In developing the calendar information that is set forth in the book *1994?*, it was possible from Biblical data to reconstruct the calendar of history in an exact and accurate fashion, all the way from creation in 11,013 B.C. to the division of the kingdom of Israel upon the death of Solomon in 931 B.C.

For a number of reasons, no attempt was made in *1994?* to justify the 931 B.C. date, which can be shown to be a very accurate date. The same is true of the year 587 B.C. when Jerusalem was destroyed by the Babylonians. The duration of the reign of the individual kings of Judah and Israel who reigned between 931 B.C. and 587 B.C. are not set forth in any way in *1994?*, simply because I had not personally reconstructed that period of history from the available Biblical data. Nor was I able to find from any other source that is dependable a reconstruction of that portion of history that was not flawed.

But now I have done my homework and am able to place, by God's mercy, each and every king's reign into its proper place· in history. This in turn has enabled us to see many more paths that focus on the birth of Jesus in 7 B.C., the crucifixion of Jesus in 33 A.D., the beginning of the final tribulation in 1988 A.D., and the extreme likelihood of the end of the world in 1994 A.D.

Later in our study, we will also show the justification that allows us to harmonize our Julian or Gregorian calendar with the calendar of the Bible which accurately sets forth the first 10,000 years of the history of the world. This will show us that the years 931 B.C. (Solomon's death) and 587 B.C. (Babylonians destroy Jerusalem) are very accurate dates.

Basic Principles

Before we begin to develop the Biblical chronology of the kings of Judah and Israel, there are certain principles we must keep in mind. These principles are derived from the Bible as we compare Scripture with Scripture.

1. All of the Biblical data must be harmonized before an accurate chronological record can be established.

2. The length of the reign of any king noted in the Bible can be:
    a. The total length of reign including the time of co-regency with the previous king or a following king.
    b. The length of time he ruled alone, excluding the years of co-regency.
    c. The length of time he ruled as the dominant king even though a co-regency was in effect.
    d. Of course, most frequently a king's reign did not include a co-regency.

3. Two methods of timekeeping were employed.
    a. The first was the accession year system. In this system, the first official year is the year following the year the king begins to reign. This first year was, therefore, the first full year of a king's reign.   Thus, the last year of one king would not be the first official year of the next king; his first official year would be the year following the year the previous king died.
    b. The second was the non-accession year system. In this system, the first official year is the year the king begins to reign. Thus, the last year of one king would also be the first official year of the next king.

Two Kinds of Timekeeping

The consequence of these two systems is that a king would officially reign one year longer by the non-accession year system than by the accession year system. The duration of each king's reign and each and every reference to a year within a king's reign must be examined from the standpoint of both systems in order to find harmony.

God carefully instructs us in this matter by an apparent contradiction that is recorded in connection with the reign of Ahaziah. We read in II Kings 8:25: "In the **twelfth year** of Joram the son of Ahab king of Israel did Ahaziah the son of Jehoram king of Judah begin to reign." But in II Kings 9:29 we read: "And in the **eleventh year** of Joram the son of Ahab began Ahaziah to reign over Judah."

The counting of years beginning with the first full year of a king's reign is called by historians the accession year system. **The years one to eleven listed on the left side of the vertical bar are in accord with the accession year system.**

The counting of years beginning with the year that a king began to reign is called by historians the non-accession year system. **The years one to twelve listed on the right of the vertical bar are in accord with the non-accession year system.**

Chart 1. Key: ☐ last year reigned; ◯ identification with Scripture notation. Accession year on left of bar; non-accession year on right of bar.

	Yr. B.C.	Joram		Ahaziah	
First full year of	853		①		← *Year Joram actually*
Joram's reign →	852	1	2		*ascended the throne*
	851	2	3		
	850	3	4		
	849	4	⑤		
	848	5	6		
	847	6	7		
	846	7	8		
	845	8	9		
	844	9	10		
	843	10	11	Ahaziah	
	842	⑪	⑫	1	← *Year Ahaziah*
	841	*First full year of* → 1	2		*actually ascended*
	840	*Ahaziah's reign*			*the throne*

An Apparent Contradiction Helps Our Understanding

The apparent contradiction in these two verses is resolved if we look at the reign of Joram from the viewpoint of both systems.

By looking at the above diagram, we can see why the year 842 B.C. is both the twelfth year of Joram and the eleventh year of Joram. It is the eleventh year by the accession year system, but it is the twelfth year by the non-accession year system.

Because God has given this apparent contradiction in connection with Joram's reign over Israel, we are enabled to harmonize many of the Biblical citations that otherwise would remain impossible to understand. Having been given this information concerning the reign of Joram, we now know that the Biblical record that gives the year of the reign of any king must be looked at both from the standpoint of the accession year system as well as from the standpoint of the non-accession year system.

In fact, we will find that in the nation of Judah, the duration of the reigns of every one of the kings was according to the accession year system. On the other hand, in the nation of Israel, the ten tribes, the duration of the reigns of the first eight kings was according to the non-accession year system and after this, all of the reigns were in accordance with the accession year system.

Nevertheless, when an event is recorded as having taken place in a certain year of a king, only by carefully harmonizing that particular event with all other events found in the Bible record of that king, can we know whether the year of the event was in accordance with the accession year system or the non-accession year system.

To say it in a different way: When an event is recorded as having taken place in a certain year of a king, was the numbering of that year started from the year he began to reign (non-accession year system), or was it started from the first full year of his reign (accession year system)? Either possibility existed and only by taking into account any other available applicable Biblical data can it be determined which numbering system was used by the citation in question.

For example, in II Kings 15:22-23, we read:

> And Menahem slept with his fathers; and Pekahiah his son reigned in his stead. In the fiftieth year of Azariah king of Judah Pekahiah the son of Menahem began to reign over Israel in Samaria, and reigned two years.

Later, when we harmonize this information with all other applicable Bible citations, we will find that the duration of the reign of Azariah (Uzziah), king of Judah, was according to the accession year system. And we will also find that the duration of the reigns of both Menahem, king of Israel, and his son, Pekahiah, were also according to the accession year system. Yet when we harmonize the above verses with all other applicable Biblical data, we will find that the fiftieth year of Azariah was his fiftieth year including the year that he became king. Thus, his fiftieth year was counted according to the non-accession year system, even though the total duration of his reign was according to the accession year system.

To further complicate matters, some of the kings are given two names in the Bible. Thus, Joram is also named Jehoram. Azariah is also named Uzziah. Additionally, there were times when the kingdoms of Judah and Israel were very friendly with each other, even contracting marriages between the royal families. For example, Athaliah the daughter of Omri, king of Israel, married Jehoram, king of Judah (II Kings 8:25-26). Consequently, they gave identical names to some of their children. Thus, for example, from 853 B.C. to 842 B.C., Jehoram was the name of the king of Judah, and the king of Israel had the same name. However, in spite of all of these difficulties and complications, by carefully comparing Scripture with Scripture, we shall be able to reconstruct with great exactness the chronological history of these two nations.

So we shall begin our study of the reigns of the kings of Judah and Israel.

Saul: The First King of Israel

Officially, Israel became a nation when Abraham was circumcised, and that was the year 2068 B.C. From 1877 B.C. to 1447 B.C., a period of 430 years, they were in Egypt. During this time, Israel grew into a nation of approximately two million people. After spending forty years wandering in the wilderness, they entered into the land of Canaan in the year 1407 B.C.

For the next 360 years, Israel was ruled over by men who were judges. However, in the year 1047 B.C., they rebelled against God and demanded a king like the kings who ruled the nations around them. God gave them a king, a man whose name was Saul.

Saul was killed in battle after a reign of forty years (Acts 13:21). Saul was followed by David, who also reigned for forty years (I Kings 2:11). During the last four years of his reign, David appointed his son Solomon to rule with him (I Kings 1:30-48). Solomon reigned for a total of forty years (I Kings 11:42), of which four years were a co-regency with David. Thus, King Saul reigned from 1047 to 1007 B.C. David reigned from 1007 to 967 B.C. Solomon reigned from 971 to 931 B.C.

Yr. B.C.	Judah Rebohoam				Israel Jeroboam		Yr. B.C.
931		1				1	931
930	1	2			1	2	930
929	2	3			2	3	929
928	3	4			3	4	928
927	4	5			4	5	927
926	5	6			5	6	926
925	6	7			6	7	925
924	7	8			7	8	924
923	8	9			8	9	923
922	9	10			9	10	922
921	10	11			10	11	921
920	11	12			11	12	920
919	12	13			12	13	919
918	13	14			13	14	918
917	14	15			14	15	917
916	15	16			15	16	916
915	16	17	Abijam		16	17	915
914	17			①	17	⑱	914
913	↑ Rehoboam		1	2	18	19	913
912	reigned 17 yrs,		2	3	19	20	912
	I Kings 14:21					**Chart 2.**	

The Kingdom is Divided into Two Nations

The division of the kingdom of Israel was decreed before Solomon died. In his old age, Solomon's wives turned away his heart after other gods, so God took ten of the tribes from Solomon's son Rehoboam and gave them to another man, named Jeroboam (I Kings 11:4-13, 11:28-40). The nation of the two tribes was called Judah and the ten-tribe nation was called Israel.

Since Solomon died in the year 931 B.C., we know that the first year of his son Rehoboam, who ruled over Judah, was 931 B.C.

We can also know that the first year of Jeroboam, whom God appointed to rule over the ten tribes, was 931 B.C. In both instances, their first year by the non-accession year system was 931 B.C., while their first official year by the accession year system was the following year, 930 B.C. (see Chart 2).

According to I Kings 14:21, Rehoboam reigned for seventeen years:

> And Rehoboam the son of Solomon reigned in Judah. Rehoboam was forty and one years old when he began to reign, and he reigned seventeen years in Jerusalem, the city which the LORD did choose out of all the tribes of Israel, to put his name there. And his mother's name was Naamah an Ammonitess.

Abijam his son reigned in his stead, I Kings 14:31:

> And Rehoboam slept with his fathers, and was buried with his fathers in the city of David. And his mother's name was Naamah an Ammonitess. And Abijam his son reigned in his stead.

According to I Kings 15:1-2, Abijam began to reign in the eighteenth year of Jeroboam and reigned for three years.

> Now in the eighteenth year of king Jeroboam the son of Nebat reigned Abijam over Judah. Three years reigned he in Jerusalem. And his mother's name was Maachah, the daughter of Abishalom.

When this information is harmonized with everything else the Bible offers on the subject, we find that the eighteenth year of Jeroboam was according to the non-accession year system (counting from the year he became king), the year 914 B.C. The seventeenth year of Rehoboam was according to the accession year system (counting from the first full year of his reign), which was also 914 B.C. Thus, the first year of Abijam was the year 914 B.C., according to the non-accession year system. According to the accession year system, his first full year of reign was 913 B.C. (see Chart 2).

In I Kings 15:8-9, we read that Asa the son of Abijam began to reign in the twentieth year of Jeroboam:

> And Abijam slept with his fathers; and they buried him
> in the city of David: and Asa his son reigned in his stead.
> And in the twentieth year of Jeroboam king of Israel
> reigned Asa over Judah.

When this is harmonized with all of the Biblical data, we discover that the twentieth year of Jeroboam that God had in view was according to the accession year system (counting from the first full year). This twentieth year, which was 911 B.C., was the third year of the reign of Abijam according to the accession year system and was the first year of the reign of Asa according to the non-accession year system (counting from the year Asa became king). The following year, 910 B.C., became the first full year of Asa according to the accession year system (see Chart 3).

In I Kings 14:20 we read that Jeroboam reigned for twenty-two years:

> And the days which Jeroboam reigned were two and
> twenty years: and he slept with his fathers, and Nadab
> his son reigned in his stead.

In I Kings 15:25 the Bible declares that Nadab the son of Jeroboam began to reign in the second year of Asa and reigned over Israel two years:

> And Nadab the son of Jeroboam began to reign over
> Israel in the second year of Asa king of Judah, and
> reigned over Israel two years.

To harmonize this information, we discover that the two years of Nadab were according to the non-accession year system as were the twenty-two years of Jeroboam, his father. The second year of Asa, when Nadab began to reign, was according to the non-accession year system.

From I Kings 15:28 we learn that in the third year of Asa, a contender for the throne of Israel, Baasha, killed Nadab and became king: "Even in the third year of Asa king of Judah did Baasha slay him, and reigned in his stead." This was the year 909 B.C. as Chart 3 shows.

I Kings 15:33 indicates that Baasha reigned for twenty-four years: " In the third year of Asa king of Judah began Baasha the son of Ahijah to reign over all Israel in Tirzah, twenty and four years."

Again, we find that the third year of Asa was according to the non-accession year system.

The Thirty-Sixth Year of Asa

In II Chronicles 16:1, we read an especially puzzling statement: "In the six and thirtieth year of the reign of Asa Baasha king of Israel came up against Judah, and built Ramah, to the intent that he might let none go out or come in to Asa king of Judah."

Yr. B.C.	Judah Rebohoam				Israel Jeroboam				Yr. B.C.
915	16	17	Abijam		16	17			915
914	[17]		①		17	⑱			914
913	↑	1	2		18	19			913
912	Rehoboam	2	3	Asa	19	20			912
911	reigned		[3]	①	⑳	21	Nadab		911
910	17 yrs,	↑	1	②	21	[22]	①	Baasha	910
909	I Kings	Abijam	2	③	↑	1	②	①	909
908	14:21	reigned	3	4	Jeroboam	↑	1	2	908
907		3yrs,	4	5	reigned	Nadab	2	3	907
906		I Kings	5	6	22 yrs,	reigned	3	4	906
905		15:1-2	6	7	I Kings	2 yrs,	4	5	905
904			7	8	14:20	I Kings	5	6	904
903			8	9	15:25		6	7	903

Chart 3.

When we examine the reigns of the kings of Judah and Israel, we find that the last year of Baasha was 886 B.C., while the thirty-sixth year of Asa was 875 B.C., eleven years after Baasha died. How can this citation, which declares that Baasha came against Asa in Asa's thirty-sixth year, be harmonized?

It can be harmonized if we realize that in this instance the thirty-sixth year of Asa was not the thirty-sixth year of his reign. Instead, it was the thirty-sixth year after the beginning of the reign of Rehoboam, when the two tribes, Judah and Benjamin, became the nation of Judah.

Since Rehoboam began to reign in 931 B.C., the thirty-sixth year would have been the year 895 B.C. (931 - 36 = 895). Since Asa's first official year was 910 B.C., the year 895 B.C. was Asa's sixteenth year.

Knowing this, we can harmonize several seemingly contradictory verses: I Kings 15:32, II Chronicles 14:1, and II Chronicles 15:19.

> I Kings 15:32: And there was war between Asa and Baasha king of Israel all their days.

> II Chronicles 14:1: So Abijah slept with his fathers, and they buried him in the city of David: and Asa his son reigned in his stead. In his days the land was quiet ten years.

> II Chronicles 15:19: And there was no more war unto the five and thirtieth year of the reign of Asa.

It appears that throughout the reigns of Asa and Baasha, there was enmity between them. However, there was a ten-year period during the early years of Asa's reign when relations between the two nations were quiet. In the sixteenth year of Asa, which was thirty-six years after Rehoboam became king, open warfare broke out between Asa and Baasha. This was brought about because many people of Israel were migrating into Judah. In II Chronicles 15:9-10, God speaks of Asa bringing together people from the nation of Israel into the nation of Judah:

> And he gathered all Judah and Benjamin, and the strangers with them out of Ephraim and Manasseh, and out of Simeon: for they fell to him out of Israel in abundance, when they saw that the LORD his God was with him. So they gathered themselves together at Jerusalem in the third month, in the fifteenth year of the reign of Asa.

The fifteenth year was the thirty-fifth year since Judah began. This was the last year of the quiet ten years because the following year (thirty-sixth from the beginning of Judah), Baasha came against Judah and built Ramah to stop the migration of people from Israel to Judah. We read in II Chronicles 16:1:

Yr. B.C.	Judah Asa		Israel Baasha				Omri		Tibni		Yr. B.C.
902	9	10	7	8							902
901	10	11	8	9							901
900	11	12	9	10							900
899	12	13	10	11							899
898	13	14	11	12							898
897	14	15	12	13							897
896	⑮	16	13	14	15th year of Asa = 35th since Rehoboam began to reign						896
895	⑯	17	14	15	16th year of Asa = 36th since Rehoboam began to reign						895
894	17	18	15	16							894
893	18	19	16	17							893
892	19	20	17	18							892
891	20	21	18	19							891
890	21	22	19	20							890
889	22	23	20	21							889
888	23	24	21	22							888
887	24	25	22	23	Elah						887
886	25	㉖	23	[24]	①	Zimri	Omri		Tibni		886
885	26	㉗	Baasha ↑	1 [②]	①		1		1		885
884	27	28	reigned	Elah ↑	Zimri	1	2	1	2		884
883	28	29	24 yrs,	reigned	reigned	2	3	2	3		883
882	29	30	I Kings	2 yrs,	7 days,	3	4	3	4		882
881	30	31	15:33	IKings	I Kings	4	5	4	5		881
880	㉛	32		16:8	16:15	5	⑥	5	[6]		880
879	32	33				6	7	Tibni ↑			879
878	33	34				7	8	must have			878
877	34	35				8	9	reigned			877
876	35	36				9	10	6 yrs,			876
875	36	37	Omri reigned 12 yrs,			10	11	I Kings	Ahab		875
874	37	㊳	I Kings 16:23 →			11	[12]	16:23	①		874

Chart 4.

In the six and thirtieth year of the reign of Asa Baasha king of Israel came up against Judah, and built Ramah, to the intent that he might let none go out or come in to Asa king of Judah.

All of the Biblical citations, therefore, which speak of the thirty-fifth or the thirty-sixth year of the reign of Asa identify with the beginning of the nation of Judah in 931 B.C. when Rehoboam became king.

Baasha, Elah, Zimri, Omri

Continuing our development of the reigns of the kings of Judah and Israel, we read in I Kings 16:6 that Baasha died and his son Elah reigned: "So Baasha slept with his fathers, and was buried in Tirzah: and Elah his son reigned in his stead."

In I Kings 16:8, we read that it was in the twenty-sixth year of Asa that Elah began to reign over Israel, and he reigned for two years: "In the twenty and sixth year of Asa king of Judah began Elah the son of Baasha to reign over Israel in Tirzah, two years."

Harmonizing the Biblical record, we find that Baasha died in the twenty-fourth year of his reign according to the non-accession year system, which was also the first year of his son, Elah, according to the same system, and the twenty-sixth year of Asa according to the same system.

We then read in I Kings 16:10 that Zimri killed Elah in the twenty-seventh year of Asa: "And Zimri went in and smote him, and killed him, in the twenty and seventh year of Asa king of Judah, and reigned in his stead."

We read in I Kings 16:15-18 that Zimri reigned only seven days and was killed by Omri.

> In the twenty and seventh year of Asa king of Judah did Zimri reign seven days in Tirzah. And the people were encamped against Gibbethon, which belonged to the Philistines. And the people that were encamped heard say, Zimri hath conspired, and hath also slain the king: wherefore all Israel made Omri, the captain of the host, king over Israel that day in the camp. And Omri went up from Gibbethon, and all Israel with him, and they beseiged Tirzah. And it came to pass, when Zimri saw that the city was taken, that he went into the palace of the king's house, and burnt the king's house over him with fire, and died.

Harmonizing this information, we find that even as Jeroboam reigned over Israel for twenty-two years according to the non-accession system, Nadab for two years by the same system, and Baasha for twenty-four years by the same system, so, too, Elah reigned for two

Yr. B.C.	Judah — Asa		Israel — Baasha								Yr. B.C.
892	19	20	17	18							892
891	20	21	18	19							891
890	21	22	19	20							890
889	22	23	20	21							889
888	23	24	21	22							888
887	24	25	22	23	Elah						887
886	25	(26)	23	24	① Zimri	Omri	Tibni				886
885	26	(27)	Baasha↑	1 ②	①	①	1				885
884	27	28	reigned	Elah↑ Zimri	1	2	1	2			884
883	28	29	24 yrs,	reigned reigned	2	3	2	3			883
882	29	30	I Kings	2 yrs, 7 days,	3	4	3	4			882
881	30	31	15:33	IKings I Kings	4	5	4	5			881
880	(31)	32		16:8 16:15	5	⑥	5	[6]			880
879	32	33			6	7	Tibni↑				879
878	33	34			7	8	must				878
877	34	35			8	9	have				877
876	35	36	Omri reigned		9	10	reigned				876
875	36	37	12 yrs,		10	11	6 yrs,	Ahab			875
874	37	(38)	I Kings 16:23 →		11	12	I Kings 16:23	①			874

Chart 5.

years by the same system. In the twenty-seventh year of Asa, by the same system, Elah was killed, Zimri reigned for seven days and was killed, and Omri began to reign. This was the year 885 B.C. (Chart 5).

Two Kings Reign Over Israel

In I Kings 16:23, we have a citation that is very puzzling. There we read that in the thirty-first year of Asa, Omri began to reign over Israel twelve years, six years at Tirzah.

> In the thirty and first year of Asa king of Judah began Omri to reign over Israel, twelve years: six years reigned he in Tirzah.

But from I Kings 16:15-16, we learned that Zimri was killed in the twenty-seventh year of Asa and Omri was made king. How can these seemingly conflicting statements be reconciled? The solution is found in I Kings 16:20-22:

Now the rest of the acts of Zimri, and his treason that he wrought, are they not written in the book of the chronicles of the kings of Israel? Then were the people of Israel divided into two parts: half of the people followed Tibni the son of Ginath, to make him king; and half followed Omri. But the people that followed Omri prevailed against the people that followed Tibni the son of Ginath: so Tibni died, and Omri reigned.

In these verses we read that upon the death of Zimri there were two kings on the throne of Israel - Omri and Tibni. The capital at that time was a city named Tirzah. Remember that the previous kings of Israel all reigned in Tirzah (Baasha, twenty-four years in Tirzah, I Kings 15:33; Elah, two years in Tirzah, I Kings 16:8; and Zimri, seven days in Tirzah, I Kings 16:15). Omri also reigned in Tirzah, for six years (I Kings 16:23), but Tibni also started to reign when Omri began to reign. However, in the thirty-first year of Asa, the Bible informs us that Omri began to reign for twelve years.

When we harmonize this information, we find that Omri reigned a total of twelve years according to the same system - the non-accession system - by which all of the previous kings of Israel reigned. In the thirty-first year of Asa, by the accession year system, which coincided with the sixth year of Omri's reign by the non-accession year system, Omri began to reign as sole king. Tibni, therefore, must have died the same year. This freed Omri so he was able to move the capital of Israel from Tirzah to Samaria. Thus, Omri began to reign in the year 885 B.C. In 880 B.C., he began to reign alone. His last year was the year 874 B.C.

Continuing to the next king of Israel, we read in I Kings 16:28-29:

So Omri slept with his fathers, and was buried in Samaria: and Ahab his son reigned in his stead. And in the thirty and eighth year of Asa king of Judah began Ahab the son of Omri to reign over Israel: and Ahab the son of Omri reigned over Israel in Samaria twenty and two years.

Harmonizing this information, we find that the thirty-eighth year of Asa, king of Judah, was according to the non-accession year system. In that year, Omri died and his son Ahab began to reign (see Chart 6).

Yr.	Judah				Israel							Yr.
B.C.	Asa				Baasha							B.C.
887	24	25			22	23	Elah					887
886	25	26			23	24	(1) Zimri	Omri		Tibni		886
885	26	(27)			Baasha↑	1	(2)	(1)	(1)	1		885
884	27	28			reigned	Elah	Zimri	1	2	1	2	884
883	28	29			24 yrs,	reigned	reigned	2	3	2	3	883
882	29	30			I Kings	2 yrs,	7 days,	3	4	3	4	882
881	30	31			15:33	IKings	I Kings	4	5	4	5	881
880	(31)	32				16:8	16:15	5	(6)	5	6	880
879	32	33						6	7	Tibni↑		879
878	33	34						7	8	must		878
877	34	35						8	9	have		877
876	35	36						9	10	reigned		876
875	36	37						10	11	6 yrs,	Ahab	875
874	37	(38)						11	12	I Kings	(1)	874
873	38	39	Jehosh-					Omri↑	16:23	1	2	873
872	39	40	aphat					reigned		2	3	872
871	40	41		(1)				12 yrs,		3	(4)	871
870	(41)		1	2				I Kings		4	5	870
869	↑Asa		2	3				16:23		5	6	869

reigned 41
yrs, II
Chron.
16:13   **Chart 6.**

A Co-Regency of Asa and Jehoshaphat

Continuing with the kings of Judah, we read in I Kings 22:41-42:

> And Jehoshaphat the son of Asa began to reign over Judah in the fourth year of Ahab king of Israel. Jehoshaphat was thirty and five years old when he began to reign; and he reigned twenty and five years in Jerusalem. And his mother's name was Azubah the daughter of Shilhi.

When we harmonize this information, we learn that the fourth year of Ahab, according to the non-accession system (counting from the year Ahab became king), coincided with the beginning of

Jehoshaphat's reign of twenty-five years, so that the first full year of the reign of Jehoshaphat, according to the accession year system, was the next year, 870 B.C. (see Chart 6). However, since Jehoshaphat's father, Asa, reigned for forty-one years, and his forty-first year was 870 B.C., it means that Asa made his son Jehoshaphat to reign with him in the year before he died. This is understandable in the light of the information recorded in I Kings 15:23. There we read that in his old age, he was diseased in his feet. II Chronicles 16:12-13 graphically explains:

> And Asa in the thirty and ninth year of his reign was diseased in his feet, until his disease was exceeding great: yet in his disease he sought not to the LORD, but to the physicians. And Asa slept with his fathers, and died in the one and fortieth year of his reign.

During the thirty-ninth year of Asa, his feet became greatly diseased so that the next year he made his son Jehoshaphat to reign with him. The following year, his forty-first year, he died (II Chronicles 16:13). So far, we might note, the length of reign of all the kings of Judah was counted by the accession year system, whereas the length of reign of all the kings of Israel was counted by the non-accession year system.

Later, we will learn that when Jehoram the son of Ahab became king, both he and all the following kings of Israel counted the length of their reigns by the accession year system even as did the kings of Judah throughout Judah's history.

A Co-Regency of Ahab and Ahaziah

Returning to the kings of Israel, we read in I Kings 22:40 and I Kings 22:51:

> So Ahab slept with his fathers; and Ahaziah his son reigned in his stead. . . . Ahaziah the son of Ahab began to reign over Israel in Samaria the seventeenth year of Jehoshaphat king of Judah, and reigned two years over Israel.

Yr. B.C.	Judah (Asa)					Israel (Omri)						Yr. B.C.
875	36	37				10	11	Ahab				875
874	37	38				11	[12]	①				874
873	38	39				Omri ↑	1	2				873
872	39	40	Jehoshaphat			reigned	2	3				872
871	40	41	①			12 yrs,	3	④				871
870	[41]	1	2			I Kings	4	5				870
869	↑ Asa	2	3			16:23	5	6				869
868	reigned 41	3	4				6	7				868
867	yrs., II	4	5				7	8				867
866	Chron.	5	6				8	9				866
865	16:13	6	7				9	10				865
864		7	8				10	11				864
863		8	9				11	12				863
862		9	10				12	13				862
861		10	11				13	14				861
860		11	12				14	15				860
859		12	13				15	16				859
858		13	14				16	17				858
857		14	15				17	18				857
856		15	16				18	19				856
855		16	17	Jehoram			19	20	Ahaziah (Jehoram)			855
854		⑰	18	①			20	21	①	Joram		854
853		⑱	19	1	②		21	[22]	1	[2]	①	853
852		19	20	2	3		Ahab ↑		Ahaziah ↑	1	2	852

Ahab reigned 22 yrs., I Kings 16:28

Ahaziah reigned 2 yrs., I Kings 22:51

Chart 7.

    When we harmonize this information, we discover that Ahaziah, the son of Ahab, began to reign in the seventeenth year of Jehoshaphat according to the accession year system. Since this was the twenty-first year of his father, Ahab, by the non-accession year system and since Ahab died in his twenty-second year, it means that Ahab made his son co-regent with him in the year before he died. Since his son Ahaziah reigned for two years, it means that Ahaziah died the same year Ahab died. This was the year 853 B.C. (see Chart 7), which is a very important year in helping us relate the Biblical calendar to the Julian calendar. We will address this matter later in our study.

Concerning the death of Ahaziah, we read in II Kings 1:2 and in II Kings 1:17:

> II Kings 1:2: And Ahaziah fell down through a lattice in his upper chamber that was in Samaria, and was sick: and he sent messengers, and said unto them, Go, inquire of Baal-zebub the god of Ekron whether I shall recover of this disease.

> II Kings 1:17: So he died according to the word of the LORD which Elijah had spoken. And Jehoram reigned in his stead in the second year of Jehoram the son of Jehoshaphat king of Judah; because he had no son.

We learn from these verses that Ahab's son Ahaziah, who had begun to reign with his father the year before Ahab died, had an accident so that he died the same year his father died. Since Ahaziah did not have a son, his brother Jehoram, who was also the son of Ahab, began to reign. The beginning of the reign of Jehoram (Joram) over Israel was the second year, by the non-accession year system, of Jehoram, king of Judah.

In II Kings 3:1, we further read:

> Now Jehoram the son of Ahab began to reign over Israel in Samaria the eighteenth year of Jehoshaphat king of Judah, and reigned twelve years.

Harmonizing this information, we discover that the eighteenth year of Jehoshaphat was according to the accession year system. Thus, Jehoram the son of Ahab began to reign in the year 853 B.C., the year Ahab died and the year his brother Ahaziah died (see Chart 7). He reigned for twelve years.

At this juncture we will note something very interesting. Until Jehoram the son of Ahab began to reign, the durations of the reigns of the kings of Israel were always reckoned by the non-accession year system. That is, the year they came to the throne was always counted as the first year. On the other hand, we might recall that all of the kings of Judah reigned in accordance with the accession year system so that the first full year of their reign was counted as the first year.

But we will find that beginning with the reign of Jehoram (Joram) the son of Ahab, the duration of the reigns of the kings of Israel will be counted by the accession year system, the same as that being used by the kings of Judah. Thus, from this time forward, all of the length of reigns of both the kings of Judah as well as those of the kings of Israel will be counted in accordance with the accession year system.

A Jehoshaphat-Jehoram Co-Regency

Returning now to the kings of Judah, we read in II Chronicles 21:1 and 5:

> Now Jehoshaphat slept with his fathers, and was buried with his fathers in the city of David. And Jehoram his son reigned in his stead. . . . Jehoram was thirty and two years old when he began to reign, and he reigned eight years in Jerusalem.

Chart 8.

Yr. B.C.	Judah — Jehoshaphat		Jehoram		Israel — Ahab		Ahaziah		Joram		Yr. B.C.
855	16	17	Jehoram		19	20	Ahaziah		(Jehoram)		855
854	⑰	18		①	20	21		①	Joram		854
853	⑱	19	1	②	21	[22]	1	②	①		853
852	19	20	2	3	Ahab ↑		Ahaziah ↑		1	2	852
851	20	21	3	4	reigned 22 yrs.,		reigned 2 yrs.,		2	3	851
850	21	22	4	5	I Kings 16:28		I Kings 22:51		3	4	850
849	22	23	⑤	6				4	⑤		849

To understand this citation, we must look very carefully at several other verses.

We must first learn that Ahaziah the son of Jehoram, king of Judah, was killed the same year that Jehoram the son of Ahab was killed. We can then fit Jehoram the son of Jehoshaphat into the chronological framework.

First, let us learn about the end of Jehoram, king of Judah, and the ascent of Ahaziah to the throne. In II Chronicles 21:4, we read of the wickedness of Jehoram:

Now when Jehoram was risen up to the kingdom of his
father, he strengthened himself, and slew all his brethren
with the sword, and divers also of the princes of Israel.

The term "risen up to the kingdom of his father" implies some
kind of change in his reign over Judah. When we harmonize all of the
Biblical citations relating to Jehoram's reign over Judah, we will discover
that for several years he had been co-regent with his father Jehoshaphat,
but during the last four years of his father's reign, Jehoram had become the
dominant king. The time he became the dominant king could have been
when he "was risen up to the kingdom of his father," at which time he
killed all of his brothers.

Because of Jehoram's great wickedness, God brought many
terrible things into his life, including the fact that all of his sons except
for the youngest, Jehoahaz (also called Ahaziah) were killed by
Arabians (II Chronicles 21:16-17). Following this, God struck him
with an incurable disease so that at the end of two years, he died (II
Chronicles 21:18-19). Upon his death, the people of Jerusalem made
his son Ahaziah (Jehoahaz) king (II Chronicles 22:1).

In II Kings 8:25-26a, we read:

In the twelfth year of Joram the son of Ahab king of
Israel did Ahaziah the son of Jehoram king of Judah
begin to reign. Two and twenty years old was Ahaziah
when he began to reign; and he reigned one year in
Jerusalem.

We learned earlier that Jehoram the son of Ahab began to reign
in the eighteenth year of Jehoshaphat, which was the year 853 B.C. The
twelfth year of Ahab's son Jehoram (Joram) was therefore either 842
B.C. or 841 B.C. Thus, Ahaziah the son of Jehoram, king of Judah,
must have begun to reign either in 842 B.C. or 841 B.C. We will learn
that it was the year 841 B.C. (Chart 9).

We also learn from these verses that Ahaziah reigned one year.

Jehu Kills Two Kings

To continue our study we must now look at the death of
Ahaziah. It took place at the same time that Joram son of Ahab was
killed. Both of these kings were killed by Jehu, who would become the
next king to reign over Israel. We read in II Kings 9:21, 24, and 27:

Yr. B.C.	Judah — Jehoshaphat				Israel — Ahab					Yr. B.C.
858	13	14			16	17				858
857	14	15			17	18				857
856	15	16			18	19				856
855	16	17	Jehoram		19	20	Ahaziah	(Jehoram)		855
854	(17)	18		①	20	21	①	Joram		854
853	(18)	19	1	②	21	22	1	②	①	853
852	19	20	2	3	Ahab↑	Ahaziah↑	1	2		852
851	20	21	3	4	reigned	reigned 2	2	3		851
850	21	22	4	5	22 yrs.,	yrs..,	3	4		850
849	22	23	⑤	6	I Kings	I Kings	4	⑤		849
848	23	24	6	7	16:28	22:51	5	6		848
847	24	25	7	8			6	7		847
846	25		8	9			7	8		846
845	↑Jehoshaphat		9	10			8	9		845
844	reigned 25 yrs.,		10	11	(Jehoahaz)		9	10		844
843	I Kings 22:42		11	12	Ahaziah		10	11		843
842		12			①		11	⑫	Jehu	842
841	Jehoram ↑ reigned		1				12	↑	1	841
840	8 yrs in Jerusalem,		↑Ahaziah		Joram		1	2		840

II Chron. 21:5. He must have reigned a total of 12 yrs., II Kings 3:1, II Kings 1:17

reigned 1 yr., II Chron. 22:2

reigned 12 yrs., II Kings 3:1

Chart 9.

II Kings 9:21 And Joram said, Make ready. And his chariot was made ready. And Joram king of Israel and Ahaziah king of Judah went out, each in his chariot, and they went out against Jehu, and met him in the portion of Naboth the Jezreelite.

II Kings 9:24 And Jehu drew a bow with his full strength, and smote Jehoram between his arms, and the arrow went out at his heart, and he sunk down in his chariot.

II Kings 9:27 But when Ahaziah the king of Judah saw this, he fled by the way of the garden house. And Jehu followed after him, and said, Smite him also in the chariot. And they did so at the going up to Gur, which is by Ibleam. And he fled to Megiddo, and died there.

From these verses, we learn that Ahaziah, king of Judah, was killed at the same time that Joram, king of Israel, was killed. Since we have already learned that Joram, king of Israel, who was the son of Ahab, began to reign in the year 853 B.C. and reigned for twelve years, his twelfth year by the non-accession year system would have been 842 B.C., or by the accession year system, 841 B.C. Thus, since he was killed by Jehu at the same time that Ahaziah, king of Judah, was killed, we know that Ahaziah, king of Judah, was killed either in 841 or 842 B.C. (Chart 9). Later we will learn that it was in the year 841 B.C. Additionally, we have learned that Jehoshaphat, king of Judah, began to reign in the year 871 B.C. and reigned for twenty-five years. Since all of the kings of Judah followed the accession year system, the year he died would have been 846 B.C.

Before we attempt to harmonize all of the above, we should add one other Biblical citation. It is found in II Kings 8:16-17:

> And in the fifth year of Joram the son of Ahab king of
> Israel, Jehoshaphat being then king of Judah, Jehoram
> the son of Jehoshaphat king of Judah began to reign.
> Thirty and two years old was he when he began to
> reign; and he reigned eight years in Jerusalem.

Harmonizing all of these verses, we discover that in Judah there was a co-regency of Jehoshaphat and his son Jehoram, which had to have begun in the seventeenth year of Jehoshaphat according to the accession year system (Chart 9). Jehoram was a co-regent with his father Jehoshaphat until 846 B.C., when his father died. He continued to reign until 842 B.C., so that his total reign must have been twelve years according to the accession year system. His son Ahaziah began to reign in 842 B.C. upon his father's death and was killed the next year, 841 B.C., by Jehu.

From 849 B.C. until 846 B.C., when his father, Jehoshaphat, died, Jehoram was the dominant king. These four years together with the four years he reigned alone add up to the eight years recorded in II Kings 8:16-17. They began in the fifth year according to the non-accession year of Joram (Jehoram), who was ruling over Israel in 849 B.C. Therefore, we have the citation of II Kings 8:16-17 that in the fifth year of Joram of Israel, Jehoram the son of Jehoshaphat began to reign. He had already been on the throne for several years as co-regent but in this year he became the dominant king. Thus, Joram of Israel began to reign in the second year of Jehoram of Judah's second year according to the non-accession year system (as II Kings 1:17 states), which was the eighteenth year of Jehoshaphat according to the accession year system (see Chart 9).

Since Jehu killed both Ahaziah of Judah and Jehoram of Israel at the same time, it would have been in the year 841 B.C.

Interestingly, II Kings 8:25 records that it was in the twelfth year of Joram son of Ahab, king of Israel, that Ahaziah son of Jehoram, king of Judah, began to reign, whereas in II Kings 9:29, we read that Ahaziah's reign began in the eleventh year of Joram, king of Israel. There is no discrepancy when we realize that the twelfth year was according to the non-accession year system, whereas the eleventh year was the same year, but figured according to the accession year system.

Jehu Becomes King of Israel

Going on with the kings of Israel, we find that when Jehu killed Joram, king of Israel (II Kings 9:24), he became king, in 841 B.C. This year, like 853 B.C. (which was the last year of Ahab, king of Israel), is also a very important year because it helps to match the Biblical calendar with the secular or Julian calendar (more on this year later).

Yr. B.C.	Jehosh-aphat	Judah				Israel					Yr. B.C.
						Ahab					
856	15	16				18	19				856
855	16	17	Jehoram			19	20	Ahaziah	(Jehoram)		855
854	17	18	①			20	21	①	Joram		854
853	⑱	19	1	②		21	22	1	②	①	853
852	19	20	2	3		Ahab ↑	Ahaziah↑	1	2		852
851	20	21	3	4		reigned	reigned	2	3		851
850	21	22	4	5		22 yrs,	2 yrs,	3	4		850
849	22	23	⑤	6		I Kings	I Kings	4	⑤		849
848	23	24	6	7		16:28	22:51	5	6		848
847	24	25	7	8				6	7		847
846	㉕		8	9				7	8		846
845	↑ Jehosh-		9	10				8	9		845
844	aphat		10	11				9	10		844
843	reigned		11	12	Ahaziah			10	11		843
842	25 yrs,	⑫		①	Athaliah			11	⑫	Jehu	842
841	I Kings	↑Jehoram	1		1			⑫		1	841
840	22:42	reigned 8	↑Ahaziah 1		2			↑ Joram 1		2	840

yrs in Jerusalem, II Chron. 21:5. He must have reigned a total of 12 yrs, II Kings 3:1, II Kings 1:17

reigned 1 yr, II Chron. 22:2

reigned 12 yrs, II Kings 3:1

Chart 10.

Concerning the death of Jehu, we read in II Kings 10:35-36:

> And Jehu slept with his fathers: and they buried him in Samaria. And Jehoahaz his son reigned in his stead. And the time that Jehu reigned over Israel in Samaria was twenty and eight years.

These verses inform us that Jehu reigned for twenty-eight years and that his son Jehoahaz followed him (Chart 11). To help place these events in their proper place, we find the following information in II Kings 11:1-3:

> And when Athaliah the mother of Ahaziah saw that her son was dead, she arose and destroyed all the seed royal. But Jehosheba, the daughter of king Joram, sister of Ahaziah, took Joash the son of Ahaziah, and stole him from among the king's sons which were slain; and they hid him, even him and his nurse, in the bedchamber from Athaliah, so that he was not slain. And he was with her hid in the house of the LORD six years. And Athaliah did reign over the land.

Wicked Athaliah Reigns Over Judah

The Bible is showing us that when Jehu killed King Ahaziah of Judah in the year 841 B.C., Athaliah, the mother of Ahaziah, became the ruler of Judah. She attempted to remove all contenders to the throne by murdering all the royal seed. Only the baby Joash, the infant son of Ahaziah, escaped. In the seventh year, the priest Jehoiada brought Joash forth and had him crowned king. II Kings 11:20-21:

> And all the people of the land rejoiced, and the city was in quiet: and they slew Athaliah with the sword beside the king's house. Seven years old was Jehoash when he began to reign.

Further help to harmonize this event with the reigns of the kings is found in II Kings 12:1: "In the seventh year of Jehu Jehoash began to reign; and forty years reigned he in Jerusalem. And his mother's name was Zibiah of Beer-sheba."

In harmonizing these verses, we learn that Athaliah began to reign over Judah in 841 B.C., and Jehu began to reign over Israel in the same year. In the seventh year of Jehu by the non-accession year system, which was the sixth year of Athaliah's reign over Judah by the accession year system, Athaliah was killed and Joash, who was also called Jehoash, began to reign. He reigned for forty years, and thus, he began to reign in the year 835 B.C.

Yr.	Judah					Israel			Yr.
B.C.	Jehoram					Joram			B.C.
843	11	12	Ahaziah			10	11		843
842	12			①	Athaliah	⑪	⑫	Jehu	842
841	↑Jehoram		1		1	12		1	841
840	reigned 8	↑Ahaziah	1	2		↑Joram	1	2	840
839	yrs in	reigned	2	3		reigned	2	3	839
838	Jerusalem,	1 yr, II	3	4		12 yrs,	3	4	838
837	II Chron.	Chron. 22:2	4	5	(Jehoash)	II Kings	4	5	837
836	21:5. He		5	6	Joash	3:1	5	6	836
835	must have		6		①		6	⑦	835
834	reigned a	↑Athaliah		1	2		7	8	834
833	total of 12	must have		2	3		8	9	833
832	yrs, II	reigned 6		3	4		9	10	832
831	Kings 3:1, II	yrs, II Kings		4	5		10	11	831
830	Kings 1:17	11:3, 20, 21		5	6		11	12	830
829				6	7		12	13	829
828				7	8		13	14	828
827				8	9		14	15	827
826				9	10		15	16	826
825				10	11		16	17	825
824				11	12		17	18	824
823				12	13		18	19	823
822				13	14		19	20	822
821				14	15		20	21	821
820				15	16		21	22	820
819				16	17		22	23	819
818				17	18		23	24	818
817				18	19		24	25	817
816				19	20		25	26	816
815				20	21		26	27	815
814				21	22		27	28 Jehoahaz	814
813				22	㉓		28	①	813
812				23	24	Jehu reigned↑ 28 yrs,	1	2	812
811	**Chart 11.**			24	25	II Kings10:36	2	3	811

The next citations are in II Kings 10:35-36 and II Kings 13:1.

II Kings 10:35-36: And Jehu slept with his fathers: and they buried him in Samaria. And Jehoahaz his son reigned in his stead. And the time that Jehu reigned over Israel in Samaria was twenty and eight years.

II Kings 13:1: In the three and twentieth year of Joash the son of Ahaziah king of Judah Jehoahaz the son of Jehu began to reign over Israel in Samaria, and reigned seventeen years.

Jehu reigned for twenty-eight years, in accordance with the accession year system. Upon his death, in 813 B.C., his son Jehoahaz began to reign and reigned for seventeen years over Israel. Thus, the seventeenth year of Jehoahaz, according to the accession year system, was 796 B.C. Jehoahaz began to reign in the twenty-third year of the reign of Judah's King Joash. The twenty-third year was in accordance with the non-accession year system (see Chart 12).

Continuing to look at the kings of Israel, we look next at II Kings 13:9-10, where the Bible reports:

> And Jehoahaz slept with his fathers; and they buried him in Samaria: and Joash his son reigned in his stead. In the thirty and seventh year of Joash king of Judah began Jehoash the son of Jehoahaz to reign over Israel in Samaria, and reigned sixteen years.

In the thirty-seventh year of Judah's King Joash, in accordance with the accession year system, Jehoash (Joash) the son of the Israelite King Jehoahaz began to reign. This was the year 798 B.C. He reigned for sixteen years. This means that Jehoash reigned for three years as co-regent with his father Jehoahaz and his last year was sixteen years later in 782 B.C.

In II Kings 14:1-2 we read that Amaziah the son of Joash, king of Judah, began to reign in the second year of Joash the son of Jehoahaz, king of Israel, and reigned for twenty-nine years.

> In the second year of Joash son of Jehoahaz king of Israel reigned Amaziah the son of Joash king of Judah.

He was twenty and five years old when he began to reign, and reigned twenty and nine years in Jerusalem. And his mother's name was Jehoaddan of Jerusalem.

The second year of Jehoash (Joash) was the second full year, the same year his father Jehoahaz died, which was the year 796 B.C. Since the last year of King Joash of Judah was 795 B.C., it means that the year before King Joash of Judah died, he made his son Amaziah co-regent with him. Thus, we know that Amaziah began to reign in the year 796 B.C. His twenty-ninth year would, therefore, have been the year 767 B.C.

Joash, Amaziah, Azariah - Jehoash, Jeroboam

To establish the reigns of the next king, following Amaziah of Judah, and the next king, following Jehoash of Israel, requires that we harmonize a number of verses. In II Kings 14:15-16, we read that Jehoash of Israel died and his son Jeroboam reigned.

Yr. B.C.	Judah — Joash (Jehoash)		Israel — Jehu			**Chart 12.**		Yr. B.C.
815	20	21	26	27				815
814	21	22	27	28	Jehoahaz			814
813	22	(23)	[28]			①		813
812	23	24	↑ Jehu	1	2			812
811	24	25	reigned	2	3			811
810	25	26	28 yrs,	3	4			810
809	26	27	II Kings	4	5			809
808	27	28	10:36	5	6			808
807	28	29		6	7			807
806	29	30		7	8			806
805	30	31		8	9			805
804	31	32		9	10			804
803	32	33		10	11			803
802	33	34		11	12			802
801	34	35		12	13			801
800	35	36		13	14	(Joash)		800
799	36	37 Joash		14	15	Jehoash		799
798	(37)	38 reigned		15	16		①	798
797	38	39 40 yrs, Amaziah	Jehoahaz	16	17	1	2	797
796	39	40 II Kings ①	reigned → [17]			②	3	796
795	[40]	← 12:1 1	2	17 yrs, II Kings 13:1			3	4	795

> II Kings 14:15-16: Now the rest of the acts of Jehoash which he did, and his might, and how he fought with Amaziah king of Judah, are they not written in the book of the chronicles of the kings of Israel? And Jehoash slept with his fathers, and was buried in Samaria with the kings of Israel; and Jeroboam his son reigned in his stead.

In the following verse, we read that Amaziah, king of Judah, lived for fifteen years after the death of Jehoash, king of Israel (Chart 13).

> II Kings 14:17: And Amaziah the son of Joash king of Judah lived after the death of Jehoash son of Jehoahaz king of Israel fifteen years.

In II Kings 14:18-21, we read that King Amaziah of Judah was killed by his people and Azariah (also called Uzziah) was made king.

> II Kings 14:18-21: And the rest of the acts of Amaziah, are they not written in the book of the chronicles of the kings of Judah? Now they made a conspiracy against him in Jerusalem: and he fled to Lachish; but they sent after him to Lachish, and slew him there. And they brought him on horses: and he was buried at Jerusalem with his fathers in the city of David. And all the people of Judah took Azariah, which was sixteen years old, and made him king instead of his father Amaziah.

According to these verses, Azariah was sixteen years old when he began to reign. This is echoed by the citation of II Kings 15:1-2, where we read that he began to reign in the twenty-seventh year of Jeroboam, the king of Israel. He was sixteen years old when he began to reign and he reigned for fifty-two years.

> II Kings 15:1-2: In the twenty and seventh year of Jeroboam king of Israel began Azariah son of Amaziah king of Judah to reign. Sixteen years old was he when he began to reign, and he reigned two and fifty years in Jerusalem. And his mother's name was Jecholiah of Jerusalem.

Yr. B.C.	Judah				Israel					Yr. B.C.
	Joash				Jehoahaz					
800	35	36				13	14	(Joash)		800
799	36	37				14	15	Jehoash		799
798	(37)	38				15	16		(1)	798
797	38	39	Amaziah			16	17	1	2	797
796	39	40	(1)			[17]		(2)	3	796
795	[40]	1	2		↑ Jehoahaz	3	4			795
794	↑ Joash	2	3		reigned	4	5			794
793	reigned	3	4		17 yrs,	5	6		Jeroboam	793
792	40 yrs,	4	5		II Kings	6	7		1	792
791	II Kings	5	6	Azariah	13:1	7	8	1	2	791
790	12:1	6	7	(Uzziah)		8	9	2	3	790
789	7	8		1		9	10	3	4	789
788	8	9	1	2		10	11	4	5	788
787	9	10	2	3		11	12	5	6	787
786	10	11	3	4		12	13	6	7	786
785	11	12	4	5		13	14	7	8	785
784	12	13	5	6		14	15	8	9	784
783	13	14	6	7		15	16	9	10	783
782	14	15	7	8		[16]		10	11	782
781	(15)	16	8	9	↑ Jehoash			(11)	12	781
780	16	17	9	10	reigned			12	13	780
779	17	18	10	11	16 yrs,			13	14	779
778	18	19	11	12	II Kings			14	15	778
777	19	20	12	13	13:10			15	16	777
776	20	21	13	14				16	17	776
775	21	22	14	15				17	18	775
774	22	23	15	16				18	19	774
773	23	24	16	17				19	20	773
772	24	25	17	18				20	21	772
771	25	26	18	19				21	22	771
770	26	27	19	20				22	23	770
769	27	28	20	21				23	24	769
768	28	29	21	22				24	25	768
767	[29]		22	23				25	26	767
766	↑ Amaziah		(23)	24				26	(27)	766
765	reigned		24	25				27	28	765
764	29 years,		25	26				28	29	764
763	II Kings 14:2		26	27				29	30	763
762			27	28				30	31	762
761			28	29				31	32	761

Chart 13.

In II Kings 15:8, we read that in the thirty-eighth year of Azariah, king of Judah, Zachariah the son of Jeroboam, king of Israel, began to reign, and he reigned for six months (Chart 14).

II Kings 15:8: In the thirty and eighth year of Azariah king of Judah did Zachariah the son of Jeroboam reign over Israel in Samaria six months.

Zachariah was followed by Shallum, who was not of Jeroboam's family, who reigned for one month during Azariah's thirty-ninth year.

II Kings 15:10: And Shallum the son of Jabesh conspired against him, and smote him before the people, and slew him, and reigned in his stead.

II Kings 15:13: Shallum the son of Jabesh began to reign in the nine and thirtieth year of Uzziah king of Judah; and he reigned a full month in Samaria.

With this much information, we can now harmonize the reigns of the Jewish kings Joash, Amaziah, and Azariah. We also can harmonize the reigns of these kings of Israel: Jehoash, Jeroboam, Zachariah, and Shallum.

As we have already learned, Amaziah of Judah was made king one year before his father, King Joash of Judah, died in his fortieth year of reign. In Amaziah's seventh full year (his eighth year counting the year he was made king), Azariah (Uzziah) became co-regent with him. This was 789 B.C. (Chart 13).

The occasion for the beginning of this co-regency between Azariah and his father Amaziah is given in IIKings 14:8-14. In these verses we read that Amaziah foolishly insisted on fighting with Jehoash the king of Israel. The consequence was the defeat of Amaziah and the plundering of Jerusalem. We read in verse 13 and 14: "And Jehoash king of Israel took Amaziah king of Judah ... and came to Jerusalem and brake down the wall of Jerusalem ... and he took all the vessels that were found in the house of the Lord ... and hostages...".

Chart 14.

Yr. B.C.	Judah — Amaziah		Azariah (Uzziah)		Israel — Jeroboam					Yr. B.C.
773	23	24	16	17	19	20				773
772	24	25	17	18	20	21				772
771	25	26	18	19	21	22				771
770	26	27	19	20	22	23				770
769	27	28	20	21	23	24				769
768	28	29	21	22	24	25				768
767	29		22	23	25	26				767
766	↑ Amaziah		(23)	24	26	27				766
765	reigned		24	25	27	28				765
764	29 yrs.,		25	26	28	29				764
763	II Kings 14:2		26	27	29	30				763
762			27	28	30	31				762
761			28	29	31	32				761
760			29	30	32	33				760
759			30	31	33	34				759
758			31	32	34	35				758
757			32	33	35	36				757
756			33	34	36	37				756
755			34	35	37	38				755
754			35	36	38	39				754
753			36	37	39	40	Zech-			753
752			37	38	40	41	ariah		Mena-	752
751			(38)	39	41		(1)	Shallum	hem	751
750			(39)	40	↑ Jeroboam	1	(1)		1	750
749			40	41	reigned 41yrs.,	↑Zechariah reigned 6 mos.,	Shallum reigned 1 mo.	1	2	749
748			41	42	II Kings 14:23	II Kings 15:8	II Kings 15:13	2	3	748

From chart 13 we see that this information can be harmonized with the reign of these kings. Undoubtedly in the seventh year of Amaziah which was the ninth year of Jehoash this foolish action took place. It surely was at this time that "the people of Judah took Azariah, which was sixteen years old and made him king instead of his father Amaziah" because of the king of Israel. Jehoash, had taken king Amaziah (2 kings 14:13) temporarily as a hostage. Thus at this time a co-regency began.

Azariah continued to be co-regent with his father Amaziah until 767 B.C., when the people of Judah killed Amaziah so that his son Azariah (Uzziah) would be sole ruler. Azariah's rule began in the year 789 B.C., when he was made co-regent with his father, and extended over a period of fifty-two years, his last year being 737 B.C. His father, Amaziah, who was killed in the year 767 B.C., lived for fifteen years after the death of Jehoash, king of Israel, who died in the year 782 B.C. (782 - 767 = 15), as declared in II Kings 14:17.

Harmonizing the kings of Israel, we learned from II Kings 15:1 that in the twenty-seventh year of Jeroboam of Israel, Azariah began to reign. The first full year that Azariah of Judah reigned alone was the year 766 B.C., the year following the death of his father Amaziah. Thus, the twenty-seventh year of Jeroboam, counting from the year he began to rule (by the non-accession year system), was the year 766 B.C. This means that he had begun to rule twenty-six years earlier, which was the year 792 B.C. But 792 B.C. was the sixth official full year (by the accession year system) of Jehoash, king of Israel, who was Jeroboam's father. This means that Jeroboam reigned as co-regent with his father Jehoash for the first ten years of his forty-one year reign (Chart 13).

Therefore, the first full year of Jeroboam as sole ruler was the year 781 B.C., which was the fifteenth full year of Amaziah, king of Judah, as II Kings 14:23 declares: "In the fifteenth year of Amaziah the son of Joash king of Judah Jeroboam the son of Joash king of Israel began to reign in Samaria, and reigned forty and one years." Since Jeroboam, king of Israel, began to reign in the year 792 B.C., and he reigned for forty-one years, he died in the year 751 B.C. In the year he died, his son Zachariah became king and was king for six months in the thirty-eighth full year (accession year system) of Azariah (Uzziah) of Judah. The thirty-eighth year of Azariah was 751 B.C., which coincides with the year Jeroboam died. (Chart 16)

Chart 15

Yr.	Judah				Israel				Yr.
B.C.	Amaziah				(Joash) Jehoash				B.C.
794	2	3			4	5			794
793	3	4			5	6	Jeroboam		793
792	4	5			6	7		1	792
791	5	6			7	8	1	2	791
790	6	7	Azariah (Uzziah)		8	9	2	3	790
789	7	8	1		9	10	3	4	789
788	8	9	1	2	10	11	4	5	788

Chart 16

Yr. B.C.	Judah — Amaziah		Azariah (Uzziah)		(Joash) Jehoash		Israel — Jeroboam		Zechariah / Shallum / Menahem	Yr. B.C.
787	9	10	2	3	11	12	5	6		787
786	10	11	3	4	12	13	6	7		786
785	11	12	4	5	13	14	7	8		785
784	12	13	5	6	14	15	8	9		784
783	13	14	6	7	15	16	9	10		783
782	14	15	7	8	16		10	11		782
781	(15)	16	8	9	Jehoash	11	11	12		781
780	16	17	9	10	reigned	12	12	13		780
779	17	18	10	11	16 yrs,	13	13	14		779
778	18	19	11	12	II Kings	14	14	15		778
777	19	20	12	13	13:10	15	15	16		777
776	20	21	13	14			16	17		776
775	21	22	14	15			17	18		775
774	22	23	15	16			18	19		774
773	23	24	16	17			19	20		773
772	24	25	17	18			20	21		772
771	25	26	18	19			21	22		771
770	26	27	19	20			22	23		770
769	27	28	20	21			23	24		769
768	28	29	21	22			24	25		768
767	[29]		22	23			25	26		767
766	↑ Amaziah	(23)	24				26	(27)		766
765	reigned	24	25				27	28		765
764	29 yrs.,	25	26				28	29		764
763	II Kings 14:2	26	27				29	30		763
762		27	28				30	31		762
761		28	29				31	32		761
760		29	30				32	33		760
759		30	31				33	34		759
758		31	32				34	35		758
757		32	33				35	36		757
756		33	34				36	37		756
755		34	35				37	38		755
754		35	36				38	39		754
753		36	37				39	40		753
752		37	38				40	41	Zechariah ... Mena-	752
751		(38)	39				[41]		(1) Shallum ... hem	751
750		(39)	40				↑ Jeroboam	[1]	[(1)] ... 1	750
749		40	41				reigned 41 yrs.,	↑ Zechariah reigned 6 mos., Shallum reigned 1 mo.,	1	2	749
748		41	42				II Kings 14:23	II Kings 15:8	15:13	2	3	748

Zechariah, Shallum, Menahem

Zechariah reigned over Israel for only six months during the thirty-eighth year of Azariah (II Kings 15:8), and was followed by Shallum, who reigned over Israel only one month during the thirty-ninth year of Azariah (II Kings 15:13). The Jewish year begins in the month of Nisan, which is March or April of our year. Therefore, Zechariah's six-month reign over Judah must have ended just before the first of Nisan in the year 750 B.C. inasmuch as the one-month rule of Shallum was in the thirty-ninth year of Azariah, which began the first of Nisan. Thus, Zechariah would have begun his reign late in 751 B.C. of our calendar and continued to March or April of 750 B.C. Shallum's reign of one month would definitely have been in 750 B.C.

We are now ready to examine a few more Biblical citations as we continue our reconstruction of the reigns of the kings of Judah and Israel.

In II Kings 15:13-14, we read that Menahem killed Shallum and became king of Israel.

> Shallum the son of Jabesh began to reign in the nine and thirtieth year of Uzziah king of Judah; and he reigned a full month in Samaria. For Menahem the son of Gadi went up from Tirzah, and came to Samaria, and smote Shallum the son of Jabesh in Samaria, and slew him, and reigned in his stead.

From II Kings 15:17, we learn that this event happened in the thirty-ninth year of Azariah, king of Judah, and that Menahem ruled over Israel for ten years.

> II Kings 15:17: In the nine and thirtieth year of Azariah king of Judah began Menahem the son of Gadi to reign over Israel, and reigned ten years in Samaria.

We have learned that the thirty-ninth full year (accession year system) of Azariah was the year 750 B.C., thus, we know that Menahem began to rule in the year 750 B.C. We will discover that the ten years of his reign are reckoned by counting from the first full year of his reign, so his tenth year would have been 740 B.C. (Chart 17).

Yr. B.C.	Judah — Azariah (Uzziah)		Israel — Jeroboam							Yr. B.C.
754	35	36	38	39						754
753	36	37	39	40						753
752	37	38	40	41	Zechariah					752
751	(38)	39	41		(1)	Shallum	Menahem			751
750	(39)	40	↑Jeroboam	1		(1)	(1)			750
749	40	41	reigned	↑Zechariah	Shallum	1	2			749
748	41	42	41 yrs,	reigned	reigned	2	3			748
747	42	43	II Kings	6 mos.,	1 mo.,	3	4			747
746	43	44	14:23	II Kings	II Kings	4	5			746
745	44	45		15:8	15:13	5	6			745
744	45	46				6	7			744
743	46	47				7	8			743
742	47	48				8	9			742
741	48	49				9	10	Pekahiah		741
740	49	(50)				10		(1)		740
739	50	51 Jotham				↑Mena-	1	2	Pekah	739
738	51	(52) 1				hem	2		(1)	738
737	(52)	(1) 2				reigned	↑Pekahiah	1	(2)	737
736	↑Azariah	2 3				10 yrs,	reigned	2	3	736

reigned 52 yrs, II Kings 15:2

II Kings 15:17   2 yrs, II Kings15:23   **Chart 17**

Going on with the Biblical citations that help us learn about the kings of Israel, we read in II Kings 15:22-23 that Menahem died in the tenth year of his reign over Israel and was succeeded by his son Pekahiah, who began his reign in the fiftieth year of Azariah, king of Judah, and reigned over Israel for two years: "And Menahem slept with his fathers; and Pekahiah his son reigned in his stead. In the fiftieth year of Azariah king of Judah Pekahiah the son of Menahem began to reign over Israel in Samaria, and reigned two years."

We find harmony when we realize that the fiftieth year of Azariah that is in view is the fiftieth year counting from the year Azariah began to reign over Judah (non-accession year system). This is the year 740 B.C., which is also the year Menahem died.

Next, we read in II Kings 15:25 that a captain of Pekahiah's army, named Pekah, revolted against Pekahiah and killed him. We read further in II Kings 15:27 that this was the fifty-second year of Azariah (Chart 17), king of Judah, and that Pekah reigned for twenty years.

II Kings 15:25: But Pekah the son of Remaliah, a captain of his, conspired against him, and smote him in Samaria, in the palace of the king's house, with Argob and Arieh, and with him fifty men of the Gileadites: and he killed him, and reigned in his room.

II Kings 15:27: In the two and fiftieth year of Azariah king of Judah Pekah the son of Remaliah began to reign over Israel in Samaria, and reigned twenty years.

Harmonizing this information, we learn that Pekahiah began to reign in 740 B.C. and was killed two years later, in 738 B.C., which was also the year Pekah began to reign. The year 738 B.C. was the fifty-second year of Azariah, king of Judah, counting from the year Azariah began to reign, 789 B.C. (non-accession year system).

As we continue to examine the reigns of the kings of Judah and Israel, we see in II Kings 15:32-33 that in the second year of Pekah, king of Israel, Jotham the son of Uzziah (Azariah) began to reign. He reigned for sixteen years.

II Kings 15:32-33: In the second year of Pekah the son of Remaliah king of Israel began Jotham the son of Uzziah king of Judah to reign. Five and twenty years old was he when he began to reign, and he reigned sixteen years in Jerusalem. And his mother's name was Jerusha, the daughter of Zadok.

On the other hand, we read in II Kings 15:30 that Hoshea killed Pekah, king of Israel, in the twentieth year of Jotham, king of Judah: "And Hoshea the son of Elah made a conspiracy against Pekah the son of Remaliah, and smote him, and slew him, and reigned in his stead, in the twentieth year of Jotham the son of Uzziah."

When we harmonize these Scripture verses we find that Pekah began to reign in the year 738 B.C. In his second year, counting from the year he became king of Israel, Jotham, who had begun the previous year to reign as co-regent with his father Uzziah, now began to reign alone as king. It becomes clear that Uzziah made his son Jotham rule with him the year before Uzziah died. According to II Chronicles 26:16-23, near the end of Uzziah's reign, he arrogantly attempted to burn incense in the temple. For this sin, he immediately became leprous.

Yr. B.C.	Judah				Israel				Yr. B.C.
	Azariah (Uzziah)				Menahem				
742	47	48			8	9			742
741	48	49			9	10	Pekahiah		741
740	49	(50)			10	①			740
739	50	51	Jotham		↑Menahem 1	2	Pekah		739
738	51	(52)	1		reigned	2	①		738
737	(52)	①	2		10 yrs,	↑Pekahiah 1	②		737
736	↑Azariah	2	3		II Kings	reigned 2	3		736
735	reigned	3	4		15:17	2 yrs, 3	4		735
734	52 yrs,	4	5			II Kings 4	5		734
733	II Kings	5	6			15:23 5	6		733
732	15:2	6	7			6	7		732
731		7	8	Ahaz		7	8		731
730		8	9	1		8	9		730
729		9	10	1	2	9	10		729
728		10	11	2	3	10	11		728
727		11	12	3	4	11	12		727
726		12	13	4	5	12	13		726
725		13	14	5	6	13	14		725
724		14	15	6	7	14	15		724
723		15	16	7	8	15	16		723
722		16	17	8	9	16	17		722
721		17	18	⑨	10	⑰	18		721
720		18	19	10	11	18	19		720
719		19	20	11	12	19	20	Hoshea	719
718		(20)	(12)	13		(20)	①	718
717		↑Jotham	13	14 Heze-		↑Pekah 1	2	717
716		reigned	14	15 kiah		reigned 2	3	716
715		20 yrs,	15	16 ①		20 yrs, ③	4	715
714		II Kings	16	1 2		II Kings 4	5	714

15:30　↑Ahaz
reigned 16 yrs,
II Kings 16:2

15:27

Chart 18

We read in verse 21: "And Uzziah the king was a leper unto the day of his death, and dwelt in a several house, being a leper; for he was cut off from the house of the LORD: and Jotham his son was over the king's house, judging the people of the land."

　　Harmonizing this information with the fact that in the second year of Pekah, Jotham began to reign, we can understand that during the last year of Uzziah, his fifty-second by the accession year system, Jotham his son began to reign as if he alone were the king.

The twentieth year of Jotham by accession year reckoning was 718 B.C., which was also the twentieth year of Pekah, who was succeeded as king over Israel by Hoshea.

To understand and harmonize the citation of II Kings 15:32-33, where it indicates that Jotham reigned for sixteen years, we need more information. This is given to us in II Kings 16:1-2, where we read that in the seventeenth year of Pekah, Ahaz the son of Jotham began to reign over Judah. He reigned for sixteen years.

> II Kings 16:1-2: In the seventeenth year of Pekah the son of Remaliah Ahaz the son of Jotham king of Judah began to reign. Twenty years old was Ahaz when he began to reign, and reigned sixteen years in Jerusalem, and did not that which was right in the sight of the LORD his God, like David his father.

The seventeenth year of Pekah, counting from the first full year (accession year system) of his reign, was 721 B.C., but the seventeenth year of Pekah was also the seventeenth year of Jotham. Therefore, some kind of co-regency existed between Jotham and Ahaz as they ruled over Judah.

We can learn more about this co-regency from the information given in II Kings 17:1, where we read that Hoshea began to reign over Israel in the twelfth year of Ahaz, king of Judah, with Hoshea ruling for nine years: " In the twelfth year of Ahaz king of Judah began Hoshea the son of Elah to reign in Samaria over Israel nine years" (Chart 18).

We have already learned that Hoshea killed Pekah in the year 718 B.C., which was also the twentieth year of Jotham's rule over Judah. Therefore, we can reconstruct this period of history and know that there was a co-regency between Ahaz and Jotham, with Ahaz beginning to reign in 730 B.C. He reigned for a total of sixteen years with his last year being 714 B.C. In the seventeenth year of Pekah, king of Israel, Ahaz became the dominant king over Judah even though Jotham had been the dominant king for the previous sixteen years. From 721 B.C., which was the year following the first sixteen years of Jotham's rule, Ahaz became the dominant king.

Yr. B.C.	Azariah (Uzziah) Judah					Israel					Yr. B.C.
						Menahem					
742	47	48				Menahem 8	9				742
741	48	49				9	10 Pekahiah				741
740	49	(50)				[10]	(1)				740
739	50	51 Jotham				↑ Mena- 1	2 Pekah				739
738	51	52	1			hem [2]	(1)				738
737	(52)	(1)	2			reigned ↑ Peka- 1	(2)				737
736	↑Azariah	2	3			10 yrs, hiah 2	3				736
735	reigned	3	4			II Kings reigned 3	4				735
734	52 yrs,	4	5			15:17 2 yrs, 4	5				734
733	II Kings	5	6			II Kings 5	6				733
732	15:2	6	7			15:23 6	7				732
731		7	8 Ahaz			7	8				731
730		8	9	1		8	9				730
729		9	10	1	2	9	10				729
728		10	11	2	3	10	11				728
727		11	12	3	4	11	12				727
726		12	13	4	5	12	13				726
725		13	14	5	6	13	14				725
724		14	15	6	7	14	15				724
723		15	16	7	8	15	16				723
722		16	17	8	9	16	17				722
721		17	18	(9)	10	(17)	18				721
720		18	19	10	11	18	19				720
719		19	20	11	12	19	20 Hoshea				719
718		(20)		(12)	13	[20]	(1)				718
717		↑ Jotham	13	14		↑ Pekah 1	2				717
716		reigned	14	15 Hezekiah		reigned 2	3				716
715		20 yrs,	15	16	(1)	20 yrs, (3)	4				715
714		II Kings	[16]	1	2	II Kings 4	5				714
713		15:30	↑ Ahaz	2	3	15:27 5	6				713
712			reigned	3	4	6	7				712
711			16 yrs,	(4)	5	(7)	8				711
710			II Kings	5	6	Hoshea reigned 9 yrs, 8	9				710
709			16:2	(6)	7	II Kings 18:10 → (9)					709

Chart 19   *The end of the ten-tribe nation of Israel*

We have learned that Hoshea began to reign over Israel in the twentieth year of Jotham, which was the twelfth year of Ahaz. This was the year 718 B.C. We then read in II Kings 18:1 that Hezekiah the son of Ahaz began to reign over Judah in the third year of Hoshea, king of

Israel. The third full year of Hoshea, counting from the first full year of his reign, was 715 B.C. This was the year, therefore, that Hezekiah began to reign. In II Kings 18:9-11, we find additional time references that relate the reign of Hoshea, the king of Israel, to Hezekiah, the king of Judah:

> And it came to pass in the fourth year of king Hezekiah, which was the seventh year of Hoshea son of Elah king of Israel, that Shalmaneser king of Assyria came up against Samaria, and besieged it. And at the end of three years they took it: even in the sixth year of Hezekiah, that is the ninth year of Hoshea king of Israel, Samaria was taken. And the king of Assyria did carry away Israel unto Assyria, and put them in Halah and in Habor by the river of Gozan, and in the cities of the Medes.

From these verses, we learn that the city of Samaria was besieged by Shalmaneser, king of Assyria, in the fourth year of Hezekiah, king of Judah, which is the seventh year of Hoshea, king of Israel. When we harmonize this information, we discover that the fourth year of Hezekiah is figured on the accession year basis (Chart 19). Likewise, the seventh year of Hoshea is figured the same way.

The End of the Ten-Tribe Nation of Israel

Moreover, we learn that in the ninth year of Hoshea, again reckoned on the accession year basis, which was the sixth year of Hezekiah reckoned the same way, Samaria was taken, and from additional language of the Bible, we can know that this was the end of the kingdom of Israel that had begun at the death of Solomon. The ninth year of Hoshea and the sixth year of Hezekiah were the year 709 B.C. (Chart 20). Later we will discuss why verse 9 tells us that it was Shalmaneser who assaulted the city, whereas in verse 10, the Bible simply declares that it was the king of Assyria who took the city.

This ends the history of the nation of Israel. Its history began when Jeroboam became their king in 931 B.C. and ended in 709 B.C., when Assyria conquered Samaria, the capital of Israel.

Because the two nations, Judah and Israel, existed during the period from 931 B.C. to 709 B.C., we have been able to reconstruct in a very precise way the chronology of the reigns of the kings of both

Yr. B.C.	Judah						Israel		Yr. B.C.
	Jotham		Ahaz				Pekah		
720	18	19	10	11			18	19	720
719	19	20	11	12		Hoshea	19	20	719
718	20		12	13		①	20		718
717	↑ Jotham		13	14			↑ Pekah	1	2	717
716	reigned		14	15	Hezekiah		reigned	2	3	716
715	20 yrs,		15	16	①		20 yrs,	③	4	715
714	II Kings		16	1	2		II Kings	4	5	714
713	15:30		↑ Ahaz	2	3		15:27	5	6	713
712			reigned	3	4			6	7	712
711			16 yrs,	④	5			⑦	8	711
710			II Kings	5	6			8	9	710
709			16:2	⑥	7			⑨		709
708				7	8		↑ Hoshea		708
707				8	9		reigned		707
706				9	10		9 yrs,		706
705				10	11		II Kings		705
704				11	12		18:10		704
703				12	13			703
702				13	14		**709 B.C.:**		702
701				14	15		**The end of**		701
700				15	16		**the ten-tribe**		700
699				16	17		**nation**		699
698				17	18	Manasseh	**of Israel**		698
697				18	19	1		697
696				19	20	1	2	**Chart 20**	696

nations. By carefully reading each and every verse that relates to the kings of Judah and Israel, we have been enabled to reconstruct this period of history with extreme accuracy. With the exception of one verse,* every single verse in the Bible that bears on the subject has been fully harmonized. The "fit" of the reigns of the kings is so exact that if the reign of even one of the kings is shifted even one year, harmony will not be possible for several other kings.

* The single verse that cannot be harmonized is that of II Chronicles 22:2. This verse says that Ahaziah, who reigned for one year over Judah, was 42 years old when he began to reign. But II Kings 8:26 declares that he was 22 years old when he began to reign. The 22 year old citation harmonizes with all the other data. However, because II Chronicles 22:2 is also the Word of God, there must be some spiritual reason why God speaks of Ahaziah being 42 years of age when 22 years is quite clearly an accurate figure.

When Israel ceased to exist as a nation, Judah continued for many years as a nation. But no longer could the chronology of the kings of Judah be harmonized with the kings of Israel. As we continue with the Bible citations, we have only the record of the kings of Judah.

However, we find that near the end of the existence of the nation of Judah, God gives us extensive information concerning the reign of the king of Babylon, who destroyed Judah in 587 B.C. We will examine some of that evidence in Chapter 10, pages 320-356. When this Babylonian information is harmonized with the Biblical information relating to Judah, we will be helped in our reconstruction of the reigns of the kings of Judah from Hezekiah to the end of Judah in 587 B.C. Furthermore, God has graciously given other Biblical evidence that focuses on 587 B.C. as the end of Judah's existence. Much of this was set forth in the book *1994?* For example, we learned in *1994?* that the path which led to 1994 as being in all likelihood the end of the world, which was based on the 1290 days of Daniel 12:11, lands squarely on 587 B.C. as well as 1994 A.D. Moreover, in this book, we will find added Biblical evidence that 587 B.C. is accurate.

But now we should return to Hezekiah.

We have learned thus far that Hezekiah began to reign in the year 715 B.C. and his sixth year was 709 B.C. In II Kings 18:2, we read that Hezekiah reigned for twenty-nine years. Therefore, his last year would have been 686 B.C. (Chart 21). II Kings 18:2: " Twenty and five years old was he when he began to reign; and he reigned twenty and nine years in Jerusalem. His mother's name also was Abi, the daughter of Zachariah."

Hezekiah and Manasseh were Co-Regents

The next king following Hezekiah was his son Manasseh, who ruled for fifty-five years, as we read in II Kings 21:1: "Manasseh was twelve years old when he began to reign, and reigned fifty and five years in Jerusalem. And his mother's name was Hephzibah."

For two reasons, we immediately suspect that during a number of these fifty-five years, Manasseh was co-regent with his father Hezekiah. The first reason is that he was a child of twelve years when he began to reign. It is true that other kings, like Joash (seven years old), and Josiah (eight years old), began to reign as children, but in their situations, their fathers who were reigning kings, were killed in

Yr. B.C.	Judah — Hezekiah		Judah — Manasseh		Yr. B.C.
702	13	14			702
701	14	15			701
700	15	16			700
699	16	17			699
698	17	18	Manasseh		698
697	18	19		1	697
696	19	20	1	2	696
695	20	21	2	3	695
694	21	22	3	4	694
693	22	23	4	5	693
692	23	24	5	6	692
691	24	25	6	7	691
690	25	26	7	8	690
689	26	27	8	9	689
688	27	28	9	10	688
687	28	29	10	11	687
686	[29]		11	12	686
685	↑ Hezekiah reigned		12	13	685
684	29 yrs, II Kings 18:2		13	14	684
659			38	39	659
658			39	40	658
657			40	41	657
656			41	42	656

Chart 21

untimely fashion. Hezekiah, who was Manasseh's father, reigned for twenty-nine years; his death was not a result of palace rebellion.

That brings us to the second reason. In Hezekiah's fourteenth year, he had become deathly ill. We read in II Kings 20:1: "In those days was Hezekiah sick unto death. And the prophet Isaiah the son of Amoz came to him, and said unto him, Thus saith the LORD, Set thine house in order; for thou shalt die, and not live."

And in II Kings 20:6: "And I will add unto thy days fifteen years; and I will deliver thee and this city out of the hand of the king of Assyria; and I will defend this city for mine own sake, and for my servant David's sake."

This event occurred in Hezekiah's fourteenth year (701 B.C.). We know this because he reigned for twenty-nine years and fifteen of these years were added at the time of his illness. Since Hezekiah knew the year of his death, it seems very appropriate that he would begin to prepare his young son Manasseh for the kingship by making him co-regent during the closing years of his life.

How many years was Manasseh co-regent with his father Hezekiah? We have no immediate information in the Bible that helps us. However, as we have already noted, near the end of Judah's history, the Bible gives us much information concerning the king of Babylon who destroyed Judah. Additionally, the secular record concerning the king of Babylon is sufficiently detailed and accurate so that we can harmonize it with the Biblical record and know that we have truth.

Based on the preceding information, which we will develop later in our study, we know that Manasseh began to reign in the eighteenth year of his father, Hezekiah, which was the year 697 B.C. His twelfth year, 685 B.C., was his first full year of reigning alone. The year of his death, which was his fifty-fifth year, was, therefore, 642 B.C. (see Chart 22).

The son of Manasseh, who reigned next, was Amon. We read in II Kings 21:18-19:

> And Manasseh slept with his fathers, and was buried in the garden of his own house, in the garden of Uzza: and Amon his son reigned in his stead. Amon was twenty and two years old when he began to reign, and he reigned two years in Jerusalem. And his mother's name was Meshullemeth, the daughter of Haruz of Jotbah.

Amon reigned for two years. Therefore, he began to reign in the year 642 B.C. His first official year was 641 B.C., and he was killed in the second year of his reign, 640 B.C. II Kings 21:23-24 records his untimely death:

> And the servants of Amon conspired against him, and slew the king in his own house. And the people of the land slew all them that had conspired against king Amon; and the people of the land made Josiah his son king in his stead.

Yr. B.C.	Judah					Yr. B.C.
	Manasseh					
655	42	43				655
654	43	44				654
653	44	45				653
652	45	46				652
651	46	47				651
650	47	48				650
649	48	49				649
648	49	50				648
647	50	51				647
646	51	52				646
645	52	53				645
644	53	54				644
643	54	55	Amon			643
642	55			1		642
641	↑ Manasseh		1	2	Josiah	641
640	reigned		2		1	640
639	55 yrs,		↑ Amon reigned	1	2	639
638	II Kings 21:1		2 yrs, II Kings	2	3	638
637			21:18-19	3	4	637
636				4	5	636
635				5	6	635
634				6	7	634
633				7	8	633
632				8	9	632
631				9	10	631
630				10	11	630
629				11	12	629
628				12	13	628
627				13	14	627
626				14	15	626
625				15	16	625
624				16	17	624
623				17	18	623
622				18	19	622
621				19	20	621
620				20	21	620
619				21	22	619
618				22	23	618
617				23	24	617
616	**Chart 22**			24	25	616

Josiah: The Last Good King

Josiah, Amon's eight year old son, was put on the throne in 640 B.C. and reigned for thirty-one years. II Kings 22:1 records that:

> Josiah was eight years old when he began to reign, and he reigned thirty and one years in Jerusalem. And his mother's name was Jedidah, the daughter of Adaiah of Boscath.

Since Josiah reigned for thirty-one years by the accession year reckoning, which was the way all of the reigns of the kings of Judah had been figured, his thirty-first year was 609 B.C. (see Chart 23). His death is recorded in II Kings 23:29-30:

> In his days Pharaoh-nechoh king of Egypt went up against the king of Assyria to the river Euphrates: and king Josiah went against him; and he slew him at Megiddo, when he had seen him. And his servants carried him in a chariot dead from Megiddo, and brought him to Jerusalem, and buried him in his own sepulchre. And the people of the land took Jehoahaz the son of Josiah, and anointed him, and made him king in his father's stead.

His son Jehoahaz reigned only three months, as we read in II Kings 23:31:

> Jehoahaz was twenty and three years old when he began to reign; and he reigned three months in Jerusalem. And his mother's name was Hamutal, the daughter of Jeremiah of Libnah.

Therefore, he reigned during the year 609 B.C.
He was deposed by Pharaoh Necho, as disclosed in II Kings 23:33-34:

> And Pharaoh-nechoh put him in bands at Riblah in the land of Hamath, that he might not reign in Jerusalem;

Yr. B.C.	Judah Josiah		Jehoahaz	Jehoiakim	(Jechoniah)		Babylon	Yr. B.C.
617	23	24						617
616	24	25						616
615	25	26						615
614	26	27						614
613	27	28						613
612	28	29						612
611	29	30			(Coniah)			611
610	30	31	Jehoahaz	Jehoiakim	(Jechoniah)			610
609	31		1	1	Jehoiachin			609
608	↑ Josiah	↑ Jehoahaz	1	2	1			608
607	reigned	reigned 3	2	3	1	2	Nebuchad-	607
606	31 yrs,	mos., II Kings	3	4	2	3	nezzar	606
605	II Kings	23:31	④	5	3	4	①	605
604	22:1		5	6	4	5	1	2	604
603			6	7	5	6	2	3	603
602			7	8	6	7	3	4	602
601			8	9	7	8	4	5	601
600			9	10	8	9	5	6	600
599			10	11	9	10	6	7	599
598	Jehoiakim reigned →	11		10	Zedekiah	7	⑧	598
597	11 yrs, II Kings 23:36	Jehoiachin ↑ reigned alone 1	½			8	9	597

3 mos. & 10 days, II Chron. 36:9. He was deposed just before Nisan in 597 B.C. Therefore, Zedekiah began to reign early in 597 B.C. which beginning at Nisan 1 was his first full year (see pg. 174).

Chart 23

and put the land to a tribute of an hundred talents of silver, and a talent of gold. And Pharaoh-nechoh made Eliakim the son of Josiah king in the room of Josiah his father, and turned his name to Jehoiakim, and took Jehoahaz away: and he came to Egypt, and died there.

We learn from II Kings 23:36 that Jehoiakim reigned for eleven years

II Kings 23:36: Jehoiakim was twenty and five years old when he began to reign; and he reigned eleven years in Jerusalem. And his mother's name was Zebudah, the daughter of Pedaiah of Rumah.

Since Jehoiakim began to reign in 609 B.C., his eleventh year was 598 B.C. (see Chart 23).

In Jeremiah 25:1, we discover the next time-reference to Jehoiakim. There we read:

> The word that came to Jeremiah concerning all the people of Judah in the fourth year of Jehoiakim the son of Josiah king of Judah, that was the first year of Nebuchadrezzar king of Babylon.

From this reference we know what year King Nebuchadrezzar began to reign. The fourth year of Jehoiakim was 605 B.C., which means the first year of the Babylonian king was also 605 B.C. (Chart 23).

The next citation we will examine is II Chronicles 36:6, where God informs us that Jehoiakim was deposed by the king of Babylon:

> Against him came up Nebuchadnezzar king of Babylon, and bound him in fetters, to carry him to Babylon.

In II Kings 24:6, we learn that Jehoiachin (also called Jeconiah and Coniah in the Bible), the son of Jehoiakim, became the next king. In II Kings 24:8, we read that he was eighteen years of age when he began to reign and he reigned for three months.

> II Kings 24:8: Jehoiachin was eighteen years old when he began to reign, and he reigned in Jerusalem three months. And his mother's name was Nehushta, the daughter of Elnathan of Jerusalem.

But II Chronicles 36:9 reports that he was eight years of age when he began to reign:

> Jehoiachin was eight years old when he began to reign, and he reigned three months and ten days in Jerusalem: and he did that which was evil in the sight of the LORD.

This apparent contradiction is resolved when we recognize that Jehoiakim made his eight-year-old son co-regent with himself almost immediately after Jehoiakim ascended the throne. In the year 609 B.C.,

Yr. B.C.	Judah Jehoiakim		Jehoiachin(Coniah, Jechoniah)			Babylon Nebuchadnezzar		Yr. B.C.
605	④	5	3	4			①	605
604	5	6	4	5		1	2	604
603	6	7	5	6		2	3	603
602	7	8	6	7		3	4	602
601	8	9	7	8		4	5	601
600	9	10	8	9		5	6	600
599	10	11	9	10		6	7	599
598	11		10		Zedekiah	⑦	⑧	598
597	↑ Jehoiakim		↑ Jehoiachin	1	1/2	8	9	597
596	reigned 11		reigned alone 3 mos. &	2	3	9	10	596
595	yrs, II Kings		10 days, II Chron. 36:9.	3	4	10	11	595
594	23:36		He was deposed before	4	5	11	12	594
593			Nisan 1 in 597 B.C.	5	6	12	13	593
592			(see pg. 174)	6	7	13	14	592
591				7	8	14	15	591

Chart 24

Jehoiakim began to reign. The next year, 608 B.C., his eight-year-old son, Jehoiachin, was made co-regent with him. Thus, ten years later, when Jehoiachin was 18 years old, he was already reigning when his father, Jehoiakim, was taken to Babylon. Jehoiachin then reigned for three months and ten days before he was taken to Babylon (Chart 24)..

Additional information concerning the deposing of Jehoiachin is given in II Kings 24:12, where we read that it was the eighth year of King Nebuchadnezzar.

> II Kings 24:12: And Jehoiachin the king of Judah went out to the king of Babylon, he, and his mother, and his servants, and his princes, and his officers: and the king of Babylon took him in the eighth year of his reign.

The eighth year of King Nebuchadnezzar was, therefore, 598 B.C.

Following the deposing of Jehoiachin, we read in II Kings 24:17-18 that the king of Babylon made a brother king of Judah in place of Jehoiachin.

> II Kings 24:17-18: And the king of Babylon made Mattaniah his father's brother king in his stead, and

Yr. B.C.	Judah — Jehoiakim		Jehoiachin			Babylon — Nebuchadnezzar		Yr. B.C.
605	④	5	3	4			①	605
604	5	6	4	5		1	2	604
603	6	7	5	6		2	3	603
602	7	8	6	7		3	4	602
601	8	9	7	8		4	5	601
600	9	10	8	9		5	6	600
599	10	11	9	10		6	7	599
598	11		10		Zedekiah	⑦	⑧	598
597	↑ Jehoiakim		↑ Jehoiachin	1	1/2	8	9	597
596	reigned 11 yrs,		reigned alone 3	2	3	9	10	596
595	II Kings 23:36		mos. & 10 days, II	3	4	10	11	595
594			Chron. 36:9. He	4	5	11	12	594
593			was deposed	5	6	12	13	593
592			before Nisan 1 in	6	7	13	14	592
591			597 B.C.	7	8	14	15	591
590				8	9	15	16	590
589				9	10	16	17	589
588				⑩	11	17	⑱	588
587				⑪		⑱	⑲	587
586						19	20	586
585	*587 B.C.: The*					20	21	585
584	*nation of Judah*					21	22	584
583	*was destroyed by*					22	23	583
582	*Babylon.*					23	24	582

Chart 25

changed his name to Zedekiah. Zedekiah was twenty and one years old when he began to reign, and he reigned eleven years in Jerusalem. And his mother's name was Hamutal, the daughter of Jeremiah of Libnah.

The End of the Nation of Judah

Zedekiah's first full year according to the accession year system was 597 B.C., and his eleventh year by the same system was 587 B.C. Since he was the last king of Judah, the year 587 B.C. ended the period of the kings of Judah.

Jeremiah 32:1 gives another citation that describes the time relationship between the reigns of Zedekiah and Nebuchadnezzar.

Jeremiah 32:1: The word that came to Jeremiah from the LORD in the tenth year of Zedekiah king of Judah, which was the eighteenth year of Nebuchadrezzar.

The tenth year of Zedekiah by the accession year system was 588 B.C., as was the eighteenth year of Nebuchadnezzar by the non-accession year system.

The end of Jerusalem is described in Jeremiah 52:12-15. The Bible describes the precise day that the city was destroyed.

Jeremiah 52:12-15: Now in the fifth month, in the tenth day of the month, which was the nineteenth year of Nebuchadrezzar king of Babylon, came Nebuzar-adan, captain of the guard, which served the king of Babylon, into Jerusalem, And burned the house of the LORD, and the king's house; and all the houses of Jerusalem, and all the houses of the great men, burned he with fire: And all the army of the Chaldeans, that were with the captain of the guard, brake down all the walls of Jerusalem round about. Then Nebuzar-adan the captain of the guard carried away captive certain of the poor of the people, and the residue of the people that remained in the city, and those that fell away, that fell to the king of Babylon, and the rest of the multitude.

In this citation, God again emphasizes that this occurred in the nineteenth year of Nebuchadnezzar (non-accession year system).

In II Kings 24:12, we read that it was in the eighth year of King Nebuchadnezzar that Jehoiachin was taken to Babylon. In Jeremiah 52:28, the Bible records that it was in the seventh year of Nebuchadnezzar that 3320 captives were taken. There is no discrepancy because the eighth year of the king is the same as the seventh year. Counting from the year 605 B.C., when King Nebuchadnezzar ascended the throne, we come to 598 B.C. as his eighth year. However, reckoning by the accession year system, the year 598 B.C. was his seventh year. Remember that in the accession year system, the year number one for a king was the first full year he reigned and, therefore, the year number one was the year immediately following the year he ascended the throne (see Chart 25).

Likewise, in Jeremiah 52:29, we read that in the eighteenth year of Nebuchadnezzar, he carried away captive 832 persons. Remember, in Jeremiah 52:12-15, we read that it was in the nineteenth year that the captain of the guard carried away certain of the poor of the city. Again there is no contradiction. The eighteenth year of King Nebuchadnezzar was the same year (587 B.C.) as the nineteenth year. The eighteenth year according to the accession year system started counting from his first full year as king (604 B.C.). The nineteenth year according to the non-accession year system started counting from the previous year (605 B.C.) when he actually became king.

By God's mercy, we have been enabled to reconstruct the calendar of history covering the entire period of the kings of Israel and Judah. Later in our study, we will show why we can be certain that our starting date of 931 B.C. and our ending date of 587 B.C. are trustworthy. Further, we will discover that this reconstruction also produces a number of paths that focus on the birth of Christ in 7 B.C., the crucifixion of Christ in 33 A.D., the beginning of the final tribulation in 1988 A.D., and the end of the world in 1994 A.D.

But now we should spend some time showing how and why God so extensively uses numbers in the Bible.

[An outline of the kings of Judah and Israel is on the following page.]

Kings of Judah		Kings of Israel	
Rehoboam	931-914	Jeroboam	931-910
Abijam	914-911		
Asa	911-870	Nadab	910-909
		Baasha	909-886
		Elah	886-885
		Zimri	885
		Tibni	885-880
		Omri	885-874
Jehoshaphat	871-846	Ahab	874-853
Jehoram	854-842	Ahaziah	854-853
Ahaziah (Jehoahaz)	842-841	Joram (Jehoram)	853-841
Athaliah	841-835	Jehu	841-813
Joash (Jehoash)	835-795	Jehoahaz	813-796
Amaziah	796-767	Jehoash (Joash)	798-782
Uzziah (Azariah)	769-737	Jeroboam	792-751
		Zechariah	751-750
		Shallum	750
		Menahem	750-740
Jotham	738-718	Pekahiah	740-738
Ahaz	730-714	Pekah	738-718
Hezekiah	715-686	Hoshea	718-709
Manasseh	697-642		
Amon	642-640		
Josiah	640-609		
Jehoahaz	609		
Jehoiakim	609-598		
Jehoiachin	608-597		
Zedekiah	597-587		

Chapter 7.
God's Use of Numbers in the Bible

We have spent considerable effort to show that every word in the Bible is God-breathed and therefore very important. We must realize that "All scripture is given by inspiration of God" (II Timothy 3:16), and this principle applies to every word, phrase, and section of the Bible. We must never take the position that words that seem irrelevant or unimportant are indeed irrelevant or unimportant. Every word and every letter of each and every word in the original autographs are given to us by God. This is true even though God utilized the personalities of humans who wrote in the context of their abilities and experiences.

Included in these words that were God-breathed are all of the numbers found in the Bible. They are just as important and just as much the Word of God as any other word recorded in the Bible. This is a truth that may be difficult to grasp because many of us do not do well with any kind of number system. Yet, as we live in this world, every human being must deal with numbers to some degree whether he likes it or not. The moment he buys food or clothing, he must deal with numbers.

Therefore, it is just as unreal to try to live in this world without ever having to relate to any numbers as it is to go to the Bible and expect to learn as much truth as possible from God's Word without taking into account the numbers of the Bible.

> *A disregard for the significance of the numbers of the Bible is bound to limit our understanding of some aspects of the Gospel message.*

In fact, the whole universe was created by the same God who has given us the Bible. If scientists were to disregard all usage of numbers in their study of the universe, their understanding would be seriously hampered. Numbers have a tremendous involvement in the design of the universe. To disregard these numbers would produce a situation in which a great amount of the intricacies and complexities of this beautiful universe that are now understood could never be understood. Likewise, without question, a disregard for the significance of the numbers of the Bible is bound to limit our understanding of some aspects of the Gospel message.

Because every word and phrase in the Bible is given to us by God, the greater our understanding of these words and phrases, the greater will be our understanding of the Bible. Likewise, because each and every number recorded in the Bible is given to us by God, the greater our understanding of these numbers, the greater will be our understanding of the Bible.

We must, of course, interpret the meaning of Biblical words and phrases by the way they are used in the Bible. Likewise, we must understand God's usage of the numbers recorded in the Bible by the criteria that God Himself gives us in the Bible.

> *We must never engage in numerology, as it is sometimes called.*

For example, we must never engage in numerology, as it is sometimes called. In this practice, number values are assigned to the letters of the Hebrew and Greek alphabets. Thus, words and phrases are associated with each other by their number values which are derived from the number value of each letter in the word or phrase. This practice has no Biblical validation whatsoever. It is entirely alien to the Bible and no Bible student who wishes to find truth should have anything at all to do with it.

We have learned that the Bible gives us one Gospel message. Sometimes the words or phrases give the Gospel message in very plain language, but many times the words and phrases are allegorical in nature so we must discover the spiritual message conveyed by them.

Not infrequently, a word or phrase that we find recorded in the Bible gives us no hint of how it may fit into the Gospel message. This does not mean that these words or phrases are unimportant. It just means that God has not yet opened our spiritual eyes to the Gospel or spiritual meaning of these words or phrases.

> *This does not mean that these numbers are unimportant. It just means that God has not yet opened our spiritual eyes to see how these numbers fit into the Gospel message.*

Likewise, there are numbers recorded in the Bible that appear to offer no help whatsoever toward giving us an understanding of the Gospel message. This does not mean that these numbers are unimportant. It just means that God has not yet opened our spiritual eyes to see how these numbers fit into the Gospel account.

Sometimes God uses words or phrases to convey the idea of size or greatness. He uses words such as "great," "large," "many," "multitude," "small," "few," etc. Likewise, God sometimes uses numbers to convey the idea of size or greatness.

For example, God tells us in Numbers 1:20-46 that in all Israel that came out of Egypt there were 603,550 men twenty years of age or older who were able to go to war. Moreover, He tells us how many of these men were in each of the individual tribes. As a minimum, these numbers give us some idea of the size of Israel when they came out of Egypt. In fact, if we compare these numbers with the numbers given in Numbers 26, when Israel was ready to go into the land of Canaan, we can calculate that the nation of Israel that came out of Egypt was about two million souls. (This calculation is not given in this book because it is not germane to this study.) Thus, we can have an additional appreciation of the size of the miracles of going through the Red Sea, receiving water from the rock, etc.

This does not mean that numbers such as these are recorded only to give us size or amount. They also might have been given to us to convey other spiritual truth of which God has not yet made us aware.

Many times God gives words or phrases in the Bible to convey time concepts. Such words include "beginning," "end," "last days," "last day," "fulness of time," etc. Likewise, God has placed many numbers in the Bible to give us precise understanding of the timetable of the earth. As we learned in the book *1994?*, the timetable of history is governed by the unfolding of God's salvation plan. Only because of the numbers given in the Bible are we able to know exactly when each of the milestones of God's salvation plan did take place.

We have learned what an enormous contribution these numbers that give calendar information are to our understanding of God's salvation plan. By their use we learned in the *1994?* study that the important Biblical historical events relating to the unfolding of God's salvation plan did not come in random fashion but followed a very precise plan. Because of this, we were enabled to project God's salvation plan into the future and discover that the year 1994 is in all probability the year when the world will end.

Words and phrases are also given in the Bible to embellish and enrich the Gospel message. Many times these words speak directly to the salvation message. For example, in Ephesians 1:5, we read:

> Having predestinated us unto the adoption of children by Jesus Christ to himself, according to the good pleasure of his will.

This verse could have simply ended with the words "according to His will." It would still be altogether a trustworthy phrase. The addition of the words "the good pleasure of" makes the verse much more meaningful. It enhances and enriches the message that God is conveying to us through this verse.

> *Likewise, God greatly enhances and enriches the Gospel presentation by inserting certain numbers into the Gospel record.*

Likewise, God greatly enhances and enriches the Gospel presentation by inserting certain numbers into the Gospel record. Later, we will examine several examples of this.

Frequently, these added words, phrases, or whole paragraphs are given in allegorical or parable form. As we learned earlier in Chapter 5, Jesus spoke in parables. Thus, many words and phrases appear superficially to be meaningless, but when their spiritual meaning is understood, they greatly add to the message being conveyed.

The Lamb of God

For example, earlier in our study, we examined John the Baptist's announcement of Jesus: "Behold the Lamb of God, which taketh away the sin of the world" (John 1:29). The announcement would have been accurate if John had declared, "Behold the one who takes away the sin of the world." This is an absolutely true statement and would appear to be an adequate announcement of Jesus.

John, speaking under the inspiration of the Holy Spirit, included in this announcement the phrase "the Lamb of God." As we learned earlier, the addition of this phrase tends to obscure the truth. Jesus was not an animal. Why was He called a lamb when this important announcement was made?

Remember, we learned that when we search the Bible to discover the spiritual meaning of the word "lamb," all kinds of Gospel meaning comes into view. Quickly, we learn that by the use of the word "lamb," Jesus is being announced as the one who would be sacrificed. He would be the one who would endure the wrath of God as payment for the sins of anyone in the whole world who would believe on Him. Thus, the announcement of Jesus by John the Baptist was greatly enriched by the addition of the allegorical phrase "the Lamb of God."

However, the added riches and spiritual depth that came with the phrase "the Lamb of God" cannot be obtained until we carefully study the whole Bible to learn how God uses the word "lamb" in unfolding the Gospel message. It is imperative that care be taken if we are to be blessed by the addition of this phrase. In fact, if we have not carefully studied the Bible to learn the spiritual meaning of the word "lamb," and instead came to a wrong understanding of the word "lamb," we could greatly diminish the import of the entire announcement of Jesus by John the Baptist.

Numbers Convey Spiritual Truth

In like fashion, God frequently inserts numbers into the Biblical account. When Jesus designed the story of the rich man and Lazarus as given to us in Luke 16, He has the rich man in hell and speaking of his five brothers (Luke 16:28). Why five? Why not a few brothers or several brothers?

When Jesus gives us the story of the ten virgins, five of whom were wise and five foolish, why does He use the numbers ten and five? Why not "a number of virgins," some of whom were wise and some were foolish?

Why does the Bible tell us that David picked up five stones on his way to fight with Goliath? (I Samuel 17:40).

Why are there two witnesses in Revelation 11:3? Why not "some" witnesses? Why the redundancy of Revelation 7:9, where the Bible speaks of all nations, and kindreds, and people, and tongues.

Why is the lamb pictured with seven horns and seven eyes in Revelation 5:6? Why not a lamb with several horns and several eyes?

Why does God introduce the terms thirteenth year and twenty-third year in Jeremiah 25:3?

Why was Isaiah to walk naked and barefoot for three years? (Isaiah 20:3). Why not two years or four years or several years?

Just as He uses words like "Lamb of God" to teach spiritual truth, so, too, through the use of numbers He teaches spiritual truth.

We begin to sense that there must be a reason for these numbers. Surely God wants them to be part of the Gospel message. And indeed each one of these numbers is placed in the Bible to enrich the Gospel message. (Just as He uses words like "Lamb of God" to teach spiritual truth, so, too, through the use of numbers He teaches spiritual truth.)

We have seen, therefore, that God frequently uses words and phrases, many times in an allegorical manner, to greatly enrich the spiritual content of the sentences in which these words and phrases are placed. Likewise, God very frequently uses numbers to achieve the same kind of goal. Many times, as we noted earlier, the number is used to give us some idea of size or amount. But frequently the number is given to also give additional spiritual truth that enriches the Gospel message. However, to achieve this goal of obtaining additional truth from numbers, we must carefully study the Bible to discover what they could mean. This is a task that must be performed before the riches in a Bible verse will be realized by the numbers found in the verse.

The procedure for discovering the spiritual meaning of numbers is identical to that which is followed to discover the spiritual meaning of words. As we learned in Chapter 5 of this book, we must discover how the word in question is used throughout the Bible. Likewise, we are to determine if there is a meaning that is a common thread that runs through the verses wherein that number is used.

The Number Three - God's Purpose or Will

For example, we find that the number 3 is used very frequently in the Bible. In connection with the trial and crucifixion of Jesus, it is used repeatedly.

A partial list of these repeated usages of the number 3 is as follows:

1. There were three crosses (Luke 23:33).
2. Peter denied Jesus three times (Matthew 26:34, 75).
3. The inscription placed on the cross, "Jesus of Nazareth, the King of the Jews," was written in three languages (John 19:19-20, Luke 23:38).
4. Jesus prayed three times that this cup might be removed (Matthew 26:39-44).
5. Three disciples went deeper into the garden with Him (Matthew 26:36-37).
6. He was crucified the third hour (Mark 15:25).
7. There was darkness three hours (Mark 15:33).
8. He was three days and three nights in the heart of the earth (Matthew 12:40).
9. Pilate asked the Jews three times, "What evil hath He done?" (Luke 23:22).
10. The sepulchre was made secure until the third day (Matthew 27:64).

The emphasis signified by the use of the number 3 is that of God's purpose or will.

Why does God repeatedly make reference to the number 3 in connection with the atonement? When we carefully examine each of the above references, we find that the emphasis signified by the use of the number 3 is that of God's purpose. It was God's purpose to pour out His wrath on Christ. It was God's purpose that Jesus alone suffered for our sins. It was God's purpose that He was to be crucified so that it would be shown that He had become cursed of God.

Wherever the number 3 is in view, the truth found in the event is enriched because we know that God is emphasizing that it was His purpose to do whatever is recorded in the context in which that number 3 is found.

Indeed, wherever we find the number 3 used anywhere in the Bible, if it signifies spiritual truth, it will be emphasizing God's purpose.

In a similar manner we find that God uses many numbers to illustrate spiritual truth. The following is a list of ways in which God uses numbers in the Bible to signify spiritual truth:

Number 2 signifies the church either as a corporate, external body or as the true believers within the church.

1. Two witnesses (Revelation 11:3).
2. Two olive trees (Revelation 11:4).
3. Two candlesticks (Revelation 11:4).
4. They were sent out two by two (Mark 6:7).

Number 3 signifies the purpose or will of God.

1. The number 3 is tremendously prominent in the atonement - 3 days and nights, 3 crosses, Jesus prayed 3 times, Peter denied Jesus 3 times, etc.
2. Paul prayed 3 times for the removal of the thorn in the flesh (II Corinthians 12:7-8).

Number 4 signifies universality.

1. Points of the compass (Revelation 21:13).
2. Revelation 17:15 (peoples, multitudes, nations, tongues).
3. Revelation 20:8 (nations in the four quarters of the earth).

Number 5 signifies God's grace (salvation or redemption).

1. Matthew 25:2, five wise virgins.
2. Numbers 18:16, five shekels were given as redemption money.
3. The five loaves that fed the five thousand (Matthew 16:9).

Number 5 signifies the judgment of God.

1. The five foolish virgins (Matthew 25:2-12).
2. The five brothers who were still under the judgment of God (Luke 16:28).
3. The five months of Revelation 9:5 signifying God's judgment on the church.

Number 6 signifies work.

1. Creation. "For in six days the Lord made heaven and earth" (Exodus 20:11).
2. Six days work (Exodus 20:9).
3. Six years planting (Exodus 23:10).
4. Christ works to provide for our redemption (Luke 23:44, John 19:14-18).

Number 7 signifies perfection or totality.

1. Seven days of creation.
2. The seven spirits of God (Revelation 5:6).
3. The seven heads of the dragon (Revelation 13:1).
4. The seven churches (Revelation 1:4).

Number 8 signifies redemption or salvation.

1. Babies circumcised on the eighth day (Gen. 17:12).
2. Eight persons in the ark (I Peter 3:20).
3. Jesus was raised on the eighth day. (The first day of the week became the eighth day when added to the previous seven days.)

Number 10 (or 100 or 1000) Signifies the Completeness of Whatever is in View

1. The ten commandments (Exodus 20).
2. The ten virgins (Matthew 25:1).
3. The ten coins (Luke 15:8).
4. The 100 sheep (Luke 15:4).
5. The 1000 years (Revelation 20:1-5).

Number 11 Signifies the Coming of Christ as Savior

1. The eleven brothers will bow down to Joseph who is a type of Christ (Genesis 37:9).
2. The eleven days' journey of Deuteronomy 1:2.
3. The eleven sons of Jacob who were born in Haran but who came with Jacob into Canaan (Genesis 32:22).

Number 12 Signifies the Fullness of Whatever is in View

1. The twelve tribes of Israel (James 1:1).
2. The twelve apostles (Mark 3:14).
3. The holy city Jerusalem has twelve foundations and twelve gates, etc. (Revelation 21:14, 21).

Number 13 Signifies Superfullness or the End of the World

1. While twelve tribes are normally featured, there were in fact thirteen tribes.
2. While twelve apostles are normally featured in the Bible, the Apostle Paul insists that he was an apostle like the others (II Corinthians 12:11-12, I Corinthians 9:1, I Corinthians 15:8-9).
3. Israel went around the walls of Jericho thirteen times before the walls fell (Joshua 6).

Number 17 Signifies Heaven or Salvation

1. Joseph was 17 years old when he had the dream that the members of his family would bow before him. In view of the fact

that Joseph was a type or figure of Christ, this event anticipates heaven when all believers will worship Christ (Gen. 37:2-10).
2. Jacob lived seventeen years in Egypt under the care and keeping of Joseph who as the second ruler of Egypt had saved him from the famine. This event points us to heaven which we obtain when we have come under the care and keeping of Christ forevermore (Genesis 47:28).
3. When Israel was about to go into captivity, Jeremiah was instructed to buy a field in the land of Israel and pay seventeen shekels for it (Jeremiah 32:9). This anticipated the future return of Israel into the land of Israel which in turn is a figure of our entrance into heaven or into salvation (Jeremiah 32:37-38).

Number 23 Signifies Judgment

1. The 2300 days when the temple is trodden under foot which points to the final tribulation period when God is judging the church (Daniel 8:13-14).
2. The 23,000 who were killed in the plague (I Corinthians 10:8).
3. The twenty-three years inclusively which began with the death of the last good king over Judah. His name was Josiah and he was killed in battle in the year 609 B.C. The remaining four kings were very wicked but reigned until 587 B.C. when Judah was completely destroyed by the Babylonians.

Number 37 Signifies Judgment

1. Jehoiachin freed by the king of Babylon in his thirty-seventh year (II Kings 25:27). This event points to the judgment on the church at the end of the world.
2. David, who typifies Christ, had thirty-seven mighty men who fought the enemies of Israel (II Samuel 23:39). These thirty-seven men typify the believers as they bring the Gospel which emphasizes that man is under judgment and who with Christ will judge the world at the end of time.
3. The number of man - 666 - equals 3 x 6 x 37. This signifies spiritually that it is God's purpose (3) that those who work (6) to get right with God (this includes everyone who is not saved), will come into judgment (37).

4. Noah and his family were in the ark 370 days (Genesis 7:11, 24; 8:4, 14-18). This is 10 x 37. It signifies that they remained in the safety of the ark until God's judgment (37) upon the earth had been completed (10). Or we could say: Because they were in the safety of the ark, they completely (10) escaped the judgment (37) of God.
5. 185,000 Assyrians who assaulted Judah in Hezekiah's reign were killed by God in one night (II Kings 19:35). 185,000 = 5 x 37 x 10 x 10 x 10. This signifies God's complete (10 x 10) judgment (37) upon the wicked who come against God's kingdom, which consists of those who are completely (10) saved (5).

Number 40 - Testing

1. Israel was forty years in the wilderness as God tested them whether they would obey Him (Deuteronomy 8:2-3, 15-16).
2. Jesus was forty days in the wilderness being tested (Luke 4:2).
3. Jesus remained on earth forty days before His ascension. This signifies a test for mankind as to whether they will believe on Him as the risen Christ (Acts 1:3).

We might note that in the foregoing list of numbers, we skipped over many numbers. These numbers can be divided into two groups.

The first group is made up of numbers that in themselves do not readily show spiritual truth. But when they are broken down to their prime numbers, by means of the spiritual truth latent within each prime number, the spiritual message (if any is intended by it), is revealed. These numbers are:

$$9 = 3 \times 3, \ 14 = 2 \times 7, \ 15 = 5 \times 3, \ 16 = 4 \times 4, \ 18$$
$$= 2 \times 3 \times 3, \ 20 = 2 \times 10, \ 21 = 3 \times 7, \ 22 = 2 \times 11,$$
$$24 = 2 \times 12, \ 25 = 5 \times 5, \ 26 = 2 \times 13, \ 27 = 3 \times 3$$
$$\times 3, \ 28 = 2 \times 2 \times 7, \ 30 = 3 \times 10, \ 32 = 2 \times 4 \times 4,$$
$$33 = 3 \times 11, \ 34 = 2 \times 17, \ 35 = 5 \times 7, \ \text{etc.}$$

The second group of numbers are in themselves prime numbers but at present sufficient Biblical information has not been found to understand their spiritual meaning (if any has been intended by God). These numbers are 19, 29, 31, 41, etc.

The Generation of Jacob

A remarkable and interesting illustration of God's use of numbers in the Bible is found in Genesis 37. In Genesis 37:2, God records:

> These are the generations of Jacob. Joseph, being seventeen years old, was feeding the flock with his brethren; and the lad was with the sons of Bilhah, and with the sons of Zilpah, his father's wives: and Joseph brought unto his father their evil report.

This verse is followed by further focus on Joseph as he dreams two dreams. In the first dream, his eleven brothers bow down to him. In the second dream, not only his eleven brothers but also his father and mother bow down before him. These events are recorded in verses 6-10, which declare:

> And he said unto them, Hear, I pray you, this dream which I have dreamed: For, behold, we were binding sheaves in the field, and, lo, my sheaf arose, and also stood upright; and, behold, your sheaves stood round about, and made obeisance to my sheaf. And his brethren said to him, Shalt thou indeed reign over us? or shalt thou indeed have dominion over us? And they hated him yet the more for his dreams, and for his words. And he dreamed yet another dream, and told it his brethren, and said, Behold, I have dreamed a dream more; and, behold, the sun and the moon and the eleven stars made obeisance to me. And he told it to his father, and to his brethren: and his father rebuked him, and said unto him, What is this dream that thou hast dreamed? Shall I and thy mother and thy brethren indeed come to bow down ourselves to thee to the earth?

This whole chapter is very strange because it is introduced as being the record of the generations of Jacob, yet it sets forth the experiences of one son, Joseph.

This whole chapter is very strange because it is introduced as being the record of the generations of Jacob, yet it sets forth the experiences of one son, Joseph. If it were truly speaking of the generations of Jacob, a list of sons and grandsons would appear in the rest of the chapter. This is done, for example, in Genesis 5:1, where God speaks of the generations of Adam. In the verses that follow Genesis 5:1, God records the descendants of Adam. Likewise, in Genesis 10:1, God speaks of the generations of the sons of Noah, and then He follows that with a list of Noah's descendants.

In a similar manner in Genesis 11:10, God speaks of the generations of Shem and then follows with a list of the descendants of Shem.

But Genesis 37:2 speaks of the generations of Jacob but no list of descendants of Jacob follows. Instead, the Bible records that when Joseph was seventeen years old, he dreamed two dreams in which it is shown that he is to be ruler over his family. What a strange follow-up on the generations of Jacob. Joseph was not the first son, and he was not the son from whom Christ descended. He was the eleventh son. But what did he have to do with the generations of Jacob?

The mystery is solved when we remember that the Bible was written with many parables - earthly stories with heavenly or spiritual meanings. It is obvious that this chapter is parabolic in nature because we must find spiritual meaning to satisfy the introduction of the chapter, where we find the words, "These are the generations of Jacob."

In the opening verses of Chapter 37, God has featured Jacob, who, we know from other Bible references, fathered twelve sons. Additionally, God teaches us that 17-year-old Joseph, who, we know from other Bible references, was the eleventh son, had two dreams. In one of his dreams the eleven brothers of Joseph, typified by sheaves of grain, bow down to him. In the second dream his eleven brothers, typified by stars, together with his father and mother, typified by the sun and the moon, bow down to him. How can we find the Gospel in all of this?

To begin, let us look at Jacob. In the Bible, Jacob is sometimes used as a picture of Christ, sometimes as a picture of the external, corporate body of believers, and sometimes as a representative of the elect of God - those who become true believers. In Romans 9:11-13, God speaks of Jacob as the elect of God. We read:

(For the children being not yet born, neither having done any good or evil, that the purpose of God according to election might stand, not of works, but of him that calleth;) It was said unto her, The elder shall serve the younger. As it is written, Jacob have I loved, but Esau have I hated.

In Deuteronomy 32:8-9, God declares:

When the Most High divided to the nations their inheritance, when he separated the sons of Adam, he set the bounds of the people according to the number of the children of Israel. For the LORD'S portion is his people; Jacob is the lot of his inheritance.

In these verses, God emphasizes that "Jacob is the lot [or line] of His inheritance." That is, the children of Israel who are to receive the inheritance are in the line of Jacob. Those who receive the inheritance are the elect of God. We, therefore, must understand that in the Genesis 37 account, Jacob represents the elect of God. We can paraphrase Genesis 37:2 by the words "these are the generations of the elect (Jacob) of God."

Whom Does Joseph Represent?

We next look at Joseph. In his dreams, his family members bowed down to him. Therefore, he must be a picture of Christ. Many of Joseph's experiences qualify him as a type or representative of Christ, and we will see that the verses we are presently examining certainly certify this.

Joseph was 17 years old. We know that the number 17, if it has any spiritual meaning, signifies heaven or salvation. Thus, Joseph at 17 years of age represents that salvation that Christ brings.

In Joseph's first dream, his brothers bowed down before him. His brothers are represented by sheaves of grain, indicating that they have been harvested. Remember, Jesus declares in John 4:35, "look on the fields; for they are white already to harvest," and He tells us to pray that the Lord would send forth reapers in Matthew 9:38: "Pray ye therefore the Lord of the harvest, that he will send forth labourers into his harvest."

> *The eleven brothers typified by sheaves of grain point to those who have become saved because Christ would come as the Savior.*

This verse speaks of God's plan to save people. Those who are harvested are those who have become saved. They bow down to Christ because He has become the Lord and King of their lives. Thus, the eleven brothers typified by sheaves of grain point to those who have become saved because Christ would come as the Savior.

The number eleven is featured in view of the fact that Joseph had eleven brothers who bowed down to him. The number eleven is also featured by the fact that Joseph was the eleventh son of Jacob. We have learned that the number eleven, if it has spiritual meaning, signifies the first coming of Christ when He came as Savior almost exactly 11,000 years after creation. As we have seen, the sheaves of grain also point to Christ coming as Savior to bring in the harvest of believers.

In the second dream, the eleven brothers are typified by stars. In Daniel 12:2-3, we read that believers will shine as the stars forever and ever:

> And many of them that sleep in the dust of the earth shall awake, some to everlasting life, and some to shame and everlasting contempt. And they that be wise shall shine as the brightness of the firmament; and they that turn many to righteousness as the stars for ever and ever.

Note that in this reference found in Daniel 12, they are identified with stars immediately after God declares that those who sleep in the dust of the earth shall awake to everlasting life. Thus, the stars point us to the end of the world when the believers are given their glorified spiritual bodies. The fact that the stars bowed down to Joseph again indicates that forevermore Christ is Lord and King of our lives.

> *There are exactly 13,000 years from creation to the beginning of the final tribulation period, at which time God's judgment of the world begins as He first brings judgment on the church.*

In the second dream, the number 13 is featured in view of the fact that his eleven brothers and his father and mother bowed down to him. Thus, the total number bowing down is eleven plus two which equals thirteen. We know the number 13 signifies the second coming of Christ. This is so because there are exactly 13,000 years from creation to the beginning of the final tribulation period, at which time God's judgment of the world begins as He first brings judgment on the church. As we have seen, the figure of stars also points to the end of the world.

Bringing all of these factors into consideration, we can know why God heads up these verses by indicating "these are the generations of Jacob." We can paraphrase this sentence of Genesis 37:2 by the language, "these are the generations of the elect, the ones God has chosen from before the foundations of the world to become saved." This spiritual genealogical line must begin with Christ who brings salvation (Joseph who is 17 years old).

Christ came in fulness of time 11,000 years after creation (Joseph was the eleventh son), to save His spiritual children (those who have and will become saved). They will worship Him and bow down to Him. They are represented by the eleven brothers of the first dream.

When Christ comes at the end of the world, all of His spiritual descendants from the entire 13,000 years of the earth's history, will worship Him. This is represented by Joseph's eleven brothers and father and mother bowing down to him.

> *Thus, we learn that the numbers 11, 13, and 17, which were either stated or implied in Genesis 37, greatly enrich the Gospel message brought forth in these verses.*

Thus, we learn that the numbers 11, 13, and 17, which were either stated or implied in Genesis 37, greatly enrich the Gospel message brought forth in these verses. Not only do they enhance the spiritual message but they greatly assist us in seeing the Gospel message hidden in the Biblical account. Thus, we are greatly encouraged to examine every number in the Bible with great care in order to obtain the teaching that God is bringing forth by use of those numbers.

How Are We to Understand Large Numbers?

But now we come to another question. What about numbers in the Bible that are found only once and yet they are in a very significant context? We immediately think of numbers such as the 153 fish of John 21:11 and the 276 men who were shipwrecked in Acts 27:37. How are we to understand these numbers? Surely they must have spiritual meaning, just as the numbers we examined in Genesis 37 definitely have spiritual meaning. Significantly, the 153 fish are the complete total of all the fish caught in the net; and the 276 men are the complete total of all who were on the ship that was destroyed. Are they then to be understood as representing the fulness of whatever is in view even as the number 12 signifies fulness?

In Revelation 21:12-13, God gives us an illustration of a larger number that is broken down to two smaller numbers:

> And had a wall great and high, and had twelve gates, and at the gates twelve angels, and names written thereon, which are the names of the twelve tribes of the children of Israel: On the east three gates; on the north three gates; on the south three gates; and on the west three gates.

In this example, the number 12 signifies fulness. The twelve tribes of the children of Israel would signify the fulness of all believers. The twelve gates signify the fulness of Christ as He provides our salvation. Remember, Jesus says in John 10:9: "I am the door: by me if any man enter in, he shall be saved, and shall go in and out, and find pasture." Thus, a door or a gate must signify Christ.

But the twelve gates are broken down to four sets of three. The number 4 signifies universality and the number 3 signifies purpose.

Thus, God is teaching us that it is the purpose of God (3) that the believers come from the whole world (4). Thereby we have the fulness of all believers.

> *God is surely teaching us that we can discover the spiritual riches of numbers by breaking them down into prime and/or significant numbers.*

By this example, God is surely teaching us that we can discover the spiritual riches of numbers by breaking them down into prime and/ or significant numbers. A prime number is one that is not divisible by any number other than by itself or the number 1. In the above illustration, the number 4 is not a prime number because it is divisible by the number 2. But the number 4 is a significant number because it signifies universality or worldwide. The number 3 is a prime number because it cannot be broken down any further.

In Revelation 21:17, the Bible speaks of a wall that is 144 cubits. Curiously, it does not say which dimension is given. We could never build the wall because we cannot tell if it is to be 144 cubits long, 144 cubits high, or 144 cubits wide. We do know, however, that God frequently uses the word "wall" to signify believers. Nehemiah, for example, took 52 days to build the wall of Jerusalem (Nehemiah 6:15), which typified the building of the whole body of Christ. We also know that the number 12 is used repeatedly in the Bible to signify fulness. For example, we have just seen that the wall had twelve gates (Revelation 21:12) and twelve foundations (Revelations 21:14). Moreover, the size of the wall was 144 cubits, which can be broken down to 12 x 12. Thus, the fact that the wall was 144 cubits in size is definitely giving us the information that it represented the fulness of all believers typified by the twelve tribes of Israel (verse 12) and by the twelve apostles (verse 14). These two verses read as follows:

> Revelation 21:12: And had a wall great and high, and had twelve gates, and at the gates twelve angels, and names written thereon, which are the names of the twelve tribes of the children of Israel.

Revelation 21:14: And the wall of the city had twelve foundations, and in them the names of the twelve apostles of the Lamb.

Thus, we have learned that by breaking down the larger number
144 into two significant numbers, 12 x 12, the 144 cubits of verse 17
greatly enriches that verse by indicating that this wall, which measured
144 cubits, represented the fulness of all believers in Christ.

If we apply the same principle, of breaking down a larger
number to its significant or prime numbers, to the 153 fish of John
21:11, we find that:

$$153 = 3 \times 3 \times 17.$$

The number 3 signifies purpose whereas the number 17
signifies heaven or salvation. Since Jesus told His disciples, "I will make
you fishers of men" (Matthew 4:19), we can understand that the 153
large fish caught in the net signify all those who will become saved. That
is, it signifies that the purpose of God (3) is to bring all those caught
in the net of the Gospel to heaven or to salvation (17).

---

*The number 153, when broken down to its prime
numbers 3 and 17, greatly enhances and enriches
the spiritual message taught by the catching of
the 153 fish.*

Therefore, the number 153, when broken down to its prime
numbers 3 and 17, greatly enhances and enriches the spiritual message
taught by the catching of the 153 fish.

Likewise, in Acts 27 God uses the number 276 which enumer-
ates every person aboard the ship that was wrecked and who were all
saved. We find that the number 276 breaks down to 12 x 23 or 3 x 4
x 23 or 3 x 2 x 2 x 23.

The number 2 signifies the church (either as it exists as a
congregation or as the true believers within the external
church).
The number 3 signifies purpose.

The number 4 signifies universality.
The number 12 signifies fulness.
The number 23 signifies judgment.

We learned in the book *1994?* that the ship that was wrecked represented the church that is under judgment during the final tribulation period. The men who were saved represent the fact that all of the true believers within the church are safe even though their congregations have become apostate.

Thus, the number 12 x 23, or 276, adds the emphasis that the fulness (12) of all true believers within an apostate congregation which has come under the judgment of God during the final tribulation period cannot lose their salvation as God is judging (23) the church.

If the number 276 is broken down to 4 x 3 x 23, we find that the added spiritual emphasis given by the number 276 is that it is the purpose of God (3) that believers who are found throughout the world (4) do not lose their salvation when the church is judged (23).

If the number 276 is broken down to 2 x 2 x 3 x 23, we find that the added spiritual emphasis given by the number 276 is that it is the purpose of God (3) that the true believers (2) who are in the corporate or external church (2) that is under God's judgment (23) during the final tribulation, will be safe.

We know, of course, that God could have declared simply that not one of the many men aboard the wrecked ship lost his life. That would have given us the main message that is being given to us by this account. But as we have just learned, the addition of the number 276 has greatly enhanced and enriched the message given in this account.

The Rebellion of Korah, Dathan, and Abiram

Another account that beautifully illustrates the principle that God frequently introduces numbers into the Biblical account is found in the Book of Numbers. Israel was in the wilderness under the leadership of Moses. But in Numbers 16 we read of rebellion against Moses that was headed up by three men, Korah, Dathan, and Abiram. We read in Numbers 16:2-3:

And they rose up before Moses, with certain of the children of Israel, two hundred and fifty princes of the assembly, famous in the congregation, men of renown: And they gathered themselves together against Moses and against Aaron, and said unto them, Ye take too much upon you, seeing all the congregation are holy, every one of them, and the LORD is among them: wherefore then lift ye up yourselves above the congregation of the LORD?

The consequences of this rebellion was the opening of the earth to swallow the families of these three men and the destruction by fire of the 250 men who rebelled. In Numbers 16:35, we read:

And there came out a fire from the LORD, and consumed the two hundred and fifty men that offered incense.

However, the next day the Israelites complained to God, in Numbers 16:41:

But on the morrow all the congregation of the children of Israel murmured against Moses and against Aaron, saying, Ye have killed the people of the LORD.

As a result of this added rebellion on the part of Israel, God sent a plague into Israel that began to kill the Israelites in great numbers. Only the timely intervention of Aaron in making an atonement for Israel kept God from killing all of Israel. We read of this terrible judgment and its remedy in the language of Numbers 16:45-48:

Get you up from among this congregation, that I may consume them as in a moment. And they fell upon their faces. And Moses said unto Aaron, Take a censer, and put fire therein from off the altar, and put on incense, and go quickly unto the congregation, and make an atonement for them: for there is wrath gone out from the LORD; the plague is begun. And Aaron took as Moses commanded, and ran into the midst of the congregation; and, behold, the plague was begun among the people: and he put on incense, and made an atonement for the people. And he stood between the dead and the living; and the plague was stayed.

> *The fire that came down and destroyed the 250 men is pointing to the judgment of God that will destroy all of the unsaved.*

In this account, rebellious Israel is representative of all of mankind who have rebelled against God. The plague that killed a great many of the Israelites and the fire that came down and destroyed the 250 men are pointing to the judgment of God that will destroy all of the unsaved. The atonement offered by Aaron as well as Aaron himself, as he stood between the dead and the living, represent Christ Himself who stopped the wrath of God from falling on all those for whom He made atonement. Thus, we see much of the Gospel of salvation in this account.

But Numbers 16:49 adds one more important piece of information. We read:

> Now they that died in the plague were fourteen thousand and seven hundred, beside them that died about the matter of Korah.

Why did God give us this information? Why didn't He simply declare that a great number of people died in the plague? Why did He number the princes of the people who rebelled against Moses and were killed by fire from heaven? Why does He bring these two numbers together in verse 49?

Let us see what the result is when we add the 14,700 who died in the plague to the 250 men who died by fire coming from heaven. The sum of these two numbers is 14,950. Does this number help us to learn anything? Indeed it does when we break it down to its prime or significant numbers. We discover:

$$14,950 = 5 \times 10 \times 13 \times 23.$$

Remember:

    5 signifies salvation or judgment
    10 signifies completeness
    13 signifies the end of the world
    23 signifies judgment

We know, too, that fire from heaven signifies the judgment of God that is to come on the unsaved at the end of the world. We read in Revelation 20:9:

> And they went up on the breadth of the earth, and compassed the camp of the saints about, and the beloved city: and fire came down from God out of heaven, and devoured them.

This verse is emphasizing God's final judgment on the enemies of God (the unsaved) as they are cast into hellfire on the last day. In Revelation 22:18 God warns of judgment utilizing the word "plagues":

> For I testify unto every man that heareth the words of the prophecy of this book, If any man shall add unto these things, God shall add unto him the plagues that are written in this book.

Thus, by the word "plague" and by the word "fire" God is indicating that the 14,950 people who are numbered in this Numbers account are a picture of those who will endure the judgment of God on the last day. But this truth is also reinforced by the use of the number 14,950 which can be broken down to $5 \times 10 \times 13 \times 23$. We can write the spiritual emphasis being made by the sentence: Those who rebel against God are under the judgment (5) of God and will experience the complete (10) judgment (23) of God at the end of the world (13).

By giving the number 14,700 and the number 250, God has greatly enriched this account by indicating that the complete judgment of God will come upon the wicked at the end of the world.

Obviously, God could have declared simply that a great many men rebelled against God and fire from heaven came upon them and destroyed them. Likewise, He could have stated simply that a large number of Israelites were killed in the plague. We surely would have received the message. But by giving the number 14,700 and the number 250, God has greatly enriched this account by indicating that the complete judgment of God will come upon the wicked at the end of the world.

The Number 37 and Noah's Flood

The account of the flood of Noah's day offers a very excellent example of the use of a larger number which when broken down to its prime numbers enriches the Gospel message. We read in Genesis 5:30 that "Lamech lived after he begat Noah five hundred ninety and five years, and begat sons and daughters." Because verse 29 indicates that Lamech "called his name Noah," we are assured that Noah was an immediate son of Lamech. Since Noah was 600 years of age when the flood began (Genesis 7:11), we know that Lamech died five years before the flood.

> *Why did God arrange the sequence of events so that Lamech would die just five years before the flood?*

The interesting fact is that Lamech was 777 years old when he died (Genesis 5:31). Why did God arrange the sequence of events so that Lamech would die just five years before the flood? And why did God take him in death at the age of 777 years? All of this could be coincidental. But on the other hand, it may be information that further enhances the Gospel account.

The number 777 breaks down into three very significant prime numbers: $3 \times 7 \times 37 = 777$. Thus, we have in view four important prime numbers:

    3 = purpose or will of God
    7 = perfection
    37 = judgment
    5 = judgment or salvation

By the time Lamech died, the ark must have been well along in construction. God had told Lamech's son, Noah, that He was going to destroy the world with the flood. The ark that Noah was building would provide salvation for those within it. By use of the above numbers, the message is further developed.

It is God's perfect (7) purpose (3) that judgment (37) would come but salvation (5) would be provided for those who trusted God.

Another use of the number 37 to emphasize judgment is vividly in view when we examine the duration of the flood. In Genesis 7:11 God indicates that the flood began "In the six hundredth year of Noah's life, in the second month, the seventeenth day of the month." In Genesis 8:3-4 God further informs us that "after the end of the hundred and fifty days the waters were abated. And the ark rested in the seventh month, on the seventeenth day of the month, upon the mountains of Ararat."

Thus, we know that in Noah's day, each month consisted of thirty days. Consequently, a year would have been 360 days.

Exactly five months by Noah's calendar had elapsed which equalled 150 days. Thus, we know that in Noah's day, each month consisted of thirty days. Consequently, a year would have been 360 days. Obviously, from time to time, an adjustment would have been required because the actual year was about 365¼ days as it is in our day. We make an adjustment every four years by adding a day in February. This is because our calendar's year is 365 days whereas the actual year is 365¼ days.

But then we read something very strange. In Genesis 8:13 we read:

> And it came to pass in the six hundredth and first year, in the first month, the first day of the month, the waters were dried up from off the earth: and Noah removed the covering of the ark, and looked, and, behold, the face of the ground was dry.

Since the face of the earth was dry one would think that Noah would come out of the ark immediately. He and his family had been in the ark for more than ten months. Certainly with all the animals aboard, the ark was plenty uncomfortable. One has no difficulty imagining the smell.

But amazingly God kept Noah in the ark for almost an additional two months. We read in Genesis 8:14-16:

> And in the second month, on the seven and twentieth day of the month, was the earth dried. And God spake unto Noah, saying, Go forth of the ark, thou, and thy wife, and thy sons, and thy sons' wives with thee.

The 27th day of the second month was one year and ten days after the flood began. And Genesis 7:12-13 tells us that it was on the that self-same day that Noah entered the ark:

> And the rain was upon the earth forty days and forty nights. In the selfsame day entered Noah, and Shem, and Ham, and Japheth, the sons of Noah, and Noah's wife, and the three wives of his sons with them, into the ark.

However, when we add ten days to Noah's calendar year of 360 days, we see the meticulous planning of God. God shut the door of the ark the day the flood waters began (Genesis 7:16). Exactly 360 plus ten days later, God commanded Noah to leave the ark. The number 370, which is the sum of 360 + 10, is made of two very important numbers.

$$370 = 10 \times 37.$$

Remember, 10 is the number that signifies completion.
Remember, 37 is the number that signifies judgment.

Thus, God is surely emphasizing that God saved Noah and his family from the complete (10) judgment God brought against the world of that day.

> *God deliberately kept Noah and his family in the ark an extra long time so that the number 37 would be prominently featured.*

We cannot help but see that God deliberately kept Noah and his family in the ark an extra long time so that the number 37 would be prominently featured, even as God took Noah's father, Lamech, in the 777th year of his life so that the number 37 would be featured. Because the number 37 signifies judgment, God used these means to underscore the awful fact of God's judgment.

The Number 666 and God's Judgment

While we are looking at the number 37, we might look once more at the number 666 recorded in Revelation 13:17-18. There we read:

> And that no man might buy or sell, save he that had the mark, or the name of the beast, or the number of his name. Here is wisdom. Let him that hath understanding count the number of the beast: for it is the number of a man; and his number is Six hundred threescore and six.

Heretofore, I have associated the number 666 with the fraction two-thirds, spoken of in Zechariah 13:8. There God divides the human race into two parts: one-third and two-thirds. The number one-third clearly relates to those who have become saved, and the number two-thirds to those who remain under God's wrath.

If two-thirds is written as a decimal, it is the number .66666 . . . . If only the first three numbers are written and multiplied by a thousand, which signifies completeness, it becomes 666.

But now that we have learned that 37 is a number signifying judgment, a great additional truth can be seen in the number 666. If we break it down into significant numbers we find that:

$$3 \times 6 \times 37 = 666.$$

> *In their rebellion and pride, every idea fostered in man's mind includes the concept that man must do something himself to be right with God.*

Remember, 6 is a number that signifies work. It points to those who are working for their salvation. That includes each and every human being who is not saved. By nature, because they were created in the image of God, they want somehow to become right with God. But in their rebellion and pride, every idea fostered in man's mind includes the concept that man must do something himself to be right with God. He must live in such a way or do such a thing that God will recognize their worthiness and save them.

These are the ones who have the number 666. And this number signifies that it is God's purpose or will (3) to bring to judgment (37) all those who are trusting in their own works (6) to become saved.

By these examples we have learned that the numbers given in the Bible are very important. They add to and enrich the Gospel message just as surely as words and phrases in the Bible add to and enrich the Gospel message. Therefore, whenever we see a number in the Bible it is a true Biblical principle to ask the question: Why did God give us that number? What spiritual truth is being conveyed by it? Can I find the meaning of this number that is in harmony with everything else God teaches us about salvation?

But now another question must be asked: Since God has given sufficient information so that we can reconstruct the calendar of history, how is the Gospel message enhanced and enriched by the numbers that describe the passage of time? We will look at this question in the next chapter.

Chapter 8
Numbers that Describe
Time Paths

We have thus far learned in this study that every word in the Bible is God-breathed and, therefore, important in conveying the Gospel message. Some of the words or phrases and even whole chapters are allegorical in nature so that we must search the whole Bible to discover the spiritual meaning taught by these words or phrases.

We have discovered that this is also true of the numbers in the Bible. Numbers frequently are written to convey chronological information. Sometimes we do not know why they are given. Sometimes they are used to teach spiritual information. Thus, the number 2 frequently signifies the church or the true believers within the church. The number 3, purpose. The number 4, universality, etc.

We have also learned the larger numbers frequently can be broken down to their significant or prime numbers. The spiritual meaning of these smaller numbers in turn conveys additional spiritual meaning to the passage in which the larger number is found.

As we continue our study of the Bible, we will find that the time paths from significant historical events to Christ's first coming or to His second coming may have great spiritual meaning. When the total number of years between the event in question and the first or second coming of Christ is broken down to its significant or prime numbers, and the spiritual meaning inherent within these significant or prime numbers is applied to the passage in which the larger number is found, the Gospel is enriched and enhanced. At the same time, this is further evidence that the historic years of Jesus' birth and crucifixion are accurate. And they also give further evidence that the year A.D. 1988 indeed must be the year when the final tribulation did begin, and the year A.D. 1994 must be the year of Christ's return.

In the book *1994?*, we discovered that there are many paths that focus on the year 1994 as the highly probable year in which the end of the world will come. Since that book was published, additional time paths have been discovered from Biblical data. In this follow-up to

1994?, I would like to detail three of these paths and then briefly outline many other paths of the same nature.

Terah: The Father of Abraham

The first path that we will examine in detail begins with the birth of Terah, the father of Abraham. When we examine the Biblical evidence concerning Terah, we find little information and, at first glance, what is given does not relate to God's salvation plan in any meaningful way. The following are all pertinent facts about Terah that can be found in the Bible.

1. He was born in the year 2297 B.C.

2. He lived most of his life in Ur of the Chaldees (Joshua 24:2).

3. While there is evidence that he and two of his sons did become believers, the Bible also records that he worshipped other gods (Joshua 24:2).

4. At the age of 70, he fathered three sons, Nahor, Haran, and Abram (Genesis 11:26).

5. Haran died in Ur of the Chaldees (Genesis 11:28) without any evidence of having become a believer.

6. Nahor left Ur of the Chaldees and lived in Haran, being the grandfather of Rebekah whom Isaac married. He like his father Terah never entered the land of Canaan.

7. Abram was born when Terah was 130 years of age (Genesis 11:32, Genesis 12:4).

8. Terah moved to Haran, where he died at the age of 205 (Genesis 11:31-32).

9. Terah, Nahor, and Haran lived on the other side of the flood (Joshua 24:2).

> *Terah is a representative of the world that never enters the kingdom of God.*

When we examine this information very carefully, we can see that Terah never came into the land of Canaan. Thus, Terah was a representative of the world that never enters the kingdom of God. The world serves other gods. The world is on the other side of the flood; that is, they (the unsaved) have not crossed the Jordan River into the promised land, Canaan, which signifies the kingdom of God. In these passages, the word flood signifies hell, which we must cross to get into the kingdom of God.

Because Jesus has taken upon Himself the sins of the believers and endured the wrath of God on behalf of those believers, it means they have crossed over the flood, which is a word like the Jordan River and the Red Sea, that represents hell. Of the family of Terah, only Abraham crossed over the flood, that is, is a representative of those who become saved.

The fact that the Bible records that Terah bore three sons at the age of 70 years (Genesis 11:26), emphasizes the perfection - number 7 - and the completeness - number 10 - (7 x 10 = 70) of the progeny of Terah as representative of the human race.

The Unsaved Are Signified by the Number Two-Thirds

In Zechariah 13:8-9, God symbolically divides the whole human race into two groups - one of the groups equals two parts and is unsaved. They will be cut off and die. One-third shall be refined by fire and will become the people of God.

Zechariah 13:8-9: And it shall come to pass, that in all the land, saith the LORD, two parts therein shall be cut off and die; but the third shall be left therein. And I will bring the third part through the fire, and will refine them as silver is refined, and will try them as gold is tried: they shall call on my name, and I will hear them: I will say, It is my people: and they shall say, The LORD is my God.

> *Christ has redeemed the one-third by enduring Hell on their behalf.*

To be refined by fire is equivalent to going over the flood or through the river. Both the flood and the river signify Hell, which we must endure as payment for our sins. This must be paid before we can go into heaven. Christ, the Savior, has been the substitute or stand-in in paying the penalty for believers. Thus, it signifies that Christ has redeemed the one-third by enduring Hell on their behalf.

Returning to Terah, we see, therefore, that this man, who served other gods, who never crossed the flood in God's perfect and complete plan, had three sons: two-thirds remained outside of Canaan and, therefore, are a picture of those who are subject to hell. But Abraham who equals one-third of the sons did enter Canaan and, therefore, is a picture of those who have become saved.

We note next that Abraham was born when Terah was 130 years of age. We know this because Terah was 205 when he died in Haran and Abraham was 75 years old when he left Haran to go to Canaan. Because of the tremendous obedience displayed by Abraham in leaving his homeland, Ur of the Chaldees, to go to Canaan, it leaves us no choice but to believe that as soon as his father died in Haran (Genesis 11:32), Abraham would immediately leave Haran to continue to go to the land of Canaan.

Genesis 12:1 records:

Now the LORD had said unto Abram, Get thee out of thy country, and from thy kindred, and from thy father's house, unto a land that I will shew thee.

Genesis 12:4 continues:

So Abram departed, as the LORD had spoken unto him; and Lot went with him: and Abram was seventy and five years old when he departed out of Haran.

The language, "So Abram departed, as the LORD had spoken unto him," assures us that Terah was 130 years old when Abram was born. We will look at the spiritual implication of this 130 presently.

We are thus looking at the timetable of the whole human race.

First, let us note the year that Terah was born was 2297 B.C. Please see the book *1994?* for the proof of this. Because Terah was so clearly a picture of the whole human race, which throughout its history gives birth to the two-thirds who remain unbelievers, and the one-third who become believers, the year 2297 B.C. in a real sense is like the beginning of time. Effectively, we are thus looking at the timetable of the whole human race. (Incidentally, remember the two-thirds and the one-third symbolize unbelievers and believers, respectively, and are in no way to be considered actual numbers of people who are saved or unsaved.)

Because the whole human race appears to be in view and because we have found so much information that focuses on the year 1994 as the end of the world (see *1994?*), we wonder how many years after the birth of Terah does A.D. 1994 come? This is easily figured. Remember, we are to add the Old Testament years to the New Testament years and then, because there is no year 0, we are to subtract one year to obtain the actual number of years between two events. Thus:

$$2297 + 1994 - 1 = 4290 \text{ years.}$$

But what is spiritually significant about 4290 years? What have we learned because of this computation?

What Biblical validation do we have that permits us to even seek spiritual truth from the fact that 4290 years elapsed between the birth of Terah and the end of the world?

In fact, what Biblical validation do we have that permits us to even seek spiritual truth from the fact that 4290 years elapsed between the birth of Terah and the end of the world? This is a most important question because if it can be shown that such a procedure is entirely justified by Biblical validation, it will open up the possibility of a great amount of Biblical corroboration to the year A.D. 1988 as the beginning of the final tribulation and A.D. 1994 as the last year of the history of the world.

If, however, such a procedure cannot be adequately justified by the Bible, it will in no way weaken any or all of the paths that were set forth in the book *1994?*, which demonstrate very clearly the extremely high likelihood that these years are certain and sure as the end of the world.

Therefore, we have much to gain and nothing to lose by carefully examining this question.

As we will learn, however, we indeed have Biblical validation to look for the spiritual truth that is inherent within the elapsed years between Terah's birth and the year that ends the world.

The Birth of Terah and the End of the World Are Spiritually Interrelated

As we have already learned, there exists an intimate relationship between the birth of Terah and the end of the world. Remember, we discovered that Terah is a picture of the entire human race. His son Abraham, who entered the land of Canaan, is a figure of all the believers who will trust in Christ as Savior. In fact, in Romans 4, God speaks of him as being the father of all believers.

Remember, we learned that Terah's other two sons who never entered the land of Canaan, a figure of the kingdom of God, are a picture of that part of the human race who never do become saved. They represent the two-thirds of Zechariah 13:8 or those who have the number 666 of Revelation 13:18.

> *There definitely is a relationship between Terah's birth and the end of the world.*

The whole human race represents every person born into this world right up to the end of the world. Therefore, Terah is intimately related to the end of the world. There definitely is a relationship between Terah's birth and the end of the world.

The Years of Terah's Birth and the End of the World Are Derived from the Bible

The year 2297 B.C. in which Terah was born was very carefully calculated from Biblical data. As we learned in the book *1994?*, God has given us sufficient time information so that we can very accurately reconstruct the calendar of history.

Likewise, we have learned that the Bible offers a great amount of information which when properly understood allows us to project the calendar to the end of the world.

Thus, when we are examining the elapsed time between the birth of Terah and the end of the world, we can know that our information has come from the Bible. We also know that any information we can learn from the Bible is given for our enlightenment. It further enriches the Gospel God has so wonderfully set forth in the Bible.

> *Therefore, we can be very comfortable in trying to learn additional spiritual truth from the number of years between Terah's birth and the end of the world.*

Therefore, we can be very comfortable in trying to learn additional spiritual truth from the number of years between Terah's birth and the end of the world.

The Elapsed Time between the Birth of Terah and the End of the World Is a Revelation from God

When God wrote in Joshua 6 that Israel was to march around Jericho once a day for six days and then seven times on the seventh day, He did not say that this made a total of thirteen times. Yet we can certainly know that God has revealed to us that they marched around the city thirteen times.

When Joseph's eleven brothers, typified by stars, and his father and mother, typified by the sun and the moon, bowed down to him, God never added this all together so that we know there were a total of thirteen individuals bowing to him. Yet we can be quite certain that God is giving us revelation including the number thirteen.

Likewise, if we have done our work accurately in discovering from Biblical data the year 2297 B.C. as the year Terah was born and the year A.D. 1994 as the year of the end of the world, then we may also believe that God has revealed to us the 4290 years from Terah's birth to the end of the world.

> *Since these 4290 years are derived from the Bible,*
> *we can confidently examine them to see if*
> *additional truth can be found in this number.*

Since these 4290 years are derived from the Bible, we can confidently examine them to see if additional truth can be found in this number.

Please note! I indicated, "if we have done our work accurately." If we have made a mistake in reconstructing the calendar showing Terah to be born in 2297 B.C. or if we have made an error in projecting the calendar to A.D. 1994, then obviously the 4290 years between Terah's birth and the end of the world is also in error.

The Years from Terah's Birth to the End of the World Can Be Broken Down to Very Significant Numbers that Signify Spiritual Truth

As we learned earlier in our study, certain numbers can convey rich spiritual truth. In analyzing large numbers, we discovered that sometimes they can be broken down to smaller numbers that have spiritual meaning. By this means, the Gospel message hidden within the larger number is revealed.

On the other hand, if a number cannot be broken down to significant smaller numbers, then we should not look for spiritual truth within that number. For example, the number 581 can be broken down to 7 x 83. While the number seven is used in the Bible to convey spiritual truth, to our knowledge, the number 83 does not convey spiritual truth. Therefore, we cannot expect to find spiritual truth in the number 581.

> *It is truth that harmonizes with the duration of man's life on the earth and definitely enriches the Gospel message.*

On the other hand, when we break down the 4290 years between the birth of Terah and A.D. 1994, we do find a series of numbers, each of which is used in the Bible to convey spiritual truth. It is truth that harmonizes with the duration of man's life on the earth and definitely enriches the Gospel message.

We, therefore, will break the number 4290 into its prime and/ or significant numbers. Doing this, we discover that:

$$4290 \text{ years} = 3 \times 10 \times 11 \times 13$$

These are all very significant numbers.

3 = purpose of God.
10 = completeness.
11 = anticipation of the fullness of God's plan, which is
       particularly realized by the coming of Christ.
13 = the overabundant fullness of God's plan, which is
       particularly realized by the end of the world, when
       Christ comes again.

The Year 11,013 B.C.

Isn't it interesting that two of these numbers are featured in the year 11,013 B.C.? Is it, in fact, merely a curiosity that creation's year is the numeral 11,013? Is this something that happened accidentally? It could very well be, but we must remember that the same all-wise God Who wrote the Bible also created the universe. As we examine the atoms, the molecules, the neutrons, the protons, etc., that are all integral parts of creation, we know that God's use of numbers is found everywhere. Everything, down to the smallest particle of matter, is precisely designed by God according to very precise number systems.

Therefore, when we carefully study God's revelation to us, we see that numbers are found everywhere. Was it accidental that the Julian calendar, which became the Gregorian calendar, when projected back to the very beginning, starts out with the year 11,013 B.C.? Was it accidental that this calendar left out the year 0 so that two paths are possible - the calendar path and the actual path - to such great events as the cross and the second coming of Christ? Was it accidental that Jesus was born in 7 B.C. rather than the year 0 or the year A.D. 1? God, Who has numbered the very hairs of our heads (Matthew 10:30), Who has created the tiniest insect, is certainly in control of how calendars are designed and implemented. Indeed, it is fully possible that the eleven and the thirteen as they are found in the year 11,013 B.C. is neither incidental or accidental.

> *What is the greatest event upon which all history focuses?*

What is the greatest event upon which all history focuses? Without the slightest hesitation, we know from the Bible that it is that God became a man so that He could be our Savior. When did this happen? Almost exactly 11,000 years after creation.

What is the other event that is equally the greatest event in all history? Without question, the end of the world, when the believers' salvation is completed, God's perfect love is complete, and the unsaved are judged and removed into Hell so that God's perfect justice is completely satisfied. When will this happen? Almost exactly 13,000 years after creation. In fact, the final judgment begins with God judging the church. That judgment begins at the beginning of the final tribulation period and transitions into the judgment of the whole world on the last day. Isn't it significant that so much Biblical evidence points to the year A.D. 1988 as the year in which the final tribulation began? The year 1988 is exactly 13,000 years after the creation year 11,013 B.C. Everything fits together so precisely!

> *So we see that in the creation year 11,013 B.C.,*
> *God's whole timetable of the earth's existence*
> *could well be anticipated.*

So we see that in the creation year 11,013 B.C., God's whole timetable of the earth's existence is anticipated. Likewise, when we look at Terah, who is a figure or picture of the whole human race, we see again these same two numbers - 11 and 13 - as we calculate the number of years from Terah's birth to the end of the world.

Note, too, the significant setting of the numbers 11 and 13 as they are found in the 4290 years from the birth of Terah to the end of the world in 1994. They are found in conjunction with the significant numbers 3 and 10. Remember that $10 \times 3 \times 11 \times 13 = 4290$. The number 3 emphasizes God's purpose. The number 10 emphasizes completeness. Thus, we see the spiritual emphasis in the number 4290. The number 4290 could thus signify: **Even as Terah is a picture of the human race that has brought forth those who are to be judged as well as those who are to be saved, so, too, in the completeness of time (10), God's purpose (3) for the human race will be realized through Christ coming as the Savior (11) and at the end of the world (13) coming as the Judge of all the earth.**

Thus, we see that the year in which Terah was born gives us a spiritual path that lands right on A.D. 1994.

We must bear in mind, however, that the fact that we have found a spiritual path that brings us precisely to A.D. 1994 is not in itself a proof that 1994 will be the end of the world. We can, for example, calculate the elapsed time from the birth of Terah to say, the year 2024. This would result in an elapsed time of 4320 years. And 4320 years break down to the very significant numbers $3 \times 10 \times 12 \times 12 = 4320$ years. What then is the value of the 4290 years from Terah's birth to A.D. 1994?

Actually, there is a tremendous difference in the two calculations. The year A.D. 2024 is unrelated to the end of the world. There is no other significant Biblical information that focuses on A.D. 2024. Therefore, the fact that the elapsed time between Terah's birth and 2024 has significant numbers within it has no value whatsoever.

The situation is entirely different with the year 1994. In the book *1994?*, we discovered numerous paths of great significance that ended on the year A.D. 1994. So much evidence was developed from the Biblical data that we concluded that there is an exceedingly high probability that the end of the world will be in the year A.D. 1994.

With that in mind, the fact that the 4290 years from the birth of Terah to A.D. 1994. results in a path of great spiritual significance allows us to conclude that it further substantiates the likelihood that 1994 will be the end of the world.

Terah: 130 Years Old When Abraham was Born

When we look at Terah a bit longer, we see something else that is most interesting in that it also utilizes the number 13.

Do you recall that when Terah was 130 years old, he gave birth to Abraham? Abraham is intimately identified with God's salvation plan. He typifies God Who gave His only begotten Son to be our Savior. He typifies all believers as he obediently leaves Ur of the Chaldees (the world) and comes into the land of Canaan (the kingdom of God). The number 130 can be broken down to 10 (completeness) times 13 (end of the world). Thus, the spiritual emphasis of the 130 years can be stated: **By the end of the world (13) the complete (10) number of all who are to believe will have been born.**

Or we can also break 130 down to 13 x 5 x 2. Remember the number 5 can signify salvation. The number 2 can signify the church or the believers. **Thus, the birth of Abraham when Terah was 130 years old emphasizes the spiritual truth that even as Abraham, the believer, was born to Terah who represents the world, so, too, by the end of the world (13) all believers (2) will have become saved (5).**

Adam: 130 Years Old When Seth was Born

Isn't it interesting that Seth was born to Adam when Adam was 130 years old? Adam's first two sons had come into terrible tragedy. Abel was dead, killed by his brother, Cain. Cain was driven away from the face of the earth (Genesis 4:13-14), having become a picture of being cast into hell. It looks like the human race has almost come to an end.

Then Seth was born. Curiously, Adam was 130 at the time (Genesis 5:3). This fact becomes a prophecy that the human race will go to its predetermined end of 13,000 years even as the year of creation, 11,013 B.C., had predicted. Moreover, even as Terah represents the whole human race, so, too, Adam represents the whole human race. And as Abraham represents all believers, so, too, Seth in this context represents all believers. Therefore, the fact that Adam was 130 years old when Seth was born carries the same spiritual emphasis that we have seen in the truth that Terah was 130 when Abraham was born. Isn't it amazing how God has featured the number 13 in Adam's life as well as in Terah's life?

Are these numbers, 13 and 130, accidental or incidental? Not so! Without question, they are all part of God's carefully developed plan for the world.

Terah's Birth Relates to the Final Tribulation

As we look a bit longer at the birth of Terah, we might wonder: Is there a relationship between the birth of Terah and the beginning of the final tribulation, 1988 A.D., when God's final judgment began to fall on the earth, when God's salvation plan had almost come to an end and Satan was loosed to become a judgment upon the church that has fallen away and rapidly continues to fall into rebellion?

We know that because Terah did not cross the river into the land of Canaan he is a picture of the whole human race that remains under the judgment of God because they never were saved. We also know that that judgment begins with the final tribulation period when God brings judgment on the church. Therefore, Terah's birth is definitely related to the beginning of the final tribulation.

But now let's investigate to determine if any of these truths are emphasized by the numbers involved. We have learned that Terah was born in 2297 B.C. The final tribulation in all likelihood began in 1988 A.D. This is also the year that without question was the 13,000th anniversary of the world. The years between these two events are:

$$2297 + 1988 - 1 = 4284 \text{ actual years.}$$

We immediately wonder: Is this number a product of significant and/or prime numbers? Indeed, it is a product of very significant prime numbers.

$$3 \times 3 \times 2 \times 2 \times 7 \times 17 = 4284.$$

3 = the purpose of God
2 = the church
7 = perfection
17 = heaven or salvation

Immediately, we see something very intriguing in these numbers. Do you recall how many fish were caught by the seven disciples in the John 21 account? There were 153 fish. This is discussed at length in the book *1994?* Do you recall that the number 153 can be broken down to $3 \times 3 \times 17$? Do you remember that the sum of all the integers up to and including the number 17 equals 153? That is:

$$1 + 2 + 3 + 4 \ldots + 15 + 16 + 17 = 153.$$

Thus, God features the number 3 twice and the number 17 twice. God insistently emphasizes that it is God's definite purpose that the 153 fish are a picture of all mankind who will become saved, and they will definitely, without fail, go to heaven.

Thus, since

$$4284 \text{ years} = 7 \times 2 \times 2 \times 3 \times 3 \times 17.$$

We should understand that the number 4284 is focused entirely on salvation. We can say it this way: Even though it is God's purpose (3) that judgment will come on the corporate, external church (2), **it is God's perfect (7) purpose (3) that all who are in God's eternal church (2) will realize salvation and be brought to heaven (17)**.

Or we could read this number this way:

$$4284 \text{ years} = 7 \times 3 \times 3 \times 4 \times 17.$$

This could spiritually signify: **Even though it is God's purpose (3) that judgment will come on the sinful world typified by Terah, it is God's perfect (7) purpose (3), that people all over the world (4) would realize salvation (17).** This statement is in beautiful harmony with the Biblical principle that the Gospel must be preached all over the world. It is entirely in accord with the Biblical principle that God is not a respecter of persons but will save people out of any kind of situation and out of any nation of the world.

Or we could read this number this way: 7 x 3 x 12 x 17. This could spiritually signify: **Even though judgment will come on this sinful world typified by Terah, it is God's perfect (7) purpose (3) that the fullness (12) of all who are to be saved will go to heaven (17).**

The very important fact to note is that the number 4284 is totally and intimately involved with salvation. It is also related to judgment because of the relationship between the number 4284 and A.D. 1988.

How does this relate to Terah's birth? Remember, Terah is representative of the whole human race. He, in sin, worshipped false gods even as the world is in sin worshipping anything and everything except the God of the Bible. But Terah gave birth to Abraham. This world gives birth to all of the believers. And God is prophesying by Terah's relationship to the year A.D. 1988, when judgment that is to transition into the final judgment begins, that God's perfect purpose of salvation will be realized even as God's final judgment is beginning to fall. It is just as certain as the fact that Abraham, who was born to wicked Terah, became a true and faithful child of God.

Indeed, as we look at Terah, we see the beautiful focus of the Bible on the years A.D. 1988 and A.D. 1994 And this is the focus of the multitude of other data that we have presented in the book *1994?*, and the other data that is found elsewhere in this book. Increasingly, we shall see that the year A.D. 1988 in all likelihood was the beginning of the final tribulation, which we have learned is God's judgment on the church. We shall also increasingly see that 1994 will in all likelihood be the last year of this earth's existence.

The big question is: *Are you ready to meet God?* The time has grown exceedingly short wherein you can still cry to God for mercy and repent of your sins. For your sake, don't delay. By God's mercy, it is still the day of salvation. But time is fast running out.

We have looked at length at Terah and have seen how marvelously God has used him as a means to additionally warn the unbelievers of the reality of 1994 being the year that ends the world. At the same time, we have seen how God has used him to encourage the believers that God's perfect purpose of bringing heaven to the believers will be realized.

Enoch and the End of the World

But now we should carefully look at another Old Testament individual. His name was Enoch. We read of him in Genesis 5:21-24:

And Enoch lived sixty and five years, and begat Methuselah: And Enoch walked with God after he begat Methuselah three hundred years, and begat sons and daughters: And all the days of Enoch were three hundred sixty and five years: And Enoch walked with God: and he was not; for God took him.

Enoch did not die but was taken by God to heaven - a dramatic illustration that points to the rapture of all believers when Jesus comes again at the end of the world.

Enoch is surely an impressive individual. He walked with God, which is a figure of speech that indicates that he was a true believer. He did not die but was taken by God to heaven - a dramatic illustration that points to the rapture of all believers when Jesus comes again at the end of the world.

Enoch lived for 365 years. Is that a significant number? Do you recall when Nehemiah built the wall of Jerusalem, he did so in the record time of fifty-two days? (See Nehemiah 6:15.) What did the building of that wall signify? Without question, it was an historic parable in which God is showing us His divine plan to save those whom He chose to save. God typifies the body of believers as a temple (Ephesians 2:19-

22, I Peter 2:5, Revelation 11:1), as a city (Revelation 21:2), and as a wall (Revelation 21:17).

But what about the fifty-two days? Does the number 52 signify anything? Indeed, it does, for two important reasons. The first reason is the fact that the number 52 can be broken down to 4 x 13 = 52. Thus, the 52 days is spiritually signifying that the believers who are typified by the wall will come from all over the world (4) and will be completed when Christ comes at the end of the world (13).

The second reason is that fifty-two days relate to the fifty-two weeks in a year. How did Jesus speak of His plan to save His people in Luke 4:18-19? There we read:

> The Spirit of the Lord is upon me, because he hath anointed me to preach the gospel to the poor; he hath sent me to heal the brokenhearted, to preach deliverance to the captives, and recovering of sight to the blind, to set at liberty them that are bruised, To preach the acceptable year of the Lord.

The acceptable year of the Lord: God's plan of salvation is the acceptable year of the Lord.

The acceptable year of the Lord: God's plan of salvation is the acceptable year of the Lord. But how many weeks did God place in a year? Yes, God designed the year to be 365.2422 days in length. This was not decided by men or by calendar makers. When God created the earth, the sun, and the moon, He firmly fixed the length of each day and the precise length of the year. These periods of time have been unchanged since the beginning of time.

Likewise, when God rested on the seventh day after doing the work of creation in six days, God firmly decreed that there are to be seven days in a week. Thus, there are to be fifty-two weeks in a year. Without question, then, as we tie together the fact of fifty-two weeks in a year, the acceptable year of the Lord as the period of salvation, and the fifty-two days to complete the wall by Nehemiah (who can definitely be shown to be a type of Christ), we see how the fifty-two days focus on the acceptable year of the Lord, that is, those fifty-two days illustrate God's entire plan of salvation.

Returning to Enoch, we have read that he lived 365 years and then was raptured. Without question, the 365 years of Enoch's life present us with the beautiful truth of the acceptable year (365 days) of the Lord, which is God's whole plan of salvation for the human race. At the end of that acceptable year, even as it was at the end of Enoch's life, the believers will be raptured.

There is more that must be said of Enoch. In Jude 14-15, we read:

> And Enoch also, the seventh from Adam, prophesied of these, saying, Behold, the Lord cometh with ten thousands of his saints, To execute judgment upon all, and to convince all that are ungodly among them of all their ungodly deeds which they have ungodly committed, and of all their hard speeches which ungodly sinners have spoken against him.

Enoch was a preacher. Even though Enoch lived about 2000 years before the flood of Noah's day, God revealed to Jude what His dominant message was. It was a message that focused on the end of the world. "The Lord cometh with ten thousands of his saints." It was a message that focused on God's judgment to come: "to execute judgment upon all."

Thus, we see that Enoch in his life focussed on the end of the world and the rapture of the believers.

Thus, we see that Enoch in his life focussed on the end of the world and the rapture of the believers. But in his preaching, he focussed on the judgment that is to come because of the sins of mankind.

Enoch's Birth Date Is Very Significant

Is there more to learn from Enoch? Indeed there is, as we look at where he fits into the history of the world. Enoch was born in the year

7106 B.C. We can be absolutely sure of this. To see how this date is obtained, see the book *1994?*

The first thing that we should note about his birth date is its relationship to the year of the Noachian Flood, which was a gigantic reminder of the judgment of God that will come upon the whole world on the last day. Therefore, because Enoch preached judgment, we would be particularly interested in discovering if there is any relation between Enoch's life and the flood of Noah's day.

We know that the flood occurred in the year 4990 B.C. (pages 295-328, *1994?*). We also know that Enoch was born in the year 7106 B.C. The time duration from the birth of Enoch to the flood is:

$$7106 - 4990 = 2116 \text{ years.}$$

When we break down the number 2116 to its significant or prime numbers, we find:

$$4 \times 23 \times 23 = 2116 \text{ years.}$$

4 = universality
23 = judgment.

How significant this is! Enoch, by means of the very year in which he was born, in that the year relates to the year of the awesome judgment upon the world, was proclaiming judgment to come. Twice the number of judgment, 23, is featured to underscore and emphasize judgment. By the number 4, God is pointing to the fact that this will be universal judgment. Indeed, with the exception of those in the ark, the flood of Noah's day destroyed everything in the whole earth that had the breath of life.

Spiritually the 2116 years between the birth of Enoch and the Noachian Flood could be saying: **Even as Enoch warned of judgment to come, so judgment definitely came (23 x 23) upon the whole world (4) in the days of Noah.**

Then we wonder: Does Enoch's birth date relate in any way to the end of the world when the final judgment will come? Let us test this question.

$$7106 \text{ (the birth of Enoch)} + 1994 - 1 = 9099 \text{ years.}$$

When we break down 9099 years into prime numbers, we obtain:

$$3 \times 3 \times 1011.$$

While 3 is a significant number, the number 1011 is not. Therefore, we can learn nothing from this.

But do you recall that God has doubled the possibility of time paths between significant events that relate to God's salvation plan by the fact that our calendar has no year 0?

A Quick Look at Abraham

For example, do you remember in the book *1994?* we learned that the year 2068 B.C. was a very significant year because it was the year when Abraham and his household were circumcised? It was pointing to the year A.D. 33, when Christ shed His blood and was cut off in the sense that He experienced hell for our sins. Circumcision was a sign pointing to the cutting away of our sins by the shed blood of Jesus. And the time relationship between 2068 B.C. and A.D. 33 is:

$$2068 + 33 - 1 = 2100 \text{ actual years.}$$

The number 2100, when broken down to its significant or prime numbers, is:

$$3 \times 7 \times 10 \times 10$$

    3 = God's purpose
    7 = perfection
   10 = completeness.

Thus, **the time relationship was pointing to the complete (10) and perfect (7) purpose (3) of God to accomplish His plan of salvation.**

Or it could be broken down to:

$$3 \times 7 \times 2 \times 5 \times 10$$

2 = church or believers

5 = judgment of God or salvation.

The time relationship then teaches the perfect (7) and complete (10) purpose (3) of God to bring salvation (5) to the believers (2).

But, do you remember that the year 2067 B.C. was also extremely important in the unfolding of God's salvation plan. It was the year Isaac was born. In Hebrews 11:17, God refers to Isaac as the only begotten of Abraham, even as He speaks of Jesus as the only begotten Son. Thus, the birth of Isaac was pointing directly to Christ because Isaac, without question, was a type or figure of Christ. This is especially reinforced when Abraham was told to sacrifice Isaac on an altar, even as God sacrificed His Son Jesus.

When we look at the time relationship between the birth of Isaac and the cross, we find that:

$$2067 + 33 - 1 = 2099 \text{ actual years.}$$

We cannot break down 2099 into any significant numbers. Therefore, this is not a significant or important time period.

But it is a significant time period when we calculate the passage of time in calendar years instead of in actual years. To arrive at actual years in calculating the passage of time requires the subtraction of one year in going from an Old Testament event to a New Testament event. This is because the calendar does not include a year 0. An event we will call "B" that happened in the year A.D. 2 is three years later than an event that we will call "A" that happened in the year 2 B.C.

2 B.C.	1 B.C.	A.D. 1	A.D. 2
↑Event A			↑ Event B

It can readily be seen that these two events are actually three years apart. To calculate this we must add the B.C. years (2) to the A.D. years (2), which equals $2 + 2 = 4$. It is then necessary to subtract 1 from the 4 to get the answer of 3 actual years.

Had the calendar been designed with a year zero, the result would have been:

2 B.C.	1 B.C.	0	A.D. 1	A.D. 2
↑Event A				↑ Event B

In that case the actual years between an Old Testament event and a New Testament event would be calculated by simply adding the Old Testament calendar years to the New Testament calendar years. The actual years and the calendar years would each equal four years.

But the Julian calendar was designed without a year 0. Therefore, the actual years between an Old Testament event and a New Testament event is always one year less than the calendar years between these two events.

When we follow this procedure in computing the calendar years between the birth of Isaac in 2067 B.C. and the cross in A.D. 33, we obtain the result:

$$2067 + 33 = 2100 \text{ calendar years.}$$

As we have just learned, 2100 years is a very significant time path. God has doubled the possibility of significant time paths by allowing or guiding the designer of the Julian calendar to leave out the year 0.

9100 Years

Returning now to Enoch, we learned that the actual number of years from his birth to the end of the world is not significant. But let us now test the question on the basis of calendar years:

$$7106 + 1994 = 9100 \text{ calendar years.}$$

And, 9100 years, when broken down to its significant or prime numbers, gives us:

$$7 \times 13 \times 10 \times 10$$

7 = perfection

13 = superabundant fullness or the end of the world when Christ completes everything

10 = completeness

Moreover, the number 7 x 13 = 91 is a unique number wherein all of the integers that are before and include the number 13 add up to 91. Thus, 1 + 2 + 3 + 4 . . . 11 + 12 + 13 = 91. God is placing a double emphasis on the number 13 in the time relationship between Enoch and the end of the world.

Utilizing the numbers in this time relationship, we can say: **Even as Enoch who typified the acceptable year of the Lord, in that at the end of 365 years he was raptured and who warned of judgment to come, so, too, in the perfect (7) completion (10) of God's timetable, the end of the world (13) will definitely come bringing both the rapture of the believers and judgment on the unbelievers.**

Or we can break down 9100 into the numbers:

$$7 \times 13 \times 2 \times 5 \times 10$$

2 = number of the believers or the church

5 = number of judgment or of salvation.

Do you recall that the rapture of Enoch at the end of his life pointed to the completion of the rapture of the believers at the end of the world? That rapture comes when the salvation of the believers is completed. We thus obtain: **Even as Enoch whose lifespan typified the acceptable year of the Lord and who was raptured at the end of his life on earth, so, too, in the perfection (7) of God's timetable, at the end of the world (13), the salvation (5) of the believers (2) will be complete (10).**

An alternative spiritual emphasis suggested by 9100 = 7 x 13 x 2 x 5 x 10 could be: **Even as Enoch who warned of the coming judgment of God, so, too, the perfect (7) completeness (10) of the end of the world (13) will bring judgment (5) on the unbelievers in the church (2).**

Or we can break down 9100 to:

$$9100 = 7 \times 13 \times 4 \times 5 \times 5$$

4 = universality.

These numbers suggest that: **At the end of the world (13) in a perfect way (7) the whole world (4) will either experience the judgment of God (5) or the salvation of God (5).**

We cannot escape the truth that the numbers hidden within the Biblical message help to increase our understanding of God's plan for the world.

As we look at the spiritual relationships inherent in the number 9100, which are the calendar years between the birth of Enoch, who in his life was a tremendous type or representative of many aspects of the salvation plan, and the end of the world, which was so clearly anticipated by Enoch, we cannot help but see that the year 1994 is very likely going to be the end of the world. We cannot escape the truth that the numbers hidden within the Biblical message help to increase our understanding of God's plan for the world.

Esau Married Two Heathen Wives

We will now examine in some detail a third historical event that is related to the Gospel message and about which we know the precise year in which it occurred. It relates to a notice we find in the Bible giving the information that Esau married two heathen wives.

In Genesis 26:34-35, we read:

And Esau was forty years old when he took to wife Judith the daughter of Beeri the Hittite, and Bashemath the daughter of Elon the Hittite: Which were a grief of mind unto Isaac and to Rebekah.

> *Esau's act of marrying two heathen wives further emphasized his rebellion against God.*

This is a very curious piece of information in that God tells us that Esau was 40 years old when he married two Hittite wives. Surely this was sin because Esau was a covenant child. He was born into a home where there was the Gospel, and believers are not to be unequally yoked with unbelievers. Even though we know that Esau personally had not become a believer, he came from believing parents and was reared with the Gospel. His act of marrying two heathen wives further emphasized his rebellion against God.

Why does God tell us that Esau was 40 years old when he married these wives? Frequently in the Bible the age of an individual is given to assist in developing the chronology of that period of time. But from that standpoint, it was a totally unnecessary fact that he was 40 years old.

It is true, as we have learned, that the number 40 is the number of testing. It seems obvious that this was a time of testing in Esau's life, and he failed the test because he married two heathen women.

But why does God focus on the act of marrying two heathen wives? Esau had committed a far greater sin previously, and God gives us no indication of Esau's age when he committed that sin. We read of that sin in Genesis 25:29-33:

> And Jacob sod pottage: and Esau came from the field, and he was faint: And Esau said to Jacob, Feed me, I pray thee, with that same red pottage; for I am faint: therefore was his name called Edom. And Jacob said, Sell me this day thy birthright. And Esau said, Behold, I am at the point to die: and what profit shall this birthright do to me? And Jacob said, Swear to me this day; and he sware unto him: and he sold his birthright unto Jacob.

> *This transaction, in which Esau despised his*
> *birthright to the degree that he sold his right to it*
> *for a bowl of soup, was an enormous sin.*

This transaction, in which Esau despised his birthright to the degree that he sold his right to it for a bowl of soup, was an enormous sin. The birthright, which was his because he was the firstborn, would have given him the rights of the firstborn, including a double share of the inheritance when his father died. Esau's action indicated that he had no concern for the future. His focus was on the here and now.

His action was a portrait of the human race that remains in sin. Even though the years we spend on earth are less than a drop in the ocean compared with eternity, that is the condition of every human being; mankind wants the here and now and cares not at all for what happens after they die. God commands mankind to believe in Christ so they might receive the inheritance of the firstborn, eternal life. But no man of himself wants to obey God. Man would rather live for the present, obeying the sensual lusts of the flesh.

Curiously, while God does not tell us when Esau committed the great sin of despising his birthright, as we have seen, He does tell us when Esau became unequally yoked with heathen women. He was 40 years old. Since we know from the chronological study set forth in the book *1994?* that Esau and Jacob were born in the year 2007 B.C., we know that it was the year 1967 B.C. when Esau committed this sin. But why is this important? We must look further in the Bible to discover why this year is so very significant.

Believers Are Not to be Unequally Yoked to Unbelievers

We should now look at Genesis 6, where we find another account of men becoming unequally yoked. By examining this passage, we will be helped in our understanding of Esau's sin. In Genesis 6:1-6 we read:

And it came to pass, when men began to multiply on the face of the earth, and daughters were born unto them, That the sons of God saw the daughters of men that they were fair; and they took them wives of all which they chose. And the LORD said, My spirit shall not always strive with man, for that he also is flesh: yet his days shall be an hundred and twenty years. There were giants in the earth in those days; and also after that, when the sons of God came in unto the daughters of men, and they bare children to them, the same became mighty men which were of old, men of renown. And God saw that the wickedness of man was great in the earth, and that every imagination of the thoughts of his heart was only evil continually. And it repented the LORD that he had made man on the earth, and it grieved him at his heart.

In these verses, the sons of God are the believers. When we become saved, we are adopted into the family of God; we become His children. This is clearly taught, for example, in Romans 8:14: "For as many as are led by the Spirit of God, they are the sons of God."

> *It is as impossible for an angel to marry a human as it is for an elephant to marry a butterfly.*

Incidentally, some have taught that the sons of God mentioned in Genesis 6 were angels who intermarried with humans, who are called the daughters of men. This is totally impossible. God created everything after its kind. Humans were created in the image of God. Angels are ministering spirits (Hebrews 1:13-14). It is as impossible for an angel to marry a human as it is for an elephant to marry a butterfly.

Returning to Genesis 6, we next learn that because believers became unequally yoked with unbelievers (the daughters of men), God was grieved at his heart (verse 6). Remember we read in Genesis 26:35 that when Esau became unequally yoked, it was "a grief of mind unto Isaac and to Rebekah." While the Hebrew word used to describe grief in Genesis 6 is different from the word used in Genesis 26, the sense is exactly the same. In the one case, it was grief to God, Who had fathered the human race. In the other case, it was grief to the parents of Esau.

Genesis 6 and Genesis 26 Show Parallel Truth

We are beginning to discover noteworthy parallels between the Genesis 6 account and the Genesis 26 account. Another parallel is seen in whom Esau represents. We read in the Genesis 25 account, in which Esau sold his birthright for a bowl of soup (verse 30):

> And Esau said to Jacob, Feed me, I pray thee, with that same red pottage; for I am faint: therefore was his name called Edom.

> *Surely in Esau's purchase of the bowl of soup at the cost of his birthright, he is a dramatic picture of mankind, who has traded the possibility of eternal life through Jesus Christ for their present sensual desires.*

The word "red" in this verse has precisely the same Hebrew spelling as the word "Adam." The name Edom was given to Esau because Edom has almost exactly the same spelling as red or Adam. In fact, in at least one instance in the Bible, Edom is spelled exactly the same as Adam. Adam is, of course, the progenitor of the whole human race. Therefore, he signifies all of mankind. Since one of the names given to Esau is Edom, which identifies with Adam, God is surely teaching us that Esau is a picture of mankind. Surely in his purchase of the bowl of soup at the cost of his birthright, he is a dramatic picture of mankind, who has traded the possibility of eternal life through Jesus Christ for their present sensual desires.

We thus see these parallels between the Genesis 6 account and the Genesis 26 account.

Genesis 6	*Genesis 26*
Mankind is tested	Esau is tested
Mankind became unequally yoked	Esau became unequally yoked
Grief to God	Grief to Esau's parents

There is another parallel between the two accounts of Genesis 6 and Genesis 26 but it is only implied in the Genesis 26 account. That is the statement of Genesis 6:2-3, where we read:

> That the sons of God saw the daughters of men that they were fair; and they took them wives of all which they chose. And the LORD said, My spirit shall not always strive with man, for that he also is flesh: yet his days shall be an hundred and twenty years.

In this succinct statement, "his days shall be an hundred and twenty years," God is indicating that the consequence of man's rebellion of becoming unequally yoked would be an end to this world. We know that this cannot be addressing the age at which a man dies, because the statement was made before the flood of Noah's day, when men lived hundreds of years. Noah lived to be 950 years old, Shem, his son, lived for 600 years, etc.

It is possible that the 120 years were to be the time between this announcement of sin and the flood that came during Noah's lifetime. Thus, effectively, God was giving Noah 120 years to build the ark in preparation for the flood.

In any case, the 120-year period is a statement that focuses on the prospect of judgment coming because mankind has become unequally yoked.

While judgment is clearly in view in the Genesis 6 account, and God has even given a timetable for it, in the Genesis 26 account, judgment is implied but not stated. But the principle that the wages of sin is death was just as applicable in Esau's day as it is today. Therefore, judgment is also in view in the Genesis 26 account, even as it is always in view wherever sin is committed.

Mankind Becomes Unequally Yoked

As we continue to unravel the significance of Esau's sin of becoming unequally yoked, we want to go to a third Biblical account that also relates very intimately to the accounts found in Genesis 6 and Genesis 26. We should go to Genesis 3, where we find the sad account of our first parents becoming unequally yoked with Satan. God had created them as perfect sons of God. He had placed them in a perfect earth with every blessing of God, and Adam fell into sin. By disobeying

God's command that he was not to eat of the forbidden tree, he had become unequally yoked with Satan. Now Satan would be the ruler of the human race.

The consequence of his sin was judgment. Not only would he die physically, but he would die spiritually. Spiritually, mankind became dead. Even worse, he became subject to the second death, eternal damnation.

We immediately see many parallels between Genesis 3 and Genesis 6 and in turn with Genesis 26.

Genesis 3	*Genesis 6*	*Genesis 26*
Adam: Represents whole human race	Mankind	Esau: Represents the whole whole human race
Adam was tested in Garden of Eden	Mankind tested by presence of beautiful daughters of men amongst sons of God	40 years signifies testing
Adam failed test	Mankind failed the test	Esau failed the test
Adam became unequally yoked	Mankind became unequally yoked	Esau became unequally yoked
Adam came under judgment, to come at last day	Mankind to be destroyed by flood	Esau to be punished at last day for his sin
Judgment at end of world: Judgment Day to come in 13,000 yrs	Judgment to come in 120 yrs	Judgment to come at the end of the world

> *Judgment on the churches is in view during the final tribulation period, which transitions into judgment on the world at the end of the final tribulation period.*

120 Years - 13,000 Years

Before we go on, we should ask the question: Is there really a parallel between the 120 years of Genesis 6 and the 13,000 years that in all likelihood separates Adam's sin and God's judgment at the end of time? In the book *1994?* we learned that the creation of the world was in the year 11,013 B.C. We also learned that the judgment at the end of the world begins with judgment on the house of God and ends with judgment on the whole world. Judgment on the churches is in view during the final tribulation period, which transitions into judgment on the world at the end of the final tribulation period. And we learned that in all likelihood the final tribulation period began in A.D. 1988, exactly 13,000 years after creation in 11,013 B.C.

How does 120 years relate to 13,000 years? Remember in the book *1994?*, we found verses in the Bible that show why these numbers are related. In Deuteronomy 32:8, God declares: "When the Most High divided to the nations their inheritance, when he separated the sons of Adam, he set the bounds of the people according to the number of the children of Israel."

In the Old Testament, the children of Israel were the twelve tribes of Israel. Invariably, whenever the tribes are listed, twelve are named. But in actuality there were thirteen tribes. This is because Joseph, who was one of the twelve sons of Jacob, had been given two tribes. These two tribes were Ephraim and Manasseh.

> *In both the Old Testament as well as in the New Testament in connection with the children of Israel, the number 12 is featured while in reality the number 13 was the fact.*

Likewise, the New Testament Israel are those who believe in Jesus Christ. They are found in the churches which began with the apostles. But while the Bible repeatedly speaks of the twelve, in actuality there were thirteen. This is because the Apostle Paul insisted that he, too, had seen Jesus and had been called to be an apostle (I Corinthians 9:1-2, I Corinthians 15:8-9). Thus, in both the Old Testament as well as in the New Testament in connection with the children of Israel, the number 12 is featured while in reality the number 13 was the fact.

Moreover, we read in Job 14:5:

Seeing his days are determined, the number of his months are with thee, thou hast appointed his bounds that he cannot pass.

In this passage, God is identifying man's days as determined in relation to months. Ordinarily, we think of twelve months in a year. But because the months in the Jewish calendar were determined by each new moon and each new moon encompassed about 29 1/2 days, some years were twelve months and some were thirteen months. The extra month was added approximately every three years to cover the time lost by twelve months of 29½ days. So again there were apparently twelve months but in actuality, from time to time, there were thirteen months. So man's days are determined by twelve months or thirteen months.

Furthermore, when we understand the calendars of the Bible, we find that there were almost exactly 11,000 years from creation to the first coming of Christ. When we add to that the 1000 years that Satan would be bound, which we read about in Revelation 20:1-3, we obtain a total time span for the earth of 12,000 years. In fact, we know that the duration of time during which Satan is bound when added to the Old Testament period is exactly 13,000 years (11,013 + 1988 - 1 = 13,000 years). This is so because Satan was bound at the cross, 1955 years before he was loosed in 1988, if indeed that was the beginning of the final tribulation period.

One other fact must be kept in mind. In one sense, the 120 years of Genesis 6 convey the same truth as 1200 years or 12,000 years. This is because spiritually the number 12 signifies the fullness of whatever is in view. Multiplying 12 by 10 or by 10 x 10 x 10 does not change the spiritual significance of the number since the number 10 signifies completeness. Thus, we obtain these relationships.

Apparent Duration of Earth	*Actual Age of Earth*
Signified by:	Signified by:
12 tribes	13 tribes
12 apostles	13 apostles
12 months	13 months
120, which = 12,000 years	13,000 years

> *The wrath of God that will eventually fall on man because of his sin will also be at the end of the world, which comes 13,000 years after Adam's sin.*

Returning to the parallels between Genesis 3, Genesis 6, and Genesis 26, we can see that in Genesis 6, God pronounced 120 years as the duration of man on earth. This 120 years signified the apparent 12,000 years of the earth's duration. The 12,000 years are actually 13,000 years before judgment would come upon the human race because of the sin of Adam (and therefore all mankind) of becoming unequally yoked. Likewise, Esau, in the Genesis 26 account, is a picture of Adam, who failed the test in the Garden of Eden. Therefore, the wrath of God that will eventually fall on man because of his sin will also be at the end of the world, which comes 13,000 years after Adam's sin.

Summarizing all of this data, we can see, therefore, that the account of Genesis 26, describing how at 40 years of age Esau married two heathen wives and thus grieved his parents, is a picture of mankind near the beginning of time coming under the wrath of God because they became unequally yoked with Satan.

The year 1967 B.C., when Esau became unequally yoked, thus identifies in a real sense with the beginning of time when Adam fell into sin.

But can we find other Biblical information that relates 1967 B.C. to the beginning when Adam fell into sin? To determine that, we have to assemble additional data from the Bible.

Missing Names in a Genealogical Account

In Matthew 1, **God gives us the genealogical line from Abraham to Joseph, who was the stepfather of Christ. We will find that in these genealogies, the significance of 1967 B.C. will come to light.**

Beginning with verse 2 and going through verse 6, we read fourteen names that follow each other. The fourteen names begin with Abraham and end with David. In verse 17, God explains that all the generations from Abraham to David are fourteen generations.

Then in verse 7, the genealogy starts with Solomon and goes to verse 11, where the last person named is Jechonias (Jehoiachin in the Old Testament), who reigned at the time they were carried off to Babylon. Again, fourteen names are given, including the names of Solomon and Jechonias. Verse 17 of Matthew 1 explains:

> So all the generations from Abraham to David are fourteen generations; and from David until the carrying away into Babylon are fourteen generations; and from the carrying away into Babylon unto Christ are fourteen generations.

When we study the fourteen names that are given in the Matthew account and their relation to each other, we find that a number of names are missing.

But when we study the fourteen names that are given in the Matthew account and their relation to each other, we find that a number of names are missing. We can know this precisely because the names listed are those of the kings who ruled over Judah from Rehoboam to Jehoiachin. When we compare this list with the Old Testament information, four kings who are definitely in the genealogical line are missing. They are Joash, Amaziah, Uzziah, and Jehoiakim. **Therefore, it is very clear that this is a contrived list, given in such a way that fourteen names result.**

> *Therefore, it is very clear that this is a contrived*
> *list, given in such a way that fourteen names result.*

We next look at the third group of names that begins with Salathiel, who is named in verse 12, and go through to verse 16, which ends with Jesus, Who was born to Mary, the wife of Joseph. In verse 17, God declares that "from the carrying away into Babylon unto Christ are fourteen generations." Again, we find that it is a very contrived list. Jesus was not the son of Joseph and therefore, strictly speaking, was not a generation following Joseph. Moreover, to obtain the number 14, it is necessary to include Jechonias, who was already part of the previous fourteen names.

One truly wonders why God placed this in the Bible in this way. There may be many reasons, but one of them is to come up with a figure of forty-two generations from Abraham to Christ.

The Bible clearly declares in verse 17 of Matthew 1:

So all the generations from Abraham to David are fourteen generations; and from David until the carrying away into Babylon are fourteen generations; and from the carrying away into Babylon unto Christ are fourteen generations.

Three times fourteen gives us a total of forty-two generations.

The Genealogical Listing of Luke 3

Let us leave this genealogical list for a moment and look at another genealogical list found in Luke 3. Again, we have a list of names that are sometimes father to son and frequently are father to grandson or to great-grandson. For example, in verses 36 and 37, the list goes from Methuselah to Lamech, but in our study of the calendar of Genesis 5, we learned that Lamech could not have been the immediate son of Methuselah.

However, when we count the names in this list of names, we find that there are 77 if we include God, Who is listed, and Christ, Who is listed. Remember that when we counted forty-two generations from Abraham to Christ in the Matthew 1 account, it required that we include the names of both Abraham and Christ. Therefore, we have complete Biblical sanction to include the names God and Christ to come to the number 77 when we look at the names in Luke 3.

Immediately, we see something interesting in the Luke 3 account. The listing goes from the very beginning - when God created Adam and Eve - all the way to the first coming of Christ. And the number 77 is made up of the two prime numbers 7 x 11.

By the number 77, God is surely pointing to the perfection of the 11,000 years that passed from creation to the coming of Christ even as the list of 77 names also goes from creation to Christ.

We sense that there is a truth being revealed by the number 77. Seven is the number of perfection, and eleven is the number that focuses on the timetable from creation to the coming of Christ as Savior. **By the number 77, God is surely pointing to the perfection of the 11,000 years that passed from creation to the coming of Christ even as the list of 77 names also goes from creation to Christ.**

What does all of this have to do with the year 1967 B.C., when Esau at the age of 40 years took to wife two heathen women? We shall find our answer, but first let us summarize what we have learned so far.

1. Esau is a picture of mankind. When he failed the test and became unequally yoked, he became representative of Adam, who, in the Garden of Eden, failed the test by becoming unequally yoked with Satan. Thus, the year 1967 B.C., when Esau failed the test, in one sense becomes equivalent to the time of the beginning of creation.

2. In Matthew 1, God in a very mysterious way focuses our attention on forty-two generations from Abraham to the first coming of Christ. Since we know from the calendar record of the Old Testament that Abraham was born in the year 2167 B.C., and we find that all of the Biblical evidence points to 7 B.C. as the year Christ was born, we can conclude, using the contrived information of Matthew 1,

that there were forty-two generations from the birth of Abraham (2167 B.C.) to the birth of Christ and His generation (7 B.C.) - a period of 2160 years. Remember that in Matthew 1, Christ's generation must be included to obtain a total of forty-two generations.

It logically follows then that the average length of each one of these forty-two generations is $^{2160}/_{42}$ years or approximately 51.5 years.

3. We know that God gives 77 names in Luke 3, going from God (Who created Adam) to Christ and His first coming.

4. The result of Esau's failing the test reaches to the end of time. We learned this when we discovered the parallels between Genesis 26 and Genesis 6, where God indicates that man's days shall be 120 years.

We Relate 42 Generations to 77 Names

Now we come to a very interesting and perhaps very significant conclusion of this whole matter. If the average generation of Matthew 1 is $^{2160}/_{42}$ years or approximately 51.5 years, what would be the result if we multiplied the 77 names of Luke 3 by this same average generation length of $^{2160}/_{42}$ years?

$$\frac{(2160 \times 77)}{42} = 3960 \text{ years}$$

The result we obtain is 3960 years.

> *Therefore, in a real sense the 77 generations of Luke 3 equivalently began with Esau becoming unequally yoked.*

Remember now that the year 1967 B.C. when Esau married two heathen women was parallel to Adam's fall into sin at the beginning of time. **Therefore, in a real sense the 77 generations of Luke 3 equivalently began with Esau becoming unequally yoked.** Thus, we wonder what the result would be if we would add the 3960 years we have just obtained to 1967 B.C., the year Esau sinned. **Amazingly, we come to the year 1994 A.D.**

Let's do this arithmetic. Remember that when we go from an Old Testament to a New Testament event, we add the number of the Old Testament years and the number of the New Testament years together and subtract one because there is no year 0. Thus:

$$
\begin{array}{ll}
\text{Esau, 40 years old:} & 1967 \text{ B.C.} \\
\text{Christ comes} & \underline{+\ 1994 \text{ A.D.}} \\
& 3961 \\
& \underline{-\ \ 1} \\
& 3960 \text{ years.}
\end{array}
$$

We surely are astounded to come exactly to the year 1994 A.D. which we have already learned is the likely year for the end of the world. But we still have a problem. The year 1994 A.D. is the end of time whereas the seventy-seven names of Luke 3 go to Christ's first coming.

Can we, in any sense, go to the end of time based on the seventy-seven names in Luke 3? We can, indeed, if we remember that those names start at God, from Whom Adam came, and then go through a whole series of names until they end with Christ. But when Christ came His was the last name that can be named. There are no names that can be named between His first coming and His second coming. Going from God through Adam and then through all the names listed in Luke 3 to Christ's second coming, is still seventy-seven names or seventy-seven generations.

We can say this a different way. God shows us in Luke 3 that there are seventy-seven generations from God to Christ. Christ's generation goes all the way from His first coming to the end of the world.

Earlier in our study (pages 224-231), we had learned that when we set forth the parallels between Esau's sin, the sins named in Genesis 6, and those of Adam in the Garden of Eden, the focus was judgment at the end of the world as a result of those sins.

Therefore, the impact of becoming unequally yoked focuses on the end of time rather than on the first coming of Christ. We thus know that we are on safe ground in going from Esau's sin of becoming unequally yoked all the way to the end of time.

> *We believe we have Biblical sanction to equate the*
> *sin of Esau in becoming unequally yoked with the*
> *sin of our first parents in becoming unequally yoked*
> *when they sinned.*

That is, we believe we have Biblical sanction to equate the sin of Esau in becoming unequally yoked with the sin of our first parents in becoming unequally yoked when they sinned. Thus, the year of Esau's sin in 1967 B.C. identifies in this sense with the beginning of time. Since the 77 names of Luke 3 start at creation and go to Christ, the beginning of these 77 names also in this same sense identify with 1967 B.C. when Esau became unequally yoked. And since God mysteriously develops in Matthew 1 a contrived list of 42 generations going from Abraham to Christ we believe we have Biblical sanction in applying the average length of each of these 42 generations to the 77 names in Luke 3 which begin in a certain sense, as we have seen, with 1967 B.C., the year Esau sinned.

> *When we harmonize all of this information, we*
> *discover that it all points to the year 1994 A.D.*
> *as the year for Christ's return and the end*
> *of the world.*

At least we are astonished that the result of all of this is a most interesting path that ends exactly at 1994 A.D. Of course, this could be coincidental even as any other path to 1994 could be coincidental. However, we strongly suspect that it is not coincidental. Instead, it could be a most beautiful way in which God has hidden truth in the Bible. We can now see one reason why God has written in the Bible the year when Esau married heathen wives. We can see a major reason why God has emphasized forty-two generations in Matthew 1. We can understand why God has carefully designed the number of names (seventy-seven) in Luke 3. **When we harmonize all of this information, we discover that it all points to the year 1994 A.D. as the year**

for Christ's return and the end of the world. This information, added to all of the other paths that we have found that focus on the year 1994 A.D., assures us of the extreme likelihood that the end of the world will come in 1994.

Or to say it another way: All this information, that focuses on 1994 as the last year of this earth's existence, means that every human being on the face of the earth must make sure that he is ready to meet God.

The Spiritual Significance of 3960 Years

Earlier we examined the years between an important Biblical event and the first or second coming of Christ. In the case of Terah's birth and in the case of the birth of Enoch, the years between these events and the end of the world were extremely significant in that those years, when broken down to their significant or prime numbers, also gave the spiritual message of the Gospel. We, therefore, wonder if there is a spiritual lesson in the 3960 years that transpired between the year that Esau married heathen wives and the end of the world.

We have learned that the two events, the sin of Esau and the end of the world in A.D. 1994, are spiritually very related to each other. But does God give us additional help in understanding this relationship by the 3960 years that separate the two events?

To discover if this is so, we have learned that we must break the number 3960 down to its prime or significant numbers. By analyzing in turn the spiritual meaning of these smaller numbers, we can begin to obtain additional Gospel insights into the spiritual relationships that exist between the sin of Esau and that most awesome event, the end of the world.

When we break the number 3960 into its prime or significant numbers, a very interesting result is obtained.

$$3960 \text{ years} = 3 \times 3 \times 2 \times 2 \times 10 \times 11$$

$$\text{Or: } 3960 \text{ years} = 3 \times 10 \times 11 \times 12$$

$$\text{Or: } 3960 \text{ years} = 3 \times 3 \times 2 \times 4 \times 5 \times 11$$

$$\text{Or: } 3960 \text{ years} = 3 \times 3 \times 4 \times 10 \times 11$$

We wonder how these numbers relate to the spiritual relationship that may exist between Esau taking two heathen wives and the end of the world, when Christ will come to complete the salvation of the believers and judge the unsaved. Remember that:

> 2 = the church or the body of believers
> 3 = the purpose of God
> 4 = universality
> 5 = salvation or judgment
> 10 = completeness
> 11 = anticipates fullness and particularly focuses on
>   Christ coming as the Savior
> 12 = the fullness of God's plan

We have learned that Esau is definitely representative of the human race, which has become unequally yoked with Satan and the world. We also know that Christ came to redeem His church when He came into the world, taking on a human nature so that He could bear the sins of those He came to save. This church comes from those who are identified with Esau before they are saved.

Doesn't Esau Represent those who Will not Become Saved?

At this point in our study someone may wish to point out that Esau is not a picture of the whole human race but only of those who will never become saved because they were never elected to salvation. This is surely the emphasis of Romans 9:10-13, where we read:

> And not only this; but when Rebecca also had conceived by one, even by our father Isaac; (For the children being not yet born, neither having done any good or evil, that the purpose of God according to election might stand, not of works, but of him that calleth;) It was said unto her, The elder shall serve the younger. As it is written, Jacob have I loved, but Esau have I hated.

> *That does not mean, however, that wherever we find the name Esau or synonyms for Esau such as Mount Seir or Edom, we can only have in mind those who can never become saved.*

It is true that in Romans 9, God is discussing the elect versus the non-elect. In this passage, God uses Esau to be representative of the non-elect and Jacob to be representative of the elect. That does not mean, however, that wherever we find the name Esau or synonyms for Esau such as Mount Seir or Edom, we can only have in mind those who can never become saved. In the narrow sense, as set forth in Romans 9, Esau represents those who will never become saved. But in the broader sense, as we have been looking at Esau in this study, Esau represents the whole human race. Even though the human race like Esau has failed the test and therefore has come under the curse of God, there is still the possibility of forgiveness, which comes with salvation. We can be sure of this when we compare a citation in Amos 9 with its fulfillment in Acts 15. We read in Amos 9:11-12:

> In that day will I raise up the tabernacle of David that is fallen, and close up the breaches thereof; and I will raise up his ruins, and I will build it as in the days of old: That they may possess the remnant of Edom, and of all the heathen, which are called by my name, saith the LORD that doeth this.

Remember Edom is another name for Esau. In Acts 15:16-17, God quotes Amos 9:11-12 but has slightly modified the words so that we can know for certain that Edom and the heathen named in Amos 9 are to be saved.

In Acts 15:16-17, the Bible assures us that these verses of Amos 9:11-12 are speaking of those who are to be saved out of the nations of the world. There we read:

> After this I will return, and will build again the tabernacle of David, which is fallen down; and I will build again the ruins thereof, and I will set it up: That the residue of men might seek

after the Lord, and all the Gentiles, upon whom my name is called, saith the Lord, who doeth all these things.

> *We know that we have complete Biblical validation*
> *in looking at Esau who became*
> *unequally yoked as a picture of the whole*
> *human race from which both the saved and the*
> *unsaved come.*

Thus, we know that we have complete Biblical validation in looking at Esau who became unequally yoked as a picture of the whole human race from which both the saved and the unsaved come. Therefore, the human race, typified by Esau, must look to Christ as the only way of escape. The alternative is that they will be confronted by Christ as the Judge of all the earth at the end of the world.

The spiritual truth being taught is that the human race must relate to Christ either as He came as our Savior or as He will come as Judge at the end of the world. So the numbers that relate to Esau's sin of becoming unequally yoked focus on Christ's coming to provide salvation and upon the end of the world when the unsaved must answer to God for his sins.

We Return to 3960 Years

As we have already learned, the number 3960 focuses on 1994, the end of the world, because it is the duration of time from Esau's sin wherein he was a type of the whole human race, which sinned from the beginning. But when 3960 is broken down to prime and significant numbers, many spiritual truths are in evidence. Let us look first at 3960 years = 3 x 3 x 2 x 2 x 10 x 11.

The number 11 stands out. This assures us that there is hope for the world in that the number 11 points to Christ coming as Savior.

The number 3 x 3 also is in evidence. Three signifies purpose and 3 x 3 further emphasizes this purpose. We could say it is God's definite purpose that Christ will come as Savior. The number 2 x 2 is featured. Since 2 is the number signifying the church or believers and a doubling of the number gives it added emphasis, we can understand that God has in mind that God is teaching that the church very definitely will be brought into existence before the end of the world.

The number 10 signifies completeness. It conveys the truth that God's salvation program will be complete in all of its aspects.

Thus, the numbers 3960 years = 3 x 3 x 2 x 2 x 10 x 11 could be understood to say spiritually: **Even as Esau who represents the whole world that became unequally yoked and who desperately needs a Savior, so, too, the definite purpose (3 x 3) of God is that certainly for the church (2 x 2) which comes from the world (Esau) that in the completeness of time (10), Christ will come (11) to provide salvation.**

The number 12 signifies fullness. Through its use God signifies that in the fullness of time and purpose all of these things will be accomplished.

Thus, the numbers 3960 years = 3 x 10 x 11 x 12 could be understood to say spiritually: **It is the complete (10) purpose of God (3) that in the fullness of time (12), Christ will come (11) to save those who are unequally yoked with Satan and the world.**

The number 4 signifies universality or something that is worldwide. It, therefore, conveys the spiritual truth that God's salvation plan which goes all the way to the end of the world is worldwide.

The number 5 signifies salvation or judgment. Thus, it could signify that because Christ is coming, salvation will be available to the whole world all the way to the end of the world. Or it could be emphasizing that the church that is brought into being because Christ came will be judged at the end of the world.

Thus, the number 3960 years = 3 x 3 x 2 x 4 x 5 x 11 could be understood to say spiritually: **It is the purpose of God (3) that believers (2) will be found in all the world (4) because it is God's purpose (3) that Christ is coming (11) to bring salvation (5) to those who are unequally yoked with Satan and the world.**

Or the number 3960 years = 3 x 3 x 4 x 10 x 11 could be understood to say spiritually: **The definite purpose of God (3 x 3) for the world (4) is that in the completeness of time (10), Christ will come (11).**

As we can see, these numbers beautifully tie into the Gospel message being taught and cause us to consider a great number of spiritual truths which are an integral part of the Gospel message.

We definitely see, therefore, that the 3960 years from the time of Esau's sin of becoming unequally yoked adds much spiritual promise and significance to the Gospel declaration. **It encourages us that God's plan of redemption is very precise and certain.** It also gives us added reason to believe that 1994 is in all likelihood the year that ends the world.

We have looked in some detail at the three examples of Terah's birth, Enoch's birth, and Esau's sin of marrying heathen wives. We have learned that in each case there is a great amount of spiritual enlightenment that the Bible gives to us, not only as we look at the words and phrases that describe these men, but also as we look at the numbers that become apparent once we accurately found their place in history and as we related that place in history to the timetable of the coming of Christ.

In fact, there are many, many other historical events in the Bible that in a very similar fashion greatly enrich our understanding of the Gospel message. This understanding is further enhanced as we place them accurately within the Biblical calendar. Indeed, they further emphasize the great likelihood that 1994 A.D. is the end of the world. We will examine these historical events in our next chapter.

Chapter 9.
Forty-Nine Calendar Milestones

In our study of the Bible, we have learned that there are many historical accounts that are actually historical parables in that when these accounts are understood spiritually, they give us further insights into God's salvation plan. In fact, many of these historical accounts are written about in the Bible in such a way that we can know precisely in which year of history the event did occur. Because it is an event that definitely relates to teaching us something about God's salvation plan, we wonder if the time information was given to help relate this event to the great events of the historic fulfillment of God's salvation plan. These events, of course, are (1) the coming of Christ as the Savior and (2) the end of the world.

In the book *1994?* we examined a few of these events and saw how they bore a definite relationship to the coming of Christ and the end of the world. In this book which is a follow-up of the book *1994?*, in Chapter 8, we looked in detail at three of these events that are milestones in the unfolding of the calendar of history. These three events were the birth of Terah, the birth of Enoch, and the time when Esau married two heathen wives.

When we summarize the whole calendar of history, we can find more than forty additional calendar milestones that are similar to the three we have more fully developed in previous chapters.* Each milestone begins at an historical event that spiritually relates to the Gospel message. Moreover, it also has a distinct connection to the fulfillment of the Gospel program. That is, the years between the event and the birth and/or crucifixion of Christ are spiritually significant, or the years between the event and the completion of the salvation program at the end of the world, A.D. 1988 and A.D. 1994, may be shown to be spiritually significant. Remember, the end of the world begins with the final tribulation period which in all likelihood commenced in A.D. 1988. This period ends in A.D. 1994 when Christ

---

* A three-page summary of these calendar milestones begins on page 311 of this book.

returns. Both A.D. 1988 and A.D. 1994 are, therefore, intimately related to the end of the world.

As we detailed the significance of the Biblical time information concerning Terah, Enoch, and Esau, the following principles were derived from the Bible. They should be carefully kept in mind as we discover this added truth from the Bible.

1. The event must have a distinct place in history. That is, we should be able to accurately place it within the Biblical calendar.

2. It should be an event that either directly, as it stands, or as an historical parable, definitely relates to the Gospel message.

3. The years should be calculated between this event and the coming of Christ (the time line):

   a. At Christ's birth in 7 B.C.
   b. At Christ's crucifixion in A.D. 33.
   c. At Christ's second coming, which began with judgment on the church in A.D. 1988.
   d. At Christ's coming on the last day in A.D. 1994.

4. The resultant time line should be such that it can be broken down to prime or significant numbers that in themselves relate to the Gospel.

5. The spiritual emphasis inherent within this time line that has been broken down should either match the spiritual message in the event, thus enriching and enhancing the spiritual message inherent within the event or, if it does not directly match, it should still add to, support, and enrich the spiritual message of the event.

We could write in detail about each of these more than forty events as we wrote in detail about Terah, Enoch, and Esau. But for now, we will simply indicate what they are and how they serve as markers in the Biblical calendar.

Please bear in mind that the spiritual emphasis brought our by the number patterns is suggestive. With an understanding of the spiritual significance of each event together with the number that is hidden within the time paths, it might be possible to write somewhat different sentences that are still in harmony with the Gospel.

Event No. 1
Creation: 11,013 B.C.

Relationship of the Event to the Gospel Message:
In the year 11,013 B.C., God created the earth and the whole universe. This was the first event required to bring to pass God's Gospel plan.

Time Line
Years to the end of world, A.D. 1988:
11,013 + 1988 - 1 = 13,000 years.

Time Line's Spiritual Emphasis:
13,000 years = 13 x 1000.
God's Gospel plan, which began with creation (11,013 B.C.), will be brought to completion (1000) at the end of the world (13). The end of the world begins with the final tribulation (A.D. 1988), as God prepares the church and the world for Judgment Day.

Or: Time Line's Spiritual Emphasis:
13,000 years = 4 x 5 x 5 x 10 x 13.
God's Gospel of salvation (5) and judgment (5) for the whole world (4) will be completed (10) at the end of the world (13). The end of the world begins with the final tribulation which prepares the world for judgment.

Or: Time Line's Spiritual Emphasis:
13,000 years = 5 x 5 x 13 x 40.

God's plan of testing (40), which results in either salvation (5) or judgment (5), goes all the way to the end of the world (13). The end of the world begins with the final tribulations as judgment begins with the house of God.

Or: Time Line's Spiritual Emphasis:
13,000 years = 2 x 2 x 5 x 5 x 10 x 13.

It is established by God will shortly come to pass (2 x 2) that God will complete (10) His Gospel of salvation (5) and judgment (5) at the end of time (13) beginning with the final tribulation period which prepares the world for the end.

Event No. 2
Seth was Born: 10,883 B.C. (Gen. 5:3-4)

Relationship of the event to the Gospel Message:
Abel (a figure of believers), was killed by Cain (a figure of the unsaved). Seth, another seed in place of Abel (Genesis 4:25), was born when Adam was 130 years old. The number 130 points to the end of the world (13). The spiritual parallel to all of this data is that the world will go to its predetermined end of 13,000 years, at which time the full amount (10) of believers will be born again.

> Time Line
> Years to the end of the world, A.D. 1988:
>   10,883 + 1988 - 1 = 12,870 years.

Time Line's Spiritual Emphasis:
12,870 years = 3 x 3 x 10 x 11 x 13.

It is the purpose or will (3) of God that Christ, Adam's seed, will come (11), and it is His purpose (3) that Christ will bring to completion (10) all of God's plan at the end of time (13).

Or: Time Line's Spiritual Emphasis

12,870 years = 2 x 3 x 3 x 5 x 11 x 13.

It is the definite purpose or will (3 x 3) of God that salvation (5) will come to the believers (2) through the coming of Christ (11) to be completed at the end of the world (13).

The last event in history is judgment which begins upon the church, beginning in A.D. 1988, preparing the way for judgment upon the world and for the creation of the new heavens and the new earth.

Event No. 3
Enoch was Born: 7106 B.C. (Gen. 5:18-24)

Relationship of the Event to the Gospel Message:
Enoch is a beautiful picture of a believer. For example, he lived 365 years. Using the Bible's analogy of a year for a day, his life span on earth points to the acceptable year when believes are saved. He was raptured, as believers will be. He walked with God, preaching the Gospel which includes the message of judgment at the end of the world, as believers do.

Time Line
Years to end of the world, A.D. 1994:
    7106 + 1994 = 9100 calendar years.

Time Line's Spiritual Emphasis:

9100 years = 7 x 13 100.

Even as Enoch's earthly life ended at the end of his years, so in the perfection (7) of God's time, believers will complete (100) their acceptable year at the end of time (13).

Or: Time Line's Spiritual Emphasis:
    9100 years = 2 x 2 x 5 x 5 x 7 x 13.
    Even as Enoch preached until the end of his life that judgment
was coming, at which time he was raptured, so in the perfection (7) of
God's time, Christ will come for the true believers (2) within the church
(2) which preaches salvation (5) and God's judgment (5) until the end
(13) when true believers will be raptured.

Event No. 4
Eber was Born: 3617 B.C. (Gen. 11:14-17)

Relationship of the Event to the Gospel Message:
    Eber is the name from which we get the name
Hebrew. From the Hebrews came the nation of Israel,
which typified the believers. Therefore, Eber's birth
pointed to the believers or the Israel of God that was
to come.

Time Line
Years to end of the world, A.D. 1994:
    3617 + 1994 - 1 = 5610 years.

Time Line's Spiritual Emphasis:
    5610 years = 3 x 10 x 11 x 17.
    Even as Eber was the progenitor of Christ who would secure
the blessings of heaven (17) for His people, so it is the will (3) of God
that in the fullness or completeness of time (10), Christ would come
(11) to accomplish this.

Or: Time Line's Spiritual Emphasis:
    5610 years = 2 x 3 x 5 x 11 x 17.
    Even as Eber was the progenitor of national Israel, so it is the
purpose (3) of God that Christ came (11) and begot spiritual Israel or
the church (2) through His work of salvation (5) and eventually gave
them the blessings of heaven (17) which would be fully accomplished
at the end of the world.

Event No. 5
Terah was Born: 2297 B.C. (Gen. 11:24-32)

Relationship of the Event to the Gospel Message:
Terah is a figure of all the people of the world. To him were born three sons, two of whom were typical of the unsaved and one of whom definitely became a believer. This proportion is highlighted as a type of all unbelievers and all believers in history ($^2/_3$ unbelievers and $^1/_3$ believers, Zechariah 13:8). When Terah was 130 years old, Abraham, the believing son, was born. Similarly, at the end of the world (13), the believers, typified by Abraham, will experience the completion (10) of their salvation.

Time Line
Years to the end of the world, A.D. 1988:
    2297 + 1988 - 1 = 4284 years.

Time Line's Spiritual Emphasis:
4284 years = 3 x 7 x 12 x 17.
It is God's perfect (7) will or purpose (3) that the fullness of all believers (12) will go to heaven (17). The destiny of believers is sure even though judgment beginning in A.D. 1988 comes upon this sinful world, typified by the two-thirds proportion of Terah's sons.

Time Line
Years to the end of the world, A.D. 1994:
    2297 + 1994 - 1 = 4290 years.

Time Line's Spiritual Emphasis:
4290 years = 3 x 10 x 11 x 13
In the completeness of time (10), God's purpose (3) for the human race will be realized at the end of the world (13) because Christ came as Savior (11).

Or: Time Line's Spiritual Emphasis:
    4290 = 2 x 3 x 5 x 11 x 13
    It is the purpose or will of God (3) that Christ would come (11) to bring salvation (5) to the believing part of the human race (2) until the end of time (13).

Event No. 6
Abraham was Born: 2167 B.C. (Gen. 11:27 to 12:4)

Relationship of the Event to the Gospel Message:
        The nation of Israel, which typified the body of believers, began with Abraham. In fact, Abraham is called the father of believers (Romans 4:16). Also, Abraham bore two sons, Ishmael, a type of people who remain unsaved, and Isaac, who represents both those who become saved and Christ Himself.

> Time Line
> Years to the coming of Christ, 7 B.C.:
>   2167 - 7 = 2160 years.

Time Line's Spiritual Emphasis:
    2160 years = 2 x 3 x 3 x 10 x 12.
    Even as Abraham was born so that the nation of Israel might come into being, so it is God's definite will (3 x 3) that Christ would come in the fulness (12) of time so that there would be brought into being the complete (10) body of believers.

Or: Time Line's Spiritual Emphasis:
    2160 years = 2 x 3 x 3 x 3 x 4 x 10.
    Even as Abraham was born so that Israel might come into being, so it is God's certain purpose (3 x 3 x 3) that, out of the whole world (4), there would be a complete (10) body of believers (2).

> Time Line
> Years to the coming of Christ, A.D. 33:
>   2167 + 33 = 2200 calendar years.

Time Line's Spiritual Significance
    2200 years = 2 x 11 x 100.
    In the completeness of time (100), Christ would come (11) so that through His sacrifice on the cross in A.D. 33, the church would be established (2).

Or: Time Line's Spiritual Emphasis:
    2200 years = 2 x 4 x 5 x 5 x 11.
    Even as Abraham bore two sons, one who typified Christ and all believers, and the other who typified all people who remain under the wrath of God, so Christ came (11) and through His sacrifice, out of the whole world (4), there would be salvation (5) for those who believed and judgment (5) upon those who would not believe.

> Time Line
> Years to the end of the world, A.D. 1994:
>   2167 + 1994 - 1 = 4160 years.

Time Line's Spiritual Emphasis:
    4160 years = 4 x 8 x 10 x 13.
    Even as Abraham was born to bring Israel into existence, so Christ's plan of salvation (8) for spiritual Israel will come into completion (10) at the end of the world (13) because Christ came.

Event No. 7
Abraham Enters the Land of Canaan: 2092 B.C.
(Gen. 12:1-9)

Relationship of the Event to the Gospel Message:
Abraham is called the father of believers. The
land of Canaan is a figure of the kingdom of God or

salvation or heaven. Therefore, this event highlights the entrance of believers into the kingdom of God when they become saved or into heaven at the end of time.

Time Line
Years to the coming of Christ, A.D. 33:
    2092 + 33 = 2125 calendar years.

Time Line's Spiritual Emphasis:

2125 years = 5 x 5 x 5 x 17.

Even as Abraham came into the promised land, so do all believers go into heaven (17) because God's salvation plan is certain and sure (5 x 5 x 5).

Time Line
Years to the end of the world, A.D. 1988:
    2092 + 1988 = 4080 calendar years.

Time Line's Spiritual Emphasis:

4080 years = 2 x 2 x 2 x 3 x 10 x 17.

It is established by God and will shortly come to pass (2 x 2) that the purpose of God (3) to bring the complete (10) number of believers (2) to heaven (17), will be fulfilled even though the final judgment begins with judgment on the house of God.

Or: Time Line's Spiritual Emphasis:

4080 years = 2 x 3 x 40 x 17.

Even as Abraham was tested as he went into the land of Canaan, so it is God's purpose (3) that the church (2) be tested (40) near the end of time before it goes to heaven (17).

Events No. 8
Abraham Circumcised: 2068 B.C. (Gen. 17)
Sodom and Gomorrah Destroyed: 2068 B.C.
(Gen. 18 & 19)

Relationship of the Event to the Gospel Message:
The circumcision of Abraham was a sign that God would provide salvation through the Lord Jesus Christ. The destruction of Sodom and Gomorrah was pointing to Judgment Day at the end of the world. These two events take place in the same year to highlight the fact that both events are similar in the sense that circumcision was a bloody ceremony that was a picture of Jesus' death and that He has experienced judgment on behalf of the elect. The events take place in the same year to also highlight the fact that the salvation for believers, to which circumcision pointed, would be completed at the same time that judgment upon unbelievers would take place.

Time Line
Years to the coming of Christ, A.D. 33:
2068 + 33 - 1 = 2100 years.

Time Line's Spiritual Message:
2100 years = 3 x 7 x 100.

It is the perfect (7) purpose (3) of God, that He would complete (100) His Gospel plan. The plan that was pictured in a shadow by Abraham's physical circumcision was certain to be fulfilled by the sacrifice of Christ in A.D. 33, when He endured the judgment of God.

Or: Time Line's Spiritual Message:
2100 years = 3 x 4 x 5 x 5 x 7.

It is God's perfect (7) purpose (3) to bring both salvation (5) and judgment (5) to the world (4). When Jesus endured the judgment of God, He guaranteed both the salvation of believers and the judgment of unbelievers.

> Time Line
> Years to the end of the world, A.D. 1988:
>   2068 + 1988 = 4056 calendar years.

Time Line's Spiritual Message:

4056 years = 2 x 12 x 13 x 13.

Even as God brought Sodom and Gomorrah to their end in judgment, so in the fulness of time (12), God will definitely bring and end to history (13 x 13) in judgment, beginning with the church (2).

Or: Time Line's Spiritual Message:

4056 years = 2 x 3 x 4 x 13 x 13.

Even as God brought Sodom and Gomorrah to their end in judgment, so it is the will (3) of God to definitely bring an end to history (13 x 13) in judgment, beginning with the church (2) including the whole world (4).

Event No. 9
Isaac was Born: 2067 B.C. (Gen. 21:1-5)

Relationship of the Event to the Gospel Message:
        Isaac, a type of Christ, was the only son born to Abraham and Sarah in their old age. His birth is dramatic proof of the sovereign grace of God, that He is wise and able to provide a Savior, as He had promised according to His will.

> Time Line
> Years to the coming of Christ, A.D. 33:
>   2067 + 33 = 2100 calendar years.

Time Line's Spiritual Emphasis:

2100 years = 3 x 7 x 100.

Even as Isaac's birth to Abraham and Sarah proved the certainty of God's promise of a seed, so it is God's perfect (7) purpose

(3) that He will complete (100) His Gospel promise to bring the Savior into the world.

Or: Time Line's Spiritual Emphasis:

2100 years = 2 x 3 x 5 x 7 x 10.

Even as Isaac's birth to Abraham and Sarah proved that God would fulfill His promise of a Savior, so it is God's perfect (7) will (3) to complete (10) His plan to bring grace (5) to His church (2).

Or: Time Line's Spiritual Emphasis:

2100 years = 3 x 4 x 5 x 5 x 7.

It is God's perfect (7) purpose or will (3) to bring both salvation (5) and judgment (5) to the world (4). When Jesus is born according to God's promise, He will bring the Gospel to the world, which will prepare some for grace and others for judgment.

Event. No. 10
Sarah Died and Abraham Bought a Grave Site:
2030 B.C. (Gen. 23)

Relationship of the Event to the Gospel Message:
In the year 2030 B.C., Abraham's wife Sarah died at the age of 127 years. To obtain a permanent tomb in which to bury her, Abraham bought the cave of Machpelah, which was the only land that Abraham ever owned. It pointed to the fact that when we die we must leave our bodies on this earth but they will be resurrected because Christ came to save our bodies as well as our souls.

Time Line
Years to Christ's first coming, 7 B.C.:
2030 - 7 = 2023 years.

Time Line's Spiritual Emphasis:
     2023 years = 7 x 17 x 17.
     In God's perfect (7) timetable, because Jesus came as our Savior in 7 B.C., not only are our souls resurrected at the moment we become saved (17) but also our bodies will be saved (17).

Event No. 11
Jacob and Esau were Born: 2007 B.C. (Gen. 25:20-26)

Relationship of the Event to the Gospel Message:
     Jacob, a son of Isaac, pointed to the seed of Abraham. That seed is Jesus, who is also referred to as Jacob in the Bible. That seed is also the church or the body of believers. In contrast, Esau, also a son of Isaac, is a picture of the unsaved people, especially unsaved people in the church.

Time Line
Years to the coming of Christ, 7 B.C.:
          2007 - 7 = 2000 years.

Time Line's Spiritual Emphasis:
     2000 years = 2 x 1000.
     The birth of Jacob pointed to the fact that in the completeness of time (1000) Christ would be born to bring salvation to believers (2).

Or: Time Line's Spiritual Emphasis:
     2000 years = 2 x 2 x 5 x 100.
     The birth of Jacob pointed to the fact that in the completeness of time (100) Christ would be born to bring salvation (5) to the believers (2) in His church (2).

Or: Time Line's Spiritual Emphasis:
     2000 years = 2 x 5 x 5 x 40.
     Even as Jacob and Esau were tested, with two different results,

so the church (2) is tested (40), which for some the result is salvation (5) and for others judgment (5).

Or: Time Line's Spiritual Emphasis:
2000 years = 2 x 4 x 5 x 5 x 10.
Because Christ was born in the church (2) and in the world (4) comes salvation (5) and judgment (5) which completes God's plan.

Time Line
Years to the coming of Christ, A.D. 33:
    2007 + 33 = 2040 calendar years.

Time Line's Spiritual Emphasis:
2040 years = 2 x 5 x 12 x 17.
The birth of Jacob pointed to the coming of Christ to bring God's salvation (5) for the fulness (12) of believers (2) and bring them to heaven (17).

Or: Time Line's Spiritual Emphasis:
2040 years = 10 x 12 x 17.
The birth of Jacob pointed to the coming of Christ, who came to complete (10) His plan for the fulness of believers (12) and realize the promise of heaven (17).

Or: Time Line's Spiritual Emphasis:
2040 years = 2 x 3 x 4 x 5 x 17.
The birth of Jacob pointed to the coming of Christ, who came for God's purpose (3) to bring His salvation (5) to believers throughout the world (4) and secure for them the promise of heaven (17).

Time Line
Years to the end of the world, A.D. 1994:
    2007 + 1994 - 1 = 4000 years.

Time Line's Spiritual Emphasis:
4000 years = 4 x 1000.
Even as Jacob, a type of Christ was born, so, too, God in the

person of the Lord Jesus came in the flesh so that in the completeness of time (1000) salvation might be provided for the world (4).

Or: Time Line's Spiritual Emphasis:
4000 years = 2 x 2 x 1000.

Even as Jacob, a type of Christ was born, so, too, God in the person of the Lord Jesus Christ came to be born and will come again at the end of the world to complete (1000) the salvation of the believers (2) within the church (2).

Or: Time Line's Spiritual Emphasis:
4000 years = 2 x 4 x 5 x 100.

The birth of Jacob points to Christ who would bring salvation (5) for the church (2) throughout the world (4) and bring it to completion (100). The salvation plan will be completed at the end of the world in A.D. 1994.

Or: Time Line's Spiritual Emphasis:
4000 years = 4 x 5 x 5 x 40.

The birth of Jacob points to Christ, who would come bring testing (40) to the whole world (4) resulting in either salvation (5) or judgment (5).

Event No. 12
Abraham Died: 1992 B.C. (Gen. 25:7-8)

Relationship of the Event to the Gospel Message:
Abraham, who is called the father of believers, died after he lived in Canaan exactly 100 years. The 100 years represent the completeness of God's salvation program, which actually will last forevermore. Abraham's physical death is the evidence that all mankind is under the curse of God. Apart from Christ, everyone is subject to judgment and eternal damnation.

Time Line
Years to the coming of Christ, A.D. 33:
    1992 + 33 - 1 = 2024 years.

Time Line's Spiritual Emphasis:
    2024 years = 2 x 4 x 11 x 23.

Jesus came (11) to endure judgment (23) on behalf of the believers (2) throughout the world (4). The 100 years Abraham lived in Canaan pointed to the eternal life which believers throughout the world received because Jesus came to endure judgment on their behalf.

Event No. 13
Esau, at 40 Years of Age, became Unequally Yoked:
1967 B.C. (Gen. 26:34-35)

Relationship of the Event to the Gospel Message:
    Esau is a picture of the whole human race that became unequally yoked with Satan when sin entered the world. (See Chapter 8, pages 232 to 252.)

Time Line
Years to end of the world, A.D. 1994:
    1967 + 1994 - 1 = 3960 years.

Time Line's Spiritual Emphasis:
    3960 years = 3 x 3 x 4 x 10 x 11.

Esau, who became unequally yoked, represents the whole human race that has become a slave of sin and Satan and therefore needs a Savior. The coming of Christ (11) as Savior showed that it is God's definite purpose (3 x 3) that His plan for the world (4) would take place because Christ came (11) and will be completed (10) at the end of the world.

Or: Time Line's Spiritual Emphasis:
    3960 years = 3 x 10 x 11 x 12.
    Esau, who became unequally yoked, represents the whole human race that has become unequally yoked with sin and Satan and therefore needs a Savior. The coming of Christ as Savior (11) in the fullness of time (12) showed that it was the purpose (3) of God to provide for salvation that would be completed (10) at the end of the world.

Or: Time Line's Spiritual Emphasis:
    3960 years = 2 x 3 x 5 x 11 x 12.
    Esau, who became unequally yoked, represents the whole human race that became unequally yoked with sin and Satan and therefore needs a Savior. It is the purpose (3) of God that through the coming of Christ as Savior (11) in the fullness of time (12) provided salvation (5) for the church (2) which comes into being all the way to the end of the world.

Event No. 14
Joseph was Born: 1916 B.C. (Gen. 30:22-24)

Relationship of the Event to the Gospel Message:
    Joseph, in many ways, was a type or picture of Christ. He was the eleventh son of Jacob, which pointed to Jesus' birth about 11,000 years after creation. Also, the fact that he saved his family and the Egyptians from famine plus the fact that he ruled over Egypt point to Jesus as Savior and King.

Time Line
Years to the end of the world, A.D. 1994:
    1916 + 1994 = 3910 calendar years.

Time Line's Spiritual Emphasis:
    3910 years = 10 x 17 x 23.
    Even as Joseph was born to save and rule, so Jesus was born

to complete (10) the plan which is to bring His people to heaven (17) and rule with a rod of iron over His enemies in judgment (23).

Or: Time Line's Spiritual Emphasis:
3910 years = 2 x 5 x 17 x 23.
Even as Joseph was born to save and rule, so Jesus brought salvation (5) to His church (2) in order to bring His people to heaven (17) and rule with a rod of iron over His enemies in judgment (23).

Event No. 15
Jacob became Israel: 1907 B.C. (Gen. 32:24-32)

Relationship of the Event to the Gospel Message:
When Jacob was 100 years old, that is, in the completeness of time, he wrestled with God at the River Jabbok. At the end of that event, his name was changed to Israel. The name Israel mean prince of God. Jacob or Israel was a great picture of both Christ, who is the Prince of God, and of the believers, who reign with Christ.

> Time Line
> Years to the end of the world, A.D. 1994:
> 1907 + 1994 - 1 = 3900 years.

Time Line's Spiritual Emphasis:
3900 years = 3 x 13 x 100.
Even as Jacob became Israel, the prince of God, so it is the purpose (3) of God to bring His Gospel plan to completion (100) at the end of the world (13), when believers will reign as princes of God forever with Christ in the new heavens and the new earth.

Or: Time Line's Spiritual Emphasis:
3900 years = 2 x 3 x 5 x 10 x 13.
Even as Jacob became Israel, the prince of God, so it is the

purpose or will (3) of God to save (5) the believers and complete their salvation (10) at the end of the world (13), when believers will reign forever as princes of God with Christ in the new heavens and the new earth.

Event No. 16
Joseph was 17 Years Old in 1899 B.C. (Gen. 37:1-11)

Relationship of the Event to the Gospel Message:
At the age of 17, Joseph dreamed two dreams that showed he would rule over his family. These dreams show him to be a picture of Christ, who is King of kings and Lord of lords, coming at the end of time to judge the world. The fact that He was 17 years old pointed to the fact that Christ would provide the blessings of heaven. In Joseph's first dream, his eleven brothers bowed down to him, pointing to the first coming of Christ 11,000 years after mankind's fall into sin. In Joseph's second dream, his eleven brothers plus his father and mother bowed down to him, pointing to the second coming of Christ 13,000 years after creation, when at the end of time, all believers will bow down before Him.

Time Line
Years to the coming of Christ, A.D. 33:
    1899 + 33 = 1932 calendar years.

Time Line's Spiritual Emphasis:
    1932 years = 3 x 4 x 7 x 23.
    As Joseph ruled over his brothers, according to his first dream, so Christ went to the cross in A.D. 33 and was judged (23) so that He could fulfill the perfect (7) will (3) of God which was to rule over His brothers throughout the whole world (4).

> Time Line
> Years to the end of the world, A.D. 1988:
>   1899 + 1988 = 3887 calendar years.

Time Line's Spiritual Emphasis:
        3887 years = 13 x 13 x 23.
        As Joseph ruled over the whole family, according to his second dream, so Christ would rule with a rod of iron over all mankind in judgment (23) at the definite end of the world (13 x 13), that judgment begins with the house of God at the beginning of the final tribulation in A.D. 1988.

Event No. 17
Isaac Died: 1887 B.C. (Gen. 35:28-29)

Relationship of the Event to the Gospel Message:
        Isaac is a great type of Christ. His death displays the fact that all men are subject to death and so He had to die for those whom He decided to release from that curse. Isaac died when he was old and full of years, reminding us that Christ died in the fullness of time.

> Time Line
> Years to the first coming of Christ, A.D. 33:
>   1887 + 33 = 1920 calendar years.

Time Line's Spiritual Emphasis:
        1920 years = 2 x 2 x 4 x 10 x 12.
        The death of Isaac reminds us that Christ died so that the complete plan of God (10) for the believers (2) in the church (2)

throughout the world (4) would be established and will come to pass in the fullness of time (12).

Or: Time Line's Spiritual Emphasis:
    1920 years = 2 x 2 x 2 x 4 x 5 x 12.
    The death of Isaac pointed to Christ who died so that in the fullness of time (12), salvation (5) would come to believers (2) in the church (2 x 2) throughout the world (4).

Event No. 18
The Seven-Year Famine in Egypt Began: 1879 B.C.
(Gen. 41:29, 30, 46)

Relationship of the Event to the Gospel Message:
        Joseph at the age of 37 (which signifies judgment) is prime minister over Egypt. It is in this year that the seven-year famine begins which is a picture of God's judgment on the world.

Time Line
Years to the coming of Christ, 7 B.C.
        1879 - 7 = 1872 years.

Time Line's Spiritual Emphasis:

    1872 years = 3 x 6 x 8 x 13.
    It is the purpose (3) of God that Christ who came as our Savior in 7 B.C. will come at the end of the world (13) to bring judgment on those who work (6) for their salvation (8).

Or: Time Line's Spiritual Emphasis:
    1872 years = 3 x 4 x 12 x 13.
    It is God's will (3) for the world (4) that in the fulness of time

(12) at the end of the world (13) Christ who came as the Savior will come as the Judge.

> Time Line
> Years to the coming of Christ, A.D. 33
> 1879 + 33 - 1 = 1911 years.

Time Line's Spiritual Emphasis:

1911 years = 3 x 7 x 7 x 13.

It is God's perfect (7) purpose (3) that Christ who at the cross endured the judgment for believers, will come at the end of the world (13) as Judge of all the earth.

> Time Line
> Years to the coming of Christ, A.D. 1994.
> 1879 + 1994 - 1 = 3872 years.

Time Line's Spiritual Emphasis

3872 years = 4 x 8 x 11 x 11.

Christ who definitely came the first time (11 x 11) to bring salvation (8) to the world (4), will come at the end of the world as Judge.

Or: Time Line's Spiritual Emphasis:

1920 years = 2 x 2 x 4 x 10 x 12.

The death of Isaac reminds us that Christ died so that the complete plan of God (10) for the believers (2) in the church (2) throughout the world (4) would be established and will come to pass in the fullness of time (12).

Or: Time Line's Spiritual Emphasis:

1920 years = 2 x 2 x 2 x 4 x 5 x 12.

The death of Isaac pointed to Christ who died so that in the fulness of time (12) salvation (5) would come to believers (2) in the church (2 x 2) throughout the world (4).

Event No. 19
Joseph Called Israel into Egypt in 1877 B.C. (Gen. 46)

Relationship of the Event to the Gospel Message:
Israel's entrance into Egypt is a picture of salvation in the sense that he was saved from starvation and came into the care of Joseph, who is a type of Christ. Jacob or Israel was 130 (13 x 10) years old and Joseph was 39 (3 x 13). These thirteens point to the end of the world when believers, the Israel of God, come into the complete care of Christ. An additional but different message is based upon Egypt as a picture of bondage to sin. Thus, Israel's entrance into Egypt is a picture of the external church, God's external Israel, spiritually coming into bondage to sin and apostasy during the final tribulation at the end of time.

Time Line
Years to the coming of Christ, 7 B.C.:
        1877 - 7 = 1870 years.

Time Line's Spiritual Emphasis:
        1870 years = 10 x 11 x 17.
        Even as Joseph saved his family from starvation, so Christ came the first time (11) to bring the blessings of heaven (17) to the complete number (10) of His spiritually starving family.

Or: Time Line's Spiritual Emphasis:
        1870 years = 2 x 5 x 11 x 17.
        Even as Joseph saved his family, so Christ came the first time (11) to save (5) believers (2) and give them the blessing of heaven (17).

Time Line
Years to the end of the world, A.D. 1988:
        1877 + 1988 - 1 = 3864 years.

Time Line's Spiritual Emphasis:
  3864 years = 2 x 3 x 4 x 7 x 23.
  Even as Israel and his family went into Egypt and eventual bondage, so it is God's perfect (7) will (3) to bring judgment (23) upon the church (2) throughout the world (4) for its spiritual bondage at the end of time.

Event No. 20
Moses was Born: 1527 B.C. (Exo. 2:1-10)

Relationship of the Event to the Gospel Message:
  Moses, who brought the law to the nation of Israel and who brought the nation of Israel out of Egypt, is both a type of the law of God and a type of Christ, the Savior.

> Time Line
> Years to the coming of Christ, A.D. 33:
>   1527 + 33 = 1560 calendar years.

Time Line's Spiritual Emphasis:
  1560 years = 10 x 12 x 13.
  Christ came to die in order to bring the complete number (10) of His people (12) out of this sin-cursed world at the end of time (13).

Or: Time Line's Spiritual Emphasis:
  1560 years = 2 x 5 x 12 x 13.
  Christ came to die in the fullness of time (12) so that He could give salvation (5) to believers (2) and deliver them out of this sin-cursed world at the end of time (13).

> Time Line
> Years to the end of the world, A.D. 1994:
>   1527 + 1994 - 1 = 3520 years.

Time Line's Spiritual Emphasis:
       3520 years = 2 x 2 x 4 x 4 x 5 x 11.
       Even as Moses was born to deliver the nation of Israel, so Christ would be born (11) into the world (4) to bring salvation (5) to believers (2) within the church (2) throughout the world (4).

Event No. 21
Israel Leaves Egypt in 1447 B.C. (Exo. 12)

Relationship of the Event to the Gospel Message:
       Israel's exodus from Egypt in 1447 B.C. is a dramatic picture of salvation. Moses led Israel out of Egypt and Pharaoh's rule, which was a picture of Christ leading His spiritual Israel out of bondage to sin and Satan. That was the time that the passover lamb was killed, a ceremony that was a picture of Christ's sacrifice that provided salvation. At that time, the nation of Israel began a forty-year testing program in the wilderness, just as spiritual Israel is tested as long as it is in this spiritual wilderness, earth.

Time Line
Years to the coming of Christ, 7 B.C.:
       1447 - 7 = 1440 years.

Time Line's Spiritual Emphasis:
       1440 years = 10 x 12 x 12.
       In the definite fullness of time (12 x 12), Christ would come to free the complete number (10) of His people.

Or: Time Line's Spiritual Emphasis:
       1440 years = 2 x 3 x 4 x 5 x 12.
       Even as national Israel was freed from Egyptian bondage, so

spiritual Israel (2) throughout the world (4) was given salvation (5) in the fullness of time (12) according to God's purpose (3).

Or: Time Line's Spiritual Emphasis:
    1440 = 3 x 12 x 40.
    Even as national Israel was tested in the wilderness, so it is God's will (3) to test (40) the fullness of His people (12).

> Time Line
> Years to the coming of Christ, A.D. 33.
>   1447 + 33 = 1480 calendar years.

Time Line's Spiritual Emphasis:
    1480 years = 2 x 4 x 5 x 37.
    Jesus would endure the wrath of God (37) to bring salvation (5) to believers (2) who are found throughout the world (4)

Event No. 22
Israel Enters Canaan in 1407 B.C. (Joshua 3)

Relationship of the Event to the Gospel Message:
    After wandering in the wilderness for forty years, national Israel entered the promised land. This was a picture of spiritual Israel entering the kingdom of God or entering heaven.

> Time Line
> Years to Christ's coming, 7 B.C.:
>   1407 - 7 = 1400 years.

Time Line's Spiritual Emphasis:
    1400 years = 2 x 7 x 10 x 10.
    Even as national Israel entered the promised land, so Jesus

came in the perfect (7) completeness (10) of time so that the complete (10) number of believers (2) could enter into the kingdom of God.

Or: Time Line's Spiritual Emphasis:
        1400 years = 2 x 2 x 5 x 7 x 10.
        Even as national Israel entered the promised land, so in God's perfect (7) time, salvation (5) would come to the complete number (10) of believers (2 x 2) so that they could enter into the kingdom of God.

Time Line
Years to Christ's coming, A.D. 33:
        1407 + 33 = 1440 calendar years.

Time Line's Spiritual Emphasis:
        1440 years = 10 x 12 x 12.
        Even as all of national Israel went into the promised land, because Christ went to the cross so in the completeness of time (10) will the fullness of all believers of all time (12 x 12) go into the kingdom of God.

Or: Time Line's Spiritual Emphasis:
        1440 years = 2 x 3 x 4 x 5 x 12.
        Even as it was God's purpose to bring all of national Israel into the land of Canaan, so because Christ went to the cross it was God's purpose (3) in the fullness of time (12) to bring salvation (5) to all believers (2) throughout the world (4).

Time Line
Years to the end of the world, A.D. 1994:
        1407 + 1994 - 1 = 3400 years.

Time Line's Spiritual Emphasis:
        3400 years = 2 x 10 x 10 x 17.
        The promised land, Canaan, was a type of heaven. In the completeness of time (10) the complete number (10) of believers will enter heaven (17).

Or: Time Line's Spiritual Emphasis:
 3400 years = 2 x 2 x 5 x 10 x 17.
 Salvation (5) will come to the complete number (10) of believers (2 x 2) so that they will go to heaven (17) at the end of time.

Event No. 23
Gideon Died and His Sons were Murdered: 1207 B.C.
(Judges 9 & 10)

Relationship of the Event to the Gospel Message:
 Gideon was a judge over Israel for forty years. When he died, a son whom he had by a concubine, murdered all except one of his other seventy sons. This sad event is a dramatic picture of the church which seems dead and without hope. This situation existed when Christ came the first time and will exist at the end of the final tribulation just before Christ comes.

Time Line
Years to the coming of Christ, 7 B.C.:
  1207 - 7 = 1200 years.

Time Line's Spiritual Emphasis:
 1200 years = 2 x 5 x 10 x 12.
 To the apparently hopeless situation of the apostate church, Christ came the first time in the fullness of time (12) to bring salvation (5) to the complete number (10) of believers (2).

Or: Time Line's Spiritual Emphasis:
 1200 years = 2 x 3 x 4 x 5 x 10.
 To an apparently hopeless situation of the apostate church, Jesus came the first time in the completeness of time (10) according to God's will (3) to bring salvation (5) to believers (2) worldwide (4).

Time Line
Years to the end of the world, A.D. 1994:
    1207 + 1994 - 1 = 3200 years.

Time Line's Spiritual Emphasis:
    3200 years = 2 x 4 x 5 x 8 x 10 x 10.
    To an apparently hopeless situation of the apostate church, Jesus Christ will come the second time, in the completeness of time (10) to the world (4) to complete (10) the salvation (8) of the believers and to bring judgment (5) on the unsaved .

Event No. 24
Upon the Death of the Judge Tola, Jair Began to Judge Israel in 1181 B.C. (Judges 10:1-5)

Relationship of the Event to the Gospel Message:
            Tola judged Israel for 23 years. When he died in 1181 B.C., Jair began to judge. Jair judged for 22 years and had 30 sons who rode on 30 ass colts and had 30 cities (Judges 10:1-4). The end of 23 years points to the end of the final tribulation period when Christ comes. Jair, therefore, is a picture of Christ as He comes at the end of the world. His 30 sons (3 x 10) represent the purpose (3) of God that the complete number of the sons of God will be saved. Riding on a colt and having a city in each case points to the complete (10) purpose (3) of God, which will be realized as all believers reign with Him forevermore.

Time Line
Years to the end of the world, A.D. 1994:
            1181 + 1994 - 1 = 3174 years.

Time Line's Spiritual Emphasis:
    3174 years = 2 x 3 x 23 x 23.
    Even as Jair came to judge after Tola judged for 23 years, so it is God's purpose or will (3) that Christ will come at the end of time to definitely judge (23 x 23) the church (2).

Event No. 25
Jephthah Began to Judge Israel in 1159 B.C.
(Judges 11)

Relationship of the Event to the Gospel Message:
    Jephthah the Gileadite (heap of witness) began to judge Israel after he had conquered the Ammonites who were oppressing Israel. Because of a vow he made to God that he would sacrifice whatever first came out of his house if God gave deliverance to Israel, he sacrificed his only daughter. Thus, he is a picture of God who gave His only Son as a sacrifice so that the Israel of God might spiritually be set free.

> Time Line
> Years to the birth of Christ in 7 B.C.:
>   1159 - 7 = 1152 years.

Time Line's Spiritual Emphasis:
    1152 years = 2 x 4 x 12 x 12.
    Even as Jephthah sacrificed his only daughter to obtain victory for Israel, so God sent His only Son, Jesus, to take on a human nature so that He could be sacrificed in the fullness of time (12). Thus, the fullness (12) of believers (2) throughout the world (4) might be delivered from sin and Satan.

Or: Time Line's Spiritual Emphasis:
    1152 years = 3 x 4 x 8 x 12.
    Even as Jephthah sacrificed his only daughter to obtain victory

for Israel, so it was God's purpose or will (3) that God sacrifice His Son so that the fullness (12) of His church throughout the world (4) might be delivered from sin and Satan.

> Time Line
> Years to the end of the world, A.D. 1988:
>   1159 + 1988 - 1 = 3146 years.

Time Line's Spiritual Emphasis:
        3146 years = 2 x 11 x 11 x 13.
        Christ definitely came the first time (11 x 11) and will come again at the end of time (13) for the sake of believers.

Event No. 26
Ibzan Began to Judge in 1153 B.C. (Judges 12:8-10)

Relationship of the Event to the Gospel Message:
        When the judge Jephthah died, Ibzan of Bethlehem began to judge and he judged Israel for seven years. He had 30 sons and 30 daughters, whom he took from abroad for his sons. His birthplace Bethlehem parallels that of Jesus who was born in Bethlehem. His 30 (3 x 10) sons emphasize the complete (10) purpose (3) of Jesus in making believers His sons. His 30 (3 x 10) daughters taken from abroad emphasize the complete (10) purpose (3) of God to have spiritual children from the whole world.

> Time Line
> Years to the end of the world, A.D. 1994:
>   1153 + 1994 - 1 = 3146 years.

Time Line's Spiritual Emphasis:
3146 years = 2 x 11 x 11 x 13.
Christ definitely came the first time (11 x 11) and will come again at the end of time (13) for the sake of all believers (2).

Event No. 27
The Ark was taken by the Philistines in 1068 B.C.
(I Sam. 4)

Relationship of the Event to the Gospel Message:
One of the saddest events in the history of Israel occurred when the ark was captured by the Philistines. This was a sign that God had abandoned Israel because of the people's wickedness.

Time Line
Years to the coming of Christ, A.D. 33:
1068 + 33 - 1 = 1100 years.

Time Line's Spiritual Emphasis:
1100 years = 11 x 100.
Jesus came (11) in the completeness (100) of time to die on the cross, at which time God no longer had a special relationship with national Israel.

Or: Time Line's Spiritual Emphasis:
1100 years = 2 x 5 x 10 x 11.
Christ came the first time (11) to die on the cross so that salvation could come to the complete number (10) of believers (2) at which time God no longer had a special relationship with national Israel.

Event No. 28
The Ark Restored to Israel: 1067 B.C. (I Sam. 6)

Relationship of the Event to the Gospel Message:
            Seven months after the ark was taken by the
Philistines, the ark was restored to Israel. This antic-
ipates Immanuel, God coming to be with His people.
The seven months anticipate the fact that Jesus came
in a perfect time.

Time Line
Years to the coming of Christ, A.D. 33:
            1067 + 33 = 1100 calendar years.

Time Line's Spiritual Emphasis:
            1100 years = 11 x 100.
            Jesus came the first time (11) in the completeness of time (100)
to be with His people.

Or: Time Line's Spiritual Emphasis:
            1100 years = 2 x 5 x 10 x 11.
            Even as the ark was restored to national Israel, so Jesus came
the first time (11) to bring salvation (5) to the complete number (10)
of believers (2) in order to be with them forever.

Time Line
Years to the end of the world, A.D. 1994:
            1067 + 1994 - 1 = 3060 years.

Time Line's Spiritual Emphasis:
            3060 years = 2 x 3 x 3 x 10 x 17.
            Even as the ark was restored to national Israel, it is the definite
purpose of God (3 x 3) that at the end of the world the complete number
(10) of believers (2) would be with Him in heaven (17) forever.

Event No. 29
Saul Becomes the First King to Rule Over Israel: 1047 B.C.

Relationship of the Event to the Gospel Message:
God brought the nation of Israel out of Egypt in the year 1447 B.C. For the next 400 years, God ruled over them through Moses and Joshua and by means of a series of judges, the last of whom was Samuel. In the year 1047 B.C., precisely 400 years after leaving Egypt, they desired a king like the other nations. God explained to Samuel that this was because they were rejecting God's rule over them. The 400 years (10 x 40) indicated that during this 400 years, they had been tested by God and had completely (10) failed the test (40).

Time Line
Years to the first coming of Christ, 7 B.C.
        1047 - 7 = 1040 years.

Time Line's Spiritual Emphasis:
        1040 years = 2 x 4 x 10 x 13.
        Christ came to the world (4) in the completeness (10) of time to be the King who would rule over the church (2) as it is to be found throughout the time (13) of the world.

Time Line
Years to Christ's first coming, A.D. 33.
        1047 + 33 = 1080 calendar years.

Time Line's Spiritual Emphasis:
        1080 = 2 x 2 x 3 x 3 x 3 x 10
        Even as God gave Israel their first king, Saul, so it is God's definite purpose (3 x 3 x 3) that in the completeness of time (10) God Himself in the person of the Lord Jesus would come to rule the church (2 x 2).

Event No. 30
David was Born: 1037 B.C. (I Sam. 17:12-17, II Sam. 5:4)

Relationship of the Event to the Gospel Message:
> *David is a great type of Christ. Therefore, his birth pointed to Christ who would be born as our Savior.*

Time Line
Years to the end of the world, A.D. 1988:
    1037 + 1988 = 3025 calendar years.

Time Line's Spiritual Emphasis:
    3025 years = 5 x 5 x 11 x 11.
    Even as David was born, Christ would definitely come the first time (11 x 11) to bring salvation (5) and judgment (5). His work would conclude at the end of time, being ushered in by the final tribulation.

Event No. 31
David Became King: 1007 B.C. (I Sam. 5:4)

Relationship of the Event to the Gospel Message:
> *David is a great type of Christ. Therefore, when he became king over national Israel, he was a picture of Christ who became King of the Israel of God.*

Time Line
Years to the coming of Christ, 7 B.C.:
    1007 - 7 = 1000 years.

Time Line's Spiritual Emphasis:
    1000 years = 10 x 10 x 10.
    Even as David ascended the throne of Israel, so it is God's will expressed in His Word, that in the completeness of time (10 x 10), Christ would come as King over the complete church (10).

Or: Time Line's Spiritual Emphasis:
    1000 years = 4 x 5 x 5 x 10.
    Even as David ascended the throne of national Israel, so in the completeness of time (10), Christ would come to rule, bringing salvation (5) and judgment (5) to the whole world (4).

Or: Time Line's Spiritual Emphasis:
    1000 years = 2 x 2 x 5 x 5 x 10.
    Even as David ascended the throne of national Israel, so in the completeness of time (10), Jesus would come to rule, bringing salvation (5) to the believers (2) and judgment (5) to the unsaved within the church (2).

Time Line
Years to the end of the world, A.D. 1994:
    1007 + 1994 - 1 = 3000 years.

Time Line's Spiritual Emphasis:
    3000 years = 3 x 10 x 10 x 10.
    Even as David ascended the throne, so it is the will and purpose (3) of God that when Jesus returns at the end of time, He will completely (1000) rule over all things.

Or: Time Line's Spiritual Emphasis:
    3000 years = 3 x 4 x 5 x 5 x 10.
    As David ascended the throne, so it is the will (3) of God, that Christ will come as King at the end of the world to complete His plan (10) of salvation (5) and judgment (5) for the whole world (4).

Or: Time Line's Spiritual Emphasis:
    3000 years = 3 x 4 x 5 x 5 x 10.

Even as David ascended the throne, so, too, it is the purpose of God (3) that Christ will come as King at the end of the world to complete (10) salvation (5) and judgment (5) for the world (4).

Event No. 32
Temple Foundation Laid: 967 B.C. (I Kings 6:1)

Relationship of the Event to the Gospel Message:
Solomon, who was a type of Christ, ruled over Israel and constructed the temple. The temple is a type or figure of God's church, both the outward organization called the church and the body of true believers who are part of the church.

Time Line
Years to the coming of Christ, 7 B.C.:
            967 - 7 = 960 years.

Time Line's Spiritual Emphasis:
            960 years = 2 x 4 x 10 x 12.
            Even as Solomon began to build the temple, so Christ came in the fullness of time (12) to begin building the complete number (10) of believers (2), who are found throughout the world, into His spiritual temple.

Or: Time Line's Spiritual Emphasis:
            960 years = 2 x 2 x 4 x 5 x 12.
            Even as Solomon began to build the temple, so did Christ come to begin building His church (2) by bringing salvation (5) to the full number (12) of believers who are found in the whole world (4).

Time Line
Years to the coming of Christ, A.D. 33:
            967 + 33 - 1 = 999 years.

Time Line's Spiritual Emphasis:

999 years = 3 x 3 x 3 x 37.

It was God's definite purpose (3 x 3) that Christ, the temple of God, would be judged (37) so that He could fulfill His purpose (3) of building His temple, the believers.

Time Line
Years to the coming of Christ, A.D. 33.
967 + 33 = 1000 calendar years.

Time Line's Spiritual Emphasis:

1000 years = 10 x 100.

In the completeness (100) of time Christ died to build the complete (10) church.

Or: Time Line's Spiritual Emphasis:

1000 years = 2 x 2 x 5 x 5 x 10.

Jesus came to die on the cross in the completeness of time (10) in order to build His church (2) of all the believers (2) as He brought the message of salvation (5) and judgment (5).

Time Line
Years to the coming of Christ, A.D. 1994
967 + 1994 - 1 = 2960.

Time Line's Spiritual Emphasis:

2960 = 2 x 4 x 10 x 37.

Jesus would complete (10) His plans for believers (2) and for the whole world (4) when judgment comes (37) at the end of time.

Event No. 33
The Kingdom of Israel Divided: 931 B.C. (I Kings 11)

Relationship of the Event to the Gospel Message:

*In his old age, Solomon did evil and went not
fully after the Lord. Therefore, upon Solomon's death,
God split the kingdom of Israel. Ten tribes to the north
formed a nation which retained the name Israel. Two
tribes to the south formed a nation which was called
Judah. God promised that Israel and Judah would
again become one nation. This prediction was fulfilled
when Christ established the kingdom of God, the real
spiritual nation of Israel.*

Time Line
Years to the coming of Christ, 7 B.C.:
    931 - 7 = 924 years.

Time Line's Spiritual Emphasis:
    924 years = 7 x 11 x 12.
    National Israel was broken because of sin, but Christ came (11)
in the fullness of time (12) to create His one perfect (7) church, spiritual
Israel.

Or: Time Line's Spiritual Emphasis:
    924 years = 2 x 2 x 3 x 7 x 11.
    National Israel was broken because of sin, but Jesus came (11)
so that His purpose (3) to establish His perfect (7) church (2 x 2) would
be fulfilled.

Time Line
Years to the end of the world, A.D. 1994:
    931 + 1994 = 2925 calendar years.

Time Line's Spiritual Emphasis:
    2925 years = 3 x 3 x 5 x 5 x 13.
    As faithful Judah was separated from wicked Israel, it is the
definite purpose of God (3 x 3) that at the end of time (13), the true
church will be given salvation (5) and the false church will be judged
(5).

Event No. 34
The Wicked King Jehoram of Judah Died: 842 B.C.
(II Kings 21)

Relationship of the Event to the Gospel Message:
    Jehoram was an especially wicked king who despised God's Word. After reigning for eight years, God struck him with a terrible illness so that the Bible records that "after the end of two years, his bowels fell out by reason of his sickness: so he died of sore diseases" (II Chronicles 21:19). Jehoram is a picture of a rebellious church that comes under the judgment of God.

Time Line
Years to the end of the world, A.D. 1994:
    842 + 1994 - 1 = 2835 years.

Time Line's Spiritual Emphasis:
2835 years = 3 x 3 x 3 x 3 x 5 x 7.
    It is God's absolute purpose (3 x 3 x 3 x 3) that perfect (7) judgment (5) will come upon the church at the end of time.

Event No. 35
Athaliah Began to Reign: 841 B.C. (II Kings 11)

Relationship of the Event to the Gospel Message:
    Athaliah murdered all but one of the royal seed, then reigned over Judah for six years. Her reign was a dramatic picture of a church that is under God's judgment.

Time Line
Years to the end of the world, A.D. 1994:
    841 + 1994 = 2835 calendar years.

Time Line's Spiritual Message:
        2835 years = 3 x 3 x 3 x 3 x 5 x 7.
        It is God's absolute purpose (3 x 3 x 3 x 3) that at the end of the world, perfect (7) judgment (5) would come upon a sinful church and world.

Event No. 36
Athaliah Died and Joash (Jehoash) Began to Reign:
835 B.C. (II Kings 11:21 to 12:1)

Relationship of the Event to the Gospel Message:
        The death of the wicked Athaliah and the beginning of the reign of the 7-year-old Joash is a picture of the judgment of Satan and the victory of Christ and His kingdom.

Time Line
Years to the coming of Christ, 7 B.C.:
        835 - 7 = 828 years.

Time Line's Spiritual Emphasis:
        828 years = 3 x 3 x 4 x 23.
        It is the definite purpose (3 x 3) of God that the birth of Christ would guarantee judgment (23) against the world (4).

Or: Time Line's Spiritual Emphasis:
        828 years = 3 x 12 x 23.
        It is the will (3) of God that in the fullness of time (12), Satan would be judged (23). The birth of Christ would guarantee this.

Time Line
Years to the coming of Christ, A.D. 33:
        835 + 33 - 1 = 867 years.

Time Line's Spiritual Emphasis:
 867 years = 3 x 17 x 17.
 Because Christ came as the Savior, He vanquished Satan even as wicked Athaliah was killed. This guaranteed that God's purpose (3) to bring believers to heaven (17 x 17) would be certain.

Event No. 37
Death of Jehoiada the Priest: 796 B.C.
(II Chron. 24:25)

Relationship of the Event to the Gospel Message:
 Jehoiada was the God-fearing priest who brought the young child to the throne upon the death of wicked Athaliah. As long as Jehoiada lived, Joash was a God-fearing king. Upon the death of Jehoiada at the age of 130 years (II Chron. 24:15), Joash became very wicked. Because of this wickedness, as a judgment God brought devastation to Judah by the Syrian army. This resulted in a diseased Joash who then was murdered by his servants. When we reconstruct the reigns of the kings of Judah (pages 129-174), we discover that the son of Joash, Amaziah, began to reign in 796 B.C., the year before Josiah died. The circumstantial evidence is very great that Jehoiada died in 796 B.C. the year Amaziah began to reign as co-regent. In that year:

 1. Joash had reigned 39 years (3 x 13).
 2. Joash was 46 years old (2 x 23).
 3. Jehoiada died at the age of 130 (10 x 13).

This year, therefore, is a dramatic picture of the end of the world (13) when God (typified by Jehoiada) has left the church, the church becomes wicked and comes under God's judgment (2 x 23) beginning with the final tribulation period.

Time Line
Years to the coming of Christ, A.D. 33
                796 + 33 - 1 = 828 years.

Time Line's Spiritual Emphasis:
828 years = 2 x 2 x 3 x 3 x 23.

Because Christ went to the cross guaranteeing judgment on the wicked, so it is God's definite will (3 x 3) to bring judgment on the churches (2 x 2) that do wickedly.

Or: Time Line's Spiritual Emphasis:
828 years = 3 x 12 x 23.

It is the purpose (3) of God that in the fullness (12) of time, judgment (23) will come upon the world. By Christ experiencing judgment at the cross, it guaranteed judgment for all the wicked of the world.

Time Line
Years to the end of the world, A.D. 1988.
                796 + 1988 - 1 = 2783 years.

Time Line's Spiritual Emphasis:
2783 years = 11 x 11 x 23.

Because Christ came the first time (11) to begin the church (11) but also guaranteeing judgment on the wicked, so it will be at the end of the world, God's judgment (23) will come and will begin in A.D. 1988 when God begins by judging the church. The death of Jehoiada underscores the withdrawal of the Holy Spirit's protection of the church.

Event No. 38
Joash (Jehoash) Died: 795 B.C.
(II Chronicles 24:24-25)

Relationship of the Event to the Gospel Message:

Joash reigned for forty years, and during most of his reign, he was a good king. But the year he died, he did very wickedly. He is a picture of the church, which finally comes under God's judgment.

Time Line
Years to the coming of Christ, A.D. 33:
795 + 33 = 828 calendar years.

Time Line's Spiritual Emphasis:
828 years = 2 x 2 x 3 x 3 x 23.
It is the definite purpose (3 x 3) of God that the church (2 x 2), which began because Christ went to the cross, will come under God's judgment (23) if it does wickedly.

Or: Time Line's Spiritual Emphasis:
828 years = 3 x 12 x 23.
It is the purpose of God (3) that in the fullness (12) of time, judgment (23) was guaranteed by Christ going to the cross.

Time Line
Years to the end of the world, A.D. 1988
795 + 1988 = 2783 calendar years.

Time Line's Spiritual Emphasis:
2783 years = 11 x 11 x 23.
Even as Joash did wickedly at the end of his life, so the church which was established by Christ going to the cross (11) will do wickedly near its end, as God begins to bring judgment (23) beginning with the church, which was established by Christ's first coming (11).

Event No. 39
Uzziah (Azariah) Began to Reign over Judah: 789 B.C.
(II Kings 15:1-2)

Relationship of the Event to the Gospel Message:

The God-fearing king Uzziah reigned over Judah for 52 years. The 52 years point to the 52 weeks in a year. Therefore, his reign typifies the reign of Christ during the whole New Testament era, which is called the acceptable year.

Time Line
Years to the coming of Christ, 7 B.C.:
    789 - 7 = 782 years.

Time Line's Spiritual Emphasis:
    782 years = 2 x 17 x 23.
    Even as Uzziah reigned over Judah, so Christ came to reign through believers (2) bringing the Gospel of the promise of heaven (17) and the threat of judgment (23) during the acceptable year.

Time Line
Years to the end of the world, A.D. 1994:
    789 + 1994 = 2783 calendar years.

Or: Time Line's Spiritual Emphasis:
    2783 years = 11 x 11 x 23.
    The coming of Christ (11 x 11) guaranteed that judgment (23) will come to the unsaved at the end of the world.

Event No. 40
Uzziah (Azariah) Died: 737 B.C. (II Chronicles 26, Isaiah 6)

Relationship of the Event to the Gospel Message:
    In the year that Uzziah died after a reign of fifty-two years, Isaiah in a vision saw the glory of God as the King and Judge over the earth; and Isaiah was qualified and was given the mandate to send forth the Gospel (Isaiah 6:1-9).

> Time Line
> Years to the coming of Christ, A.D. 33:
>   737 + 33 = 770 calendar years.

Time Line's Spiritual Emphasis:
     770 years = 7 x 10 x 11.
     In the perfect (7) completeness (10) of time, Christ would come (11) to bring into reality God's plan of salvation for the world.

Or: Time Line's Spiritual Emphasis:
     770 years = 2 x 5 x 7 x 11.
     In the perfection (7) of God's timetable, Christ would come as the Savior (11) to bring salvation (5) to the believers (2).

> Time Line
> Years to the end of the world, A.D. 1994:
>   737 + 1994 - 1 = 2730 years.

Time Line's Spiritual Emphasis:
     2730 years = 3 x 7 x 10 x 13.
     It is God's purpose (3) that in the perfection (7) of God's plan, the end of the world (13) will come, which completes (10) the acceptable year of the Lord.

Or: Time Line's Spiritual Emphasis:
     2730 years = 2 x 3 x 5 x 7 x 13.
     It is God's purpose (3) that in the perfection (7) of God's plan, salvation (5) will come for the church (2) throughout the acceptable year of the Lord, even to the end of the world (13).

Event No. 41
Hezekiah Threatened by Assyrians and by Death: 701 B.C. (II Kings 16 to II Kings 20)

Relationship of the Event to the Gospel Message:

In King Hezekiah's fourteenth year (701 B.C.), two momentous events occurred. The Assyrians had surrounded Jerusalem with an army of 185,000 men, and Hezekiah was dying. God gave him victory over the Assyrians by causing the 185,000 men to die overnight, and God gave Hezekiah fifteen additional years of life. His experience is representative of the end of the world when Satan surrounds the camp of the saints, typified by Jerusalem in Hezekiah's day, and when it looks like the church is dying typified by Hezekiah, as he was dying. But then God gave victory to the church and eternal life to the believers, typified by the additional fifteen years (3 x 5) given to Hezekiah the third day he prayed. Thus, through Hezekiah, God is showing that it is His purpose (3) to give salvation (5) to all those who have trusted in Christ.

Time Line
Years to the end of the world, A.D. 1988:
$$701 + 1988 - 1 = 2688 \text{ years.}$$

Time Line's Spiritual Emphasis:

2688 years = 2 x 2 x 3 x 4 x 7 x 8.

It is God's purpose (3) that at the end of the world, He will bring Satan against the church (2) all over the world (4) during the final tribulation period, but finally God's perfect (7) salvation (8) plan will be realized for the believers (2).

Time Line
Years to the end of the world, A.D. 1994:
$$1994 + 701 = 2695 \text{ calendar years.}$$

Time Line's Spiritual Emphasis:

2695 years = 5 x 7 x 7 x 11.

It is God's perfect (7) plan of salvation (5) that because Christ went to the cross (11) He provided perfect (7) salvation from the enemies.

Event No. 42
Jehoiakim was Cursed by God and Nebuchadrezzar became King over Babylon: 605 B.C.

Relationship of the Event to the Gospel Message:
Jehoiakim was a wicked king of Judah. In the fourth year of his reign (Jer. 36:1), he was cursed by God so that "He shall have none to sit upon the throne of David" (Jer. 36:30). In the same year Nebuchadrezzar (also called Nebuchadnezzar) began to rule over Babylon (Jer. 25:1) and began to rule over Judah (Jer. 25:9). This is a picture of Satan being loosed at the beginning of the final tribulation to rule over the apostate church.

Time Line
Years to the birth of Christ, 7 B.C.
605 - 7 = 598 years.

Time Line's Spiritual Emphasis:
598 years = 2 x 13 x 23.

Jehoiakim had none to sit upon the throne of David, but Jesus came as the son of David to rule over the church (2) in judgment (23) at the end of time (13).

Time Line
Years to the cross, A.D. 33.
605 + 33 - 1 = 637.

Time Line's Spiritual Emphasis:
637 = 7 x 7 x 13.

In the perfection (7) of time, Jesus went to the cross in accordance with God's perfect (7) plan so that at the end of time (13) He could come to end Satan's reign.

Time Line
Years to the end of the world, A.D. 1988
605 + 1988 - 1 = 2592

Time Line's Spiritual Emphasis:
2592 = 3 x 6 x 12 x 12.

It is God's will (3) that in the fullness (12) of time God judged the works (6) of the Old Testament church by allowing Nebuchadrezzar to rule, so He would judge the New Testament church in the fullness (12) of time by allowing Satan to rule.

Event No. 43
Israel (Judah) was Destroyed by Babylon: 587 B.C.
(II Chronicles 36)

Relationship of the Event to the Gospel Message:
        In 587 B.C., Babylon ended the existence of Israel as an independent nation when it conquered Jerusalem and destroyed the temple and the city. It was a picture of God's judgment on the church during the final tribulation. In fact, the last twenty-three years of Israel's existence (609-587 B.C., inclusive), are a type or figure of the final tribulation.

Time Line
Years to the end of the world, A.D. 1988:
        587 + 1988 - 1 = 2574 years.

Time Line's Spiritual Emphasis:
        2574 years = 2 x 3 x 3 x 11 x 13.

It is the purpose of God (3) that Christ would come (11) to build His church (2), but it is also the purpose (3) of God that at the end of the world (13), judgment will come upon the church, beginning with the final tribulation period in A.D. 1988.

Event No. 44
The 23rd Year of Nebuchadrezzar: 582 B.C.
(Jeremiah 52:28-30)

Relationship of the Event to the Gospel Message:
In the seventh year (597 B.C.) Nebuchadrezzar took 3023 Jews captive. In his eighteenth year when Jerusalem was destroyed (587 B.C.), he took an additional 832 captives. In his 23rd year (582 B.C.), he took 745 people captive, making a total of 4600 captives (3023 + 832 + 745 = 4600). Nebuchadrezzar was used of God to bring judgment on Jerusalem and Judah even as God uses Satan during the final tribulation to bring judgment on the church. The 4600, which equals 2 x 23 x 10 x 10, emphasizes the definite completeness (10 x 10) of this judgment (23) on the church (2). The 23rd year of Nebuchadrezzar further emphasizes this judgment.

> Time Line
> Years to the first coming of Christ, 7 B.C.
> $$582 - 7 = 575 \text{ years.}$$

Time Line's Spiritual Emphasis:
575 years = 5 x 5 x 23.
Christ came to bring salvation (5) to this world. But because He bore the judgment (5) of God for the sins of those who become saved, He guaranteed judgment (23) upon the world, which would begin with judgment on the church even as Israel came into judgment.

> Time Line
> Years to the end of the world, A.D. 1994:
> $$582 + 1994 = 2576 \text{ calendar years.}$$

Time Line's Spiritual Emphasis:
2576 years = 2 x 2 x 4 x 7 x 23.

Even as God used Nebuchadrezzar to bring judgment on Judah, so, too, at the end of the world, God will use Satan to bring judgment (23) on the church (2 x 2) as it is found throughout the world (4).

Event No. 45
Jehoiachin Freed from Prison: 560 B.C.
(Jeremiah 52:31-34)

Relationship of the Event to the Gospel Message:
Jehoiachin, the son of Jehoiakim, reigned ten years with his father. However, because of Jehoiakim's arrogant destruction of God's Word, God decreed that none of his seed would sit on the throne of David (Jeremiah 36:30). Therefore, three months and ten days (II Chronicles 36:9) after Jehoiakim was taken prisoner by the Babylonians, Jehoiachin was also taken captive by the Babylonians in the year 597 B.C. Thirty-seven years later, the King of Babylon freed Jehoiachin from prison and made him a ruler in Babylon. This is a dramatic picture of Satan who is given authority to rule over the church during the final tribulation period. In so doing, it will be the apostate leadership of the church, typified by Jehoiachin, that will make the church into a spiritual Babylon as its rulers come under the authority of Satan. This is a judgment on the church that transitions into the judgment of the last day.

Time Line
Years to Christ's first coming, A.D. 33.
$$560 + 33 - 1 = 592 \text{ years.}$$

Time Line's Spiritual Emphasis:
$592 = 2 \times 2 \times 4 \times 37.$
In God's plan for the church (2) all over the world (4) Jesus

would come to bear the wrath of God (37) even as there is to be judgment at the end of the world upon the church (2).

Time Line
Years to the end of the world, A.D. 1988:
    560 + 1988 = 2548 calendar years.

Time Line's Spiritual Emphasis:
    2548 years = 2 x 2 x 7 x 7 x 13.
    In God's perfect (7) plan for the church (2) at the end of the world (13), beginning with the final tribulation period, God will use Satan to rule over the church (2) so that the church and the world will be perfectly (7) prepared for Judgment Day.

Time Line
Years to the end of the world, A.D. 1994.
    560 + 1994 - 1 = 2553 years.

Time Line's Spiritual Emphasis:
    2553 = 3 x 23 x 37.
    It is God's purpose (3) to bring judgment on the world (37) beginning with judgment (23) on the church which was typified by Jehoiachin's release from prison and rule over Babylon.

Event No. 46
Ezra Brings the Law to Jerusalem: 458 B.C.
(Ezra 7)

Relationship of the Event to the Gospel Message:
        In 458 B.C., Ezra was commissioned by the king of the Medes and Persians to go to Jerusalem and teach the law of God. This is a picture that points to the building of the City of God, which is the church or the body of believers.

> Time Line
> Years to the coming of Christ, A.D. 33:
>   458 + 33 - 1 = 490 years.

Time Line's Spiritual Message:
490 years = 7 x 7 x 10.

In the perfect (7) completeness (10) of God's timetable, Christ would go to the cross in A.D. 33 to perfectly (7) provide for the building of the spiritual house of God.

Or: Time Line's Spiritual Emphasis:
490 years = 7 x 7 x 2 x 5.

In the perfection (7) of God's timetable, Christ would go to the cross in A.D. 33 to perfectly (7) provide for the salvation (5) of the church (2), which is the City of God.

Event No. 47
Jesus was Born: 7 B.C.

Relationship of the Event to the Gospel Message:
In 7 B.C., God in the person of the Lord Jesus took on a human nature, by being born of Mary, so that He could be the Savior.

> Time Line
> Years to the cross, A.D. 33:
>   7 + 33 = 40 calendar years.

Time Line's Spiritual Emphasis:
40 years = 4 x 10.

In the completeness of time (10), Jesus was born of a woman so that He could go to the cross to be the Savior of the world (4).

Or: Time Line's Spiritual Emphasis:

40 years = 4 x 2 x 5.

Jesus was born of a woman so that He could go to the cross to provide salvation (5) for the church (2), which comes from the whole world (4).

> Time Line
> Years to the end of the world, A.D. 1994:
> 7 + 1994 - 1 = 2000 years.

Time Line's Spiritual Emphasis:

2000 years = 2 x 10 x 10 x 10.

It was the purpose of God that in the completeness of time (10), Christ would be born so that He could provide a complete (10) salvation for a complete (10) church (2) that would be brought in all the way to the end of the world.

Or: Time Line's Spiritual Emphasis:

2000 years = 4 x 5 x 5 x 2 x 10.

In the completeness of time (10), Jesus came so that He could guarantee salvation (5) for the church (2) and judgment (5) for the world (4).

Or: Time Line's Spiritual Emphasis:

2000 years = 40 x 5 x 5 x 10.

In the completeness of time (10) Jesus came, placing all those who hear the Gospel under a testing (40) program. Those who believed were saved (5). Those who did not believe remain under judgment (5).

Event No. 48
Jesus went to the Temple: A.D. 7

Relationship of the Event to the Gospel Message:
Jesus was born in the fall of 7 B.C. Therefore, He became 13 years of age in the fall of A.D. 7 (7 + 7 - 1 = 13). He went to Jerusalem at the Passover time when He was still 12 years old, which, therefore, was

in the year A.D. 7. He was there to do His Father's business (Luke 2:49). Thus, He was anticipating the time when He would be the Passover by going to the cross.

Time Line
Years to the time of the cross, A.D. 33:
          33 - 7 = 26 years.

Time Line's Spiritual Emphasis:
          26 years = 2 x 13.
          It was Jesus' business to provide salvation for the church (2), which would be brought in to Christ's kingdom all the way to the end of the world (13).

Event No. 49
Christ was Crucified and God Began to Evangelize the World: A.D. 33

Relationship of the Event to the Gospel Message:
          This is the centerpiece of the Gospel. Christ's crucifixion brought salvation and heaven to the believers but it guarantees judgment on the unsaved.

Time Line
Years to the end of the world, A.D. 1988:
          1988 - 33 = 1955 years.

Time Line's Spiritual Emphasis:
          1955 years = 5 x 17 x 23.
          The program of the Gospel is that Christ was crucified so that the world could be evangelized. As the Gospel of salvation (5) goes forth, it brings heaven (17) to those who believe but judgment (23) upon those who do not believe.

[A summary is presented on the next three pages.]

# Year B.C. Event	To 7 B.C. Jesus' Birth	To 33 A.D. Jesus Crucified	To 1988 A.D. Begin Final Trib.	1994 A.D. End of World
1. 11013 Creation			13000 yrs 13 x 10 x 10 x 10	
2. 10883 Shem born			12870 yrs 10 x 3 x 3 x 11x13	
3. 7106 Enoch born				9100 yrs* 7 x 13 x 100
4. 3617 Eber born				5610 yrs 3 x 10 x 11 x 17
5. 2297 Terah born			4284 yrs 3 x 12 x 7 x 17	4290 yrs 3 x 10 x 11 x 13
6. 2167 Abraham born	2160 yrs 2 x 3 x 12 x 3 x 10	2200 yrs* 2 x 11 x 100		4160 yrs 2x2x2x4x10 x 13
7. 2092 Abraham enters Canaan		2125 yrs* 5 x 5 x 5 x 17	4080 yrs* 2 x 10 x 12 x 17	
8. 2068 Abraham circumcised. Sodom & Gomorrah destroyed		2100 yrs 3 x 7 x 100	4056 yrs* 2 x 12 x 13 x 13	
9. 2067 Isaac born		2100 yrs* 3 x 7 x 100		
10. 2030 Sarah dies	2023 7 x 17 x 17			
11. 2007 Jacob born	2000 yrs 2 x 1000	2040 yrs* 10 x 12 x 17		4000 yrs 4 x 1000
12. 1992 Abraham dies		2024 yrs 2 x 4 x 11 x 23		
13. 1967 Esau 40 yrs old				3960 yrs 3 x 10 x 11 x 12
14. 1916 Joseph born				3910 yrs* 10 x 17 x 23
15. 1907 Jacob becomes Israel				3900 yrs 3 x 13 x 100
16. 1899 Joseph 17 yrs old		1932 yrs* 4 x 3 x 7 x 23	3887 yrs* 13 x 13 x 23	

* This is the calendar period obtained by adding the Old Testament years to the New Testament years. The actual period that elapsed between these two events is one year less than the calendar year because there is no year 0. In addition to the evidence shown in this chart that Jesus was crucified in 33 A.D., there is much more evidence found in the Bible that this is so. Therefore, we can know that we are faithful to Scripture in understanding that God ties important spiritual events together both by the use of actual years as well as by the use of calendar years.
NOTE: Keep in mind that the numbers in the multiples each represent a spiritual truth.

#	Year B.C. Event	To 7 B.C. Jesus' Birth	To 33 A.D. Jesus Crucified	To 1988 A.D. Begin Final Trib.	To 1944 A.D. End of World
17.	1887 Isaac dies		1920 yrs 4 x 4 x 10 x 12		
18.	1879 Famine begins	1872 yrs 12 x 12 x 13	1911 yrs 3 x 7 x 7 x 13		3872 yrs 4 x 8 x 11 x 11
19.	1877 Israel enters Egypt	1870 yrs 10 x 11 x 17		3864 yrs 2 x 7 x 12 x 23	
20.	1527 Moses born		1560 yrs* 12 x 13 x 10		3520 yrs 2 x 4 x 4 x 10x11
21.	1447 Israel leaves Egypt. Law given at Mt. Sinai	1440 yrs 12 x 12 x 10	1480 yrs* 2 x 2 x 10 x 37		
22.	1407 Israel enters Canaan	1400 yrs 2 x 7 x 100	1440 yrs* 12 x 12 x 10		3400 yrs 2 x 17 x 100
23.	1207 Gideon diea & his sons killed	1200 yrs 12 x 100			3200 yrs 2 x 4 x 4 x 100
24.	1181 Jair judges				3174 yrs 2 x 3 x 23 x 23
25.	1159 Jephthah judges	1152 yrs 2 x 2 x 2 x 12x12		3146 yrs 2 x 11 x 11 x 13	
26.	1153 Ibsen judges				3146 yrs 2 x 11 x 11 x 13
27.	1068 Ark taken by Philistines		1100 yrs 11 x 100		
28.	1067 Ark restored		1100 yrs* 11 x 100		3060 yrs 2 x 3 x 10 x 17x3
29.	1047 Saul becomes king	1040 yrs 2 x 4 x 10 x 13	1080 yrs* 2 x 2 x 3 x 3 x3x10		
30.	1037 David born			3025* yrs 5 x 5 x 11 x 11	
31.	1007 David becomes king	1000 yrs 10 x 10 x 10			3000 yrs 3 x 1000
32.	967 Temple foundation laid	960 yrs 2 x 2 x 2 x10x12	1000 yrs* 10 x 10 x 10. 999 yrs 3 x 3 x 3 x 37		2960 yrs 2 x 4 x 10 x 37
33.	931 Kingdom divided	924 yrs 7 x 11 x 12			2925 yrs* 3 x 3 x 5 x 5 x 13

Continued next page . . .

# Year B.C. Event	To 7 B.C. Jesus' Birth	To 33 A.D. Jesus Crucified	To 1988 A.D. Begin Final Trib.	To 1944 A.D. End of World
34. 842 Jehoram dies				2835 yrs 5 x 3 x 3 x 3 x 3x7
35. 841 Athaliah begins to reign				2835 yrs* 5 x 7 x 3 x 3 x 3x3
36. 835 Athaliah dies	828 yrs 3 x 12 x 23	867 yrs 3 x 17 x 17		
37. 796 Jehoiada dies		828 yrs 3 x 12 x 23	2783 yrs 11 x 11 x 23	
38. 795 Joash dies		828 yrs* 3 x 12 x 23	2783 yrs* 11 x 11 x 23	
39. 789 Uzziah begins to reign	782 yrs 2 x 17 x 23			2783 yrs* 11 x 11 x 23
40. 737 Uzziah dies		770 yrs* 10 x 7 x 11		2730 yrs 10 x 3 x 7 x 13
41. 701 Hezekiah saved from Assyrians			2688 yrs 2 x 2 x 8 x 7 x 12	2695 yrs* 5 x 7 x 7 x 11
42. 605 Jehoiakim's line is cursed	598 yrs 2 x 13 x 23	637 yrs 7 x 13 x 7	2592 yrs 2 x 3 x 3 x 12 x 2	
43. 587 Jerusalem destroyed			2574 yrs 2 x 3 x 3 x 11 x 13	
44. 582 23rd yr of Nebuchadnezzar	575 yrs 5 x 5 x 23			2576 yrs* 2 x 2 x 4 x 7 x 23
45. 560 Jehoiachin freed from prison		592 yrs 2 x 2 x 4 x 37	2548 yrs* 2 x 2 x 7 x 7 x 13	2553 yrs 3 x 23 x 37
46. 458 Ezra brings the law to Jerusalem		490 yrs 7 x 7 x 10		
47. 7 Jesus born		40 yrs* 4 x 10 39 yrs 3 x 13		2000 yrs 2 x 1000
48. A.D. 7 Twelve-year-old Jesus goes to temple		26 yrs 2 x 13		
49. A.D. 33 Jesus goes to the cross. New Testament era begins			1955 yrs 5 x 17 x 23	

Is there an Alternative Year that We should Examine as Back-Up to A.D. 1994?

In this study, we have outlined forty-nine significant events of history that relate to the first or second coming of Christ by the intimate relationship that exists between that event and the first coming of Christ or by the second coming of Christ. Additionally, these events relate to the first or second coming of Christ by the spiritual meaning of the number of years that have transpired between these two events.

Each one of these forty-nine events is intimately related to either the first coming or second coming of Christ both by the character of the event as well as by the spiritual meaning of the number path that it outlined. Therefore, each one could be expanded and detailed even as we have done with the events of the birth of Terah, of Enoch, and the incident of Esau taking two wives.

To say it another way, the Biblical evidence pointing to A.D. 1988 and 1994 almost becomes overwhelming. God has given us so much information.

In fact, the number of paths from these forty-nine events to either the first or second coming of Christ is as follows:

To the first coming of Christ at His birth in 7 B.C.: 17 events.

To the first coming of Christ at His crucifixion in A.D. 33: 26 events.

To the second coming of Christ at the beginning of the final tribulation in A.D. 1988: 16 events.

To the second coming of Christ at the end of the world in A.D. 1994: 26 events.

We can be quite certain that 7 B.C. is the year in which Jesus was born. We can also be absolutely certain that A.D. 33 was the year Christ was crucified. We must, therefore, be quite impressed by the fact that there are about the same number of paths (sixteen) to the year A.D. 1988 as there are to the birth of Christ in 7 B.C. (seventeen). In each case these are separate and distinct paths.

Equally impressive is the fact that there are twenty-six paths to the year A.D. 1994 and twenty-six paths to A.D. 33. Surely this should emphasize very strongly the likelihood of the end of the world coming in A.D. 1994.

But having said this, we must realize that a number of paths of this nature can be found which also go to years other than A.D. 1988 and A.D. 1994. For example, if we had some reason to believe that Christ's return would not be in the Jubilee year A.D. 1994, but instead in the following Jubilee year which would be A.D. 2044, a number of paths would be found from these forty-nine calendar milestones to the year A.D. 2044. The year A.D. 2044 is being offered as an example because the evidence of the Bible points so strongly to the return of Christ in a Jubilee year. It is also being mentioned because more paths from these forty-nine calendar milestones would go to it than to any other year **other than the years A.D. 1988 and A.D. 1994.**

Must we, therefore, consider the year A.D. 2044 as an alternative possibility for the end of the world and the return of Christ? **The answer must be a resounding NO!**

This is so for two very important reasons. The first is that the number of paths from the forty-nine calendar milestones to A.D. 2044 is less than half of those that point to A.D. 1994. Thus, the year A.D. 2044 is not at all like the year A.D. 33 on which twenty-six paths focus or like the year A.D. 1994 on which twenty-six paths focus. In fact, any years that can be named will always have far fewer paths focused on them (even fewer than on A.D. 2044) than the years A.D. 1988 or A.D. 1994.

Only the years A.D. 1988 and A.D. 1994 are in the same league with the numerous paths that go to the year A.D. 33, the year when Christ was crucified.

A.D. 1988 and A.D. 1994 stand entirely apart from any and every other year insofar as the great number of paths from these forty-nine calendar milestones. Only the years A.D. 1988 and A.D. 1994 are in the same league with the numerous paths that go to the year A.D. 33, the year when Christ was crucified.

The second reason the year A.D. 2044 as well as any other year other than A.D. 1994 must be rejected as having any possibility of being the year of Christ's return is the fact that none of these will harmonize with the numerous Biblical time paths that were identified in the book *1994?*

In the book *1994?*, we discovered many paths that focused very uniquely on A.D. 1988 and A.D. 1994. These included paths such as those derived from the forty and 390 days of Ezekiel 4, the 1290 days of Daniel 12, the precise 13,000 years from creation to the beginning of judgment in A.D. 1988, and the precise 2000 years from the birth of Christ to His return in 1994.

Indeed, the twenty-six time paths, most of which were not mentioned in the book *1994?*, give a great amount of added reason why we can in such great likelihood expect Christ's return in A.D. 1994.

But now we must accomplish one more task as we complete this book. We would like to know what kind of evidence there is that allows us to accurately relate the Biblical calendar to the secular calendar, which is our Julian or Gregorian calendar. We will continue our study by setting forth this data.

Chapter 10.
The Secular Record and
The Biblical Record

In the book *1994?* as well as in this volume, we have very carefully studied the Biblical evidence that gives us the timetable of the history of the world. Because the Bible speaks very precisely and because we can trust it implicitly by virtue of the fact that it is God's Word, we have been enabled to develop the Biblical calendar from the beginning of time all the way to the end of the nation of the ten tribes of Israel, which were destroyed in 709 B.C. by the Assyrian king.

If we are to extend the calendar into our time, we must have a trustworthy means of relating our secular calendar to the Biblical calendar. When we use the language of our calendar in dating creation or any other Biblical event, how do we know we have made a correct and accurate tie between the Biblical calendar and the secular calendar?

This is an extremely important question because a great many of the time paths that focus on 1994 as the likely end of the world are based on a belief that an accurate tie has been established between the two calendars.

There is, of course, one great proof that such a tie between these two calendars has for certain been accurately established. That is the fact that the birth of Jesus in 7 B.C. and His return to heaven in 33 A.D. are both years that coordinate exceedingly well with the time paths that proceed from events that come from the Biblical calendar. If a correct tie had not been established, there is no possibility that so many time paths and interrelations of ancient Biblical events could focus on 7 B.C. and 33 A.D. In fact, the multitude of time paths that focus on 33 A.D. for the crucifixion of Christ and on 1994 A.D. as the end of the world assure us that the linking of the Biblical calendar to the secular calendar has been done exceedingly accurately.

It isn't that we need further corroboration. The Biblical information is so extensive and so consistent in tying the timing of significant Biblical events to the first coming and the second coming of Christ that we really do not need more proofs. But because the focus of the time line of history as developed from the Bible and presented in the book *1994?* and in this volume is so awesome, so incredibly important, we desire to seek out and weigh every shred of evidence that bears on this tremendously important subject.

Therefore, we still want to know: How do we begin to tie the Biblical calendar to the secular calendar? Apart from the corroborating evidence of the Biblical time paths, has this procedure been done accurately as the Biblical calendar is interrelated with the secular calendar, which we call the Julian or Gregorian calendar?

> *The first principle that should be declared is that*
> *the measurement of time is not in the hands of men.*

The Measurement of Time Is Controlled by God

As we study the question of the calendar, the first principle that should be declared is that the measurement of time is not in the hands of men. The length of a day and the length of a year are carefully controlled by God. It is not mankind who has decided on the length of a day or that there are 365.2422 days in a year. God has done that. On the fourth day of creation, God placed the timekeepers in the sky, including the sun, the moon and the stars. We read in Genesis 1:14-18:

> And God said, Let there be lights in the firmament of the heaven to divide the day from the night; and let them be for signs, and for seasons, and for days, and years: And let them be for lights in the firmament of the heaven to give light upon the earth: and it was so. And God made two great lights; the greater light to rule the day, and the lesser light to rule the night: he made the stars also. And God set them in the firmament of the heaven to give light upon the earth, And to rule over the day and over the night, and to divide the light from the darkness: and God saw that it was good.

With this information in hand, we know that regardless of how man marks off the passage of time, he can never change the fact that there are 365.2422 days in the year. Using sophisticated equipment, astronomers can measure the movements of the celestial timekeepers, but they cannot change the results.

> *The fact that the movements of the heavenly bodies*
> *as well as that of the earth are entirely under the*
> *control of God and are designed by God to give*
> *mankind absolute timekeepers, provides the means*
> *by which the Biblical calendar can be harmonized*
> *with and tied into the secular calendar.*

The fact that the movements of the heavenly bodies as well as that of the earth are entirely under the control of God and are designed by God to give mankind absolute timekeepers, provides the means by which the Biblical calendar can be harmonized with and tied into the secular calendar.

The movements of the various heavenly bodies follow very precise paths that were established by God. These paths never vary. Thus, astronomers can predict with great accuracy when, for example, an eclipse will occur, when there will be a new moon, etc. He not only can predict similar future events with great accuracy, but he can also reconstruct with identical accuracy what has been the case at any time in the past.

All of this becomes relevant when we realize that God has enabled man to keep records. Of course, no human record can approach the perfect accuracy of the Biblical record; nevertheless, the movement of the heavenly bodies has greatly increased the accuracy of the record keeping of the secular writers.

Thus, if an ancient historian, in writing about the pharaohs of ancient Egypt, recorded that on such and such a day, in the third year of the reign of a particular pharaoh, there was a solar eclipse, we can immediately know what the possible years are for the third year of this pharaoh. This is so because astronomically during that period of history, there were only certain very precise days when a solar eclipse did occur.

Thus, even though the ancient secular record cannot be nearly as accurate as the Biblical record, these astronomical citations enable us to harmonize the two records.

It might be noted that secular records, as seen in the ancient stelae and even in entire libraries uncovered by archaeologists, give evidence of the extreme interest that ancient nations have had in astronomical events.

The Bible Gives Information Concerning Heathen Kings

The second fact that greatly helps us to accurately tie the Biblical calendar to the secular calendar is that of the Biblical notices concerning heathen kings. As we carefully search the Bible, we sometimes discover bits of information that concern heathen kings and sometimes it is precise information.

For example, the Bible is very clear that the pharaoh who resisted God's plan for the people of Israel to leave Egypt, died the same day that the Israelites crossed the Red Sea.

Another example is that the Bible declares in II Kings 24:12 that it was in the eighth year of the king of Babylon that King Jehoiachin was taken from the throne of Judah. In Nehemiah 2:1, God ties another Biblical event to the twentieth year of the reign of Artaxerxes, king of the Medes and Persians.

Citations of this kind, coupled with astronomical data that has been found in the ancient secular writings, assure us that we can accurately mesh the Biblical record with the secular calendar. As we continue our study, we will examine a number of tie-in points.

Information from Assyria and Babylon

The records of the kings of Assyria and Babylon provide us with a number of excellent contacts between the Biblical record and the secular record. We will look first at the available information that relates to the kings of Israel. Thus far in our study, we have found that their first king was Jeroboam, who began to reign in 931 B.C., and their last king was Hoshea, who was killed in 709 B.C., at the time the ten tribes of the nation of Israel and their capital in Samaria ceased to exist.

Can we find a tie-in between these years and the secular record?

The first tie we will find relates the secular record to the Biblical record in connection with two kings who reigned over Israel, Ahab and Jehu. We have found that if we are correct in indicating that the first king, Jeroboam, began to reign in 931 B.C., then, working very carefully through all the Biblical notices, we find that the last year of Ahab was 853 B.C. and the first year of Jehu was 841 B.C. (see pages 144-148 of this study). Is there any corroborating evidence in the secular records?

The reigns of Assyrian kings during the period from 891 B.C. to 727 B.C. are given very accurately in terms of our calendar. This is because of lists of kings that archaeologists have found that are quite complete for that period of time. They are tied very directly to the Julian calendar because of an eclipse of the sun that took place on June 15, 763 B.C., which is in the archaeological records of the eponymy of Bur-Sagale.[1] This astronomical fix has enabled archaeologists to know the precise years of the reigns of Assyrian kings who reigned earlier than 763 B.C. as well as kings who reigned later.

In the Monolith Inscription of Shalmaneser III (an earlier Shalmaneser than the one recorded in the Bible), who reigned from 858 to 824 B.C., his victory over a Syrian coalition of twelve kings at Qargar is recorded and "Ahab, the Israelite," is named as one of these kings. This battle is placed in the sixth year of the Assyrian king, which would be 853 B.C.[2] Therefore, Ahab must have been alive and reigning in that year.

Additionally, on the Black Obelisk of Shamaneser III, the Assyrian records the taking of tribute from the Israelite king, Jehu. This is dated in this ancient record as having taken place in the Assyrian king's eighteenth year or 841 B.C.[3] Thus, Jehu must have been reigning in the year 841 B.C.

> *This indicates an exact synchronization between the Biblical calendar and the Julian calendar.*

When we went through the Biblical record, we found that the last year of Ahab was 853 B.C. We also found that the first year of Jehu was 841 B.C. This indicates an exact synchronization between the Biblical calendar and the Julian calendar. This is so because if the two calendars were shifted even one year in either direction from each other, either Ahab or Jehu would no longer identify with both the Biblical and the secular calendars.

We thus have one very exact "fix" between the secular and the Biblical calendars.

A Second "Fix"

A second exact "fix" between the two calendars will be found in connection with the destruction of Samaria in 709 B.C. The Biblical record based on 931 B.C. being the first year of Jeroboam's reign over Israel indicates that Israel's last king, Hoshea, was conquered in 709 B.C. by the Assyrian king.

The Biblical record of the end of Israel is found in II Kings 17:1-6 and II Kings 18:9-10.

> II Kings 17:1-6: In the twelfth year of Ahaz king of Judah began Hoshea the son of Elah to reign in Samaria over Israel nine years. And he did that which was evil in the sight of the LORD, but not as the kings of Israel that were before him. Against him came up Shalmaneser king of Assyria; and Hoshea became his servant, and gave him presents. And the king of Assyria found conspiracy in Hoshea: for he had sent messengers to So king of Egypt, and brought no present to the king of Assyria, as he had done year by year: therefore the king of Assyria shut him up, and bound him in prison. Then the king of Assyria came up throughout all the land, and went up to Samaria, and besieged it three years. In the ninth year of Hoshea the king of Assyria took Samaria, and carried Israel away into Assyria, and placed them in Halah and in Habor by the river of Gozan, and in the cities of the Medes.

> II Kings 18:9-10: And it came to pass in the fourth year of king Hezekiah, which was the seventh year of Hoshea son of Elah king of Israel, that Shalmaneser king of Assyria came up against Samaria, and besieged it. And at the end of three years they took it: even in the sixth year of Hezekiah, that is the ninth year of Hoshea king of Israel, Samaria was taken.

Significantly, in this citation, Shalmaneser, king of Assyria (he is Shalmanezer V of the archaeological record), began the assault on

Samaria. However, when the city was taken, Shalmaneser is not named. Rather, the Bible declares that the king of Assyria took Samaria. There is a very important reason why Shalmaneser is not named as the Assyrian king who took Samaria, but that reason is known because of information given in the secular record.

As indicated earlier in this study, because of the lists of kings that have been discovered on ancient tablets and because of the astronomical fix of 763 B.C., the Assyrian kings who reigned from 891 B.C. to 727 B.C. are given quite accurately. Actually, archaeologists have found an accurate list of kings all the way to 648 B.C.,[4] but they have one error and that is in connection with the reign of Shalmaneser V. Apparently, few records from his reign have been found. However, a Babylonian tablet written during the reign of King Darius (500-499 B.C.), which covers Assyrian and Babylonian history, states that Shalmaneser V died in the tenth month of the fifth year of his reign and his immediate successor was Sargon II.[5] Based on this record, which was recorded more than two hundred years after Shalmaneser reigned, archaeologists place his reign from 727 to 722 B.C., and Sargon's reign from 721 or 722 to 705 B.C.

Because the Bible clearly states that Shalmaneser came against Hoshea, and because archaeologists place more credence in the archaeological record than in the Biblical record, they try hard to prove that Samaria was taken by Shalmaneser in the year 722 B.C. To accomplish this, they ascribe errors to the Bible, and try to show that Hoshea reigned twelve years earlier than the Bible says he did.[6]

> *When we start with the correct premise, that the Bible only is absolutely dependable, then we find beautiful corroboration between the Biblical and the secular record.*

But when we start with the correct premise, that the Bible only is absolutely dependable, then we find beautiful corroboration between the Biblical and the secular record. Indeed, we discover another "fix" that ties the Biblical calendar to the secular or Julian calendar. Let us develop this information.

The King of Assyria - Sargon

As has already been indicated, the archaeological record, based on the statement of an historian who lived more than 200 years later, shows that Shalmaneser reigned for five years and was followed by Sargon. While there is little more known about Shalmaneser, considerable more is known about Sargon.

Two tablets from Assyria indicate that the thirteenth year of Sargon as king of Assyria was his first year as king of Babylon. The secular record shows that 709 B.C. was the thirteenth year of Sargon. Thus, 709 B.C. was the year Sargon also became ruler of Babylon.

The archaeological record coming from the reign of Sargon is very extensive, because Sargon built the city Khorsabad in the closing years of his reign. Thiele reports:[7]

> Here in the final series of documents coming from the closing years of his reign, the capture of Samaria "at the beginning" of Sargon's rule is featured in great prominence for all posterity to remember. Thus it was on the annals appearing on the wall slabs of three of the halls of his newly constructed palace at Khorabad. Thus also it was on the so-called Display Inscription (German, Prunkinschrift) found on the walls of rooms IV, VII, VIII, and X of the palace of Khorsabad, giving a review of the events from Sargon's accession to his fifteenth year. Once more this was the case on the Display Inscription of room XIV, where again Sargon claims to have plundered the city of Samirina (Samaria) and the whole land of Israel. Yet again, on the Bull Inscription where he recounts the building of his famous palace at Dur Sharrukin he claims Samaria's overthrow. And finally, on the Pavement Inscriptions carved at the base of the palace gates, Sargon in a résumé of the accomplishments of his reign vaunts himself as the conqueror of Samaria and of the whole land of Bit-Humria.

One of the records from the city of Khorsabad declares:[8]

At the beginning of my royal rule, I the town of the Samarians I beseiged, conquered . . . for the god . . . who let me achieve this my triumph.

> *And 709 B.C., according to the archaeological record, was the year Sargon became ruler of Babylon.*

Curiously, archaeologists have not been able to harmonize this information with the Biblical record, which shows that Samaria was taken in 709 B.C. **And 709 B.C., according to the archaeological record, was the year Sargon became ruler of Babylon.** Even though he had ruled Assyria to some degree for the previous twelve years, in his thirteenth year, there was a substantial change in his rulership. First of all, it was the year he became ruler over Babylon. What else could have changed in that year?

We know from the secular record that Sargon reigned over Assyria from 722 to 705 B.C. There appears to be sufficient information available from the archaeological record to demonstrate this. But we know from the Biblical record that Shalmaneser also reigned over Assyria at least during the first seven of the years of the reign of Hoshea, and Hoshea's reign was in the years 718-709 B.C. Therefore, it is obvious that there was some kind of co-regency between Shalmaneser and Sargon, beginning in the year 722 B.C.

In fact, there is some evidence that Sargon may have been the brother of Shalmaneser.[9] Because Sargon speaks of 709 B.C. as his first year, it may be that in the previous year, 710 B.C., Shalmaneser died. Thus, in the year 709 B.C., for the first time, Sargon was the sole ruler. It is possible that he died in his conflict with Samaria. In any case, it was Sargon who was the Assyrian-Babylonian king who conquered Samaria in 709 B.C. Possibly, little is found from the reign of Shalmaneser because Sargon could have destroyed much of the historical evidence of Shalmaneser's reign. The records of his exploits found in the city of Khorsabad strongly suggest that he was a very vain man. Therefore, it surely would be in character for him to remove evidence that Shalmaneser, who had been co-regent with him for twelve years, would get any credit for this notable victory over Samaria. It's interesting that God turned the record around and names Shalmaneser and speaks of Sargon only as the king of Assyria.

In any case, I believe that we have a very solid "fix" between the Biblical record and the secular record, because of the extensive information from Sargon's reign that he destroyed Samaria. The placement of this event in the secular record is 709 B.C., which accords perfectly with the Biblical record.

A Third "Fix"

The third "fix" that ties the Biblical record to the secular record relates to Hezekiah, king of Judah, in the year 701 B.C. We read in II Kings 18:13:

> Now in the fourteenth year of king Hezekiah did Sennacherib king of Assyria come up against all the fenced cities of Judah, and took them.

And in II Kings 18:17:

> And the king of Assyria sent Tartan and Rab-saris and Rab-shakeh from Lachish to king Hezekiah with a great host against Jerusalem. And they went up and came to Jerusalem. And when they were come up, they came and stood by the conduit of the upper pool, which is in the highway of the fuller's field.

In the secular record, reference to this event has been found, which also dates it at 701 B.C. Dr. Finegan reports:[10]

> In the annals of Sennacherib (704-681 B.C.) the record of his "third campaign" (701 B.C.) describes a siege of Jerusalem, doubtless conducted during the summer of that year, which may be the same as the siege which II K 18:13 and Is 36:1 put in the fourteenth year of King Heaekiah.

Dr. Finegan uses the phrase "may be the same" because, as we learned earlier, archaeologists have dared to say that errors have come into the Bible, particularly in connection with the end of the nation of Israel. Since the Bible teaches so clearly that Hezekiah began to reign in the third year of Hoshea (II Kings 18:1), any reconstruction of the place of Hoshea in the chronological timetable is bound to weaken the trust of these archaeologists as to the place of Hezekiah in the chronological timetable.

> *When the Biblical record and secular record agree, we have evidence that the archaeologists and the astronomers have done their work accurately.*

We know that the Bible is absolutely true. We see this again when the archaeological record places the campaign of Sennacherib against Jerusalem in 701 B.C., even as does the Biblical record. Remember that the secular record ties into the Julian calendar because of astronomical evidence. When the Biblical record and secular record agree, we have evidence that the archaeologists and the astronomers have done their work accurately.

There is additional Biblical evidence that the year 701 B.C. is the fourteenth year of Hezekiah. It is found in II Kings 19:29 in connection with the Bible's account of the siege of Jerusalem by Sennacherib. There we read:

> And this shall be a sign unto thee, Ye shall eat this year such things as grow of themselves, and in the second year that which springeth of the same; and in the third year sow ye, and reap, and plant vineyards, and eat the fruits thereof.

We have learned that the Jubilee years of the Old Testament are always those years that end in 57 or 07. Thus, we are certain that the year 707 B.C. was a Jubilee year. The next six years, 706, 705, 704, 703, 702, and 701, were normal years, and the seventh year, 700 B.C., was a Sabbath year.

It was in the year 701 B.C. that Sennacherib laid siege to Jerusalem. Therefore, because of the siege, there would have been no planting or harvesting during the year 701 B.C.

Because the next year, 700 B.C., was a Sabbath year, there was not to be any planting or harvesting that year. This was to be so even though the siege of Jerusalem was no longer taking place in 700 B.C.

Thus, the prophet Isaiah told Hezekiah that in this year (701 B.C.), since, in view of the siege, there could have been no planting, they were to eat what grew of itself. Since the second year was a Sabbath year, they could not plant, but God gave them permission to eat what grew of itself. The third year was a normal non-Sabbath year, so they could again plant and harvest.

> *By this citation, God has given additional evidence by which we are able to check the accuracy of the chronology, from the period starting with the entrance of Israel into Canaan in 1407 B.C., all the way to 701 B.C.*

By this citation, God has given additional evidence by which we are able to check the accuracy of the chronology, from the period starting with the entrance of Israel into Canaan in 1407 B.C., all the way to 701 B.C. If an error of one or more years had crept in, the statement of II Kings 19:29 would not fit.

So we have found three excellent "fixes" that relate the Biblical calendar to the Julian calendar. When we add those that identify with the pharaohs of Egypt and which we will presently examine, we can believe with the utmost confidence that we can project our Julian calendar all the way back to creation in 11,013 B.C.

Information from Babylon

We should now tie the Biblical record to the secular record so that we can know that the death of Josiah was in 609 B.C. and the end of Judah came in 587 B.C.

A number of cuneiform texts from Babylon have been discovered and are now in the British Museum. One of them records that battle in which the king of Assyria, together with a large army of Egypt, tried to re-conquer Haran, which the Babylonians had taken the previous year.[11] This battle took place in the summer of 609 B.C. This harmonizes with the account of II Kings 23:29:

In his days Pharaoh-nechoh king of Egypt went up against the king of Assyria to the river Euphrates: and king Josiah went against him; and he slew him at Megiddo, when he had seen him.

The Bible records that the son of Josiah, Jehoahaz, then became king, but after three months, the king of Judah took Jehoahaz captive and placed his brother Jehoiakim on the throne.

In Jeremiah 46:2, we find the record of the defeat of the Egyptians by Nebuchadrezzar, king of Babylon, in the fourth year of Jehoiakim.

Jeremiah 46:2: Against Egypt, against the army of Pharaoh-necho king of Egypt, which was by the river Euphrates in Carchemish, which Nebuchadrezzar king of Babylon smote in the fourth year of Jehoiakim the son of Josiah king of Judah.

The secular record indicates that in September, 605 B.C., Nebuchadnezzar became king of Babylon.

This is an important citation because according to the secular record, Nebuchadnezzar was the son of the Babylonian king, Nabopolassar. It was while Nebuchadnezzar was engaged in conquering the Egyptian forces, which were in the Euphrates River area, that he received word that his father had died. Thus, the secular record indicates that in September, 605 B.C., Nebuchadnezzar became king of Babylon. Jeremiah indicates that this was in the fourth year of Jehoiakim. In Jeremiah 25:1 the Bible speaks of this year as the first year of Nebuchadrezzar, king of Babylon.

Jeremiah 25:1: The word that came to Jeremiah concerning all the people of Judah in the fourth year of Jehoiakim the son of Josiah king of Judah, that was the first year of Nebuchadrezzar king of Babylon.

Because Nebuchadrezzar ascended the throne in September of 605 B.C., his first year by the non-accession year system was 605 B.C. On the other hand, his official first year by the accession year system was the next year, 604 B.C. Thus, the year 587 B.C., when he conquered Judah was his nineteenth year by the non-accession year system, and it was his eighteenth year by the accession year system.

A Problem has Arisen in Calendar Alignment

In our effort to be as careful as possible to set forth any and all information that bears on our study, a problem must be introduced. Isn't it true that the secular and sacred calendars cannot be exactly aligned because each calendar has a different beginning month, and doesn't that create serious problems in aligning the two calendar records? Let's examine that question.

It is true that there is no precise alignment between the Jewish calendar and the secular calendar. The first month of the Julian calendar is January, but the first month of the Jewish calendar is Nisan, which approximates our March or April. Remember that the Jewish months are governed by the moon. Each year a new moon, which begins a new month, comes at a different time. Therefore, we must speak of Nisan as coming some time in March or April. Therefore, any historical event that occurred between March-April and December 31 is always the same year, whether identified with the Jewish calendar or the Julian calendar.

On the other hand, an event that occurred between January 1 and March-April would be recorded as being one year earlier by the Jewish calendar than by the Julian calendar.

In almost all calendar calculations, this fact becomes of no consequence. All of the important feast days, from the Passover all the way through to the end of the feast of tabernacles, occurred after March-April (Nisan 1) and before December 31. Therefore, they would have been recorded as the same year by both the Jewish calendar and the Julian calendar.

Moreover, with rare exceptions, warfare occurred during the period from late spring to the fall of the year. Since it was in battle that kings were frequently killed, changes in rulership are, therefore, recorded as the same year by both calendar systems.

Furthermore, since Nisan 1 to December 31 is approximately a nine-month period, whereas January 1 to Nisan 1 is approximately three months, the likelihood of an event happening during the nine-month period, when the years by both calendars are equal, is far greater than an event occurring during the three-month period, when the calendars are one year apart.

The Bible Guides Us through the Problem Years

In addition, as we carefully study the Bible, we discover that God indicates in more than one instance that we should know that an historical event took place during the three-month period from January 1 of our calendar and Nisan 1 of the Jewish calendar, so that we will remain accurate when meshing the two calendars together.

For example, we read the account that God has given us is in connection with the reign of Jehoiachin and the reign of Zedekiah, who followed him. We know from the Biblical record that Jehoiachin's father reigned for eleven years, and the last year of his reign was 598 B.C. We are then instructed by the Bible that Jehoiachin, his son, reigned for three months and ten days. Jehoiachin was followed by his uncle, Zedekiah, who reigned for eleven years.

With no further information, we might then conclude that Jehoiakim's last year was 598 B.C. Jeconiah's (Jehoiachin) last month was probably also in 598 B.C., and Zedekiah's initial year was also 598 B.C., with his first official year being 597 B.C., because that was his first full year.

However, God gives us a little bit more information and also has supplied through the secular record even more detailed information so that we can more accurately know that Jehoiakim's last year was 598 B.C. But Jeconiah's reign of three months and ten days began in December of 598 B.C. and ended in the early spring of 597 B.C. We can know with certainty that Zedekiah's reign began in the early spring of 597 B.C., so that according to the Julian calendar, both his accession year and his first official year by the accession year system was the year 597 B.C.

The clue to this detail is given in the Bible in II Chronicles 36:9-10, where we read:

Jehoiachin was eight years old when he began to reign, and he reigned three months and ten days in Jerusalem: and he did that which was evil in the sight of the LORD. And when the year was expired, king Nebuchadnezzar sent, and brought him to Babylon, with the goodly vessels of the house of the LORD, and made Zedekiah his brother king over Judah and Jerusalem.

The significant phrase is "when the year was expired." By the Jewish calendar, a year is expired just before Nisan 1. Therefore, approximately on Nisan 1, Jehoiachin was deposed and Zedekiah was made king. From the Biblical record alone, we know that it had to be shortly before Nisan 1 when this event occurred. If it had occurred after Nisan 1, there would be no harmony between Zedekiah's eleventh year and Nebuchadrezzar's nineteenth year, when Jerusalem was destroyed.

This citation does indicate, however, that Zedekiah was made king in 597 B.C. and 597 B.C., by the Julian calendar, was also his first official year. It also indicates that the bulk, if not all, of Jehoiachin's reign of three months and ten days was in 597 B.C. by the Julian calendar.

More Information from Babylon

The secular record gives a bit more information so we know that we have understood the Bible correctly. A tablet from Babylon records:[12]

In the seventh year, the month of Kislimu, the king of Akkad mustered his troops, marched to the Hatti-land, and encamped against the city of Judah and on the second day of the month of Addaru he seized the city and captured the king. He appointed there a king of his own choice, received its heavy tribute and sent them to Babylon.

We know that by accession reckoning, the seventh year of Nebuchadrezzar, the king of Akkad, was 598 B.C. (his eighth year by the non-accession-year reckoning). We are advised that the second day of the month Addaru was March 16, 597 B.C. Three months and ten days earlier than March 16 was December 9, 598 B.C., which must have been the day Jehoiachin began to reign alone. Remember that the Bible gives evidence that Jehoiachin had been co-regent the previous ten years.

Thus, with this added information, we know that Jehoiakim reigned until December, 598 B.C., this being his eleventh year. Early in December, he was deposed and his son Jehoiachin, who had been reigning with him for ten years as a child co-regent, became king at the age of eighteen. Three months and ten days later, shortly before the beginning of the next Jewish year, he was taken to Babylon and his uncle, Zedekiah, was placed on the throne. Thus, Jehoiachin reigned alone for a few days in 598 B.C. and for almost three months in 597 B.C.

His uncle, Zedekiah, began to reign a few days before the end of the Jewish year that began in the spring of 598 B.C. His first full year or first official year thus began in the spring of 597 B.C. Therefore, in accordance with the secular or Julian calendar, he ascended the throne early in 597 B.C. and his first official year was 597 B.C.

It surely is significant how God gives this extra detail concerning the end of the reign of Jehoiachin. It assures us that we can accurately relate the Julian calendar to the Biblical calendar.

We have discovered a number of "fixes" between the Biblical calendar and the secular calendar. This assures us that we can accurately relate the Biblical events all the way from creation to our modern calendar.

The evidence we have presented is not exhaustive. For example, several "fixes" can be found in connection with the ancient Egyptian records. As we continue our study, we will examine some of these.

Information from Egypt

Many years ago, I published a book entitled *Adam When?*, in which the calendars of Genesis 5 and Genesis 11 were first set forth. In that book, considerable information was offered that showed the precise calendar agreement between key events in the lives of three pharaohs of ancient Egypt and the Biblical calendar. This agreement could only result from an accurate meshing of the Biblical calendar with our present Julian or Gregorian calendar.

Because a concern of this present book is to disclose as much information as possible that demonstrates the extreme accuracy which has been obtained in meshing the Biblical and the secular calendars together, and because the book *Adam When?* is not bookstores, I have taken the liberty to reprint in this book the chapters that relate to this meshing.

To begin, we should look at the pharaoh who was reigning at the time Joseph was freed from prison.

Joseph lived in Egypt in the first year of one of the greatest pharaohs of the Twelfth Egyptian Dynasty, which is also known as the Middle Kingdom. The year of the accession of this pharaoh, Sesostris III, can be calculated from astronomical data. When we compare his accession year with the Biblical record, we discover concordance with the Biblical chronology.

The Secular Records Date

Let us discover the accession year of Sesostris III by means of the astronomical and archeological evidence.

A tablet has been discovered from the reign of Sesostris III that indicates that in the seventh year of his reign, there was a Sothis festival on the sixteenth day of the eighth month. The festival celebrated a heliacal rising (simultaneous with the sun) of the star Sothis (Sirius).[13] This gives us a time clue, for a heliacal rising of Sirius occurs on any particular day of the year once every 1460 years. Dr. Jack Finegan records that in 139 A.D., a celebration occurred on the first day of the first month (the month Thoth), commemorating such a rising.[14] Since it took 1460 years for the festival to pass through the Egyptian calendar to come again to the same day and month, the previous time when the Sothic Festival was celebrated on the first day of the first month would have been 1322 B.C. on July 20. Finegan arrived at a date of 1321 B.C., as did Breasted. The conclusion of 1321 B.C. appears to be in error by one year, and is apparently due to a lack of consideration of the fact that there is a loss of one year in going from B.C. to A.D. G. H. Wheeler,[15] however, arrived at a date of 1322 B.C., as we did.

Since Sesostris III commemorated a Sothic rising on the sixteenth day of the eighth month, we can work backwards from July 20, 1322 B.C. to discover the year when this celebration occurred.

There are 140 days between the first day of the first month (Thoth 1) (July 20) and the sixteenth day of the eighth month (Pharmuthi). Since the Sothic rising shifts one day each four years, we can multiply this 140 days by four to give 560 as the number of years earlier than 1322 B.C. when the festival was held during the seventh year of the reign of Sesostris III. Consequently, it was the year (1322 + 560) or 1882 B.C. when the recorded festival was held. Since this was the seventh year of Sesostris III, his first year was then 1888 B.C.

The Biblical Record Date

Let us now see if we can find information in the Bible that could possibly relate to the first or accession year of Sesostris III. When we study the experience of Joseph, we do find the desired facts. The clue that supplies the answer is found in Genesis 41:13, which reads as follows:

> And it came to pass, as he interpreted to us, so it was; me he restored unto mine office, and him he hanged.

The background to this verse includes the fact that Joseph was cast into prison because he refused to sin with Potiphar's wife. While in prison, he correctly interpreted the dreams of the chief butler and the chief baker.

The dream revealed that in three days, the butler was to be restored to the butlership, and the baker was to be taken from prison and hanged. These events actually took place on the third day when Pharaoh gave a birthday feast. While in prison, Joseph's request to the butler was that he would remember him to the Pharaoh (Gen. 40:14). Chapter 40 closes with the information that the chief butler forgot about Joseph. Then two whole years passed (Gen. 41:1-7), after which Pharaoh had the dreams of the seven fat and seven skinny cows and the seven plump and seven thin ears of corn. Finally, because Pharaoh was seeking an explanation of his dream, the butler remembered poor Joseph in the dungeon. His speech to Pharaoh is very significant, which we read in Genesis 41:9-13:

Then spake the chief butler unto Pharaoh, saying, I do remember my faults this day: Pharaoh was wroth with his servants, and put me in ward in the captain of the guard's house, both me and the chief baker: And we dreamed a dream in one night, I and he; we dreamed each man according to the interpretation of his dream. And there was there with us a young man, an Hebrew, servant to the captain of the guard; and we told him, and he interpreted to us our dreams; to each man according to his dream he did interpret. And it came to pass, as he interpreted to us, so it was; me he restored unto mine office, and him he hanged.

The Pronoun "He" Conveys Significant Information

In verse 9 we discover that the chief butler, who had been freed from prison two years earlier, talked to Pharaoh and said that Pharaoh (v. 10) had put both the butler, himself, and the baker into prison when Pharaoh was angry. To speak directly to Pharaoh as he did in verse 10 and use the proper name or title, "Pharaoh," rather than a personal pronoun, "you," was very common. For example, Moses used this form of address in Exodus 8:29, where we read:

And Moses said, Behold, I go out from thee, and I will entreat the LORD that the swarms of flies may depart from Pharaoh, from his servants, and from his people, tomorrow: but let not Pharaoh deal deceitfully any more in not letting the people go to sacrifice to the LORD.

Verse 13 of Genesis 41, however, presents a very difficult problem. When Moses was speaking to Pharaoh about Pharaoh he used either the formal title, "Pharaoh," or he used the personal pronoun "you" (Exodus 8:9 and 8:29). Moses never used the third person pronoun, "he," as the butler did talking to Pharaoh in verse 13. In fact, it makes no sense at all for the butler to talk to Pharaoh about what he, the Pharaoh, had done years before and then use the pronoun "he" as it is used in this passage, **that is, unless the Pharaoh who put the baker and the butler in jail was a different Pharaoh from the one the butler was addressing in Genesis 41:9-13**. If the Pharaoh of

Chapter 40 was the father of the Pharaoh of Chapter 41, then the speech of the butler in Genesis 41:9-13 would make exact sense. In other words, the butler would have said: "Pharaoh (your father) put us in prison. He restored me and hanged the baker." This could happen only if another Pharaoh began to reign between the time of the butler's release from prison and the Pharaoh's dream two years later. This must have been the true state of affairs.

Since the Biblical account indicates this change in rulers, let us determine the Biblical timetable for this event. When we look at the Biblical chronology, we discover that Jacob and his family entered Egypt in 1877 B.C.[16] This is in the second year of the famine (Gen. 45:6), which followed seven years of plenty, as prophesied by Joseph. Since the seven years of plenty began virtually immediately after the interpretation of the dreams (Gen. 41:32), the butler was speaking to the Pharaoh nine years earlier than 1877 B.C., or 1886 B.C. Since the butler was let out of prison two whole years earlier than this, he must have been restored to office in the year 1888 B.C. Therefore, in 1888, shortly after the Pharaoh's birthday feast, the Pharaoh who put the butler in prison died, and his son ascended the throne. This son must have been Sesostris III who, as we have computed, commemorated a Sothic rising in his seventh year, the year 1882, thus making his first year 1888 B.C.

We have thus discovered from Biblical data that a Pharaoh began to reign probably in the year 1888 B.C. He was the Pharaoh who two years later made Joseph the Prime Minister of Egypt. Also, we have discovered that the archeological record indicates that a great Pharaoh of the twelfth dynasty of Egypt, named Sesostris III, came to power in 1888 B.C. We know that the Pharaoh who elevated Joseph to power could only have been this Sesostris III. How marvelous that, because of the Bible's precise and accurate use of the pronoun "he" in Genesis 41:13, we are able to discover the synchronization between the sacred and the secular records.

Was the Father of Sesostris III Murdered?

There is further evidence to indicate that there was a change of Egyptian kings soon before Joseph was freed from prison. The archeological record indicates that Sesostris II, the father of Sesostris

III, in all probability, reigned 19 years.[17] His father, Amenemhet II, reigned 35 years, and his grandfather, Amenemhet I, reigned 30 years. His son, Sesostris III, the pharaoh who made Joseph prime minister, reigned 38 years, and his grandson, Amenemhet III, reigned 48 years.

In light of the long reigns of the Pharaohs before and after Sesostris II, his 19 year reign seems to be quite short. Could it be that Sesostris II came to an untimely end either through illness, or what is more likely, murder? Could it be that Sesostris II feared for his life, perhaps afraid of death by poisoning, and, therefore, he put the two men most capable of poisoning him, the chief butler and the chief baker, into prison? Or was he ill at this time and feared that his end was near? Could it be that very shortly after this, his last birthday feast of Genesis 40:20, during which the baker was hanged and the butler restored, those who wanted him murdered succeeded? Certainly, his early demise, together with all of the events surrounding the installation of the new Pharaoh, could easily have caused the butler to forget his promise to remember Joseph.

It could also be that Sesostris III began to reign, upon the early death of his father, as a comparatively young man, and that he would have welcomed the possibility of help from the young Hebrew, who was close to his age and had already shown such great wisdom. Furthermore, we read in Genesis 45:8 that Joseph told his brothers that he was as a father to the Pharaoh, which strengthens the point that Sesostris III was young when he began to reign.

Let us return briefly to our study of the timing of the reign of Sesostris III. With the evidence that is presently available, if we use only secular information, it appears that it would be impossible to date the first year of Sesostris III's reign to one and only one year, although 1888 B.C. seems to be the most likely year. If the archeological evidence is reliable, that a Sothic festival celebrating the heliacal rising of Sirius occurred on Thoth 1, 139 A.D. (and the Biblical synchronization of Sesostris III attests to its reliability), then as we saw earlier, such a festival would also have occurred on Thoth 1, 1322 B.C., on the 16th day of the 8th month in 1882 B.C. This date, the 16th day of the 8th month, is in the archeological record. However, such a festival also could have been held on the 16th day of the 8th month of the three succeeding years, 1881, 1880, and 1879, because the heliacal rising of Sirius moves through the calendar one day each four years. Since the recorded festival occurred in the seventh year of the king, his first year could have been 1888 or 1887 or 1886 or 1885 B.C. As we have seen, either 1888, 1887, or 1886 satisfy the Biblical record. Since a known festival celebrating a Sothic rising occurred in 139 A.D., and this brings us back to 1888 B.C. as the first year of Sesostris III, we suspect that the most weighty secular evidence points to it as being the correct year.

Moreover, the phrase "at the end of two full years" in Genesis 41:1 also places the emphasis on 1888 B.C., that is, if this phrase has any reference to the reign of Pharaoh. The context surely suggests this, because the verse is talking about Pharaoh. Let us see why this is so. We know that Jacob and his family arrived in Egypt about March/April of 1877 B.C. This is known because the Israelites left Egypt "the selfsame day," 430 years later (Exodus 12:41), and they left on Nisan 15, which was about March/April, 1447 B.C. The Bibles testifies that the famine had been in the land for two years and five years remained. Genesis 45:6 reads:

> For these two years hath the famine been in the land: and yet there are five years, in the which there shall neither be earing nor harvest.

The implication is that at the end of two years, just before the beginning of the remaining five years of famine, was the time when Jacob entered Egypt. Since we know that he entered Egypt in March/April of 1877 B.C., the seven good years must have begun about nine full years earlier in March/April of 1886 B.C., which would then be the date of Joseph's release from prison. The release of the baker and the butler two full years earlier would be March/April, 1888 B.C., probably just before the death of Sesostris II. His son, Sesostris III, would thus have reigned two years when he had his dreams about cows and corn. This sequence of time satisfies all Biblical possibilities.

The timetable would look like this: Sesostris III's first year ended Thoth 1 (August/September), 1888 B.C.[18] He began to reign either as a co-regent with his father on Thoth 1, 1889 B.C.,[19] or he began to reign immediately upon his father's death. There is reason to believe that his father died on the 14th day of the 8th month (March/April).[20] The birthday feast of Genesis 40 occurred shortly before March/April of 1888 B.C.. Two full years later (Gen. 41:1), Sesostris III, who was now in the third year of his reign, had his dreams and released Joseph about March/April, 1886 B.C. In the seventh year of

Sesostris III, on the 16th day of the 8th month (March/April), 1882 B.C., Sesostris III celebrated the Sothic festival. This coincided with the beginning of the 5th year of plentiful harvest under Joseph's rule as prime minister. In March/April of 1879 B.C., the seven years of plenty came to an end, and two years later, in March/April, 1877 B.C., Jacob arrived in Egypt.

A Slave Becomes Prime Minister

Does it make any sense to believe that young Sesostris III would appoint a slave, Joseph, to the high office of prime minister or "grand vizier"? The answer comes from the archeological record that indicates that beginning especially with the 12th Dynasty, during which Sesostris III reigned, large changes occurred in the method of government and in the appointment of those governed.

The practice of appointing people who were not of royal blood to high office apparently was common during the 12th Dynasty. Archeologists have shown that men who were called "viziers" and who also often held the title of monarch, ruled over the various provinces of Egypt. The office of monarch was often an hereditary office. During the 12th Dynasty, however, there were many changes. Simpson writes that:

> the viziers of the Twelfth Dynasty evidently belonged neither to the ruling family . . . nor to the class of hereditary monarchs.[21]

The Biblical picture of the increased power of the central government during Joseph's era is also verified by secular sources. Hayes declares:

> It appears to have been in the reign of King Senworsret III of the Twelfth Dynasty that the administration of the provinces of Upper and Lower Egypt was taken out of the hands of the hereditary monarchs and reorganized into units called "wrwt," which functioned as departments of the central government.[22]

Simpson also writes:

> Students of the Twelfth Dynasty have frequently noted the loss of power suffered by the monarchs in this reign. This situation certainly requires further study and perhaps reappraisal, but it cannot be seriously questioned.[23]

We see that the archeological evidence appears to indicate that at about the time of Sesostris III, the power of administration was transferred more clearly to the central government and out of the hands of the monarchs. This could well have been a result of the palace intrigue and ferment that resulted in his father's death or it could have been a result of the total power that was given to Joseph, or both. In any case, the archeological information of a central government ruling over all of Egypt, beginning with the Twelfth Dynasty, agrees precisely with the Biblical information of Joseph ruling over all of Egypt as Prime Minister.

The Secular Data Accords with Joseph's Long Rule

When we examine the reigns of Sesostris III and his son Amenemhet III, we notice that both had long reigns (38 years and 48 years, respectively). Since Joseph died 80 years after he became Prime Minister, he died in 1806 B.C. He outlived Sesostris III and died four years before Amenemhet III. Amenemhet III died 1802 B.C.

This long period of Joseph's life together with the long reigns of the Pharaohs under whom he was Prime Minister would have contributed to a very stable government. Was this in fact the situation? The answer seems to be yes, because during these two reigns, the land was prosperous and tranquil. Breasted writes of this period:

> It was thus over a nation in the fullness of its powers, rich and productive in every avenue of life, that Amenemhet III ruled; and his reign crowned the classic age which had dawned with the advent of his family.[24]

Amenemhet III was especially concerned with the water resources of Egypt. During his reign, a large dam and lake were constructed, called Fayum Lake (Lake Moeris).[25] It is very interesting that the canal that supplied water to this lake was named "Bahr Yusuf" or Joseph's Canal.[26] We thus see that the archeological evidence and the Scriptural record dovetail very neatly and provide an exact chronological reference point for this period of history.

In this chapter we have discovered the exquisite reliability of the Bible, all the way to a small pronoun, "he." This should encourage us to believe anew in the infallible, God-breathed nature of God's Word. We should see afresh that the Bible is trustworthy when it speaks in the area of salvation and also when it speaks on historical questions.

We saw how the Biblical account, with its perfect chronology, gives us an exact timetable for the secular account, and the latter record accords altogether with the sacred, once the data from both accounts have been synchronized. Secular information about the practice of appointing "grand viziers" from other than the ruling class, the short reign of Sesostris II, the long and tranquil reigns of Sesostris III and Amenemhet III, all match the Biblical record. Even the construction of Joseph's Canal pointedly calls our attention to the beautiful relationship that exists between the sacred and secular records.

Let us continue our search to see if additional meshing of the two records is possible.

The Hyksos: Shepherd Kings

We saw the precise agreement that exists between the secular and sacred records as we studied the timetable of the Pharaoh, Sesostris III, who ruled during the middle of the Twelfth Dynasty of Egypt, beginning in 1888 B.C. We saw that he was the young Pharaoh who made Joseph Prime Minister or "Grand Vizier." By this particular study, we achieved new proof of the validity of the chronology set forth in this volume.

Before we look for another point of chronological synchronization, we should spend a few moments with the secular record of the Egyptians during the Israelites' sojourn in Egypt. This is the period from 1877 B.C. to 1447 B.C., as established by Biblical reckoning. It covers the period of Egyptian history from the middle of the 12th Dynasty to the middle of the 18th Dynasty. In this chapter, we will not discover any precise synchronization between the secular and sacred records, but we will provide some insights into puzzling archeological evidence. We shall also provide a background for clearly identifying the Pharaoh of the Exodus, who will be presented in the next chapter.

The Hyksos

Archeological evidence reveals that during the period between the 12th and 17th Dynasties, Egypt had foreign rulers, called Hyksos. They were apparently of Asiatic, Palestinian, or Hurrite origin, as indicated by the names of the rulers, as well as by pottery and other archeological evidence. Archaeologists have commonly described the entrance of these people into Egypt as an invasion of some kind. They have also suggested that it was their presence that provided the sympathetic and warm reception for Jacob and his family when they arrived in Egypt.

Since many Bible scholars as well as archaeologists believe that Jacob went to Egypt about 1720 B.C.[27] and that the Hyksos were already reigning at that time, it can readily be seen why most scholars indicate no identification between the Hyksos and the Israelites. Archbishop Usher's chronology, which appears in the margins of many Bibles, undoubtedly has done much to foster this idea. He gives the date 1729 B.C. as the date of Joseph's arrival. This would accordingly place Jacob's arrival at about 1720 B.C., which is near the time when the Hyksos began to reign as Pharaohs. This has been a very unfortunate calculation by Usher.

There is considerable evidence to show that the Hyksos were the Israelites. Let us examine this, because in so doing, we will learn something about the Israelites' conduct in Egypt and the conditions that led to their enslavement.

The Timing of the Hyksos

Most archaeologists believe that the Hyksos began to reign about 1720 B.C. The noted archeologist, Raymond Weill, however, indicates that in his judgment, the Hyksos were already present in the latter part of the Twelfth Dynasty. In a carving from the reign of

Amenemmes IV, a representation of a god is shown, which is like the god of Seth or Sutekh. Weill, therefore, writes:

> The assimilation is extremely remarkable, in view of the fact that in the older period there is no evidence of local cults of Seth in Lower Egypt, where he was first installed, in all likelihood by the "Hyksos" kings in Tanis, Avairs . . . . This identification in the time of Amenemmes IV seems to indicate clearly that these Asiatic intruders and all the things that came with them were already present in the Delta during the Twelfth Dynasty; and it thus appears to demonstrate the truth of the view recently put forward that the settlement of these foreigners in Egypt began at least as early as that central part of the Middle Kingdom.[28]

He also writes:

> . . . It now appears . . . that the "Asiatic" or "Hyksos" period in Lower Egypt extends chronologically beyond the Dynasty of the Apopis at each end, and thus this Dynasty was but an episode in a much vaster development in time and perhaps in territory. Let me observe further in support of this statement that since 1929 it has been recognized the "Hyksos" period, that is to say, the incursion of Asiatics and Egypto-Asiatic culture in Lower Egypt, will have begun immediately after the end of the Twelfth Dynasty, if not during that Dynasty itself.[29]

There is, therefore, good reason to believe that the Hyksos were already in Egypt during the Twelfth Dynasty, that is, prior to 1788 B.C. This accords with our premise that the Hyksos were the Israelites, who had been in Egypt since the middle of the Twelfth Dynasty. It is possible that they did not assert themselves until many years after Joseph's death in 1806 B.C.

How Did the Hyksos Seize Power?

Many archaeologists believe that the mysterious people who came into power between the 12th and 17th Dynasties of Egypt invaded Egypt and seized power by force, but within the last couple of decades, closer analysis of the archeological evidence has begun to reveal that possibly there was no invasion of Egypt by the Hyksos. Rather, it appears that the foreign rulers simply represented change in the ruling class from among those people who lived in Egypt. Moreover, as we have stated, there is increasing evidence that the Hyksos were in Egypt as early as the latter part of the 12th Dynasty. While apparently none of these later writers identify the Hyksos with the Hebrews, but they do express great puzzlement regarding the precise origin of the Hyksos, the evidence they have been presenting increasingly points to the Hyksos as being substantially identical with the Hebrews. Let us look at some of the evidence and see how it relates to the Biblical record.

For the archeological fact that this was not an invasion by foreign Asiatics, we turn to the testimony of T. Save-Soderbergh and John Van Seters. T. Save-Soderberg writes:

> The only literary source that describes how the Hyksos came into power is the History of Egypt written by Manetho in the second century B.C., i.e., about 1500 years after the event. Thus, it is a very late source, but derived from earlier documents. It is, however, a typical trait of all the late sources regarding the Hyksos that they are strongly tinged by propaganda against the foreigners. In fact, the later the text, the more hostile it is to the Hyksos.[30]

He writes additionally:

> Now who were the Hyksos? The Egyptian term is hk32h3swt, which means "rulers of foreign countries." This seems to have been a usual designation of the sheikhs in Palestine and Syria as early as the beginning of the Twelfth Dynasty. For instance, such a sheikh who came with 37 Asiatics to bring their products to Egypt is depicted in a tomb at Beni Hasan. In the accompanying inscription he is called "the ruler of a foreign country" (hk3h3st) Abishi -- . . . . This term gives us the impression that the Hyksos were only a little group of foreign dynasts rather than a numerous people with a special civilization. According to Manetho's version, it also seems as if the Hyksos rule only

meant a change of political leaders in Egypt; and not a mass-invasion of a numerically important foreign ethnic element. This view is corroborated by contemporary evidence. There are a great many tombs from the Hyksos period in Egypt, but there is nowhere a clear indication of an invasion of a foreign people from the north.[31]

We thus learn that the archeological information concerning the Hyksos is from the record penned by Manetho, some 1500 years after the time when they were in Egypt. This should caution us to use great care in accepting Manetho's conclusions. T. Save-Soderbergh's conclusion is that there was no invasion by the people called the Hyksos, but rather that there simply occurred a change of the political rulers. He continues:

> To sum up, the analysis of the archeological evidence gives a somewhat negative result, but rather supports the view, mentioned above, that the Hyksos rule was only a change of political leaders, and not an invasion by a numerically important ethnic element with a superior technique and a special civilization. On the other hand, the Hyksos had close connections with Asia, and seem to have favoured the introduction of innovations from this area more than their Egyptian predecessors. But it is only towards the end of their rule in Egypt that they introduce a number of improvements in military technique in an attempt to uphold their political power against the growing Egyptian opposition. Then first the horse drawn chariots, new types of daggers and swords, bronze weapons, the strong compound Asiatic bow, etc., are imported from the dates of the actual finds of these innovations in Egypt, since they are unknown until the very end of the Hyksos rule.[32]

Although no evidence of chariots as early as the 12th Dynasty (about 2000 B.C. to 1788 B.C.), has been found yet by archaeologists, the Bible says very clearly that when Joseph went to Palestine to bury his father, "there went up with him both chariots and horsemen: and it was a very great company" (Gen. 50:9). We thus should expect such evidence to be forthcoming from archaeologists. It was as late as 1960 that archaeologists found evidence of horses that relates to the 12th Dynasty.[33]

Van Seters, who calls the Hyksos people Amurrites (people of Syria, Palestine), writes:

> The long period of acculturation of coastal Syria and Palestine to Egyptian arts and crafts fully prepared the "foreign rulers" and their supporters for taking control of Egypt. This was achieved, not by a sudden coup d'etat from without, but in cooperation with a fifth column Amurrite group already established in the Delta. The strong Amurrite princes of Syria-Palestine became heir to the Egyptian throne in a time of the latter's dynastic weakness.[34]

He continues:

> There was active cooperation between the Asiatics and the Egyptians within Egypt itself in the Amurrite coup d'etat. Disloyalty by important noble families may be understood in light of the strong centralization of administration by the Pharaohs of the late Twelfth Dynasty. In the period of dynastic weakness, these families reasserted themselves. With the breakup of the land into the three departments of the previous Middle Kingdom administration, an Egyptian, Nehesy, had control of the North, probably with Asiatic cooperation. It was merely a step for Amurrite princes themselves to take control of Lower Egypt and, in time, the whole of Egypt. No great military conquest was needed to accomplish this, and it is doubtful that any occurred. All that was required for the land to become an Amurrite dynasty was the recognition, by a sufficient number of the Egyptian nobility, of a strong foreign king in the strategic city of Avaris and submission to him as vassals (to their own economic advantage.)[35]

The information above indicates that there was in all probability no invasion of Egypt by Asiatic foreigners but rather some kind of internal change in rulers. And this accords quite well with the premise that the Hyksos were the Israelites. If we go back for a moment to our earlier contact between the Pharaoh of the Bible of Joseph's day and the Pharaoh discovered by the archeological evidence, we can see what could have happened.

We saw that in the middle of the Twelfth Dynasty, the year 1888 B.C. to be exact, Sesostris III began to reign. In 1886 B.C., he made Joseph Prime Minister, and the central government took on increased strength, especially as a result of the seven years of famine when so much of the land came under ownership of the central government. It was for these reasons that, in all probability, the hereditary monarchs ceased to have rule over the provinces as they had before. These conditions prevailed when, in 1877 B.C., Jacob and his family came to Egypt and began to grow into a nation.

During the life of Joseph, who died in 1806 B.C., the two greatest Pharaohs of the Twelfth Dynasty reigned (Sesostris III and Amenemhet III), and the kingdom prospered. With the death of Amenemhet III in 1802 B.C., the reigns of two more rulers brought the Twelfth Dynasty to a close. These latter two reigned a few years (Amenemhet IV, nine years, and Sebeknefrure, four years). The next period of some 208 years was the period of the Thirteenth to the Seventeenth Dynasties, during a part of which the rulers were Semitic or Asiatic.

Following the end of the Twelfth Dynasty, a new house took control, seemingly in a very tranquil fashion.[36] However, the reigns of succeeding pharaohs were short and the empire began to dissolve. Breasted writes:

> Rapid dissolution followed, as the provincial lords rose against each other and strove for the throne. Pretender after pretender struggled for supremacy.[37]

In this kind of atmosphere, the kings with Semitic names began to reign. These were the so-called "Hyksos." We must remember now that the Israelites under Joseph had become an important part of Egyptian government. If Joseph continued in office until his death (a period of eighty years), he probably was the most outstanding government employee in the land. Because of his wisdom, he was probably highly respected. Also, he would have had much opportunity for training and introducing many of his fellow Israelites into government service. Consequently, following Joseph's death and the end of the Twelfth Dynasty several years later, the jockeying for political power by the Egyptians with no strong ruler asserting himself from their number, would have given the Israelites who had any governmental ambition at all, the opportunity to gain the rulership. Their aspirations and achievements would amply fulfill the speculative suggestions of T. Save-Soderbergh, Van Seters, and others that this was an internal coup d'etat. Because of Joseph's superb relationship to the Egyptians, as well as his dynamic leadership as Prime Minister for so many years, many of the later Egyptians would probably have been equally happy to side with the aspiring Hebrews during those troubled times.

The Land of Goshen and the Hyksos

The Bible states that the Israelites were given the land of Goshen to live in by Sesostris III (Genesis 46:34). Does this help identify them in any way with the Hyksos? It does indeed, for Goshen was in the northern part of Egypt. The city of Avaris, which was later called either Tanis or Qantir, was the capital of the Hyksos and was located in the land of Goshen. It probably was made a seat of government during Joseph's term as prime minister. Van Seter's conclusion is very pertinent to this question:

> Taking the archeological evidence together with this, it seems safe to assert that Senwosret III created an important center of government in the North, a balance and perhaps even a rival to Thebes.[38]

Thus, the identification of the land of Goshen with the capital of the Hyksos both as to location and as to time gives added proof that the Hyksos were indeed the Israelites.

One additional fact might be offered concerning Avaris. It is also commonly identified with the Biblical Zoan. We thus can find a reason for the Biblical statement of Numbers 13:22, "Now Hebron was built seven years before Zoan in Egypt." The statement that Hebron was built seven years before Zoan does provide circumstantial evidence regarding the premise that the Hyksos were the Israelites. Hebron is the city where Abraham purchased land to bury Sarah (Genesis 23:19). Since it is the only land purchased by Abraham, Hebron becomes a type or figure of a down payment or first fruits of the promise that God's people would inherit that land. Zoan, therefore, regardless of its importance in the minds of the Israelites as a place that gave evidence of the Hebrews' triumph in Egypt, was inferior to God's city Hebron (although Hebron was not occupied by Israelites at that time). So as we consider that in everything God has preeminence, we realize why the Bible ties the founding of Zoan to Hebron. God would not let Israel, who founded Zoan, or Avaris, forget that He had already decided on their inheritance.

Another interesting sidelight that possibly links the Hyksos to the Israelites is afforded by noting what gods the Hyksos served. The archeological evidence clearly indicates that their dominate god was Seth or Seth-Baal, which was of Canaanish origin. This particular god had become so highly integrated into the Egyptian religious idea that Rameses II, who reigned more than 150 years after the Exodus, identified himself with this god "Seth." "Seth" is shown on a stela of Rameses II to be a god represented in foreign attire, wearing a high conical cap with gazelle horns protruding from the front.[39] However, Seth is also represented as a bull. He is called the "bull of Retjenu" (Syria).[40]

In the Egyptian pantheon, Seth is augmented by two Asiatic goddesses as consorts, Anat and Astarte.[41] Anat seems to be represented on scarabs of the Hyksos period as a nude deity with cow ears, horns, and Hathor curls.[42] However, even as Seth is represented as a bull, so Anat, the female god, is represented as the "milch cow of Seth."[43] Thus, the Egyptians actually worshipped a god named Seth that was represented by a bull. And they also worshipped a god related to Seth that was represented by a cow.

If we look now to that sinful experience of the Israelites when Moses was on Mount Sinai, we see that they asked Aaron to make a calf. When the golden calf was made, the Israelites said very strangely, "These be thy gods, O Israel, which brought thee up out of the land of Egypt" (Exodus 32:4). But why would he use the plural "gods" when there was only one calf to worship? The difficulty ceases if we see in this calf "Seth, the bull of Retjenu" as well as "Anat the milch cow of Seth." These were the gods the Israelites served in Egypt. One calf could equally represent both gods.[44]

Joseph Identifies the Hyksos with the Hebrews

While archaeologists have generally indicated their belief that the Hyksos could not have been the Israelites, the reputable archeologist Breasted, at least, suggests that there did exist some kind of relationship between the Hyksos and the Israelites. He writes:

> That was a Semitic empire we cannot doubt, in view of the Manethonian tradition and the subsequent conditions in Syria-Palestine. Moreover, the scarabs of a Pharaoh who evidently belonged to the Hyksos time, give his name as Jacob-her or perhaps Jacob-El, and it is not impossible that some chief of the Jacob-tribes of Israel for a time gained the leadership in this obscure age. Such an incident would account surprisingly well for the entrance of these tribes into Egypt, which on any hypothesis must have taken place at about this age; and in that case the Hebrews will have been but a part of the Beduin allies of the Kadesh or Hyksos empire. . . . Likewise, the naive assumption of Josephus, who identifies the Hyksos with the Hebrews, may thus contain a kernel of truth, however accidental.[45]

Breasted therefore concludes that the Hyksos were Semitic in origin and that the Israelites could somehow have been involved in the Hyksos movement. He suggests that the presence of the Hyksos provided a satisfactory environment for the entrance of Jacob and his family. Other archaeologists have echoed these ideas. But hardly anyone has seriously suggested that the Hyksos are one and the same as the Israelites, that is, no one except Josephus, as we have seen from Breasted's writings.

The End of the Hyksos

What does the secular record indicate regarding the end of the Hyksos in Egypt? That record indicates that as the years passed, they were more and more coming into disrepute with the Egyptians. Finally, about 1600 B.C., their removal from political leadership began to take place. Avaris, the capital in the north, fell after a siege of some years and the power of the Hyksos was broken. This was near 1580-1560 B.C., during Ahmose I's reign. He was the first king of the Eighteenth Dynasty, the dynasty during which in later years the Israelites departed from Egypt.

The conclusions of Van Seters regarding the end of the Hyksos must be identified with the Israelites. He writes:

> The defeat of the foreign dynasty was the result of a civil war, and the foreign population which was probably not very numerous simply continued to live in the Eastern Delta.[46]

Can this secular solution offered by Van Seters and others regarding the expulsion of the Hyksos from Egypt be correlated with the Israelites? It probably can.

The first king of the Eighteenth Dynasty was Ahmose I. He began to reign about 1580 B.C. One of his first efforts was to remove the Asiatics or Hyksos from political office. Because some of them had become rulers of the kingdom itself, this amounted almost to civil war. Since we are suggesting that these Hyksos are the Israelites, let us reconstruct this bit of history with this thought in view. Following Joseph's death, the Israelites became increasingly prominent in politics; some became rulers in the land. In 1580 B.C., Ahmose I began to correct this situation. Under his energetic leadership, the warlike elements of the Israelites were driven from the land. He probably stripped the Israelites of all political authority and may even have begun to enslave them. Ahmose I was followed by his son Amenhotep I who reigned at least ten years and consolidated the gains of his father.

No evidence is presently available as to whether Amenhotep's successor, Thutmose I, was his son. But in 1540 or 1535 B.C., Thutmose I began to reign. One of his major tasks was to bring into subjection the land of Nubia and following that the land of Syria, in which the fires of potential rebellion were burning. Biographies of two of his soldiers indicate that his conquest was carried into northern Palestine and possibly beyond to the Euphrates River. The battle that followed resulted in a "great slaughter of Asiatics followed by the capture of a large number of prisoners." [47] This battle did not solve the problem of potential revolt by Syria (Palestine) for it was not until after twenty years of warfare under Thutmose III that Syria was finally completely crushed and placed securely under Egyptian domination.[48]

This probably sets the background for the Biblical statement of Exodus 1. Joseph had died in 1806 B.C., about 270 years earlier. After Joseph's death, the Israelites gradually came into disrepute because of the desire of some of them to rule the country. Possibly as a result of Ahmose I's victory over these Israelite leaders, the people of Israel were already in a condition of servitude. Thutmose I undoubtedly realized that these Israelites, who were increasing in number, had to be forcibly removed from power. Moreover, they were originally of the land of Palestine, which was a part of Syria and which was giving him so much difficulty. Therefore, he made his decision. We read in Exodus 1:9-11:

> And he said unto his people, Behold, the people of the children of Israel are more and mightier than we: Come on, let us deal wisely with them; lest they multiply, and it come to pass, that, when there falleth out any war, they join also unto our enemies, and fight against us, and so get them up out of the land. Therefore they did set over them taskmasters to afflict them with their burdens. And they built for Pharaoh treasure cities, Pithom and Raamses.

It could be that Thutmose I concluded that only by making complete slaves of the Israelites would they be prohibited from ever being able to rise again in power or enabled to join with the Asiatics of Palestine to attempt an overthrow of Egypt. All knowledge of the benevolent leadership of Joseph had ceased to exist. The Israelites had become a threat to the kingdom and had to be dealt with harshly. But the more they were oppressed, the more they multiplied. The Bible records that finally the king decreed that all of the firstborn males were to be killed. And so we are introduced to Moses and Princess Hatshepsut.

A Queen Is King

Thutmose I, the Pharaoh who fathered Thutmose III, had two sons and two daughters by his queen Ahmose. She was the royal descendant of Ahmose I who was the first king of the Eighteenth Dynasty. Both sons and one of the daughters of Thutmose I died in their youth or at birth. The surviving daughter, Makere-Hatshepsut, was thus the only child of the old line. And because of her direct descent from Ahmose I, she was heir to the throne, even though Thutmose I had two additional sons by other queens. One of these other sons was to become Thutmose II and the other Thutmose III.

Hatshepsut is of special interest to us because the timetable of her reign coincides with the time of the Biblical events that involve Moses, and she was the daughter of Pharaoh. The Bible records that the daughter of Pharaoh drew the baby Moses from the water and adopted him as her son. This would have been eighty years before the Exodus, the year 1527 B.C. The secular record shows that Hatshepsut began to reign about the same time as Thutmose III, which we will see must have been in 1501 B.C.,[49] and that she reigned either twenty or twenty-one years. Thus, she must have died about 1480 B.C. The archeological record furthermore shows that she was a strong, forceful, and energetic ruler. Unfortunately, no information has been found that gives her life span or age when she became ruler, but her mature actions as a ruler together with the relatively short duration of her reign suggest that she was not too young when she began to reign. If she was about 15 years old when Moses was born, she would have been in her early forties when she became ruler and in her early sixties when she died. In any event only she could have been the Pharaoh from whom Moses fled after he killed the Egyptian, as we shall presently see. This kind of action in attempting to kill Moses is quite in agreement with that of a ruler who as a young princess had made the mistake of sparing one of the hated Hebrews who now threatened the kingdom.

Princess Hatshepsut, in all probability, named the Hebrew baby Moses because her own family name on one side was Ah<u>mose</u> and her father's name was Thut<u>mose</u>. <u>Mose</u> in these names actually means <u>son</u>. Ahmose was thus "son of Ah." Thutmose was "son of Thoth." It is true that "Moses" coincides quite closely with the Hebrew word "mashah," which means "to draw out," but it does not necessarily follow, as many would suggest, that this is the reason he was called Moses.[50] Moreover, it would be strange indeed if an Egyptian princess gave her adopted son a name that identified him for life with the hated Hebrews. More probably, the emphasis of the Biblical statement "she called his name Moses: and she said, Because I drew him out of the water" (Exodus 2:10), should be on the "I" rather than on the "drew him out of the water." <u>She</u> had found the baby. It was to be <u>her</u> son. Therefore, "Moses" would fit perfectly.

This suggests a very interesting thought. Jesus identified Himself with Israel by the phrase "Out of Egypt have I called my son" (Hosea 11:1, Matthew 2:15). Moses was one of the great types of Christ. He, too, was called out of Egypt. Does his name Moses, which means "son" further identify him with Christ? He, too, was a "son" (Moses) called out of Egypt.

The next incident in the Biblical passage that relates Hatshepsut to Moses occurred forty years later. Moses was 40 years old when, after killing an Egyptian, he was forced to flee from Egypt because the Pharaoh sought to kill him (Exodus 2:15). Who was this Pharaoh? As we have already indicated, it could not have been Thutmose III who began to reign in 1501 B.C. and, we believe, died in the Red Sea, for the Bible declares that the Pharaoh who sought to kill him died while Moses was in Midian (Exodus 2:23 and Exodus 4:19).

The solution to our problem is simply that a co-regency existed at the time Moses fled from Egypt. Two kings were on the throne. One was Thutmose III who had begun to reign fourteen years earlier, in 1501 B.C., and as we have already seen, the other was none other than Hatshepsut. Because of her royal blood lines, Thutmose III was forced to acknowledge her as co-regent. She, in fact, became the dominant ruler because of her superior royal blood lines and actually was given the title "king" even though she was a woman.[51] A typical inscription concerning her reign is that of a base inscription found on the Karnak Obelisks from Hatshepsut's reign. There we read:

> Live the female Horus . . . daughter of Amon-Re, his favorite, his only one, who exists by him, the splendid part of the All-Lord, whose beauty the spirits of Heliopolis fashioned; who hath taken the land like Irsu, whom he hath created to wear his diadem, who exists like Khepri (Hpry), who shines with crowns like "Him-of-the-Horizon," the pure egg, the excellent seed, whom the two sorceresses reared, whom Amon himself caused to appear upon his throne in Hermonthis, whom he chose to protect Egypt, to "defend" the people, the female Horus, avengeress of her father, the oldest (daughter) of the "Bull-of-his-Mother," whom Re begat to make for himself excellent seed upon earth for the well-being of the people; his living

portrait, King of Upper and Lower Egypt, Makere (Hatshepsut), the electrum of kings.[52]

Even though he was not a true son of King Hatshepsut, Moses' position in the palace must have been of the highest stature. When Moses killed the Egyptian, Queen (or King) Hatshepsut no doubt realized the enormous risk she had taken in saving the Hebrew baby from death and raising him as her son. He had manifested superior wisdom and leadership qualities in the Egyptian court (Acts 7:22). At the age of 40 he showed clearly where his sympathies lay, and that was with the slaves, the Israelites, his own people. All the fears that had been expressed by her father concerning a potential uprising by the Israelites returned to her. What had she done? The only solution was to have her adopted son killed. King Hatshepsut then was no doubt the king who sought to kill Moses. No wonder he fled to the wilderness of Midian to tend sheep. No wonder he hesitated to return even after forty years. That King Hatshepsut was preoccupied with the Israelites is clearly indicated in one of her inscriptions: "I raised up that which had gone to pieces formerly, since the Asiatics were in the midst of Avaris of the Northland." "Asiatics" is a reference to the Israelites. Avaris is the same area of Egypt as the land of Goshen.

According to the archeological record, Hatshepsut died about 1481 B.C.,[53] which would have been approximately six years after Moses fled. The Bible records this fact in Exodus 2:23. Thutmose III continued to reign as sole ruler almost until Moses returned to lead the Israelites from Egypt, as we shall see. Thus, only she could have been the Pharaoh who sought to kill Moses and who died while he was in Midian.

Summary

We have seen some of the events that occurred within Egypt as Israel grew into a nation of possibly two million souls. We cannot positively identify them with the Hyksos. However, to find no record of this great nation, which grew up in Egypt, would seem very strange indeed. When we remember that they began with one of the greatest prime ministers Egypt ever had, Joseph, it would seem even more strange if no record of this people was available. On the other hand, what are we to think of all the archeological findings about these mysterious Asiatics or "Hyksos," whose arrival and removal is so clouded, and who were present in Egypt when the Israelites were there? Also, it seems suspicious that the Hyksos capital was in Avaris or Zoan in the land of Goshen where the Israelites lived. It certainly appears that the two peoples must be one and the same.

It could be argued that the Exodus is unrecorded in the ancient secular records. If that is true, why should we expect the Israelites' residence in Egypt to be noted in any of the archeological records? There is a major difference between them, of course, for secular records can be consciously altered to suit the purposes of whoever writes them. The Exodus was a shattering and dreadful defeat for Egypt, which had not one ray of victory. There just would not be any reason or compulsion to keep records of such an overwhelming and shameful defeat by a nation of slaves. There is, however, indirect archeological testimony to the Exodus as we shall see in greater detail in the next chapter.

We have introduced a number of pharaohs and dynasties into our discussion. Let us summarize by historical timetable the information thus far presented.

1888 B.C.:

Sesostris III became pharaoh. He was part of the Middle Kingdom or Twelfth Dynasty of Egypt. His father, Sesostris II, probably had reigned during the previous nineteen years and possibly came to an untimely death.

1886 B.C.:

Joseph became Prime Minister or Grand Vizier of Egypt under Sesostris III.

1877 B.C.:

The family of Joseph came to Egypt and took up residence in the land of Goshen. The city of Avaris (Zoan in the Bible), which later was called Tanis or Qantir, was their capital.

1850 B.C.:

Sesostris III died after an exceedingly successful reign of thirty-eight years. He was succeeded by another great Twelfth Dynasty pharaoh named Amenemhet III. Under his reign, Joseph continued as Prime Minister. A canal bearing Joseph's name was constructed at this time.

1806 B.C.:

Joseph died.

1802 B.C.:

Amenemhet III died after a forty-eight year reign. During his reign, Egypt was prosperous, tranquil, and productive. He was succeeded by Amenemhet IV, who reigned for nine years. During his reign, there was much internal strife for royal supremacy.

1791 B.C.:

Amenemhet IV died and was succeeded by the last pharaoh of the Twelfth Dynasty, Sebeknefrure.

1787 B.C.:

Sebeknefrure's brief reign of four years ended and with it ended the Twelfth Dynasty. The Thirteenth Dynasty began. The reigns of succeeding pharaohs were short and the empire began to dissolve. The Israelites, who no doubt are the Hyksos of archeological fame, took advantage of the internal struggles to acquire a strong hand in the Egyptian government and indeed some of them may have reigned as pharaohs during this period.

1580 B.C.:

(Approx.) Several dynasties have ruled over Egypt since 1787 B.C. At this time, Ahmose I began to reign as the first king of the Eighteenth Dynasty. He forcibly began to remove the Israelites (Hyksos) from political power. The most war-like Israelites were driven from the land and the Israeli nation began to be severely oppressed. Either this pharaoh or a closely succeeding pharaoh, such as Thutmose I, could well have been the king who "knew not Joseph" (Exodus 1:8).

1560 B.C.:

(Approx.) Ahmose I was followed by his son Amenhotep I. Amenhotep I consolidated the gains of his father.

1540 B.C.:

(Approx.) Thutmose I began to reign as king.

1535 B.C.:

He, too, was a continuation of the Eighteenth Dynasty. He continued and probably intensified the oppressive measures against the Israelites, for he was ruling when Moses was born. His animosity towards the Israelites was probably heightened by his troubles with Palestine and Syria. His reign was followed by that of his son Thutmose II.

1527 B.C.:

Moses was born at a time when a royal edict condemned all the boy babies to be destroyed. Princess Hatshepsut, a daughter of the king, found him in the bulrushes and raised him as her son.

1501 B.C.:

Thutmose III began to reign as the greatest king of the Eighteenth Dynasty. For approximately the first twenty-five years of his reign, he was co-regent with Princess Hatshepsut. She regarded herself as a king and was the dominant ruler during this co-regency.

1487 B.C.:

Moses fled from Egypt. King Hatshepsut, who had raised him to be her son, sought to kill him because of his evident loyalty to the Israelites.

1481 B.C.:

(Approx.) King Hatshepsut died and Thutmose III continued to reign until the time of the Exodus.

NOTES

[1] Edwin R. Thiele, *The Mysterious Numbers of the Hebrew Kings,* Rev. Ed. (Grand Rapids: William B. Eerdmans, 1965), page 41.

[2] Jack Finegan, *Handbook of Biblical Chronology* (Princeton, New Jersey: Princeton University Press, 1964), page 196.

[3] Finegan, page 196.

[4] Thiele, page 42.

[5] Finegan, page 197.

[6] Thiele, page 118 ff.

[7] Thiele, page 145 [From Daniel David Luckenbill, *Ancient Records of Assyria and Babylon*].

[8] Finegan, *Light of the Ancient Past*, page 209.

[9] *Light from the Ancient Past*, page 29.

[10] Finegan, ¶308, page 198.

[11] Finegan, ¶311, page 199.

[12] Finegan, ¶ 319, page 204.

[13] W. F. Edgerton, "Chronology of the Twelfth Dynasty," in "Journal of Near Eastern Studies" (Chicago, Univ. of Chicago Press, 1942), pp. 308-309.

[14] Finegan, p. 127.

[15] G. H. Wheeler, "The Chronology of the Twelfth Dynasty," in *Journal of Egyptian Archeology*, pp. 198-199.

[16] See Chapter IV of this volume.

[17] James H. Breasted, *A History of Egypt*, Charles Scribner's Sons, Second Edition (1937), pp. 598-599.

[18] In early Egyptian history the Pharaoh's reigns coincided with the calendar year, which began on Thoth 1. See Finegan, Jack, op. cit., p. 25.

[19] A. H. Gardiner, "Regnal Years and Civil Calendar in Pharaonic Egypt," in *Journal of Egyptian Archeology*, Vol. 31 (1945), p. 27.

[20] *Ibid.*, p. 27.

[21] W. V. Simpson, "Sobhemhet, A Vizier of Sesostris III," J.E.A., Vol. 43 (1957), p. 27.

[22] William C. Hayes, "Notes on the Government of Egypt in the Lake Middle Kingdom," J.N.E.S., Vol. 12 (1953), p. 31.

[23] Simpson, *"Vizier of Sesostris III,"* p. 27.

[24] James H. Breasted, *A History of Egypt*, Charles Scribner's Sons, second ed. (1973), p. 208.

[25] Ibid., p. 193.

[26] Arthur Weigall, *A History of the Pharaohs* (New York, E. P. Dutton & Co., 1927), pp. 114-115.

[27] See Chapter VII for the correct date of Joseph's arrival in Egypt.

[28] Raymond Weill, "The Problem of the Site of Avaris," in *Journal of Egyptian Archeology*, Vol. 21, 1935, p. 25.

[29] *Ibid.*, p. 23.

[30] T. Save-Soderbergh, "The Hyksos Rule in Egypt," in *Journal of Egyptian Archeology* (1951), p. 55.

[31] T. Save-Soderbergh, *"Hyksos Rule,"* p. 55.

[32] T. Save-Soderbergh, "The Hyksos Rule in Egypt," in *Journal of Egyptian Archeology* (1951), p. 60.

[33] John A. Van Seters, *The Hyksos*, Yale Press, 1966, p.185.

[34] *Ibid.*, p. 190.

[35] *Ibid.*, p. 192.

[36] James H. Breasted, *A History of Egypt*, Charles Scribner's Sons, 2nd Ed. 1937, p. 211.

[37] *Ibid.*, p.211.

[38] Van Seters, *The Hyksos*, p. 94.

[39] *Ibid.*, p. 174.

[40] *Ibid.*, p. 175.

[41] *Ibid.*, p. 175.

[42] *Ibid.*, p. 178.

[43] *Ibid.*, p. 175.

[44] The Egyptians had two other gods represented by cattle but they have not been identified with the "Hyksos." They are "Apis" the bull of Egypt and "Hathor" the cow goddess. See page 12, Georges Posener, *A Dictionary of Egyptian Civilization*, Methvan and Co., Ltd., 1962.

[45] James H. Breasted, *A History of Egypt*, Charles Scribner's Sons, 1909, p. 220.

[46] *A Dictionary of Egyptian Civilization*, p. 194.

[47] Breasted, *A History of Egypt*, p. 263.

[48] *Ibid.*, p. 259.

[49] A text at Karnak describes Hatshepsut's assumption of the kingship in year 2 of Thutmose III - William C. Hayes, "Chronology," *The Cambridge Ancient History*, Cambridge University Press (1964), p. 18.

[50] Merrill F. Unger, *Archeology and the Old Testament*, Zondervan, 1965, p. 136.

[51] James H. Breasted, *A History of Egypt*, Charles Scribner's Sons, 1909, p. 269.

[52] James H. Breasted, *Ancient Records of Egypt*, Vol. II, Univ. of Chicago Press, 1906, p. 130.

Chapter 11.
The Exodus

We have arrived in our discussion to the time of the Exodus of the Israelites from Egypt. This great event occurred in the year 1447 B.C., according to the Biblical chronology reported earlier in this study. Earlier we saw precise agreement between the secular record of the great Sesostris III of Egypt's Twelfth Dynasty and the Biblical statement concerning Joseph, who became Prime Minister during his reign. We also saw much circumstantial evidence that related the Hyksos to the Israelites. While no precise chronological evidence such as astronomical data is available, the Biblical and secular records do mesh so closely that we feel justified in identifying the Hyksos and the Israelites as one and the same people, even as did the historian Josephus. Moreover, we believe we have identified the pharaoh who sought to kill Moses and who died while Moses was in Midian.

Can we find concordant information that ties the secular to the sacred record in connection with the Exodus? In this chapter, we will examine that question and in so doing, we will find that there is indeed exceedingly close meshing of the two records. In fact, we will discover another astronomical "fix" even as we did with Sesostris III.

Let us begin our search by attempting to identify the pharaoh who would not permit Moses to lead the Israelites from Egypt. Two men are frequently set forth as possible candidates for the pharaoh who refused to let the Israelites go. Conservative scholars often suggest that Amenhotep II, the pharaoh who followed the great Thutmose III, was the pharaoh to whom Moses actually appeared. Under this arrangement, Thutmose III was the pharaoh who oppressed the Israelites but who must have died before Moses returned to Egypt. The problem with this solution is that secular sources show that Amenhotep II died about 1422 B.C. This date does not come within two decades of the Exodus.

On the other hand, a great many archeologists have sought to prove that the Exodus occurred about 150 or more years later, during the reign of Rameses II. Their major argument is that the Israelites could not have arrived until the Hyksos were ruling in Egypt (about

1720-1580 B.C.), and thus the days of Thutmose III and Amenhotep II were far too early. Furthermore, the Bible declares in Exodus 1:11 that the Israelites built the cities of Pithom and Raamses. Since no archeological information has been discovered that mentions a city named Raamses prior to the Nineteenth Dynasty when the Rameses were kings, these chronologists argue that the Israelites must have still been in Egypt during the reign of Rameses II in the thirteenth century B.C.

It appears that this latter solution must also be discarded. There is no specific evidence in the available secular data on Rameses II that particularly identifies him with the Israelites. And his death date does not coincide in any way with any kind of a reasonable Biblical date for the Exodus. The fact that there is no archeological evidence of a city called Raames existing before his dynasty (the nineteenth), should not be surprising. The archeological record provides at best fragmentary evidence. For example, until a few years ago, there was no archeological evidence of horses in Egypt before the middle of the so-called Hyksos period (Thirteenth to Seventeenth Dynasties), even though the Bible says very clearly that Joseph exchanged food for horses (Genesis 47:17) even before the Israelites were in Egypt. Now, however, there is evidence of horses in Egypt in the Middle Kingdom (Twelfth Dynasty), as revealed by the skeleton of a horse found at Buhen in a Middle Kingdom context.[1]

Actually, the Bible called the area where the Israelites dwelt "the land of Rameses" already in Joseph's day (Genesis 47:11). Furthermore, names with "Ra" were exceedingly common centuries before Rameses II.[2] The god Re, from whom Rameses II took his name, was a god of the Egyptians way back in the Fifth Dynasty.[3] We must conclude, therefore, upon the Biblical and secular evidence, that Raames was a name given to a province or town of Egypt hundreds of years before Rameses II lived, and that the Israelites built or rebuilt a city of this name, years before the Exodus, with no particular relationship to Rameses II or the Nineteenth Dynasty.

But if neither Rameses II nor Amenhotep II was the pharaoh of the Exodus, who was? Can we find agreement between the Bible and archeology? The facts offered by the sacred and the secular must agree. Let us see how these two records can be wonderfully meshed.

The Pharaoh of the Exodus - Thutmose III

We will show that the pharaoh of the Exodus was the great Thutmose III, who reigned during the flower of the Eighteenth Dynasty. We shall see that his life as well as his death coincide with the Biblical record of Exodus. Let us first of all examine the available evidence concerning the timetable of his reign.

The studies of R. A. Parker are extremely helpful.[4] He has shown that the accession year of Thutmose III must be one of five dates. This is based on the discovery of the record of a helical rising of the star Sirius during his reign as well as on two lunar dates, which require these narrow limits for his succession year. The possible dates are 1515 B.C., 1504 B.C., 1501 B.C., 1490 B.C., and 1479 B.C. While any one of these dates is acceptable according to astronomical evidence, most archeologists favor the period from 1504 B.C. to 1490 B.C. because of other secular evidence. For example, William C. Hayes[5] favors the 1504 B.C. date although he believes 1490 B.C. is also a possibility. Sir Leonard Wooley[6] also favors 1504 B.C. but concludes that with the present evidence it is impossible to determine with absolute certainty the chronology of the New Empire.

Thus far, then, we know that our candidate for the pharaoh of the Exodus probably began to reign in one of three years: 1504 B.C., 1501 B.C., or 1490 B.C. Since the Biblical record is concerned with his death, we must know the length of his reign in order to tie his accession year to his death year. This is available from the archeological record. On the wall of the tomb of one of his officers, Amenemheb by name, the notice is given that Thutmose III died in the fifty-fourth year of his reign.[7] We will look more closely at this text a bit later.

With the time span of his reign known, we can know that if he began to reign in 1504 B.C., he must have died in 1450 B.C. If his reign commenced 1501 B.C., his death would have occurred in 1447 B.C., and if his reign began 1490 B.C., the year 1436 B.C. must have been his death year.

Returning to the Biblical record, we have already seen that 1447 B.C. was the date of the Exodus. And, of course, 1447 B.C. is also one of the three possible dates of the death of Thutmose III in accordance with the secular record. Thus, we can begin to see that he is indeed a leading contender for the dubious honor of being the pharaoh of the Exodus.

Immediately a problem arises, however. If he was the king who died in the Red Sea, who then is the king who sought to kill Moses forty years earlier and who, according to the Biblical notice, died while Moses was tending sheep in Midian? How could Thutmoses III be the man we are looking for if he reigned fifty-four years? He would have been king when Moses fled from Egypt. And if he were king, how could he have died while Moses was in Midian and yet be alive when the Israelites left Egypt? We have already seen that this was King Hatshepsut who reigned as co-regent with Thutmose III and who died about 1480 B.C. or about six years after Moses fled from Egypt.

The Napoleon of Egypt

Thus far we have found synchronization between the secular and sacred records concerning the princess who drew Moses from the water, the king who sought to kill Moses and who died while Moses was in Midian, and the death date of Pharaoh Thutmose III, which coincides with the Biblical date of the Exodus. Let us continue our examination of the record of the great Pharaoh Thutmose III.[8] Does he really qualify as the king to whom God said through Moses: "And in very deed for this cause have I raised thee up, for to shew in thee my power; and that my name may be declared throughout all the earth" (Exodus 9:16)?

Abundant archeological materials are available concerning this question. They show that he was a great military man. He extended the boundaries of Egypt to the greatest extent Egypt had ever known. He personally conducted seventeen different military campaigns. Historians often call him the "Napoleon of Egypt." *The Encyclopaedia Britannica* offers the following summary:

> The immense energy of Tothmosis III now found its outlet in war. Syria had revolted, perhaps in the years of inactivity following Tothmosis I's death; now the young king was ready to lead his army against the rebels. Unlike his predecessors, who merely overran one after another a series of isolated city-states, Tothmosis had to face the organized resistance of a large combination, embracing the whole of western Syria and headed by the city of Kadesh on the Orontes. Six carefully planned

campaigns had to be fought in order to reach and capture that city. In the 33rd year of his reign he marched through Kadesh, fought his way to Carchemish, defeated the forces that opposed him there and crossed the Euphrates into the territory of the Hurrian king of Mittanni. His annals record 17 separate campaigns in Palestine and Syria and list the immense booty and tribute obtained from that rich country. Egypt was master of an empire reaching to the Amanus mountains, and the neighboring great powers hastened to send diplomatic presents. In the intervals of war Tothmosis III proved himself a wonderfully efficient administrator, with his eye on every corner of his dominions. The Syrian expeditions occupied six months on most of his best years, but the remaining time was spent in activity at home, repressing robbery and injustice, rebuilding and adorning temples with the labour of his captives and the plunder and tribute of conquered cities, or designing with his own hand the gorgeous sacred vessels of the sanctuary of Amon. In his later years some expeditions took place into Nubia. The children of the subdued princelings is Asia and elsewhere were taken as hostages to Egypt and there educated to succeed their fathers with a due understanding of the might of the Pharaoh both to protect and to punish. Thus was an empire established on a sound basis, probably for the first time in history. Tothmosis died in the 54th year of his reign. His mummy, found in the cachette at Dair al-Bahri is remarkable for the low forehead; yet we consider him the greatest of all Pharaohs.[9]

His personal activity as a military man provides another touchstone between the secular and sacred records. We read in the Bible: "And he made ready his chariot, and took his people with him: And he took six hundred chosen chariots, and all the chariots of Egypt, and captains over every one of them" (Exodus 14:6-7), when he pursued the people of Israel. This is completely in accord with the personality of this pharaoh. On a tablet describing a battle at Megiddo in which Thutmose III captured 924 chariots, we read: "His Majesty set forth in a chariot of fine gold, being adorned with his panoply of war like Horns the Strong-armed, Lord of Action, and like Mont of Thebes, his father Amun strengthening his hands."[10] He had conducted seventeen successful and glorious campaigns before that. This, his last and eighteenth, was to end in terrible defeat.

As the archaeological record presents the character of this pharaoh, there is much that suggests he may be the one. For example, pictures have been found showing this pharaoh in a position of mastery over slaves. He was a great builder, and in regards to his building activity, Petrie writes:

> We see thus the extraordinary activity in building; and probably dozens of minor temples have passed away which are quite unknown to us, as little suspected as the temples of Kom el Hisu, Gurob, and Nubt were a few years ago. As it is, we can count up over thirty different sites, all of which were built on during this reign.[11]

Certainly this could be the pharaoh whom God allowed to become great for some purpose. Certainly there was no other kingdom whose destruction would so clearly reveal God's power and His mighty Name. In so many ways, this pharaoh identifies with the Biblical account of the pharaoh who died in the Red Sea.

Thutmose III Dies

Continuing our examination of Thutmose III, let us look at how vividly the Bible describes his death in the Red Sea.

> Exodus 14:5-8: And it was told the king of Egypt that the people fled: and the heart of Pharaoh and of his servants was turned against the people, and they said, Why have we done this, that we have let Israel go from serving us? And he made ready his chariot, and took his people with him: And he took six hundred chosen chariots, and all the chariots of Egypt, and captains over every one of them. And the LORD hardened the heart of Pharaoh king of Egypt, and he pursued after the children of Israel: and the children of Israel went out with an high hand.

Exodus 14:10: And when Pharaoh drew nigh, the children of Israel lifted up their eyes, and, behold, the Egyptians marched after them; and they were sore afraid: and the children of Israel cried out unto the LORD.

Exodus 14:28: And the waters returned, and covered the chariots, and the horsemen, and all the host of Pharaoh that came into the sea after them; there remained not so much as one of them.

Psalms 136:15: But overthrew Pharaoh and his host in the Red sea: for his mercy endureth for ever.

An Unfinished Tomb

The language of the Bible relating to the cause and manner of the death of this pharaoh is very plain indeed. Since the pharaoh of the Exodus experienced such a catastrophic death, one wonders if there is any archeological evidence of this sudden end. There is. We can see this circumstantially by examining his tomb. In spite of the fact that each pharaoh considered the construction of his own tomb of paramount importance, and thus planning and constructing it in the greatest detail, the tomb of Thotmosis III was never finished. This fact is especially interesting and significant since the great pharaoh did more building and reigned longer than did other pharaohs. We quote Weigall:

> This tomb is excavated in a "chimney" of rock at the southeast corner of the valley. From the custodian's house one walks southwards, turning to the left at the junction of the paths, and thus leaving the tombs of Septah (47), Bay (13), and Tausert (14) on one's right. The path terminates in a flight of steps leading up to the "chimney." Ascending these, and crossing a platform of rock, one finds in the far corner the mouth of the tomb, which is approached by a steep flight of steps. The situation is most impressive, and repays a visit; but the descent of the tomb is somewhat difficult. The coffin and mummy of the great Pharaoh, Ra-men-kheper Thothmes III (B.C. 1501-1447) were found at Der el Bahri, where they had been hidden

by the priests . . . The tomb has been left partly unfinished, as though the king, occupied by the administration of the great empire he had built up, had not bothered to give much attention to his last resting place.[12]

An unfinished tomb is totally out of character with the pharaohs, unless of course, a pharaoh happened to die unexpectedly! When the pharaoh of the Exodus led his great army in pursuit of the Israelites, he obviously had no idea that within the next few days the sea would close over his head! Thus, his unfinished tomb supports the truth of an unexpected demise for this pharaoh. Please note, in passing, the accuracy of Weigall's date for Thutmose III.

But the archeological record indicates the finding of the mummy of Thutmose III. How could this be if he drowned in the Red Sea? God provides the necessary information. We read in Exodus 14:30:

Thus the LORD saved Israel that day out of the hand of the Egyptians; and Israel saw the Egyptians dead upon the sea shore.

The Egyptians obviously hastened to find the body of their dead king to give it a proper burial.

The Month and Day of Pharaoh's Death

Could there be even more evidence linking Thutmose III with the pharaoh of the Exodus? Wonderfully, the well-preserved and extensive records of these early Egyptian civilizations together with the marvelous accuracy of God's Word gives us one final confirmation. We previously saw that the Exodus occurred in 1447 B.C., which was also the year Thutmose III died. We shall now show that the date of Thutmose III's death as recorded in the archeological page coincides to the very month and time of the month of the passage of the Israelites through the Red Sea. The following passages of Scripture help us in naming the month in which the Israelites escaped from Egypt.

Exodus 12:1-3, 6: And the LORD spake unto Moses and Aaron in the land of Egypt, saying, This month shall be unto you the beginning of months: it shall be the first month of the year to you. Speak ye unto all the congregation of Israel, saying, In the tenth day of this month they shall take to them every man a lamb, according to the house of their fathers, a lamb for an house: . . . And ye shall keep it up until the fourteenth day of the same month: and the whole assembly of the congregation of Israel shall kill it in the evening.

Exodus 16:1: And they took their journey from Elim, and all the congregation of the children of Israel came unto the wilderness of Sin, which is between Elim and Sinai, on the fifteenth day of the second month after their departing out of the land of Egypt.

Exodus 23:15: Thou shalt keep the feast of unleavened bread: (thou shalt eat unleavened bread seven days, as I commanded thee, in the time appointed of the month Abib; for in it thou camest out from Egypt: and none shall appear before me empty).

Numbers 33:3: And they departed from Rameses in the first month, on the fifteenth day of the first month; on the morrow after the passover the children of Israel went out with an high hand in the sight of all the Egyptians.

It is apparent from the above that Abib, the month in which the Israelites left Egypt, became the first month in the original Hebrew calendar. On the fourteenth day of this month at even, they celebrated the Passover, and very early on the morning of the fifteenth, the Exodus from Egypt began. One month later they arrived at the wilderness of Sin. During this thirty-day period, the company of men, women, and children, with their flocks and herds, had traveled to the Red Sea, passed miraculously through it, rested briefly at Elim, and arrived at the wilderness of Sin. The journey to the Red Sea would have required at least ten days, and at least another ten days would have been required to trek to the wilderness of Sin. Obviously, then, the death of Thutmose III had to occur sometime between the 25th of the first month Abib and the 5th of the second month Ziv. Does the archeological record relate to this date? Indeed it does.

Let us first relate the Egyptian calendar to the Israelite calendar. The following correlation[13] between the Macedonian and Egyptian calendars is reported by Finegan:

THE MACEDONIAN CALENDAR IN EGYPT
(Corresponding names of the month in sequence)

Macedonian	Egyptian	Julian Dates in a Com. Year
1. Dios	Thoth	Aug. 29-Sept. 27
2. Appellaios	Phaophi	Sept. 28-Oct. 27
3. Audynaios	Hathyr	Oct. 28-Nov. 26
4. Peritios	Choiak	Nov. 27-Dec. 26
5. Dystros	Tybi	Dec. 27-Jan. 25
6. Zanthikos	Mecheir	Jan. 26-Feb. 24
7. Artemisios	Phamenoth	Feb. 25-Mar. 26
8. Daisios	Pharmuthi	Mar. 27-Apr. 25
9. Panemos	Pachon	Apr. 26-May 25
10. Loos	Pauni	May 26-June 24
11. Gorpiaios	Epeiph	June 25-July 24
12. Hyperberetaios	Mesore	July 25-Aug. 23
Epagomenal days		Aug. 24-Aug. 28

We are indebted to the same author for this earlier correlation of the "Macedonian Calendar in Palestine."

THE MACEDONIAN CALENDAR IN PALESTINE

Macedonian Months	Jewish Months	Julian Equivalents[14]
1. Artemisios	Nisan	Mar./Apr.
2. Daisios	Iyyar	Apr./May
3. Panemos	Sivan	May/June
4. Loos	Tammuz	June/July
5. Gorpiaios	Ab	July/Aug.
6. Hyperberetaios	Elul	Aug./Sept.
7. Dios	Tishri	Sept./Oct.
8. Appellaios	Marheshvan	Oct./Nov.
9. Audynaios	Kislev	Nov./Dec.
10. Peritios	Tebeth	Dec./Jan.
11. Dystros	Shebat	Jan./Feb.
12. Zanthikos	Akar	Feb./Mar.

A careful appraisal of the above calendar correlations makes it obvious that the Macedonian month *Artemisios* is equivalent to the Egyptian month *Phamenoth* and to the Jewish month *Nisan*. Hence, the first month Nisan, or Abib, as it is rendered in the Hebrew, corresponds to the seventh month of the Egyptian calendar, Phamenoth.

We have now established from the Biblical record the fact that the Israelites left Egypt on the fifteenth day of the seventh Egyptian month, Phamenoth (the Hebrew Abib or Nisan), and that the pharaoh must have died at the time of the crossing of the Red Sea somewhere between the 25th of Phamenoth and the 5th of the eighth month, Pharmuthi (the Hebrew Ziv). What can we find from the secular record that relates?

Petrie has provided the following remarkable inscription, which has direct bearing on the death of Thutmose III. It appears in early Egyptian records as the work of an officer named Amenemheb who served Menkheperra (Thutmose III) (see page 125 of Petrie's *History of Egypt*). It gives the significant truth that Thutmose III died on the 30th day of Phamenoth, which is the 30th day of Abib.

> Behold the king had ended his time of existence of many good years of victory, power, and justification from the 1st year to the 54th year. In the 30th of Phamenoth of the majesty of the king, Menkheperra deceased, he ascended to heaven and joined the sun's disc, the follower of the god met his maker.

> When the light dawned and the morrow came, the disc of the sun arose and heaven became bright. The king Aa-kheperu-ra, son of the sun, Amenhotep, the giver of life, was established on the throne of his father, he rested on the ka name, he struck down all the thrust.

Thutmose III was a ruler in Egypt, Thutmose III was a great builder; Thutmose III died suddenly in 1447 B.C. on the 30th of Phamenoth, the equivalent of the Hebrew Abib, the precise time when the Israelites went through the Red Sea. Thutmose III was the pharaoh of the Exodus! The correlation of the Egyptian history and the facts as recorded in the Bible could not be more exact!

The World Hears

As we continue a bit longer to compare the sacred and secular records relating to the Exodus, we might recall that when Thutmose I was king, there was an ever-present possibility of revolt by Syria and the nations of northern Palestine. This probably occasioned the increased oppression of the Israelites and the killing of their newborn sons. Then under the energetic leadership of Thutmose III, Syria and all of Palestine were brought under complete control so that his seventeenth campaign, which was conducted in his forty-second year, was followed by twelve years of peace. His successor, Amenhotep II, who as we shall see was co-regent with him for the last four months of his life, was immediately faced with revolt. Breasted reports:

> Syria, of course, revolted on the death of Thutmose III, and already in his second year we find his energetic son, Amenhotep II, on the march into northern Syria to quell the rebellion. Doubtless the harbor cities had also rebelled, and hence the young king is forced to proceed by land. Leaving Egypt in April, as his father had done on the first campaign thirty-three years before, he had already in May won a battle at Shemesh-Edom in northern Palestine.[15]

This great disaster clearly must have been the signal for the nations of Palestine-Syria to revolt. No wonder Amenhotep II was so busy with quelling rebellion. For the news of Egypt's defeat in the Red Sea would have spread like fire to the nations who were potential enemies of Egypt. One thinks of Rahab's word to the spies in Joshua 2:10:

> For we have heard how the LORD dried up the water of the Red sea for you, when ye came out of Egypt.

That the dissemination of this news was God's intention is reflected in Exodus 9:16, as He declared to pharaoh:

> And in very deed for this cause have I raised thee up, for to shew in thee my power; and that my name may be declared throughout all the earth.

The Tenth Plague

One other Biblical comment will be examined, and then we will be finished with the question of the pharaoh of the Exodus. The Bible declares that as a result of the tenth plague, the firstborn of all the Egyptians died, including the firstborn of pharaoh. Is there any evidence of this in the archeological findings? There surely appears to be. At the time of the Exodus, two pharaohs were on the throne. The great Thutmose III was reigning in his fifty-fourth year. His son Amenhotep II, who apparently had just reigned four months as co-regent with his father, was also reigning. The archeologist Gardiner makes reference to this fact:

> A difficulty arises, however, from the fact that the well-known biography of Amenemhab (Urk IV, 895, 16) places the death of Tuthmosis III in his 54th year on the last day of the seventh month, and affirms that Amenophis II, his son and successor, was already on the throne. The next morning . . . possibly - it even amounts to a probability - is that Amenophis II for exactly four months before the latter's death . . . the most important evidence is that in the Thebean tomb of Dedi (No. 200), where the two kings were shown enthroned and inspecting a military display together.[16]

The archaeological evidence thus points to the condition of a co-regency of the aged Thutmose III and his young son Amenhotep II (Amenophis II). Amenhotep II obviously was not the firstborn of Thutmose III or he would have died in the tenth plague. The Bible declares very plainly in Exodus 12:29:

> And it came to pass, that at midnight the LORD smote all the firstborn in the land of Egypt, from the firstborn of Pharaoh that sat on his throne unto the firstborn of the captive that was in the dungeon; and all the firstborn of cattle.

The concept that Amenhotep II was not a firstborn son, even though he was the next ruler, is acceptable if we study the record concerning similar situations. A later pharaoh, Rameses II, who also reigned for a long period of time - sixty-seven years - was followed by a son who was his fourteenth. Likewise, Amenhotep II could have been a much later child than the firstborn of his father, Thutmose III.

If Amenhotep II was not a firstborn son, who was the firstborn of a pharaoh who died in the tenth plague? The secular record appears to provide an answer. Co-regent Amenhotep II was followed many years later by his son Thutmose IV, but there is evidence that Thutmose IV was not a firstborn son. In the book *Bible and Spade* we read:

> On an immense slab of red granite near the Sphinx at Gizeh it is recorded that Thotmes IV, while yet a youth, had fallen asleep under the famous monument and dreamed a dream. In this the Sphinx appeared to him, startling him with a prophecy that one day he would live to be King of Egypt, and bidding him clear the sand away from her feet in token of his gratitude, which on his accession, he did. It is clear from this inscription that Thotmes' hopes of succession had been remote, which proves, since the law of primogeniture obtained in Egypt at the time, that he could not have been Amenhotep's eldest son. In other words, there is room for the explanation that the heir apparent died in the manner related in the Bible.[17]

In other words, at the time of the Exodus, there were two pharaohs on the throne. The one was Thutmose III who died in the Red Sea. The other was Amenhotep II who was probably a son of Thutmose III, but obviously not the firstborn, for then he would have died in the plague. And since the next ruler, Thutmose IV, appears by the foregoing evidence to be a son born after the firstborn, one can readily assume that it was his brother, the firstborn of his father Amenhotep II, who was the son who died in the plague.

We see, therefore, that there is circumstantial evidence that young Amenhotep II, who ascended the throne just four months prior to the Exodus, lost his firstborn in the tenth plague even as the Bible declares. His aged father, Thutmose III, who was co-regent with him, died in the Red Sea as the Bible shows. The correlation of Egyptian history and the facts as recorded in the Bible is very precise indeed. All these puny efforts have only verified what has always been true: God's eternal Word. Let God be found true. . . .

As we continue our study, we will examine the historical record of one more pharaoh. In his lifetime, an event occurred which provides further meshing of the sacred and secular calendar.

The Israel Stela: A Stela Speaks

We have identified the pharaoh who killed the firstborn males as Thutmose I, the princess who drew Moses from the water as Hatshepsut, the daughter of Thutmose I, the pharaoh who sought to kill Moses as King Hatshepsut, the pharaoh who would not let the children of Israel go and who was drowned in the Red Sea as Thutmose III, and the pharaoh whose firstborn was killed in the tenth plague as Amenhotep II. How wonderfully the sacred record provides foundation truth for the secular and the secular record provides fill-in information to the sacred.

Thus far in our attempt to mesh the sacred record with the secular we have discovered two very important astronomical dates that positively tie the two records together and provide a solid basis for expanding the secular dating of the pharaohs. The first was the first year of the great Pharaoh Sesostris III of the Twelfth Dynasty, whose first year was 1888 B.C. as determined by a Sothis rising during his reign. That year precisely met the Biblical chronological requirement of being two years before Joseph was made Prime Minister.

The second was the first year of the greatest pharaoh of the Eighteenth Dynasty, Thutmose III, whose last year, 1447 B.C., is established by a Sothic rising as well as two lunar dates during his reign. This coincides exactly with the Biblical date of the Exodus.

Because the sacred record is absolutely trustworthy, we should expect other synchronizations with the secular evidence, especially when the secular chronological evidence is tied down by astronomical observation. We shall now examine a third tie point. In doing so, we shall provide an explanation to one of the most puzzling but yet significant tablets discovered in the ruins of antiquity.

Among the tablets that have been unearthed in the archeological diggings, there is only one that speaks explicitly of Israel. Archeologists discovered that it was written during the fifth year of Pharaoh Merneptah, who ruled near the end of the thirteenth century B.C. Because this stela mentions Israel, archeologists have been ready to conclude that Israel was an independent nation at that time. But why Israel is mentioned in the stela is not easily determined. Had Egypt conquered Israel during Merneptah's reign? The stela records that "Palestine has become a widow for Egypt" and that "Israel is desolated, his seed is not." Let us study this stela to ascertain the chronological tie-in point between Israel and Egypt.

The stela reads as follows:

The kings are overthrown, saying: "Salam!"
Not one holds up his head among the Nine Bows.
Wasted is Tehenu,
Kheta is pacified,
Plundered is Pekanan, with every evil,
Carried off is Askalon
Seized upon is Gezer
Yenoam is made as a thing not existing.
Israel is desolated, his seed is not.
Palestine has become a widow for Egypt.
All lands are united, they are pacified;
Everyone that is turbulent is bound by King
Merneptah given life like Re, Every day.[18]

Israel Is without Seed

The great archaeologist Breasted concludes that the phrase "Palestine has become a widow for Egypt" must mean "Palestine has no protector against Egypt." This makes abundant sense, as we shall presently see. But can we be helped in our chronological synchronization with anything else on this stela?

The phrase "Israel is desolated, his seed is not" is the all-important phrase. At what time in Israel's history was this nation without seed? **There was indeed just such a time.** It is recorded in the Book of Judges. The Bible records the exploits of one of the greatest of the judges, Gideon. Under his leadership, 120,000 of the enemy had fallen (Judges 8:10). The men of Israel were so happy with his ability that they wanted him and his descendants to rule over them (Judges 8:22). Gideon did in fact rule as judge for forty years, during which time the land had rest (Judges 8:28). No doubt in the eyes of the world this great leader was tantamount to a king. In fact, his son Abimelech did reign as a king for three years (Judges 9:16 and 22).

But upon Gideon's death, a terrible tragedy occurred. Abimelech, a son of Gideon by a concubine, murdered the seventy sons of Gideon, "upon one stone" (Judges 9:5), in order to have no competitors for the kingship. Only one son escaped. Thus, Israel was plunged into terrible tragedy. Almost the entire ruling family had been murdered. Surely, this is the event to which Merneptah makes reference when he states, "Israel is desolated, his seed is not." This heinous and terrible crime against the family that had brought peace and tranquility to the nation of Israel must surely have been a national tragedy of the gravest consequence. Insurrection, anarchy, and civil war were all possible results of this great murder. Israel was without seed. There was no longer a ruling family except for the murderer and one son who hid himself. No wonder Merneptah concluded that Palestine was without a protector and ripe for conquest.

But when did this event, recorded on the Israel stela in the fifth year of Merneptah, occur? In the Biblical chronology we determined that Gideon died in the year 1207 B.C. This must have been the fifth year of Merneptah. His first year then must have been either 1212 B.C. or 1211 B.C., depending upon what time of the year he became king.

The information we have thus far developed seems to be of no particular help in synchronizing the secular account with the sacred. Actually, it appears as if we are on the wrong track because most archeologists choose a date of 1225 B.C. or earlier for Merneptah's first year.

When we look to his father's reign, however, we see the precise concordance that does exist. Merneptah's father was the famous Rameses II, the pharaoh who so many have incorrectly felt was perhaps the pharaoh of the Exodus. We know two very important facts of his life that do relate to the question we are presently considering. The first is that he reigned for a total of sixty-seven years. This means that if our assumption is correct, that Merneptah began to reign in 1212 or 1211 B.C., then Rameses II must have become king in 1279 or 1278 B.C. The other fact that we know from his life is the information that in his fifty-second year a new moon occurred on II prt 27.[19] There are only a few years within the possible limits of his reign when the new moon could have occurred on this date. Parker shows that these are: 1253, 1250, 1239, 1228, and 1225 B.C. Accordingly, since these are the only years that could have been his fifty-second year, the only years that could have been his first year are 1304, 1301, 1290, 1279, and 1276

B.C. Most archeologists have looked at 1304 and 1290 B.C. as the most logical choices for his first year.

The dates 1304 and 1290 B.C., while exact possibilities because of the astronomical "fix," are not necessarily in either case the correct choice of the five possible dates named above. Archeologists have opted for 1304 and 1290 B.C. because of very sketchy and incomplete information from the Assyrian and Babylonian chronologies. While these are quite helpful back to about 1100 B.C., they are of more doubtful value earlier. From the earliest period, the Assyrians named their years after an annually appointed official called a "limmu." Accurate lists of these officials were compiled. They were especially accurate from June 15, 763 B.C., a date fixed by a record of an eclipse of the sun, back to the eleventh century B.C. Earlier than the eleventh century no "limmu" lists have been preserved with an accuracy within a few decades or less. This is a result of king lists that have been found that are demonstrably based on earlier "limmu" lists. The Babylonian chronology has been figured back to about 1350 B.C. with a maximum margin of error of about fifty years either way. Thus, the Assyrian chronology for the period of Merneptah's reign does not help with precise dating.

When we turn to the Biblical record, however, we will discover a wonderful synchronization. Let us again recall that the secular evidence based upon astronomical information gives five possibilities as the first year of Rameses II, who ruled for sixty-seven years and was followed by Merneptah, who wrote the Israel Stela in the fifth year of his reign. These five years are 1304, 1301, 1290, 1279, and 1276 B.C. Let us begin with one of the five possible years, the year 1279 B.C. as the first year of Rameses II. He then would have died sixty-seven years later, in 1212 B.C., at which time his successor Merneptah would have ascended the throne. Merneptah's fifth year, when the Israel Stela which describes terrible tragedy in Israel was written, would then have been 1207 B.C. And 1207 B.C. coincides exactly with the terrible tragedy that enveloped the nation of Israel upon the death of Gideon.

Thus, we must conclude that Rameses II began to reign in 1279 B.C. This is in agreement with the astronomical data and is permitted by the background information available from the Assyrian and Babylonian records. By means of the Biblical chronological record, it alone is proven to be the correct date.

After a reign of sixty-seven years, Rameses II died and was followed by Merneptah, who began to reign in 1212 B.C. In Merneptah's fifth year, the year 1207 B.C., Gideon, the ruler over Israel, died, and seventy of his sons were murdered. Merneptah took note of this sad and tragic event by recording it on what has become known as the Israel Stela.

We see, therefore, not only the precise agreement between the language recorded on the Israel Stela and the reasons for this, but we also see the perfect synchronization that occurs between the sacred and secular records once we have accepted the Bible as being scientifically and historically trustworthy. It is indeed wonderful that God has given us so many dates, which reach back almost 4000 years, that provide a means of accurately meshing the Biblical calendar with the Julian or Gregorian calendar. We were certain that we had correctly meshed the secular and the Biblical calendars without the evidence set forth in these chapters. But it is indeed pleasing that when we examine the secular record, we find such perfect meshing with the Biblical calendar.

NOTES

[1] John Van Seters, *The Hyksos*, Yale Univ. Press, 1966, p. 185 (New York, Charles Scribner and Sons, 1899).

[2] W. M. Flinders Petrie, *History of Egypt*, Vol. 1, pp. 260-262. In this index, Petrie lists at least 150 names that begin with "Ra," all found on tablets dating before the Eighteenth Dynasty.

[3] *Ibid.*, p. 69.

[4] R. A. Parker, "The Lunar Dates of Thutmose III and Rameses II, *Journal of Near Eastern Studies*, Vol. 16 (1957), p. 41.

[5] William C. Hayes, "Chronology," *The Cambridge Ancient History*, Cambridge Univ. Press (1964), p. 17.

[6] Sir Leonard Wooley, *The Beginning of Civilization*, The New York American Library, 1965, p. 105.

[7] W. M. Flinders Petrie, *History of Egypt*, New York, Charles Scribner's Sons (1904), p. 125.

[8] He is variously called Thutmoses III, Thutmos III, Thutmosis III, Tothmosis III, etc.

[9] *The Encyclopedia Britannica* (1959 ed.), p. 58.

[10] R. O. Faulkner, "The Battle of Mediggo" in *The Journal of Egyptian Archeology* (London, The Egypt Exploration Soc., 1942), p. 4.

[11] W. M. Flinders Petrie, *A History of Egypt during the XVIIth and XVIIIth Dynasties*, New York, Charles Scribner's Sons (1904), p. 136.

[12] Arthur E. P. Weigall, *A Guide to the Antiquities of Upper Egypt*, The MacMillan Co. (1920), pp. 219-220.

[13] Jack Finegan, *Handbook of Biblical Chronology*, Princeton University Press, 1964.

[14] The Julian equivalents in the above table are doubtful. It seems as if the Macedonian month *Artemisios* should be placed opposite the Feb./Mar. equivalent as it appears in the Egyptian table. This is further suggested by the Early Roman Calendar depicted on page 74 of Finegan's book, *Handbook of Biblical Chronology*, where March is shown as the first calendar month.

1. Martius	7. Septembris
2. Aprilis	8. Octobris
3. Maius	9. Novembris
4. Junius	10. Decembris
5. Quintilis	11. Januaris
6. Sextilis	12. Februarius

The logic behind this reasoning is clearly seen in the Latin prefixes and the corresponding numeral.

[15] Breasted, *Ancient Records of Egypt*, Vol. II, p. 34.

[16] Alan H. Gardiner, *Reginal Years and Civil Calendar in Pharaonic Egypt*, Vol. 31 (1945), p. 27.

[17] Stephen L. Gaiger, *Bible and Spade*, Oxford University Press, London, 1936, p. 74.

[18] James H. Breasted, *Ancient Records of Egypt*, Vol. III, Univ. of Chicago Press, 1906, p. 263.

[19] Richard A. Parker, "The Lunar Dates of Tutmose III and Rameses II" in *Journal of Near Eastern Studies*, Vol. 16, 1957, p. 41.

Conclusion

Hopefully, in this sequel to the book *1994?*, we have answered a number of questions that might be in the minds of those who want to be very careful with the Word of God. We began with an examination of seven significant signs that were prophesied in the Bible as being evidence that the end of the world is very near. While these signs, which are clearly in evidence in the world today, do not give us any specific year or month when Christ could return, they do reinforce the calendar information contained in the Bible, which shows us the great likelihood that September, 1994 is the time of the end.

We then spent some time becoming better acquainted with the methods by which God presents the Gospel message. We learned that everything in the Bible is intimately involved with the Gospel message. When a word, a phrase, or an event does not appear to relate to the Gospel message, we have come to realize that it is probably to be understood as an allegorical word or phrase or as an historical parable. We learned that there are definite Biblical rules which we must follow as we search out these Scriptures to discover their spiritual content.

We then spent some very careful time with the kings of Judah and Israel, unravelling the complex and frequently apparently contradictory language of the Bible until we were able to harmonize all of the Biblical citations. In so doing, we were able to reconstruct a very precise chronology for these kings. This in turn helps us to see the wonderful precision with which God has crafted the Bible.

Once the task of the chronology was finished, we began to study with great care the numbers in the Bible. Because we had already learned that everything in the Bible is intimately related to the Gospel message, we knew that God did not insert various numbers into the Biblical statement accidentally or incidentally. We learned that the numbers not only could give us much more detailed historical information but also, when they were properly understood, they served to spiritually enrich and enhance the Biblical statement into which God had placed them.

With all of this significant information concerning the ways in which God utilized the numbers recorded in the Bible, we looked in some detail at three historical events, the birth of Terah, the birth of

Enoch, and the marriage of Esau with heathen wives. We discovered that each of these events was an historical parable that was emphasizing an aspect of the Gospel message. Each event bore a distinct relationship to the two greatest events in history - the first and second comings of Christ. When the time line from the year of the event to the coming of Christ was calculated, the number of years within that time line further enriched the spiritual messages in these events and their relationship to the return of Christ.

Following the same procedures, we then examined an additional forty-six events, each of which directly or as historical parables had a definite relationship to the Gospel message and the coming of Christ either as Savior or as Judge of all the earth. The Bible discloses the specific year in history when each of these took place, like the three events: the birth of Terah, the birth of Enoch, and Esau's marriage to heathen wives. The time line from each of these events to the coming of Christ was then calculated. We discovered that when these time lines were broken down to significant or prime numbers, each of which in itself conveys spiritual truth, the spiritual message in the event was greatly supported, enriched, and enhanced by the time line itself. We found by its spiritually significant time line that:

a. Seventeen of the events focused on the birth of Christ in 7 B.C.

b. Twenty-six of the events focused on the crucifixion of Christ in A.D. 33.

c. Sixteen of the events focused on the likely end of the world which begins with judgment on the church in A.D. 1988.

d. Twenty-six of the events focused on the likely year of Christ's return as A.D. 1994.

Each of these events was of such significance that, if space permitted, it could have been written about in detail similar to that which was written concerning the birth of Terah and the birth of Enoch.

We might note one significant finding of this study. There are so many paths that focus on A.D. 1994 as the probable year of Christ's return, that even if we had never been able to calculate the calendar from creation to the time of Abraham, we would still be greatly convinced of the extreme likelihood that A.D. 1994 will be the end of the world.

The fact that the Bible has permitted us to accurately reconstruct the calendar all the way back to creation in 11,013 B.C. further solidifies the conclusion that A.D. 1994 is the likely end of the world.

We closed our study by setting forth the accurate meshing that has been made of the Biblical and secular calendars. Tie-in points in the Egyptian history as well as in the Assyrian-Babylonian history were indicated and discussed. Both because of the harmonious interrelationships of the Biblical dates as well as the many tie points that allow us to firmly and accurately mesh the secular with the Biblical calendar assure us of the reliability of our reconstruction of the whole calendar of history in terms of our modern calendar.

In this book, we have been able to greatly add to and support the conclusions set forth in the book *1994?* Thus, we dare to say that we must be only months away from the end of the world.

But can it really be true that September, 1994, will be the last month this world will ever know? The world seems so solid. It seems so secure. True, earthquakes, famines, hurricanes, wars, murders, etc., etc., repeatedly occur. But any or all of these events put together have impacted our planet throughout history and yet it continues to be a relatively secure place for mankind. Scientists tell us that the sun is good for more than another million years. And with all our new technology together with growing awareness of such global threats as the dangers of destroying rain forests and ozone depletion, etc., we can and will solve these problems so that this world can continue millions of years longer.

The big problem with man's thinking is that he does not take into account God. If it is true (and it absolutely is) that 13,000 years ago, God created the whole universe in six days of twenty-four hours and if He declares that there will come a time when the whole universe will be utterly destroyed so that God can create a new perfect universe, **then it is going to happen**.

God created this universe 13,000 years ago, and 6023 years later, He covered the whole face of the earth with water so that everything with the breath of life was destroyed, that is, everything except the eight people who believed God and prepared for this flood. They, together with the animals which God instructed Noah to place in the ark, were the only survivors. Noah and his family survived because they implicitly trusted God, and they obediently built a huge boat that God declared was to be about 450 feet long, about 75 feet wide, and was to have three decks. Imagine the apparent utter foolishness of this family who no doubt spent decades building this huge vessel on dry land. No one in the world of that day would have appeared more ridiculous and insane than they. And Noah warned the people what was going to happen. But no one but his own children listened. Finally, the huge boat was finished, and Noah began to gather the animals which were to be placed in the ark. We can be sure that the fame of this insane preacher had reached the ears of tremendous numbers of people. We can be sure that as it became apparent that the time had come near that all of these animals were to be placed in this boat, the inhabitants of the world were watching. Never had they seen a spectacle like this. This Noah was apparently really insane.

And then Noah gave the final warning. God had told him that in seven days, the end would come. Not a soul believed it. We can be sure that they watched with incredulous eyes as two or more of every kind of animal were brought into the ark. And then on the seventh day, the door into the ark was shut. The Bible says that God shut the door. And then the rain began to fall. This was no ordinary rainstorm. The water was rising several feet per hour. Surely we can imagine that the people finally got the message. This monstrous rain with its flooding waters was going to destroy them! We can see them desperately pounding on the ark, "Let me in! I don't want to die!" But it was too late. God had shut the door. Not one human being or animal on the whole earth that was not on the ark survived. **That destruction had been predicted and it did happen.**

Approximately 2800 years later, God came to a wicked city named Sodom in the land of Canaan. God warned that God was going to destroy it because of its wickedness. The next day, Sodom and its three sister cities, Gomorrah, Admah, and Zeboim, were totally destroyed by God, the only survivors being the righteous man Lot and his two daughters. Even Lot's wife was destroyed because she loved this world more than she loved God. **That awful destruction did occur.**

Approximately 1250 years after God had completely destroyed these four cities, God sent a prophet to the great capital of probably the greatest nation of that day. The city was Nineveh. The prophet had a terrible message of doom and gloom: In forty days, God was going to destroy Nineveh.

How could this be? Nineveh was the great city. None of the gods of Nineveh would agree with the wild assertion of this seemingly crazy Israelite prophet, Jonah.

But mysteriously,, the king of Nineveh got the message. The Bible graphically describes his reaction. It is recorded in Jonah 3:6-9:

> For word came unto the king of Nineveh, and he arose from his throne, and he laid his robe from him, and covered him with sackcloth, and sat in ashes. And he caused it to be proclaimed and published through Nineveh by the decree of the king and his nobles, saying, Let neither man nor beast, herd nor flock, taste any thing: let them not feed, nor drink water: But let man and beast be covered with sackcloth, and cry mightily unto God: yea, let them turn every one from his evil way, and from the violence that is in their hands. Who can tell if God will turn and repent, and turn away from his fierce anger, that we perish not?

The king of Nineveh had surely heard reports that some 4000 years earlier, there had been a terrible destruction by a flood that covered the whole earth. The historians of his day wrote about such a flood. Perhaps he had heard about Sodom and the neighboring cities in the land of Canaan that some 1200 years earlier had been completely destroyed in one day.

In any case, he believed Jonah and did what no proud king would have done. He stripped off his royal garments, clothed himself with sackcloth, and sat in the ash pit. He was broken. He had gotten the message. And God spared that great city. In fact, the Bible reveals in the New Testament that many of the people of Nineveh became saved and will spend eternity with Christ in the new universe which God is going to create when this present universe is destroyed.

Approximately 2800 years after Nineveh, the warning again comes: this time, as in Noah's day, to the whole world. God is going to destroy planet earth and the whole universe by fire. Far worse than that, every one who has not trusted in Christ as his Savior must stand before the Judgment Throne of God to answer for his sins. Because every human being is a sinner, he will be found guilty. Before the piercing eye of God, every sin this person has ever done or thought will be revealed. And the Bible tells us about the awful punishment - eternity in Hell under the awful fury of God's wrath.

But there is still time to repent and cry to God for mercy. It is true, Judgment Day will not be delayed. God has a foreordained timetable for that. But individually any person can escape that awful judgment if he becomes saved.

Thus, the big question is: **Are you ready?** The God who created the universe in six days 13,000 years ago is going to bring it to an end. It is going to happen even as the judgments of the past absolutely did happen. Don't be misled by your feelings that it can't happen. Don't be misled by scientists who try to convince themselves and the rest of the world that this universe exists apart from a creator God. Don't be misled by theologians who are still looking for some kind of utopia to develop on this present earth. Don't be misled by your fears so that you don't want to even think about it.

Don't be misled by the idea that the God who created this huge universe in six days cannot bring it to an end in a moment.

Don't be misled by your love for the things of this earth - your career, your family, your home, your money, your anything that this earth has brought you. It is all going up in smoke very, very soon.

This is a time for stark reality. This is a time when we must look truth in the eye as the king of Nineveh did.

How wonderful it is that it is still the day of salvation. We can still follow the lead of the king of Nineveh. We can still get into the safety of the ark.

But the moment will soon be here when it is too late. God will shut the door. Where will you be? Will you be in the safety of God's grace because you have trusted in God's grace? Or will you be outside with no hope? Will you be one of the billions of individuals who will stand personally before the Judgment Throne of God to answer for your sins?

Whatever you do, DON'T DISREGARD THIS WARNING. Don't hope that this is just an idle threat. Don't argue with yourself that your church and/or your pastor do not teach this. Don't listen to the scientists who insist so confidently that this universe is millions or billions of years old.

The likelihood of September, 1994 being the end of this world is so very great that the alarm must be taken very seriously. If you are not truly a child of God, if you do not trust the Bible very implicitly, you are at great risk. To be damned eternally by God is a terrible matter.

But now you can still plead with God. You can humbly beg of Him for salvation. You can beseech Him that He will break your will so that Christ has become truly the Lord and King of your life.

Remember the king of Nineveh.

"But let man . . . cry mightily unto God . . . turn every one from his evil way . . . Who can tell if God will turn and repent, and turn away from his fierce anger, that we perish not?" (Jonah 3:8-9).

The big question I leave with you is:

ARE YOU READY TO MEET GOD?

Appendix I

Event	*Year B.C.*
Creation of Adam...11013	

Birth of Seth. Adam was 130 when Seth was born (Gen. 5:3)........... 10883

Birth of Enosh. Seth was 105 when Enosh was born (Gen. 5:6)....... 10778

End of Enosh's period 905 years after his birth (Gen. 5:11), which
is the year Cainan was born and which began his period 9873

End of Cainan's period 910 years after his birth (Gen. 5:14). This
is the year Mahaleel was born and the beginning of his period. 8963

End of Mahaleel's period 895 years after his birth (Gen. 5:17). This
is the year Jared was born and the beginning of his period. 8068

End of Jared's period 962 years after his birth (Gen. 5:20). This
is the year Enoch was born and the beginning of his period........... 7106

End of Enoch's period 365 years after his birth (Gen. 5:23). This
is the year Methuselah was born and the beginning of his period.......6741

End of Methuselah's period 969 years after his birth (Gen. 5:27). This
is the year Lamech was born and the beginning of his period.........5772

Birth of Noah. Lamech was 182 when Noah was born (Gen. 5:28-29) 5590

The flood. Noah was 600 when the flood came (Gen. 7:6) 4990

Death of Shem 502 years after the flood (Gen. 11:10-11). This
is the year Arphaxad was born and the beginning of his period........ 4488

End of Arphaxad's period 438 years after his birth (Gen. 11:12-13). This
is the year Salah was born and the beginning of his period.... 4050

End of Salah's period 433 years after his birth (Gen. 11:14-15). This
is the year Eber was born and the beginning of his period. 3617

End of Eber's period 464 years after his birth (Gen. 11:16-17). This
is the year Peleg was born and the beginning of his period........... 3153

The Tower of Babel incident must have occurred between 3153 & 2914 (Gen. 10:25).

End of Peleg's period 239 years after his birth (Gen. 11:18-19). This
is the year Reu was born and the beginning of his period............ 2914

End of Reu's period 239 years after his birth (Gen. 11:20-21). This
is the year Serug was born and the beginning of his period. 2675

End of Serug's period 230 years after his birth (Gen. 11:22-23). This
is the year Nahor was born and the beginning of his period. 2445

End of Nahor's period 148 years after his birth (Gen. 11:24-25). This
is the year Terah was born and the beginning of his period. 2297

Birth of Abram to Terah, when Terah was 130 years old 2167

Circumcision of Abraham when he was 99 years old
(Gen. 17:1, 23-24). 2068

Birth of Isaac. Abraham was 100 years old when Isaac was born
(Gen. 21:5). 2067

Birth of Jacob. Isaac was 60 years old when Jacob was born
(Gen. 25:26). 2007

Jacob's name changed to Israel when Jacob was 100 years old. 1907

Jacob's family arrived in Egypt when Jacob was 130 years old
(Gen. 47:9). 1877

Exodus from Egypt 430 years later (Exo. 12:40). 1447

Entrance into Canaan 40 years later (Exo. 16:35). 1407

Solomon's temple construction is begun 480 years after Exodus
(I Kings 6:1). 967

Division of kingdom at death of Solomon 36 years later
(I Kings 12, II Chron. 10) 931

Appendix II

Event	Years
The Exodus	1447 B.C.
Entrance into Canaan	1407 B.C.
Initial 40 year period in Canaan	1407-1367 B.C.
During this period the conquest of Canaan occurred under Joshua and Othniel delivered Israel	
Next 80 year period in Canaan	1367-1287 B.C.
During this period Ehud and Shamgar delivered Israel	
Next 40 year period in Canaan	1287-1247 B.C.
Deborah and Barak were deliverers during this period	
Gideon judged	1247-1207 B.C.
Abimelech rules	1207-1204 B.C.
Tola judged	1204-1181 B.C.
Jair judged	1181-1159 B.C.
Jephthah judged	1159-1153 B.C.
Ibzan judged	1153-1146 B.C.
Elon judged	1146-1136 B.C.
Abdon judged	1136-1128 B.C.
Samson judged	1128-1108 B.C.
Eli judged	1108-1068 B.C.
Ark in Philistines' hands	1068-1067 B.C.
Samuel judged	1067-1047 B.C.
Saul reigned as king	1047-1007 B.C.
David reigned	1007-967 B.C.
Solomon reigned	971-931 B.C.
Foundation of temple laid in fourth year of Solomon's reign	967 B.C.
Division of kingdom of Israel	931 B.C.
End of northern kingdom of Israel	709 B.C.
Israel comes under dominion of Egypt upon Josiah's death	609 B.C.
Israel destroyed by Babylon	587 B.C.
Babylon conquered by Medes and Persians	539 B.C.

Appendix III

Kings of Judah		Kings of Israel	
Rehoboam	931-914	Jeroboam	931-910
Abijam	914-911		
Asa	911-870	Nadab	910-909
		Baasha	909-886
		Elah	886-885
		Zimri	885
		Tibni	885-880
		Omri	885-874
Jehoshaphat	871-846	Ahab	874-853
Jehoram	854-842	Ahaziah	854-853
Ahaziah (Jehoahaz)	842-841	Joram (Jehoram)	853-841
Athaliah	841-835	Jehu	841-813
Joash (Jehoash)	835-795	Jehoahaz	813-796
Amaziah	796-767	Jehoash (Joash)	798-782
Uzziah (Azariah)	769-737	Jeroboam	792-751
		Zechariah	751-750
		Shallum	750
		Menahem	750-740
Jotham	738-718	Pekahiah	740-738
Ahaz	730-714	Pekah	738-718
Hezekiah	715-686	Hoshea	718-709
Manasseh	697-642		
Amon	642-640		
Josiah	640-609		
Jehoahaz	609		
Jehoiakim	609-598		
Jehoiachin	608-597		
Zedekiah	597-587		

Appendix IV
Family Radio Stations and
"Open Forum" broadcast times

Alabama 9:00-10:30 pm
Birmingham WBFR 89.5 FM

Arizona 8:00-9:30 pm
Phoenix KPHF 88.3 FM

California 7:00-8:30 pm
Chico KHAP 89.1 FM
El Cajon KECR 93.3 FM
El Cajon KECR 910 FM
Eureka 103.1 FM
Fresno KFNO 90.3 FM
Le Grand KEFR 89.9 FM
Long Beach KFRN 1280 AM
Palm Springs 105.5 FM
Paso Robles 105.5 FM
Sacramento KEBR 1210 AM
Sacramento KEBR 89.3 FM
San Luis Obispo 94.3 FM
San Francisco KEAR 106.9 FM
Santa Maria 104.9 FM
Santa Cruz 89.3 FM
Santa Barbara 92.7 FM
Stockton 88.1 FM
Ukiah KPRA 89.5 FM

Connecticut 3-4:30 pm
Vernon WCTF 1170 AM

Florida 10:00-11:30 pm
Jacksonville WJFR 88.7 FM
West Palm Beach WWFR 91.7 FM
Okeechobee WWFR 91.7 FM
Okeechobee WYFR Shortwave
    5985 kHz
    9505 kHz
    (heard all over the United
    States and Canada)
St. Petersburg WFTI 91.7 FM

Georgia 10:00-11:30 pm
Columbus WFRC 90.5 FM

Illinois 9:00-10:30 pm
Chicago WJCH 91.9 FM
Joliet WJCH 91.9 FM

Iowa 9:00-10:30 pm
Ames 89.1 FM
Cedar Rapids 95.1 FM
Des Moines KDFR 91.3 FM
Fort Dodge 89.1 FM
Iowa City 93.1 FM
Shenandoah KYFR 920 AM

Continued

Maryland 10:00-11:30 pm
Annapolis WFSI 107.9 FM
Baltimore WFSI 107.9 FM
Washington WFSI 107.9 FM
Hagerstown 93.5 FM

Massachusetts 10:00-11:00 pm
Boston WEZE 1260 AM

Michigan 9:00-10:30 pm
Grand Rapids WFUR 1510 AM

Nebraska 9:00-10:30 pm
Omaha KYFR 920 AM

New Jersey 10:00-11:30 pm
Atlantic City 89.3 FM
Camden WKDN 106.9 FM
Newark WFME 94.7 FM

New York 10:00-11:30 pm
Albany 90.7 FM
Buffalo WFBF 89.9 FM
New York WFME 94.7 FM
Poughkeepsie 90.5 FM
Smithtown WFRS 88.9 FM
Webster WFRW 88.1 FM

Ohio 10:00-11:30 pm
Cuyahoga Falls WCUE 1150 AM
Toledo WOTL 90.3 FM
Youngstown WYTN 91.7 FM

Oregon 7:00-8:30 pm
Eugene KQFE 88.9 FM
Grants Pass 97.7 FM
Medford 107.1 FM

Pennsylvania 10:00-11:30 pm
Erie WEFR 88.1 FM
Johnstown WFRJ 88.9 FM
Philadelphia WKDN 106.9 FM
Pittsburgh 97.7 FM

South Carolina 10:00-11:30 pm
Charleston WFCH 88.5 FM

Texas 9:00-10:30 pm
Beaumont KTXB 89.7 FM

Utah 8:00-9:30 pm
Salt Lake City KUFR 91.7 FM

Washington 7:00-8:30 pm
Kirkland KARR 1460 AM
Longview KJVH 89.5 FM

Wisconsin 9:00-10:30 pm
Milwaukee WMWK 88.1 FM

Scriptural Index

About the Author

Harold Camping was born in Colorado and at an early age moved with his family to California. He earned a B.S. degree in civil engineering from the University of California at Berkeley in 1942. In 1958 he helped found Family Radio and some years later gave up a successful construction business to devote full time to the Christian radio ministry, which now broadcasts worldwide. He and his wife, Shirley, have raised seven children; they make their home in the San Francisco Bay area. He is the Family Radio president and general manager and participates in the broadcasts by teaching on the Family Bible Study program and by serving as host of the Open Forum, a live call-in program. A forty-year student of the Bible, he has been steadfast in his attempts to provide Biblical answers to questions posed by Open Forum listeners.

He has written other books and booklets, including *Adam When?*, "The Biblical Calendar of History," *Feed My Sheep, The Fig Tree, The Final Tribulation, First Principles of Bible Study*, "Galatians Chapter One," "Galatians Chapter Two," "Galatians Chapter Three," "The Glorious Garden of Eden," "God's Magnificent Salvation Plan," *The Gospel: God's Covenant of Grace*, "Let the Oceans Speak," "The Seventy Weeks of Daniel 9," "Sunday: The Sabbath," *What God Hath Joined Together*, "What Is The True Gospel," and "When Is The Rapture?" These publications are available from Family Radio, Oakland, CA 94621. *1994?* is available in bookstores.

Readers with questions or comments may call during the Open Forum program, which is aired weekday evenings on Family Radio stations (see Appendix IV). The toll-free number is 1-800-322-5385.